King Jesus Claims His Church

King Jesus Claims His Church

A Kingdom Vision for the People of God

This book was given to me by Valerie Miller in September 2020

by Finny Kuruvilla

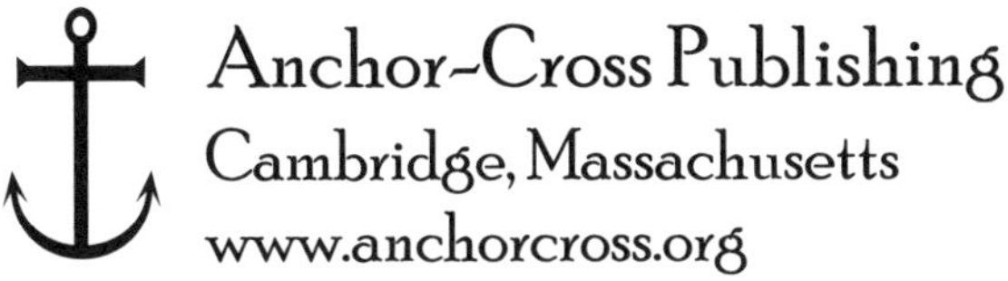

Anchor-Cross Publishing
Cambridge, Massachusetts
www.anchorcross.org

Anchor-Cross Publishing
P.O. Box 381682
Cambridge, MA 02238
www.anchorcross.org

Printed in the United States of America.

ISBN 10: 0-9742727-9-5
ISBN 13: 978-0-9742727-9-5

To maintain consistency with the NKJV convention, divine pronouns have been capitalized in Scripture, even when other translations follow a lower case convention.

When quoting non-biblical authors, all italicized portions are original unless otherwise indicated.

This book is printed on acid-free paper.

Table of Contents

Interpreting Christ's message too much as a political message distracts from the truth of what he is saying.

Preface

Perhaps no other passage in Scripture better describes the glory of the habitation of God's people than the following passage:

> Great is the LORD and greatly to be praised
>   in the city of our God!
> His holy mountain, beautiful in elevation,
>   is the joy of all the earth,
> Mount Zion, in the far north,
>   the city of the great King.
> Within her citadels God
>   has made Himself known as a fortress.
> For behold, the kings assembled;
>   they came on together.
> As soon as they saw it, they were astounded;
>   they were in panic; they took to flight.
> Trembling took hold of them there,
>   anguish as of a woman in labor.
> By the east wind You shattered
>   the ships of Tarshish.
> As we have heard, so have we seen
>   in the city of the LORD of hosts,
> in the city of our God,
>   which God will establish forever.   Selah
> We have thought on Your steadfast love, O God,
>   in the midst of Your temple.
> As Your name, O God,
>   so Your praise reaches to the ends of the earth.
> Your right hand is filled with righteousness.
>   Let Mount Zion be glad!
> Let the daughters of Judah rejoice
>   because of Your judgments!
> Walk about Zion, go around her,

number her towers,
consider well her ramparts,
go through her citadels,
that you may tell the next generation
that this is God,
our God forever and ever.
He will guide us forever. (Ps. 48)

This Psalm describes the strength of the habitation of God's people: in our age, the church. While many decry the low state of the church, the coolness of its members, its invasion with all manner of heresy, and lack of missionary progress, none of these things need be so. Indeed the Spirit has given to His church the power to overcome, so that its enemies would be "astounded, and in panic, take to flight." The church's beauty—with its breathtaking towers, ramparts, and citadels—should motivate humanity to tell the next generation that God reigns forever. It should be the city on a hill that draws the world.

Far too little has been written on the doctrine of the church. Any tabulation of Christian books according to subject area will reveal this neglect. While many more have focused on personal holiness, as admirable as that is, any attempt at personal holiness will be woefully incomplete without individuals having a local congregation to reinforce their convictions and receive encouragement. Much has been written concerning techniques of evangelism. But Jesus Himself taught that the compelling force behind His message was the church (John 13:34-35, 17:20-21). The church is Jesus' evangelism program.[1]

The New Testament sustains architectural imagery for God's people, likening the church to a building that is laid upon the foundation of the apostles and prophets, a structure in which each member is a stone carefully placed to form a dwelling place for the Holy Spirit. In the same way that God gave Moses a detailed plan for Israel's temple, the New Testament contains a surprising amount of detail on the architecture of the new temple, the church. Many people, not realizing how much the Scriptures actually teach on this subject, either fall into dead traditions or unjustly innovate. It is great audacity to innovate where God has prescribed. It is great tragedy to lapse into human traditions and thereby desecrate the abode of Almighty God. Either position will rob the church of the life God intended.

Many churches and denominations have a "statement of faith" or "confession"—a capsule summary of their theology. But usually this is

[1] Paraphrased from Mark Dever.

only about abstract theology. Others might add a "discipline," a summary of acceptable practice, which unfortunately often resembles a list of "dos and don'ts" that fail to win the heart. Few have a vision statement, a document that seeks to inspire the church by drawing out truths from Scripture and showing how these truths should form the identity of the group and lead to Christ-honoring practice. *King Jesus Claims His Church* strives to be such a vision statement. To that end, my hope is that this book serves as a focusing lens on Scripture. Just as the lens cannot be seen by its wearer, but brings clarity to other objects, so this book should be almost invisible as it brings into focus Jesus and His word. The reader is urged to read the Scripture quotations carefully, as they form the kernel of this work.

Reinforcing imagery from passages like Psalms 48, Jesus describes His disciples as a city on a hill. Thus we can safely liken the church to a city (a city-state would be more accurate). Because this book is a vision statement, my goal is to give you a memorable and accurate tour of this special city, the church as God intends it. Touring a large city can be daunting and exhausting. Which attractions should you visit? How much time should you spend at a particular museum? What about soaking up local culture? Often you find that you could have spent several more days at a place you quickly passed through. While the tour is intended to be broad rather than deep, I have naturally focused the tour on points that have been of interest throughout the ages. There is a logic to the sequence of our tour: despite the temptation to jump ahead, I ask that you move through in order. Many of our stopping points will be in ruin and I will ask your help to restore them. Doubtless, we could have lingered more at various locations or moved more quickly through others. To warn you now, this is a fatiguing book. We will visit many locations, each having its own unique importance. Just as any good tour of a city is interspersed with rest, my hope is that the book will be digested slowly and thoughtfully, then stimulate additional prayer, study, and discussion.

Our tour will draw on much Scripture and history. The historically minded reader will discover in these pages affinity to the theology and practice of the suffering, persecuted churches of history. This includes the early church, the Waldensians, the followers of John Wycliffe, and the Anabaptists. But labels often encourage compartmentalization and a consequent complacency: "Whew, so you're one of those, thankfully your tradition is different from mine." Part of my thesis is that these groups have helped carry the true faith that was once delivered to the saints. Thus this book is directed at all professing Christians, irrespective of label or affiliation.

Every several hundred years the church seems to arrive at insights that are great advances, obvious in hindsight, and vital for forward progress. For example, the Great Commission was broadly forgotten for centuries, but recovered as the Anabaptists, Zinzendorf, and Carey rediscovered it in Scripture. We today benefit from this understanding of missions—almost taking it for granted. Yet the church is always in need of reformation and rediscovery: as the historic plea goes, *ecclesia semper reformanda*. To that end, the mandate for our generation is clear: to recover a vision for the church that comes from correctly reading Scripture. May later generations not have to bear the cost of further neglect of this important subject.

Many people today say, "I'm spiritual, but not religious." Such language veils a hunger for God but a distaste for the church. Even in the church, Christians are asking, "Is this what church is supposed to be?" Many Christians sense deep down that there is supposed to be something more, but are unsure of what that something is. These longings can be fulfilled only by discovering God's true intent for His people. When studying the eye, one practically falls down in worship in perceiving the genius of God's design. Similarly, we should fall down on our knees in praise as we see how marvelously God designed the church to advance the gospel of His anointed King. We must not be content with any goal less than every tribe on this world having a faithful Christian witness. Once the church properly discovers its identity, purpose, and form as the pillar and ground of truth, the knowledge of God will spread over this world as the waters cover the seas.

Finny Kuruvilla
Cambridge, Massachusetts
August 2013

Acknowledgments

My dear wife Laura deserves immense credit for this book. Over the years, she has served as my discussion partner as we wrestled with Scripture and compared our conclusions to the diverse churches that we have attended. Those conversations and the journey of our shared experience sparked my desire to write. Her extra work on the weekends in caring for our four children provided the time for me to write. When we met, Laura was working on her PhD in English at Harvard, though she resigned from the program to stay home with our first child. I did not fully appreciate it at the time, but our marriage was God's way of bringing about a special partnership. My passion for ideas and the church married to her intelligence and patient service have birthed this book.

Carl Swartzentruber of Shalom Bible Fellowship provided the forum to present some of these ideas publicly for the first time. The ensuing discussions proved very helpful in sharpening the presentation in the book. David Bercot, Matthew Milioni, Paul Lamicela, Mahlon Fisher, Seth Gorczyca, Charles Pike, and Paul Rinear played important roles of editing and encouragement. Though I have never met the following men, several chapters have been heavily influenced by F. D. Bruner, Robert Coleman, Jonathan Leeman, Scott McKnight, Stuart Murray, Robert Picirilli, and Timothy Ward. I happily and humbly acknowledge my debt to them.

Finally, may the Lord be glorified through these pages: "Not to us, O Lord, not to us, but to your name give glory, for the sake of Your steadfast love and Your faithfulness!" (Ps. 115:1)

Part I

The Good News of the Nation

Politics change throughout time, with their focus and direction shifting with each generation. But Christ's message, and its universal applicability to the human condition, does not.

Chapter 1

A young carpenter builds a nation

You are…a holy nation. (1 Peter 2:9)

The seeds of the church were planted with the first recorded words of Jesus' ministry, "The kingdom of God is at hand. Repent, and believe in the gospel" (Mark 1:15). Unfortunately these words have been either trivialized from romanticized overuse or obscured by the fog of historic distance. Presumed understanding has led to confusion. Yet God's vision for His church must be firmly anchored in an accurate understanding of what Jesus meant with this rich expression. "Repent and believe" deeply needs revisiting.

When the young carpenter traveled throughout Galilee proclaiming, "Repent and believe, for the kingdom of God is at hand," Jesus was employing profoundly political language. He was not crucified for His teachings on love but because His enemies felt threatened by the possibility that He was gathering a new, rival nation around Himself.

Disciples today must recognize the significance of the political language that Jesus used. Far too often, we take the call of the gospel in a private, individualistic sense as a call for personal salvation and reform. While that understanding remains a valid derivative application, such a focus misses much of the significance of the gospel—and of the church's very essence.

When I was in college, I used to stand on a street corner in California and ask passersby what the word *gospel* means. Nearly everyone quite confidently answered, "truth." Because of the expression "gospel truth," most people apparently assumed that the two words are synonymous. What is more tragic is how poorly this question is answered not by those on the street, but by those in the church.

Some churchgoers might know that gospel means "good news," but the more pressing question is, "What exactly is the good news?" To understand good news to a first-century Jew, we find an excellent starting point in the book of Psalms:

> Give the king Your justice, O God,
> and Your righteousness to the royal Son!
> May He judge Your people with righteousness,
> and Your poor with justice!
> Let the mountains bear prosperity for the people,
> and the hills, in righteousness!
> May He defend the cause of the poor of the people,
> give deliverance to the children of the needy,
> and crush the oppressor!
> May they fear You while the sun endures,
> and as long as the moon, throughout all generations!
> May He be like rain that falls on the mown grass,
> like showers that water the earth!
> In His days may the righteous flourish,
> and peace abound, till the moon be no more!
> May He have dominion from sea to sea,
> and from the River to the ends of the earth!
> May desert tribes bow down before Him,
> and His enemies lick the dust!
> May the kings of Tarshish and of the coastlands
> render Him tribute;
> may the kings of Sheba and Seba
> bring gifts!
> May all kings fall down before Him,
> all nations serve Him!
> For He delivers the needy when he calls,
> the poor and him who has no helper.
> He has pity on the weak and the needy,
> and saves the lives of the needy.
> From oppression and violence He redeems their life,
> and precious is their blood in His sight.
> Long may He live;
> may gold of Sheba be given to Him!
> May prayer be made for Him continually,
> and blessings invoked for Him all the day!
> May there be abundance of grain in the land;

> on the tops of the mountains may it wave;
> may its fruit be like Lebanon;
> and may people blossom in the cities
> like the grass of the field!
> May His name endure forever,
> His fame continue as long as the sun!
> May people be blessed in Him,
> all nations call Him blessed!
> Blessed be the LORD, the God of Israel,
> who alone does wondrous things.
> Blessed be His glorious name forever;
> may the whole earth be filled with His glory!
> Amen and Amen! (Ps. 72:1-19)

Good news to an Israelite was a righteous King. The prayer of Psalms 72 describes this just King, who brings abundance and peace. This King would show compassion on the poor, needy, and oppressed. By virtue of His faithful leadership, all nations bless Him. This was the prayer of ancient Israel—they understood the importance of godly leadership. The books of Samuel, Kings, and Chronicles vividly portray how the nation fared under the leadership of both godly and wicked kings. To first-century Jews under Roman oppression, this prayer would have been the daily cry of their hearts.

Deep down, we all understand the importance of leadership. Millions of people have immigrated into one country from another to escape corrupt leadership and enjoy more favorable governance. A person's life in the United States, Saudi Arabia, China, Venezuela, Switzerland, North Korea, or the Congo would be quite different in these places because of the nature of their leaders. "When the righteous are in authority, the people rejoice; But when a wicked man rules, the people groan" (Prov. 29:2 NKJV).

Because kings have so often gone astray, the tendency since the 1700s in the West has been to strip power from their leaders and institute "checks and balances" to prevent kings from holding too much sway. Typically even the terms that rulers may hold is limited in time. Most of the world has learned its lesson that humans make bad kings.

Yet by stripping leaders of their power, the world is moving into a period more like the book of Judges, where everyone does "what is right in his own eyes" (Judges 21:25). In places like the United States, abortion and violence have claimed millions of lives. Leaders cannot be truly godly and express biblical views or they will be voted down. (Note how even supposedly Christian presidents must extol how Islam is a "great religion" and be seen holding a Qur'an.) Children are sent like sheep to the slaughter to supposedly neutral schools where they are indoctrinated with worldviews hostile to God. Propaganda runs free course stealing the hearts of the people to pleasure and materialism. While perhaps "less bad" than nations with cruel dictators, those looking upon developed Western countries with a spiritual perspective should weep.

The world needs a righteous king—not another tyrant, nor each person doing what is right in his own eyes. Israel's history, and the sweep of the Old Testament, point to this conclusion. The prayer of Psalm 72 should be our prayer too.

The first-century Mediterranean world was a period of great reflection about politics, especially in Israel. In the previous four centuries, Israel had been ruled by the Persians, the Greeks, experienced brief independence under two dynasties, and was then conquered by Rome. One of Israel's rulers was Antiochus Epiphanes, one of the most brutal leaders to ever live. And as the Israelites knew very well, religion was always intermingled with politics (as today, though we may pretend otherwise). One of Julius Caesar's titles from 63 BC was *pontifex maximus*, which means chief priest. Cicero would say in a speech in 57 BC: "Many things, O priests, have been devised and established with divine wisdom by our ancestors; but no action of theirs was ever more wise than their determination that the same men should superintend both what relates to the religious worship due to the immortal gods, and also what concerns the highest interests of the state, so that they might preserve the republic as the most honourable and eminent of the citizens, by governing it well, and as priests by wisely interpreting the requirements of religion."[1]

From this vortex of politics and religion, under Roman oppression and with Caesar as monarch and high priest, the young carpenter from Nazareth began to preach. Jesus' gospel, or good news, can now be summarized.

> **The Good News of the Nation**: God's intention at creation was for humanity to benevolently rule the earth. But because Adam and Eve rejected God's command, the Lord chose Abraham, Isaac, Jacob, Moses, and David to be instruments by which He would establish His own nation through covenant to bless the world and draw humanity to Himself. Because Israel failed in its mandate, Jesus founded a new nation—the church—with Himself as

[1] Cicero, *De Domo Sua*, 1.

> the reigning king to accomplish what Israel did not. Jesus' nation is marked by righteousness and peace. Joining this new nation involves following a radical new "constitution," the covenant of King Jesus, and requires a radical break from one's previous lifestyle. Disciples are baptized into a new social order, the church. Through Jesus' death and resurrection, members of the new nation receive liberation from Satan, forgiveness of sins, the power of the Spirit, and eternal life. The good news of Jesus' reign culminates with His nation emerging victorious, and His citizens being co-regents with Him forever. All other nations and their kings will eventually be conquered, and all will declare that Jesus is the King of kings and Lord of lords.

Put in another way, the gospel is good news because of three interlocking truths:

- The world finally has a righteous king. A new nation under King Jesus' leadership has been birthed. Citizens of this new nation live the abundant life and demonstrate to the world the radiant presence of God among them.
- Israel's story has been brought to fulfillment. Jesus' death is the ultimate sacrifice foreshadowed by the Torah and the prophets. What was promised to the ancient prophets finds its realization in Jesus as the seed of Abraham, the true Israel, the new Moses, the greater David, and the last Adam.
- The decay of this world has been undone through the resurrection of King Jesus. At the resurrection, He was coronated King over all and imparts sin-crushing, death-overcoming power to His citizens. (Personal salvation is certainly a very important consequence of this gospel, but it is not the centerpiece, as we have often been told. The centerpiece is King Jesus.)

As will be seen in later chapters, correctly understanding the church as a nation—in fact a rival nation to all other earthly nations—brings clarity to a host of issues. Here the word *nation* is used instead of *kingdom*, because *nation* is also a biblical word applying to all followers of Jesus (1 Pet. 2:9) and better captures what the word *kingdom* did in the first century. While most people in the first century lived in political entities known as kingdoms, most people today live in political entities known as nations. Saying that Jesus founded a nation is more intelligible to modern ears and better portrays the subversive character of Jesus' gospel message.

First, however, a brief survey is needed, demonstrating that the claims of the gospel are in fact political, or perhaps better described as counter-political:

1. The phrase "repent and believe" itself has political overtones. The first-century historian Josephus describes a fascinating story where he learns that a brigand chief is plotting to kill him. He tells this brigand to abandon his efforts and "repent and believe in me [Josephus]", or translated otherwise "repent and show loyalty to me."[2] The underlying language is nearly identical to that which Jesus employs in Mark 1:15.[3] Other political uses of "repent and believe" can be found in multiple sources from 100 BC-150 AD.[4]
2. Jesus chose the term church (Greek: *ekklesia*) instead of synagogue (Greek: *synagoge*) for his followers. The term *ekklesia* was the common term used for the political gatherings of the Greco-Roman city-state. The word was also used in the Septuagint for the assemblies of national Israel. It is remarkable that He would select such a political term when the more familiar term of synagogue was more palatable and perhaps more natural given the Jewish womb from which Christianity sprang.
3. Jesus selected twelve apostles, an obvious reference to the twelve tribes of Israel (Luke 22:30). His enemies correctly perceived the audacity of Jesus' numerical selection. Jesus was proclaiming in His deeds that He was assembling a political nation, a new Israel, around Himself.
4. Jesus' enemies asked His disciples if He taught that they should continue to pay taxes. These enemies understood that Jesus' followers might perceive themselves to be a rival nation.
5. The accusation brought to Pilate was, "Everyone who makes himself king opposes Caesar" (John 19:12 ESV). This opposition between Jesus and Caesar continues in the book of Acts: "These who have turned the world upside down have come here too. Jason has harbored them, and these are all acting contrary to the decrees of Caesar, saying there is another king—Jesus" (Acts 17:6-7).
6. "Jesus is Lord" was a politically subversive phrase because the slogan "Caesar is Lord" was already in circulation. An appropriate

[2] Flavius Josephus, *The Life of Josephus*, 110. Brill's translation is "change his thinking and become loyal to me." Whiston's is "repent of it, and be faithful to me."

[3] In Greek, *metanoesin kai pistos emoi* in Josephus compared to *metanoeite kai pisteuete* in Mark 1:15.

[4] Qumran is one source of notable examples.

analogy might be for someone to say "Jesus is President" in the United States, despite another person holding that office.

7. The apostle Peter describes the early Christians as a "holy nation" (1 Pet. 2:9) and as part of a "Dispersion" or Diaspora (1 Pet. 1:1), borrowing language used for national Israel.
8. James refers to Christians as the "twelve tribes which are scattered abroad" (James 1:1), also a description in continuity with political Israel.
9. Paul urges believers to understand that their citizenship is in heaven (Phil. 3:20).[5] Also earlier in the letter, "Only live as citizens worthy of the gospel of Christ." (Phil. 1:27).[6]
10. Old Testament prophecies about the Messiah include that "the government will be on His shoulder" (Isa. 9:6) and that He will crush the kings of the earth (Ps. 2).

Let us return to the question from the beginning of the chapter, "What does the word *gospel* mean?" *The gospel, or good news, is a declaration of Jesus' kingship.* These two words, *Jesus' kingship*, probably capture the essence of the gospel better than any other expression. When Jesus came to this earth, He announced and founded the nation over which He now rules. By tempting Jesus, Satan tried to derail Jesus' work by polluting the burgeoning nation. He wanted Jesus' nation to be founded on laxity, idolatry, and glamor (the three temptations of breaking the fast, devil worship, and flamboyant landing in the temple courts, respectively), rather than devotion, righteousness, and suffering.

The importance of understanding the church as a nation (or kingdom) can hardly be overstated. Other metaphors such as bride, building, and body are used in the New Testament—but the church is not literally a woman in a wedding dress, a building made of stones, or a large human body. But the church is literally a kingdom.[7] If the church does not have this self-understanding, it becomes vulnerable to drift and damage by morphing into a club or a social gathering. The church has already lost many profound insights into its identity and way of life by losing sight of what the young carpenter was building. But with

[5] The KJV misses the mark by translating Phil. 3:20 as "our conversation is in heaven." Normally the KJV translates a different Greek word, *anastrophe*, as "conversation," to mean one's way of life. Here, however, a different word is used. The NKJV corrects this.

[6] Author's translation. Few translations accurately capture that the underlying Greek verb of Philippians 1:27 is a cognate to the word "citizen" used in Philippians 3:20. Literally, "citizen yourselves worthy of the gospel of Christ."

[7] Jonathan Leeman, *Church Membership*, Crossway (2012), p. 70.

the proper infrastructure of its kingdom identity, the church can be securely joined to the solid foundation of King Jesus and His words.

Chapter 2

Relationship through covenant

The friendship of the L*ORD* *is for those who fear Him,*
And He makes known to them His covenant. (Psalms 25:14)

We long for relationship. One hardly needs to go to Scripture to affirm this truth. Our thirst for friendship, marriage, children, and even pets manifests our desire for relationship. Children create vivid imaginary friends to accompany them. Most adults can remember times in their lives when they ached for a relationship, such as for a friend in school or a lifelong marriage partner.

Not surprisingly then, slogans like "Christianity is not a religion but a relationship" have met with enthusiastic reception. These slogans reflect our broader desire to have relationship, with the seen and the unseen. The spirit behind "Christianity is not a religion but a relationship" has, however, led to unfortunate consequences. Not least of which is that the slogan contradicts Scripture itself, "Pure and undefiled religion before God and the Father is this: to visit orphans and widows in their trouble, and to keep oneself unspotted from the world" (James 1:27). Scripture uses the term *religion* in a positive light.[1] Yet this will not do for today's generation. A deep impulse seeks to cast off "rules" and "law," captured in that mean, old, and repressive term "religion." Very prominent Christian ministers regularly bash "religion" to the approving faces of their congregations. Ministers and congregations, some-

[1] The etymology of the word is also positive. Both Lactantius and Augustine wrote about the Latin word *religati* or *religare*, from which we get the English word religion. They contended that the word was derived from "to bind," meaning to bind oneself to God.

times subconsciously, are eager to throw off the restraints and baggage of religion and instead be perceived by the world as "fresh" and "authentic."

Yet the proverbial baby has been lost with the bathwater. Holiness and the intense desire to obey God have evaporated. As the pollsters have shown, there is little measurable difference between professing Christians and unbelievers in most areas of life, ranging from the divorce rate to horoscope reading. The songs of the church are styled after contemporary pop, bluegrass, or whatever else is fashionable, with a message not far from "Jesus is my boyfriend." The fear of God has been replaced with a casual spirit never before found in the history of the church. We have sown the wind and reaped the whirlwind.

With all this talk of "relationship," curiously enough the word never appears in the pages of Scripture.[2] What then have we to say about how Scripture views this deep longing of our hearts? What constitutes our relationship to God? Is there a corrective to the modern distortion?

Scripture offers another concept that integrates relationship with obedience, pairing fulfillment with corrective. As we will see, Scripture's concept makes our relationship to God more thrilling, rich, and mysterious than the modern church's poor substitute. That concept is *covenant.*

Kingdom and covenant

> The idea of covenant is fundamental to the Bible's story. At its most basic, covenant presents God's desire to enter into relationship with men and women created in his image. This is reflected in the repeated covenant refrain, "I will be your God and you will be my people" (Exodus 6:6-8; Leviticus 26:12 etc.). Covenant is all about relationship between the Creator and his creation. The idea may seem simple, however, the implications of covenant and covenant relationship between God and humanity are vast.[3]

Many people have noted that the organizing theme of Scripture is covenant. Such a claim is essentially identical to saying that the organizing theme is kingdom. Covenant is the instrument that the King has chosen to relate to His people, who form His kingdom.

---

[2] The word cannot be found in the KJV, NKJV, or ESV.

[3] Alistair Wilson and Jamie Grant, quoted in Peter Gentry and Stephen Wellum, *Kingdom through Covenant*, Crossway (2012), p. 21.

During the Old Testament period, God's relationship to His people was ordered as a king to his subjects, with covenants according to the patterns of suzerain-vassal treaties.[4] Ancient Near East covenants were composed of structured components: preamble, history, stipulations, document clause, witnesses, and sanctions. The Torah contains interlocking examples of these Ancient Near Eastern covenants, in places such as the Book of the Covenant (Exod. 19-24, containing the Ten Commandments), and the entire book of Deuteronomy:

1. Preamble: introduction of the speaker. "And God spoke all these words" (Exod. 20:1; also see Deut. 1:1-5).
2. History:[5] a description of what the King has done on behalf of the people. "I am the LORD your God, who brought you out of the land of Egypt, out of the house of slavery" (Exod. 20:2). Deuteronomy 1:6-4:43 contains an extensive history.
3. Stipulations: the obligations of the people are enumerated, often in general form first, then in a lengthier detailed form. The Ten Commandments are the compact set of stipulations (Exod. 20:3-17), followed by a detailed set (Exod. 21-23). Similarly, Deuteronomy 4:44-11:32 presents general stipulations while Deuteronomy 12:1-26:19 the detailed form.
4. Document clause: describes the public reading of the documents and their ratification. Sometimes, provisions are given on how the written documents were to be stored and how often they were to be read, with the goal of promoting the bond between King and people. (Exod. 24; Deut. 27:1-10)
5. Witnesses: legal documents called for witnesses. "I call heaven and earth to witness against you this day" (Deut. 30:19; also see Deut. 27:11-26, Exod. 24:4, Josh. 24:27).
6. Sanctions: the blessings of obedience and the curses of disobedience. (See Deut. 28.)

This covenantal form radiates out from the Torah into the rest of the Old Testament. For example, the books of Judges, Samuel, Kings, and Chronicles are history, narrating God's sustenance and provision for Israel:

> The post-Pentateuchal historical narratives...rehearse the continuing benefits bestowed by Yahweh as faithful Protector of his vassal kingdom. They tell how he graciously

[4] Gentry and Wellum's book provides a helpful overview.

[5] Sometimes called historic prologue.

> intervened for their preservation and enrichment, championing their cause in conflict, even as of old he brought them out of the iron furnace of Egypt to the covenantal table at Sinai. They relate how he staffed their ranks with judges and kings, priests and prophets, for the development of the kingdom after the pattern that had been prescribed in the constitutional stipulations of the Pentateuch. At the same time Old Testament historiography pursues the countertheme of Israel's repeated covenant-breaking and the consequent infliction on them of the evils delineated beforehand in the curse sanctions of the Mosaic treaties, particularly in Deuteronomy.[6]

In this covenantal framework, the Old Testament prophets have an important function: "The peculiarly prophetic task was the elaboration and application of the ancient covenant sanctions. In actual practice, this meant that their diplomatic mission to Israel was by and large one of prosecuting Yahweh's patient covenant lawsuit with his incurably wayward vassal people."[7]

This covenantal structure is so woven into the Hebrew Scriptures that when Paul describes his fellow Jews reading the Old Testament, they are reading "the old covenant" (2 Cor. 3:14 ESV). The rich fabric of covenant carries forward into the New Testament. The apostles call themselves "ministers of the new covenant" (2 Cor. 3:6). The cup of the Lord's table is the blood of the New Covenant (Matt. 26:28). The word that is translated as "Testament," *diatheke*, is the same word translated as "covenant." Hence the Old and New Testaments could properly be referred to as Old and New Covenants. The Bible is the Book of Covenants.

The very structure of the New Testament is covenantal. The Gospel accounts contain preamble (identity of the King), history (the story of the King's saving acts for the people), and stipulations (commands, such as in the Sermon on the Mount). The epistles correspond to the Old Testament prophetic books, wherein the apostles call the churches to covenant faithfulness. The epistles also contain document clauses, to promote the bond between King and people by regular reading of the covenant. "Devote yourself to the public reading of Scripture" (1 Tim. 4:13 ESV). Apocalyptic books such as Revelation portray the sanctions of the covenant. "Apocalyptic writing demonstrate graphically the full

[6] M. Kline, *The Structure of Biblical Authority*, second edition, Wipf & Stock (1989), pp. 54-55.

[7] Kline, pp. 58-59.

reality of the present and ultimate consequences of either blessing or cursing that follow from obedience or disobedience to the covenant."[8]

Covenants are centered on kings. Just as the Old Testament preamble and history emphasize YHWH as Lord and King, the Gospel accounts emphasize Jesus as Lord and King. The very word *gospel* (in Greek, *euangelion*) was used in extrabiblical literature to announce the birth or victory of a King. This observation merits study of the most common title ascribed to Jesus.

Understanding the title of Christ

The royal dimensions of the New Testament have been greatly neglected. So much energy has been spent "proving" Jesus' divinity—certainly a correct doctrine—that we have forgotten that the New Testament places far more emphasis on Jesus' kingship. Many historic councils and creeds focused considerable energy onto Jesus' divinity, coinciding with debates of their age. Because we too often read Scripture through the lens of creeds, and not *vice versa*, we are made vulnerable to distortion.

These distortions can be more subtle, involving the content we subconsciously pour into words. The word *Christ* (from the Greek word *christos*) serves as an excellent example. A provocative case has been made that by the time of the first century, the term Christ would have widely been understood as King, or more fully, God's anointed King.[9] We will briefly look at some of these arguments.

While an introductory Greek course will teach that the word *christos* means "Anointed One" and *basileus* means "King," today the word *Christ* has effectively become a proper name. Even knowledgeable theologians and ministers make this error in their speaking and writing. Some less trained churchgoers even think that Christ was Jesus' last name, as if Joseph and Mary were Mr. and Mrs. Christ. Even Bible translations betray this proper name bias. While proper names are normally *transliterated* across languages (Mary in English, Miriam in Hebrew, Maria in Spanish), titles, being ordinary nouns should be *translated* (*king* in English, *melech* in Hebrew, *basileus* in Greek). Remarkably though, the word Christ is nearly always transliterated into other languages, as if it were a proper name (Christ, Cristo in Spanish, Kristo in Swahili). Christ has become for all practical purposes a proper name.

Some newer translations (TNIV, HCSB) recognize that Christ has

[8] Timothy Ward, *Words of Life*, InterVarsity Press (2009), p. 55.

[9] Christopher Gorton, *The Problem with Christ* (2013).

lost its force as a title, and use Messiah instead. While slightly better, this amounts to switching from transliterated Greek to transliterated Hebrew.

Part of the problem derives from how words and phrases change over time. For example, in King James English, "by and by" meant immediately, while today the word means eventually or slowly—nearly the opposite meaning. "Careful" in King James English means anxious or nervous, while today careful means attentive to detail. These sorts of changes, happening in less than four hundred years, should caution us against assuming that the meanings of words of the Bible remained static for over 1500 years (from Moses to Jesus). Even the Scriptures attest to changes in word meanings, "Formerly in Israel, when a man went to inquire of God, he spoke thus: 'Come, let us go to the seer'; for he who is now called a prophet was formerly called a seer" (1 Sam. 9:9).

The Greek word *christos* (from which we get Christ) represents the translation of the Hebrew word *mashiach* (from which we get Messiah). In its usage in the Torah, *mashiach* meant to rub, smear, or pour with oil. That usage pattern changes in the following centuries, so that by the time of the prophets, *mashiach* meant a person—God's king. It was used to describe David in Psalm 18:50, for example. By the time of the New Testament, the term is firmly entrenched as a royal title, parallel to king (Matt. 2:1-4, also compare Acts 17:3 to 17:7).[10]

For a profitable exercise, substitute "King" or "God's anointed King" for the word "Christ." This brings a new meaning and force to familiar texts:

> You therefore must endure hardship as a good soldier of King Jesus. (2 Tim. 2:3)
>
> Bear one another's burdens, and so fulfill the law of the King. (Gal. 6:2)
>
> If then you were raised with the King, seek those things which are above, where the King is, sitting at the right hand of God. (Col. 3:1)
>
> Blessed and holy is he who has part in the first resurrection. Over such the second death has no power, but they shall be priests of God and of the King, and shall reign with Him a thousand years. (Rev. 20:6)

[10] See Gorton's work for an elaboration of the historic development of *mashiach*, as well as flaws in BDAG's definition of *christos*.

Understanding the term Christ to mean God's anointed King highlights the New Testament's focus upon the kingdom of God, and upon Jesus as King. The state-church, born in the fourth century with Emperor Constantine's rise to power, minimized the focus on Jesus' kingship for self-serving reasons:

> In the Constantinian era..., the increasing distance between Jesus' lifestyle and that of many church leaders required a marginalization of Jesus' humanity. No longer was he the example whom Christians should imitate, at least as citizens. For state Christianity, Jesus of Nazareth was difficult to assimilate. He not only taught radical discipleship rather than patriotic citizenship, he was even executed by the state. Consequently, in the fourth century Jesus was recast as a celestial figure, his divinity was emphasized, and the dangerous memory of the Nazarene was allowed to fade.[11]

Implications of covenant

The implications of covenant are vast, and should forge the identity the church and every believer.

First, through covenant, we relate to God primarily as a group—corporately—not primarily in an individualistic sense. When Jesus teaches His disciples to pray, He instructs them to pray "*Our* Father." Sadly, many of the creeds begin with "*I* believe."[12] To relate to God is to relate to Him as a subject would to a King, with full awareness of standing among fellow citizens seeking to honor their King. Our increasingly "me-centered" society has led to a highly privatized faith, alien to the New Testament. Our preaching, songs, and books cater to whatever increases our personal estate and esteem. That old hymn "It is mine" could perhaps be sung in double-time, "It is mine, mine, mine, mine!"

Relating to God in a corporate sense should not lessen our worship of God, or diminish our understand of His love to us. Rather, it should heighten it. Knowing that God sees all of His children, bearing their

[11] Stuart Murray, *Biblical Interpretation in the Anabaptist Tradition*, Pandora Press, co-published with Herald Press (2000), p. 223.

[12] John D. Martin's insightful contrast. The Apostle's Creed begins with "I believe in God the Father almighty creator of heaven and earth. I believe in Jesus Christ, His only Son, our Lord..."

burdens, tenderly caring for each one, should only magnify God's greatness and the enormity of His love in our eyes. Too often we project our own limits of attention and love onto God and subconsciously believe that God's love to another means less love to us. Such thinking is misguided and should be countered with prayer to understand how wide, long, high, and deep the love of the King truly is.

Relating to God in a corporate sense also should encourage a sense of solidarity with other believers on the journey of faith. We are part of a cloud of witnesses that spans centuries and boundaries. Those who understand the concept of covenant thus are far more motivated to study church history and understand contemporary missions. Church history and missions is our family story, after all. Even reading the Bible takes on a new light when one views oneself in solidarity with the men and women of Scripture.

Second, relating to God as King in a covenantal fashion naturally incorporates the concept of obedience. The terms king, kingdom, and covenant imply obedience, loyalty, and a certain type of law. All nations have governance and laws, for the protection and well-being of their citizens. Followers of King Jesus abide by His law (Gal. 6:2). Not only does covenant reinforce obedience, it makes obedience a delight. One's kingdom is the range of one's will. To relate to God as King through covenant induces our hearts to yearn for His will to have free course, that is, for His kingdom to expand.

Third, relating to God as King through covenant implies warfare and conquest. God's kingdom is at war with forces of evil, and we are engulfed in that struggle. As drafted soldiers, we are endowed by the King with supernatural power to overcome sin and demonic forces, giving a mandate and purpose to our lives.

With its attendant concepts of solidarity, obedience, and conquest, the concept of covenant stands far above the bland term "relationship." Yet one more dimension to covenant must be explored.

Being found in God's anointed King

One of the apostles' favorite expressions is the phrase "in Christ."[13] We will render this as "in God's anointed King" or as "in the King," given the fuller understanding of the term Christ.

[13] The expression is especially common in in the book of Ephesians, where it is found 36 times. Notable references in the New Testament include: John 15:4; Rom. 6:11, 8:1, 12:5; 1 Cor. 1:30; 2 Cor. 1:21, 2:14; Gal. 3:28; Eph. 1:1, 1:3, 2:7, 4:32; Phil. 1:1, 3:3; Col. 1:2, 1:28; Philem. 1:6; and 1 Pet. 5:14.

What does it mean to be "in the King"? This idea can scarcely be found in the Old Testament, where the suzerain was far removed from his vassals. The space between king and subject gaped so wide that being found "in the King" would have been inconceivable. Yet in the New Covenant, not only is the gap erased, but a *union* is repeatedly stressed between King Jesus and His followers. He is in them and they are in Him. The expression implies that we can partake of King Jesus' nature. His power enables us to live faithfully and to overcome.

Being in the King also implies that we can partake of the love that the Father gives to the Son. For before God loved the world, God loved His Son. The depth of this prior love far exceeds human comprehension and motivates a gift. That gift to His Son is the world. A beautiful symmetry expresses both facets of the Father's love:

> The Father loves the world, so He gives His Son to the world (cf. John 3:16).
>
> The Father loves the Son, so He gives the world to His Son (cf. Ps. 2:8).

When Jesus announces that the kingdom of God is breaking forth upon the earth, He announces this gift. The Father is reclaiming that which is rightfully His, which then becomes the inheritance of the Son. The reward that Jesus is granted for his faithful obedience is nothing short of being granted the world itself.

Yet this gift to the Son is accompanied by a stunning truth: by being found "in the King," we receive what is given to Jesus Himself. The teaching of being "in the King" so often found in the New Testament represents perhaps the most glorious truth in all of the Bible—that we can be placed into King Jesus, and so receive the blessings that He receives and be seated with Him in heavenly places! Christians therefore receive the love the Father gives to the Son.

When disciples contemplate the concept of union with King Jesus, there should be no limit to their joy. This is why the apostle can say with confidence: "For I am persuaded that neither death nor life, nor angels nor principalities nor powers, nor things present nor things to come, nor height nor depth, nor any other created thing, shall be able to separate us from the love of God which is in Christ Jesus our Lord" (Rom. 8:38-39). The love of God is found in King Jesus. Because Jesus' disciples are "in the King," the same bond that unites God to His Son unites disciples to God. Could there be any greater truth to ignite the interests and passions of our souls?

I'm not sure I really understand the point ~~of~~ all this. The author wants the reader to place more emphasis on the 'king' connotation in the term "Christ", ~~and~~ he wants us to interpret the concept of 'church' as 'nation'?

I can see the way this emphasis calls our attention to certain details. But if its given too much weight, it will also detract from other important parts of the picture.

Chapter 3

New Testament family as strong-group

Whoever does the will of My Father in heaven is
My brother and sister and mother. (Matthew 12:50)

Just as Jesus proclaimed a new nation, a rival nation, He proclaimed a new family. The gospel writers carefully highlight this new family, including several remarkable passages that would have been nothing short of scandalous to the first-century hearer. Their scandalous nature forced hearers to begin "counting the cost" and to contemplate the dramatic change in relationships that would come from following Jesus. The thesis of this chapter has five components:

1. Family in the first century represented a "strong-group" or collectivist concept where the group's priorities stood above the individual's. In contrast, most families and nations in the West are "weak-group" institutions driven mostly by individualist thinking.
2. In a series of dramatic passages, Jesus taught allegiance to His family of disciples above one's natural family, in a strong-group sense. Much of the New Testament uses "brother" and "family" to describe Jesus' followers.
3. Commitment to the church has weakened because of an erosion of the strong-group mindset.
4. Strong-group status is enabled by seven elements: shared convictions of unique truths, new and close relationships, economic solidarity, separation, distinct rites and ceremonies, claims of spiritual descent from God's true people, and persecution resulting from bold advance.

5. The potential abuse of strong-groups is countered by a plurality of leaders and a biblical commitment to truth and critical thinking.

First century family as strong-group

The word "brother" in the first century was infused with significance that most modern Westerners do not grasp. Indeed, one of the prevailing themes of this book concerns the meanings that we pour into words. Often we subconsciously inject our own definitions into a word and miss the corrective potential that the Scriptures have for our lives: "Unless we understand New Testament social history sympathetically within its cultural settings—which are ancient and alien to ours—we are predisposed to misinterpret the social realities reflected there. The result is that we will superimpose our modern questions and social agendas onto the ancient texts in order to receive the answers we expect back again clothed in biblical authority."[1]

Concerning the word "family" and "brother," most simply do not understand what those terms meant in the first century. Family in the first-century Jewish setting was a "strong-group" model. Strong-group, or "collectivist," is a precise term used by anthropologists to mean:

- Individuals putting the concerns, honor, and interests of the group above their own.
- Individuals deriving their identity from their standing within the group more than from personal accomplishments.
- Individuals seeing themselves as responsible to the group for their actions.

Manifestations of a strong-group orientation from the Bible include:

- When children were to be married, the spouse was typically chosen by the parents in a so-called "arranged marriage" (which occurs to this day in strong-group societies). Isaac's marriage to Rebekah was determined by Abraham (Gen. 24). Children's willingness to submit to such an arrangement is proportional to the strong-group quality of their society.
- The number and length of genealogies in the Bible. A person's identity was located within their ancestry and tribe.

[1] Russ Dudrey, quoted in David deSilva, *Honor, Patronage, Kinship, & Purity*, IVP Academic (2000), p. 18f.

- Entire tribes would become circumcised in one day if a leader made the request (Gen. 34:24).
- So remarkable a man as David is remembered in the Psalms as "son of Jesse" rather than "king of Israel" (Ps. 72:20).
- Family land was intended to be permanent, because it would be restored each Jubilee if it had been lost through debt (Lev. 25:10).
- Moses demonstrated collectivism over individualism. After the Israelites' sin, God offers to make Moses into a great nation. Moses refuses and pleads to the Lord that the Israelites be spared. Moses' prays that YHWH's name would not be mocked by the Egyptians (Exod. 32:9-12). He goes on to pray one of the most remarkable prayers in Scripture, "Alas, this people has sinned a great sin. They have made for themselves gods of gold. But now, if You will forgive their sin—but if not, please blot me out of Your book that You have written" (Exod. 32:31-32). Moses is willing to forsake his own life for the sake of the group.
- Paul expresses a similar spirit as Moses, "For I could wish that I myself were accursed from Christ for my brethren, my countrymen according to the flesh" (Rom. 9:3).
- When Jesus does mighty works and speak with authority, the people reflexively question His stock. "Is this not the carpenter's son? Is not His mother called Mary? And His brothers James, Joses, Simon, and Judas?" (Matt. 13:55)
- When the Philippian jailer was converted, his entire family follows his path on that very same night (Acts 16:33).

The last two hundred years have seen an acceleration of individualism, radiating from the West outward. However, collectivism, or strong-group thinking, is still found in much of the Middle East and Asia. A simple illustration captures this difference. When a person begins a conversation in a Western setting, one of the first questions asked is, "What do you do?" In an Eastern setting, one of the first questions is, "Whose son are you?" This contrast illustrates how identity is perceived in a weak-group or individualist society (identity derived from accomplishment) versus in a strong-group or collectivist society (identity from family membership).

Strong-group societies hold up honor as a cardinal virtue. Weak-group societies hold up pleasure as a cardinal virtue. The "honor versus pleasure" spectrum serves as a useful scale to measure a society's strong-group status. Residents of the United States generally strive after pleasure. Much of Asian society is rooted in honor.

Both the Old and New Testaments are steeped in an honor-based value system. Scripture repeatedly commands us to honor God's name and treat Him as holy. The first line of the Lord's prayer is a plea that God's name will be revered. Regarding interpersonal treatment, the New Testament emphasis on honor is pervasive. Non-Christians would "subject the early Christians to censure and shaming techniques, designed to bring these deviant people back in line with the values and behaviors held dear by the surrounding culture (whether Jewish or Greco-Roman). The authors of the New Testament devote much of their attention, therefore, to insulating their congregations from the effects of these shaming techniques, calling the hearers to pursue lasting honor before that court of God whose verdict is eternal."[2] For example, "Blessed are you when men hate you, and when they exclude you, and revile you, and cast out your name as evil, for the Son of Man's sake" (Luke 6:22). See also Matthew 10:24-25 and Hebrews 10:32-24. These passages manifest the honor-based worldview that New Testament authors shared. Honor was a core value of the people of God, supporting the strong-group orientation of the Old and New Testaments.

Jesus' family as the new strong-group

When Jesus calls James and John, the Gospel accounts record that they leave their father in the boat (Matt. 4:22, Mark 1:20). While easy to pass over for a modern Western reader, the first-century audience, especially the first-century Jewish audience, would have been stunned. To leave one's own father in such a manner would have been scandalous—an egregious violation of the honor due to a parent. Another passage says, "Then another of His disciples said to Him, 'Lord, let me first go and bury my father.' But Jesus said to him, 'Follow Me, and let the dead bury their own dead' " (Matt. 8:21-22). In the Old Testament, a proper burial of the father testified to the honor of the family. The dying wish of Jacob himself was to receive a proper burial near the bones of Abraham and Isaac (Gen. 49:29-33). Righteous Joseph left Egypt to personally carry out this burial request (Gen. 50:4-10). The final wish of the patriarch of Israel left no small impression on the consciousness of this people. Hence Jesus' remarks to this disciple would have seemed cold, hostile, and scandalous because it violated customary filial duties. But Jesus was no hypocrite, for He treated His family as He asked others to do: "While He was still talking to the multitudes, behold, His mother and brothers stood outside, seeking to speak with Him. Then one said to Him, 'Look, Your mother and Your brothers are standing

[2] deSilva, p. 43.

outside, seeking to speak with You.' But He answered and said to the one who told Him, 'Who is My mother and who are My brothers?' And He stretched out His hand toward His disciples and said, 'Here are My mother and My brothers! For whoever does the will of My Father in heaven is My brother and sister and mother' " (Matt. 12:46-50). This passage, when read in a first-century Jewish home, would have caused hearers to gasp. For Jesus to subject His mother and brothers to this kind of public disgrace makes this account perhaps the most memorable of all the passages on family in the Gospel accounts.

At this point, any reasonable listener to Scripture should tremble at the sacrifice that Jesus models and asks His disciples to bear. Any "counting of the cost" should appreciate the sacrifice that the first disciples were asked to make. Jesus asked His disciples to relegate two strong-groups, family and nation, in order to devote themselves to a new strong-group, the church. One's biologic family would have likely been the weightier cost. In this context, Jesus said, "If anyone comes to Me and does not hate his father and mother, wife and children, brothers and sisters, yes, and his own life also, he cannot be My disciple. And whoever does not bear his cross and come after Me cannot be My disciple" (Luke 14:26-27). The close bonds to natural family are to be as hatred relative to our love for Jesus and His family. At the same time, Jesus is not asking disciples to abandon their families or their duties to them. Just as the call to a new citizenship does not abrogate one's earthly citizenship, so Jesus upheld honoring one's parents and caring for their needs (Mark 10:10-12). If we are to honor and obey the state, much more are we to honor and obey our natural parents. However Jesus advocates *primary* strong-group allegiance toward His new family, those who do the will of the Father in heaven. When the two collide, Jesus' family must be chosen. Moreover, the strong-group nature of biologic family is not lost—it is instead *transferred* from natural family to Jesus' family. The following passage describes that transferal: "Then Peter began to say to Him, 'See, we have left all and followed You.' So Jesus answered and said, 'Assuredly, I say to you, there is no one who has left house or brothers or sisters or father or mother or wife or children or lands, for My sake and the gospel's, who shall not receive a hundredfold now in this time—houses and brothers and sisters and mothers and children and lands, with persecutions—and in the age to come, eternal life' " (Mark 10:28-30).

The first-century hearer would have thus looked at joining Jesus' nation, or Jesus' family, as adoption into a new family. For this reason, the New Testament most commonly designates Christians as "brothers," a feature particularly prominent in the epistles. One example will suffice:

"Brethren, pray for us. Greet all the brethren with a holy kiss. I charge you by the Lord that this epistle be read to all the holy brethren" (1 Thess. 5:25-27). Within a short span, Paul uses "brethren" three times in addressing the congregation. The practice seen in the epistles derives from Jesus Himself who describes God more as "Father" than by any other title. Jesus also pronounced to His disciples, "You are all brethren" (Matt. 23:8), inspiring the title of address so often found in the epistles.

Weak-group behaviors eroding the church

Sociologists employ surveys to measure the degree of individualism or collectivism present in a society. These and other metrics include:

1. Are there arranged marriages in that society?
2. What percentage of people live alone?
3. What percentage of the elderly live alone or in nursing homes versus with their children?
4. What percentage of commuters are car-pooling?
5. How often are older people addressed as sir, ma'am, Mr. or Mrs.?
6. How far away do children reside from their parents?

Sociologists have found that society has been growing more individualistic with time (the expression "rugged individualism" was introduced in the twentieth century). In parallel, dozens of surveys have found profoundly weaker commitment to church, less identity found in the church, and more of a consumerist approach: "I like the preaching there, the building over there, the people over there, and the singing more here." Pastors complain of "church dating" and "church hopping." Few are willing to place themselves under authority. More people say they love God and Jesus but want nothing to do with the life of the church. Such sentiments are the epitome of individualism and weak-group behavior.

The rise of weak-group society and the erosion of commitment to church life are closely related. As individuals increasingly consider their own interests to be paramount, the interests of other groups like family or church naturally erode.

Enabling strong-group status

The book of Acts offers the clearest paradigm for church life. Miracles demonstrated the presence of the Holy Spirit among them. Their purity and growth was renowned. Elements that enabled their strong-group status are described in a compact passage from Acts:

> And with many other words he testified and exhorted them, saying, "Be saved from this perverse generation." Then those who gladly received his word were baptized; and that day about three thousand souls were added to them. And they continued steadfastly in the apostles' doctrine and fellowship, in the breaking of bread, and in prayers. Then fear came upon every soul, and many wonders and signs were done through the apostles. Now all who believed were together, and had all things in common, and sold their possessions and goods, and divided them among all, as anyone had need. So continuing daily with one accord in the temple, and breaking bread from house to house, they ate their food with gladness and simplicity of heart, praising God and having favor with all the people. And the Lord added to the church daily those who were being saved. (Acts 2:40-47)

Seven elements that enable strong-group status can be found in this passage and the subsequent chapters of Acts. They are:

1. Shared convictions of unique truths. "They continued steadfastly in the apostles' doctrine and fellowship" (v. 42). The early disciples believed the teachings of Jesus and the apostles; doctrines like Jesus' resurrection, forgiveness through His blood, and nonresistance were unique truths that were foreign to that land.
2. New and close relationships. Their lifestyle was marked with "fellowship" and the "breaking of bread" (v. 42). Also it says, "Breaking bread from house to house, they ate their food with gladness and simplicity of heart" (v. 46). They shared their lives with each other *in their homes.* Far from restricted to a Sunday morning gathering in a neutral hall, their fellowship knew no bounds. These meetings were the spontaneous overflow of their love of Jesus and the brotherhood.
3. Economic solidarity. They "had all things in common, and sold their possessions and goods, and divided them among all, as anyone had need" (vv. 44 and 45). As all natural families do, they shared their resources. This practice followed what the disciples had with Jesus when they shared a common purse (Luke 8:3; John 12:6, 13:29).

4. Separation. Only one line of Peter's sermon is preserved in this section, presumably a summary of a longer exposition, "Be saved from this perverse generation" (v. 40). The early disciples recognized the perverseness of their generation and responded with holy living and separation from the world.
5. Distinct rites and ceremonies. Unique practices like baptism and breaking bread in the Lord's Supper strengthened their unity.
6. Claims of spiritual descent from God's true people. The apostles believed that they were the true Israel. Their sermons declared that Jesus' followers are the true successors of the people of God throughout the ages. Thus Christians follow in the lineage of Abraham, Isaac, Jacob, Moses, David, and the prophets. Jesus' crucifixion placed Him as the last and greatest prophet to be martyred. Surrounded by a great "cloud of witnesses," the followers of the Way drew instruction, encouragement, and identity from those who had gone before them.
7. Persecution resulting from bold advance. Thousands were added to the church (including priests) as the gospel boldly advanced. Acts also records that Peter and John were arrested. Stephen was stoned. James was killed by the sword. Paul would experience persecution and hardship throughout his life, including beatings and imprisonments.

These are the elements that potentiate strong-group status. Modern Christianity abounds with churches that trumpet their desire for greater "community" or fellowship, but virtually none are willing to embrace the cost modeled by Jesus and the apostles to attain the strong-group status of this movement that turned the world upside-down.

Abuse of strong-group and biblical correctives

Deep in our hearts there is a hunger for community—a hunger to know and be known. This hunger existed in Eden before sin came into the world. Because this hunger is God-given, it should be cherished. The Trinity itself consists of the persons of the triune God in unity and community. Because humans are made in the image of God, this desire for unity and community is stamped into our very souls.

Yet this hunger offers the capacity for exploitation, manipulation, and abuse. Strong-groups therefore represent powerful forces that can be bent toward evil. For example, gangs exploit the deep hunger that young people have to be part of a strong-group; they offer identity and purpose in life. Examining the definition of a strong group offered above, note how well gangs meet the criteria:

- Individuals putting the concerns, honor, and interests of the group above their own.
- Individuals deriving their identity from their standing within the group more than from personal accomplishments.
- Individuals seeing themselves as responsible to the group for their actions.

Other examples of worldly strong-groups abound. Recreational activities or hobbies can become idolatrously elevated as part of an attendant strong-group. Motorcycles groups, surf clubs, athletic leagues, fraternities, sororities, and countless other groups draw people into the pursuit of vanities in strong-group manners.

Religious strong-groups have a concerning potential for abuse. Extreme examples of cults (such as those at Jamestown or Waco) are cited by the world as the "dangers of religion." Many religious groups use tactics to draw or retain members that involve coercion or unquestioning submission to authority.

Scripture presents two correctives to check the abusive potential of strong-groups. First, leadership should be plural. This subject is covered at length in a subsequent chapter. Many abusive strong-groups have rested on the charisma and authority of a single man. Scripture in contrast always describes a *plurality* of elders.[3] These elders are nearly always unnamed individuals, quietly serving the church and providing stability. Moreover, as will be described later, scriptural leadership is primarily about service, not about power.

The second corrective offers even greater force to counter the abusive power of strong-groups. This corrective concerns the manner of influence: *biblical strong-groups are truth-based, not leadership-dominated.* Several examples illustrate this:

1. The Bereans challenged Paul with Scripture when he preached in their synagogue. They "searched the Scriptures daily to find out whether these things were so" (Acts 17:11). Challenging an apostle was commended, not reproved. Interestingly, this sort of examination caused more people with non-Jewish backgrounds

[3] Throughout the book of Acts, the word *elders* is used in the plural, and never in the singular (Acts 11:30, 14:23, 15:2, 15:4, 15:6, 15:22, 15:23, 16:4, 20:17, 20:18, 24:1). The epistles bear similar witness (1 Tim. 5:17; Titus 1:5; James 5:14; 1 Pet. 5:1, 5:5).

to become disciples, including the prominent in society: "Therefore many of them believed, and also not a few of the Greeks, prominent women as well as men" (Acts 17:12).

2. Scripture commands critical thinking: "Test all things; hold fast to what is good" (1 Thess. 5:21).
3. Even prophets are to be "weighed," "sifted," or "judged" (1 Cor. 14:29).[4]
4. Jesus uses logic applied to Scripture to devastate the challenges of his opponents.[5]
5. Jesus modifies the beloved *Shema*, "You shall love the Lord your God with all your heart, with all your soul, and with all your strength" (Deut. 6:5). He adds "mind" to the list, "You shall love the Lord your God with all your heart, with all your soul, with all your strength, and with all your mind" (Luke 10:27). Surely no accident, by this addition Jesus invites His disciples to follow His own pattern of sharp logic and clear thinking.

Hence a mark of a scriptural strong-group is its commitment to truth and investigation. A biblical strong-group will not fear critical thinking but embrace it. Studying languages like Hebrew and Greek would not be looked down upon but welcomed. While knowledge and critical thinking have the capacity to be cause for pride, when applied toward Scripture, they should instead drive disciples toward love and service.

Teachers hold sway, not because of their titles, but because they are capable expositors of truth. These teachers invite challenge and questioning. Instead of being bound together by charismatic personality, hierarchical leadership, scare tactics, or manipulation, biblical strong-groups are bound together by truth in Jesus as they strive to serve their King.

[4] Varying translations of *diakrinetosan*.

[5] D. Willard's paper *Jesus The Logician* (1999) examines texts like Matt. 12:1-8, Luke 20:27-40, and Luke 20:42-43 to illuminate this point.

Chapter 4

Discipleship as intensive companionship

Follow Me. (Matthew 4:19)

Dale was a sincere eighteen year old man who had some familiarity with Christianity from attending Sunday school as a boy.[1] His parents were not devout, attending a nearby Roman Catholic church a few times a year, especially for Christmas and Easter. Dale was generally sympathetic to Jesus' teachings, but faith made only a small impact on his life. His parents watched a good deal of television, so Dale did as well. He grew particularly fond of certain shows and began to imitate the speech, dress, and habits of those he admired. In the public schools, Dale learned the ways of the world firsthand and began to dabble in pornography. He felt guilty every time he looked at pornography, but it was easy to get access through his phone or computer. A powerful addiction grew in strength over the years. He graduated from school and worked at a gasoline station. His old school friends would often party and drink, and Dale, being quite lonely, joined them. But another friend invited him to some small group Bible studies, meetings which touched him deeply. A preacher invited him to come forward in an altar call, and he responded. Dale committed his heart to the Lord, confessing his sins, including his addiction to pornography. He even had an accountability partner, with whom he met every Saturday morning.

Though he did well for a while, Dale could not break his addiction to pornography. The repeated failures discouraged him greatly. His accountability partner prayed for him, and even helped him put a filter onto his computer. But Dale still found ways to feed his addiction. His

---

[1] This is a true story, but names and other details have been changed.

old friends kept inviting him to parties, which he resisted for several months. But after failing with pornography after several occasions, he went back to the party lifestyle. He made numerous attempts to get back on course, but eventually reverted back to his old lifestyle. Today Dale is spiritually colder than before; having "tried Jesus" he is now hardened against the gospel. Now addicted to pornography and pleasure more than ever before, Dale has managed to create in his mind a quasi-religious framework that gives respect to God but does not meaningfully challenge him to a life of obedience or devotion.

What went wrong with this young man? His story, with slight variations, is the story of thousands, perhaps millions, of people today. The core problem is that *Dale experienced a failure of discipleship*. While he studied the Bible, went to church meetings for a season, and had an accountability partner, there was a lack of biblical discipleship—the process that turns a convert into a disciple. What is more worrisome is that no one walking alongside Dale would have identified that something was wrong from the beginning of Dale's journey of faith. Hence no one could have done any differently in helping him. People today simply do not know what discipleship looks like.

Our age is in the midst of a crisis of discipleship. Many supposedly have a conversion, yet their lives are not transformed. Nearly all evangelistic efforts, from mass evangelistic campaigns to private, less formal efforts, typically produce proselytes who experience change for a short season and then slowly fall back into their own ways. Discouragement sets in when a believer supposedly leads a person to the Lord who then falls away. The zealous Christian, once filled with desire to tell the world about the Savior, after experiencing such setbacks eventually cools into lukewarm stagnation. Without discipleship, evangelism jades both Christians and the world.

Jesus as the model

Because of the broad lack of success in discipleship, many are simply apathetic, never having seen examples that inspire them. Others focus on getting people to "pray the sinner's prayer" and have little idea what to do next. Their training is oriented toward coaxing others to make a decision, not to making disciples. Still others, while understanding the importance of discipleship, have failed by turning to the wrong models. Modern discipleship methods nearly always draw upon models other than Jesus'. Countless techniques have been advocated that draw from academic training, the business world, or human psychology. Yet the solution to this grievous problem is right under our very noses, in the example of Jesus' strategy in making disciples. "This is one of the marvels of his strategy. It is so unassuming and silent that it is unnoticed by the hurried churchman. But when the realization of his controlling method finally dawns on the open mind of the disciple, he will wonder how he could have ever failed to see it before."[2]

Jesus implied that His disciples should follow His method of discipleship, "As the Father has sent Me, I also send you" (John 20:21). Christians today have been sent into the world, just as Jesus was sent into the world. Jesus' discipleship pattern thus becomes our paradigm. "For I have given you an example, that you should do as I have done to you" (John 13:15).

We must make disciples according to Jesus' example. Jesus' ministry was bracketed with discipleship: it began with a call for disciples (Mark 1:16-20) and ended with a command to make disciples (Matt. 28:19-20). In between, His earthly ministry was characterized with passionate, relentless effort to make disciples:

> His life was ordered by his objective. Everything he did and said was a part of the whole pattern. It had significance because it contributed to the ultimate purpose of his life in redeeming the world for God. This was the motivating vision governing his behavior. His steps were ordered by it. Mark it well. Not for one moment did Jesus lose sight of his goal. That is why it is so important to observe the way Jesus maneuvered to achieve his objective. The Master disclosed God's strategy for world conquest. He had confidence in the future precisely because he lived according to that plan in the present. There was nothing haphazard about his life—no wasted energy, not an idle word. He was on business for God (Luke 2:49). He lived, he died, and he rose again according to schedule. Like a general plotting his course of battle, the Son of God calculated to win. He could not afford to take a chance. Weighing every alternative and variable factor in human experience, he conceived a plan that would not fail.[3]

Let us therefore examine God's strategy for world conquest. The implications are revolutionary.

---

[2] Robert Coleman, *The Master Plan of Evangelism*, Revell (1993), p. 18.

[3] Coleman, pp. 17-18.

People were His purpose and men were His method

Jesus' mission was for people—not for programs, funds, or buildings—but people. As He walked the roads of Israel, it was the plight of humanity that moved Him to action. He came to rescue humankind from the grip of Satan. He lived and died for people. People were His purpose.

The all-consuming passion of Jesus for souls leaps out on every page of the Gospel accounts: "When He saw the multitudes, He was moved with compassion for them, because they were weary and scattered, like sheep having no shepherd. Then He said to His disciples, 'The harvest truly is plentiful, but the laborers are few. Therefore pray the Lord of the harvest to send out laborers into His harvest' " (Matt. 9:36-38). When Jesus saw people, He was moved with compassion. Because He looked past the outward appearance and into the inward reality, Jesus saw lostness, sin, and death. The sight of the multitude prompted Jesus' only recorded prayer request in the Gospel accounts. He asked His disciples to pray that God would send out laborers to reap souls into the harvest of His kingdom.

The most precious commodity of the kingdom is laborers. Money, buildings, and programs pale in comparison to the worth of faithful laborers. Jesus understood the great scarcity of laborers, so His heart could not but overflow in prayer for that great need. He could not help but invite His disciples to do the same. What flows out of Jesus' compassion for the multitudes? Two things. First, the prayer request for laborers. Second, Jesus' call for a group of men to be with him. Men were his method to change the world.

Specific selection

The sequence of events in Matthew 9:35-10:4 is no accident. Jesus traveled throughout Israel's cities and villages, teaching, preaching, and healing. But when He sees the multitudes, He is moved with compassion because they lacked godly leadership. Next, He asks His disciples to pray that God would send out workers into the harvest field. Jesus then names twelve men to be his disciples (Matt. 10:1). Jesus thus converts His compassion into action by choosing people to be with Him.

This must be our pattern of converting compassion into action: by bringing people to be with us. Not many people, but only a few.

Many believers have noted paradoxes in Scripture: servants shall be leaders, the humble shall be exalted, victory is gained through death, gain comes through loss, and strength through weakness. Yet another paradox has drawn insufficient attention: *to win the many, focus on the few.*

Jesus sees the multitudes, then turns around and focuses on the few. He turns His gaze from the thousands to only a dozen. Most have the opposite impulse—to start great campaigns or build grand buildings, attempting to reach many people quickly. Yet such responses are not rooted in the pattern of the Savior. Jesus spent most of His ministry with a small number of men, and this pattern only intensifies as the time of His death drew near. *He focused His time and energy on only a very few men.*

After Jesus died, many probably wondered if His little band would be extinguished. Yet Jesus' genius eluded the small minds of men—He laid a strong foundation for something much greater.

Immediately after this passage, the names of the disciples are given. This detail could easily go unnoticed but merits careful reflection. Jesus made it clear who the twelve were. After this selection event, there was a clear, definite circle of men who understood themselves to be Jesus' disciples. Today such clarity is often lacking. Many ministers simply hope that people will "figure it out," and are left without clear discipling relationships. For fear of being overbearing, fear of failure, lack of confidence, or even wrong-headed notions of "following the Spirit," leaders today often fail by not providing the clarity of specific and intentional selection.

While there were many people who followed Jesus, He makes it clear who His specially appointed apostles were. He did not fear offending the crowd by omitting some people from the twelve, but understood that this step was vital for the propagation of the gospel.

The substance of discipleship

An abbreviated definition of discipleship is *intensive companionship.* An expanded definition could be: a spiritually mature individual providing intensive companionship and instruction to a person seeking a new way of life. "Follow me" succinctly captures discipleship. The Gospel accounts explicitly give Jesus' reasons for calling the twelve: "Then He appointed twelve, that they might be with Him and that He might send them out to preach, and to have power to heal sicknesses and to cast out demons" (Mark 3:14-15). At the head of the list, being "with Him" represents the essential content of discipleship. The Gospel accounts narrate what it meant to be with Jesus. "He ate with them, slept with them, and talked with them for the most part of his entire active ministry. They walked together along the lonely roads; they visited together in the crowded cities; they sailed and fished together on the Sea of Galilee; they prayed together in the deserts and in the mountains; and they worshiped together in the synagogues and in the temple."[4] Leading by example, Jesus seemed to be especially eager to teach His disciples how to pray:

> More than twenty times the Gospels call attention to Jesus' practice of prayer. It is given special mention during events of momentous decision in his life—baptism (Luke 3:21); the selection of the twelve apostles (Luke 6:12); on the Mount of Transfiguration (Luke 9:29); the Last Supper (Matt. 26:27); in Gethsemane (Luke 22:39-46); and on the cross (Luke 23:46). The [apostles] also were impressed to record the Lord's intercession in connection with their own ministry—the confession of his messiahship (Luke 9:18); on hearing their reports of evangelism (Luke 10:21-22); teaching them to pray (Luke 11:1); the great high-priestly prayer before he goes to die (John 17:6-19); the loving concern for Peter (Luke 22:32); and at the home of the two disciples in Emmaus after the resurrection (Luke 24:30). Prayer is prominent also in the exercise of his power-working miracles—healing the multitudes (Mark 1:35); feeding the five thousand (Mark 6:41; Matt. 14:19; Luke 9:16; John 6:11); later feeding the four thousand (Mark 8:6; Matt. 15:36); healing the deaf-mute (Mark 7:34); and raising Lazarus from the dead (John 11:41). Moreover, prayer is on the lips of Jesus as he looks at the multitudes whom he came to save—before conflict with religious leaders (Luke 5:16); in the discussion with the Greeks who came to see him (John 12:27); after sending away the five thousand who had been fed (Mark 6:46; Matt. 14:23); blessing little children (Mark 10:16); and finally for those who nailed him to the cross (Luke 23:34).[5]

Prayer was not taught through books but by observing a living example. They learned nearly everything this way. The apostles learned how to handle Scripture by studying Jesus' incredible skill. His virtues of kindness, boldness, and compassion were transmitted over these years of continual observation and imitation.

---

[4] Coleman, p. 37.

[5] Coleman, p. 116.

Jesus' pattern of intensive companionship stands in stark contrast to modern methods. Many hope that through Sunday services, and perhaps with additional cell group meetings or prayer meetings, that discipleship can be attained. Jesus did not spend three or four hours per week with His disciples. He spent His whole day with them. If the Son of God spent essentially all of His time for over three years with a small group of people, dare we imagine that through far less time we can make disciples?

Jesus' way of making disciples was continued by the apostles. One apostle wrote, "Imitate me, just as I also imitate Christ" (1 Cor. 11:1, see also 1 Cor. 4:16). This profound sentence beautifully captures the essence of discipleship. It forces those embarking on the task of discipleship to first look at their own lives and ask, "Am I worthy of being imitated? Am I imitating Jesus?" Discipleship cannot begin without a godly life worth imitating.

Intensive companionship was not an afterthought—it was at the very foundation of their ministry and preaching. "You know, from the first day that I came to Asia, in what manner I always lived among you" (Acts 20:18; see also Acts 20:34-35 and 1 Thess. 1:5). The apostles' flock may have learned as much about the faith in the sweaty shops of labor as in cool evenings of the Lord's day gatherings.

The shallow efforts of the modern church at discipleship often do more harm than good. A false security is instilled into new converts by these mislabeled programs. Because new converts do not recognize that they are not being discipled, they easily fall prey to the Enemy.

Dale had no idea that he was not being discipled according to Jesus' example. He falsely imagined that he was on a path of discipleship by going to a Sunday meeting and meeting with his accountability partner on Saturday morning. He was actually being discipled by those with whom he was spending the most time: his unbelieving friends from school and worldly co-workers at the gas station.

Strong-group discipleship

When the disciples heed Jesus' call to follow Him, they leave their livelihoods. At the very beginning of Jesus' ministry, Mark describes that Simon, Andrew, James, and John *immediately* leave their nets to follow after Jesus (Mark 1:16-20). In order to be with Jesus, they make great sacrifice. For years they live under difficult conditions, having to subsist from a shared purse (Luke 8:3; John 12:6, 13:29). The life of sacrifice continues in the early church as described in Acts. Even today, discipleship generally involves changing one's occupation and place of residence.

The world's structures are hostile to biblical discipleship. With material prosperity and technology has come greater isolation physically and socially—opposing intensive companionship. The post-industrial rise of education outside the home has caused young people to be socialized by peers. At tender moments in time when identity is formed, young people are thrust into college environments where they are taught the importance of career and the world's set of values. As families plant roots, a comfortable house is the priority—not sacrificing to be near fellow believers. The world's patterns of "this present evil age" are arrayed against Jesus' way of discipleship in more ways than we imagine.

Separation from the world (2 Cor. 6:17) represents essentially the same concept as biblical discipleship. The Corinthians were spending time in the pagan temples, which represented the center of life in the first century. Birthday celebrations, special occasions, stimulating conversation, and basic socialization took place in the temple environment. The command to separate from the world must be understood in this context. Separation is merely the flip side of discipleship. While easy to make a negative term, separation should also be understood as a positive term. Separation is being separated into the church, a new social order demonstrating to the world how God intends humanity to live.

Strong-group churches uniquely have the ability to disciple as Jesus did. Consider again the seven elements that enable strong-group status:

1. Shared convictions of unique truths
2. New and close relationships
3. Economic solidarity
4. Separation (the twin truth to discipleship)
5. Distinct rites and ceremonies
6. Claims of spiritual descent from God's true people
7. Persecution resulting from bold advance

Discipleship as thoroughgoing resocialization should be understood from this matrix of church life. And when the gospel call goes forth, "counting the cost" should be evident by observing the lives of strong-group Christians.

Discipleship re-imagined

Let us revisit Dale's story and imagine how it might have gone differently. When Dale heard the gospel call, he saw a group of people in the congregation who had made sacrificial choices. Many had changed occupations in order to work with each other as a brotherhood. He saw that the families lived close to each other and spent a great deal of time going house to house. He observed a family, in a strong-group sense. Thus Dale understood the gospel call to repentance by way of the gap he saw between his life and what he saw practiced in the congregation.

After he responded affirmatively, one young family offered that he could move into a bedroom attached to their house. The young father, Ethan, asked if he could disciple Dale. Dale accepted because he was taught at the outset that discipleship was the substance of the Christian walk. Ethan worked with fellow brothers in a grocery store, and Dale was given the opportunity to stock shelves in the store. So he quit his job at the gas station. He spent virtually all his time with Ethan on the job, as well as the fellowship of believers in the evenings. On the job, by working closely with other believers, he began to understand how to respond to frustration in a godly manner. Over many years, he caught their love for God's word and for prayer. Dale never really had the time or opportunity to spend time with his old school friends any more. Eventually he lost the desire to party. As he matured in his walk, he began to speak more frequently in the Lord's day gathering of the saints. He even helped play a role in bringing another person into the kingdom. Dale eventually married a young lady in the church and began a family of his own.

This type of discipleship requires sacrifice. The congregation first had to make sacrifices in their own lives, by changing jobs to work with each other and moving near one another, providing a testimony to the world around them. They fought against the world's structures to become a strong-group family. They truly shared life together. Dale understood those testimonies and examples to be overlaid onto the words of the gospel message, creating a "leave your nets" moment. Dale had to sacrifice his old job and living arrangement when he decided to follow Jesus. Ethan and his family had to make sacrifice in receiving Dale into their home.

But the sacrifices were worth it.

This sort of discipleship lacks glamor; it is demanding and slow. One can usually only point to only a few changed lives. But Jesus' way of discipleship bears lasting fruit for generations to come. It represents His way to conquer the world.

The heart of *discipleship* is not and should not be primarily about belonging to a somewhat insular church community. Close Christian community is good. That is how the early churches were and how all churches should be. But *discipleship itself* goes way beyond that. My understanding is this: it is also closely related to spreading God's word *after* one has joined a church community than merely being a part of that community. It is about, I think, fully embracing the *faith* *of* *Christ* more so than immitating his manner of fellowship, though this is certainly a part of it too.

Chapter 5

Equality among brothers

Beloved, let us love one another, for love is of God; and everyone who loves is born of God and knows God. (1 John 4:7)

In 2003, a nineteen year old boy in New Jersey named Bruce was found looking through the garbage for food. He weighed 45 pounds and stood only four feet tall.[1] Severely malnourished, Bruce and three of his brothers were eating insulation and wall board to satisfy their hunger. Bruce left home to look for food and was found looking through a trash bin at 2:30 AM. When police investigated Bruce's home, they found a total of seven children: three siblings were healthy and fed while four were grossly neglected and malnourished (the four malnourished boys, aged nine to nineteen, weighed 136 pounds combined: Michael, age nine, weighed 23 pounds; Tyrone, age ten, weighed 28 pounds; and Keith, age fourteen, weighed 40 pounds). One wonders how such stark inequities could exist within a single family.

Yet this true story illustrates a no less dire condition of the church today. While all believers are members of one family, some are prosperous and well fed while others are destitute and hungry.

The least of these My brothers

The Gospel according to Matthew presents the clearest vision of the church functioning as a new family, with attendant strong-group qualities. A thread is woven through Matthew's text, beginning with a promise of blessing to those who receive Jesus' disciples: "He who receives you receives Me, and he who receives Me receives Him who sent

[1] This true story was reported by the *New York Times* on October 27, 2003.

Me. He who receives a prophet in the name of a prophet shall receive a prophet's reward. And he who receives a righteous man in the name of a righteous man shall receive a righteous man's reward. And whoever gives one of these little ones only a cup of cold water in the name of a disciple, assuredly, I say to you, he shall by no means lose his reward" (Matt. 10:40-42). Who are the little ones? According to Matthew 11:25 and 18:14, the little ones are not children, but disciples.[2] This terminology captures their vulnerability as sheep among wolves (Matt. 10:16). When someone gives to a little one "in the name of a disciple," (an idiomatic expression meaning "because he is a disciple"), they will receive a reward.

Earlier we read that Jesus calls His disciples His "brothers" and "sisters" (Matt. 12:48-40). Jesus' disciples form a new family, of which He is the eldest brother. This understanding penetrates to language used on the day of judgment: "Then the righteous will answer Him, saying, 'Lord, when did we see You hungry and feed You, or thirsty and give You drink? When did we see You a stranger and take You in, or naked and clothe You? Or when did we see You sick, or in prison, and come to You?' And the King will answer and say to them, 'Assuredly, I say to you, inasmuch as you did it to one of the least of these My brethren, you did it to Me' " (Matt. 25:37-40).

This passage is often misunderstood to be about the general poor. But in Matthew's vocabulary, the "least of these My brethren" combines two expressions used earlier: "little ones" (10:42) and "brother" (12:50, also cf. 28:10), both of which refer to disciples. Therefore, in this passage, the "least of these My brethren" means the poor and mistreated Christians.[3] The historic interpretation of this passage is that it applies to destitute believers, while in the twentieth century it was often applied the general poor, irrespective of faith status. "[The] 'Serving Christians' interpretation of 'the least' was the majority view in church history *until* modern times."[4] Jesus teaches that the day of judgment will be about how a person has treated the helpless and vulnerable Christians who are naked, hungry, and imprisoned.

---

[2] Also note that one of John's favorite titles for Christians is "little children." He uses the expression nine times in 1 John.

[3] On exegetical grounds, when unpacking the meaning of *elachistos* used in Matthew 25:37-40 in light of 10:40-42 and 18:6-14, most recent commentators favor the view that "little ones" refers to Christians. These scholars include R. T. France (NICNT), Donald Hagner (WBC), and Leon Morris (PNTC).

[4] F. D. Bruner, *Matthew: A Commentary, Volume 2*, Eerdmans (2007), p. 575. However, as noted in the prior footnote, over the last two decades, exegetes have moved to favor the historic interpretation of this passage.

Put another way, judgment day will be about equity within the family of God. Judgment will involve whether supposed members of the family were strong-group, keeping watch over the totality of the body, or whether they selfishly followed their own interests. Seen in this light, the sharing passages in Acts 2:44-46 and 4:32-35 become *fulfillments* of Matthew 25. Paul's charge to "remember the poor" (Gal. 2:10) and his collection for the famine-ravaged Jerusalem Christians were also fulfillments of this dramatic description of the last day.

Sharing instead of giving

When the people came to the Jordan river to hear John the Baptist, he said about repentance, "Whoever has two tunics is to share with him who has none, and whoever has food is to do likewise" (Luke 3:11 ESV). While some translations say "give to him who has none," more accurate translations of this verse say "share with him who has none." "Sharing" is what families do, while "giving" is typically done to those whom one may never see again. Sharing is more difficult because it involves relationships, and learning to live and relate with one's neighbor or brother. Acts describes a model that was sharing—note that the expression "all things in common" is used both in Acts 2:44 and 4:32. Giving certainly has an important place (Luke 12:33), but the major activity that disciples carry out is sharing.

Sharing also connotes that a person's possessions belong to another. Sharing connotes a shared claim. What father "gives" a couch to his son? No, the healthy family shares its possessions. The vocabulary of sharing conveys that when you join the family of God, your possessions become that family's. This understanding harmonizes with Jesus teaching: "Then Peter began to say to Him, 'See, we have left all and followed You.' So Jesus answered and said, 'Assuredly, I say to you, there is no one who has left house or brothers or sisters or father or mother or wife or children or lands, for My sake and the gospel's, who shall not receive a hundredfold now in this time—houses and brothers and sisters and mothers and children and lands, with persecutions—and in the age to come, eternal life' " (Mark 10:28-30).

The tithe becomes the whole

In the Old Testament, a tithe was the standard of giving (Lev. 27:30; Deut. 14:22-23). Yet in the New Testament, a new standard is given: "Whoever of you does not forsake all that he has cannot be My disciple"

(Luke 14:33). When a person joins the family of God, he is giving up *all* of his possessions. The mentality of a tithe is foreign to the spirit of the New Testament because all is demanded.

In the Sermon on the Mount, Jesus offers a challenging vision for His disciples on their attitude toward earthly possessions: "Do not lay up for yourselves treasures on earth, where moth and rust destroy and where thieves break in and steal; but lay up for yourselves treasures in heaven, where neither moth nor rust destroys and where thieves do not break in and steal. For where your treasure is, there your heart will be also" (Matt. 6:19-21). Instead of accumulating treasure on earth, disciples are taught to put treasure in heaven. By giving their possessions to others, they are storing up treasures in heaven (also see Luke 16:9). As Paul taught, "For what is our hope, or joy, or crown of rejoicing? Is it not even you in the presence of our Lord Jesus Christ at His coming? For you are our glory and joy" (1 Thess. 2:19-20). How many Christians understand that their crown of rejoicing is supposed to be other disciples? Some hymns teach that our glory and joy is in Jesus alone. Yet the parable of the sheep and the goats, as well as the instruction from 1 Thessalonians 2:19-20, teaches that our glory and joy, and very standing before God, is largely based in our fellow disciples.

A corollary of the New Testament principle of equality could be stated as "share more than you can spare." We should "feel" our giving and sharing because it costs us dearly. Our sharing should be sacrificial, causing us to live differently than we otherwise would. Can we point to activities or possessions that we have consciously forsaken for the sake of helping out a brother or sister in the family of God? If not, our giving and sharing is almost certainly insufficient.

Insurance

Many will be surprised to find a discussion of insurance in a book like this. For most of my life, I viewed insurance as most do: we have "security" by interacting remotely with a faceless organization or the government, paying money each month and drawing on a pool of money should a need arise. As a physician, I interacted with insurance companies on behalf of patients and learned a great deal about how the system worked. But my views completely changed when my wife and I attended a church where the members declined traditional insurance and assumed this function as a group. With a few thousand members across dozens of churches, this brotherhood had been successfully filling this role for decades. When a need arose, a minister would discreetly describe that there had been a car accident or serious illness. He would name the deficit involved, and the members would contribute. I was skeptical at first; but after watching the brotherhood sacrificially meet need after need over four years, I was deeply impressed—melted would be a better word. I had never imagined that this aspect of the early chapters of Acts was even possible in today's world. Seeing a living example made me revisit Scripture with fresh eyes.

While traditional insurance systems have certainly helped people in their hour of need, it is not the paradigm given in the New Testament. Insurance systems long precede the New Testament, being found in the Code of Hammurabi (ca. 1750 BC) and Greco-Roman benevolent societies (ca. 600 BC).[5] Not unlike modern insurance companies, a variety of first-century guilds and societies functioned to provide benefits to its members. Funeral benefits are one such example, "The poorer population used funeral associations, to which they made monthly payments, to assure themselves of a proper burial."[6] In the midst of these competing systems, Jesus ordained that His disciples would care for one another: "A new commandment I give to you, that you love one another; as I have loved you, that you also love one another. By this all will know that you are My disciples, if you have love for one another" (John 13:34-35).

Jesus, mindful of the difficulties involved, teaches that *this* command will be what the world uses as its litmus test to judge whether a person truly is a disciple of Jesus. He recognized that while His commands on Sabbath or oath taking were important, they were not the persuasive force that love and care for one another would be. It is as if Jesus says, "The world knows my teaching and will not be convinced that you are really My followers unless they see you put this into action. This teaching carries the power to convince the world that you truly are Mine."

Jesus' followers taking care of one another was intended to be the defining and persuasive mark of discipleship. This basic principle was reiterated elsewhere (Mark 10:29-30), and put into practice by the apostolic church (Acts 2:44-45, 4:32-35). Members of the early church held goods in common, selling possessions as there were needs. The church organized its own system for caring for widows and providing for its poor. In the book of Acts, we see the apostolic interpretation and ful-

[5] On the history of insurance, see the book compiled by the Prudential Insurance Company of America, *The Documentary History of Insurance, 1000 BC- 1875 AD*, published in 1923.

[6] James Jeffers, *The Greco-Roman World of the New Testament Era: Exploring the Background of Early Christianity*, InterVarsity Press (1999), p. 45.

fillment of Jesus' teaching.

The insurance landscape and its associated statutes are rapidly changing; we need to be gracious and flexible in our approach. A beautiful principle of church life can become ugly when enshrined as a rigid law. But unless the church can point to radically different ways in which it cares for its own, the world will not believe the church sincerely follows Jesus. Achieving this kind of love presents a difficult task. The world's structures are naturally bent toward individualism, ease, security, and reliance upon faceless organizations or governments. By following the dominant insurance systems of the age, the church struggles to fulfill John 13:34-35 and makes little impression on the world.[7] The world simply cannot believe that the church contains disciples of Jesus.

There may be instances that the law requires insurance (medical malpractice, liability insurance, etc.), but when possible, the brotherhood should strive to assume this role. Some churches in the United States have successfully petitioned the government for exemption in health care and automobile insurance and have successfully met the needs of their members for decades. Those churches have often grown more rapidly and achieved strong-group status more successfully.

Until critical mass is achieved, a smaller group will be unable to carry out these functions. However, a biblical church should strive to assume these functions once it reaches the necessary size.

Summary applications

1. The New Testament advocates a model where a believer's possessions belong to fellow children of the King. In harmony with this, Jesus says, "whoever of you does not forsake all that he has cannot be My disciple" (Luke 14:33).
2. On the day of judgment, people are judged for the degree that they pursued equity within the church, particularly how they have relieved the plight of the least of Jesus' brothers.
3. Remembering the call to simplicity (those with two tunics should share with those who have none), and the principle of equality in 2 Corinthians 8, each family should determine the minimal amount required for food, shelter, clothing, etc. Money received past this should "raise one's standard of giving, not one's stan-

[7] Besides the church we attended, there are other examples of churches forgoing secular insurance and caring for their own, particularly among conservative Anabaptist denominations.

dard of living."[8] Past this amount, sharing should become the default, not keeping.

4. To help calibrate our standards, disciples should have as much contact as possible (through reading, personal visits, and church-organized interchange) with the global brotherhood to understand the church's conditions, plights, and needs. By understanding others' needs and living conditions, Christians can better gauge what is truly essential and modify their own lifestyles.
5. Large sums of money have been wasted by the church on buildings and expenses rather than on the needy. Our money should flow toward needy people, not toward unnecessary goods that fatten prosperous churches.
6. "Now godliness with contentment is great gain. For we brought nothing into this world, and it is certain we can carry nothing out. And having food and clothing, with these we shall be content. But those who desire to be rich fall into temptation and a snare, and into many foolish and harmful lusts which drown men in destruction and perdition. For the love of money is a root of all kinds of evil, for which some have strayed from the faith in their greediness, and pierced themselves through with many sorrows" (1 Tim. 6:6-10). Believers should strive for contentedness and avoid pursuing incomes greater than required. They should minimize or avoid debt. Many of the problems that Christians have can be traced to excessive income or debt, which should never have been taken on.
7. Instead of using conventional insurance systems, church members should organize to provide for the brotherhood as needs arise. Because needs often surpass what a local congregation can provide, this bolsters the case for churches functioning closely together, seeing themselves in economic solidarity.
8. The brotherhood should hold each member accountable in loving watchfulness. Materialism is one of the most blinding sins, perhaps the greatest, and thus the brotherhood plays a vital role.

Followers of the Way should not marvel at the generosity of billionaires who give millions away but live in luxury, but instead remember Jesus' teaching about the poor widow, who in God's eyes gave more than everyone else at the temple that day. It has been well said, "Our generosity is measured not by what we give but by what we keep."

May Jesus' disciples keep but little in this life.

[8] Randy Alcorn, *Money, Possessions, and Eternity*, Tyndale House Publishers (2003), p. 218.

The author seems to advocate a very insular view of the church, in which we don't give to the poor but "share" with other believers.

The "least of these" are those in our greater faith community, according to this view.

This seems to completely ignore how Christ helped the gentile woman's daughter and the Centurion's servant.

Jesus taught us to love both our friends and our enemies. The author's take seems to completely disregard Matthew 38-48

Part II

The Great Battle of the Nation

Chapter 6

The battle for spirit and life

The words that I speak to you are spirit, and they are life. (John 6:63)

The greatest battle raging today *within* the church is how to understand and interpret the Scriptures. This battle affects practically everything: one's view of God, the gospel, obedience, and the church. It has even been said that the history of the church is the history of biblical interpretation. For this reason, a book on the subject of the church should address fundamental principles of biblical interpretation.

The great temptations of Scripture—Adam and Eve's temptation by the serpent in the garden, and Jesus' temptations by Satan in the wilderness—were centered on interpretations of God's word. Emblematic of humanity's constant struggle, these temptations have morphed in character but not in goal. The goal is to kill and destroy humanity by warping God's word. The stakes can hardly be overstated.

Because this battle is at the center of church life, it is the focus of the second part of this book. This second part, the Great Battle of the Nation, is also the most technical and laborious. Most Christian books that are aimed at application tend to be breezy and simplified. While that is sometimes acceptable, the church has too often catered to a spirit of laziness and superficiality. The world's military academies demand rigorous training—being a solider of King Jesus should be no less challenging! The church needs to recover a discipline of the mind as it confronts formidable issues that have led to the church's decline. These are complex problems with solutions that require careful training and thought. So this second part of this book will be the most demanding.

The modern battle over the interpretation of the Scriptures erupted in the universities and seminaries in the 1800s. Now having permeated the pews, many churchgoers today hold views not far removed from articulate scholars opposed to the faith. Higher criticism and groups like the Jesus Seminar undermine the miraculous, promoting the idea that the Bible contains as much mythology as history. These ideas often come from behind a pulpit, from supposedly Christian teachers. Such views have been widely adopted by professing Christians. It has become fashionable today to point out supposed contradictions in the Scriptures. Concerning just the resurrection accounts, scholars believe that the Gospel accounts contain "contradictions of the most glaring kind," "a jumble of contradictory statements," and present an "impossible" challenge of harmonization.[1] Much of the Bible is widely regarded by scholars as uninspired and humanly flawed. Today's churchgoers hold these views in a slipshod manner, blissfully unaware of the history or impact of these ideas.

Over many decades, ideas move from philosophy to art to music to general culture to, last of all, theology.[2] Ideas flow predictably and inexorably down this waterfall. What is fashionable in theology today was fashionable in philosophy yesterday. Many of the church's problems can be traced through such a progression. One should therefore not dismiss biblical interpretation as a merely academic subject.

The following story illustrates the significance of ideas, even seemingly academic ones. There was a philosopher and psychologist who lived in a heady world of scholarly discussions and lectures. Caught up in his academic pursuits, he lived the apparently harmless life of an intellectual. But one day the philosopher was called for the criminal trial of one of his former students, now accused of murder. The former student, while in prison awaiting trial, wrote how the discussions with his teacher had supplied him with the liberating doctrines to support his crime. His teacher was stunned. But ideas can surprisingly manifest themselves in grotesque and harmful ways. "World as well as individual events ride upon the waters of an ideational sea. The killing fields of Cambodia come from philosophical discussions in Paris."[3]

---

1 Statements by critical scholars, quoted in John Wenham's *Easter Enigma: Are the Resurrection Accounts in Conflict?*, Paternoster (1992), pp. 9-10. This book represents an excellent starting point to understand how to respond to these types of charges. Wenham, who taught Greek at Oxford University, lived in Jerusalem for a number of years and demonstrated that the lazy reading of Scripture finds contradictions in the resurrection accounts, while the careful reading finds unity.

2 Francis Schaeffer, *Escape from Reason*, InterVarsity Press (1968), p. 43. A major theme of Schaeffer's corpus was this movement, and the profound consequences of ideas.

3 Illustration and quotation from Dallas Willard, *The Divine Conspiracy*, HarperOne (1997), pp. 6-7.

Modern attitudes toward Scripture

The battles of the two prior centuries have led to devaluation of the Scriptures within the modern church. The devaluation has occurred in subtle ways, often couched in biblical terms. One attack on traditional faith is that it represents *bibliolatry*, or worship of the Bible. Critics charge that Christians effectively worship the Bible instead of God, and that discipleship has become more about mental comprehension exercises than encountering the living God. After all, Jesus sought to make disciples, not bookworms.[4] Critics allege that modern Christianity has become more about Pharisaical pursuits and needless anxiety over gnats, missing the wider themes of love and justice.

Others say something like, "I don't need doctrine because I have Jesus." While some groups have veered onto courses too intellectual, this statement is nonsensical. The word *doctrine* simply means instruction or teaching. To contrast Jesus with teaching is a classic example of a false dichotomy. A person might as well say, "I don't need aerodynamics and planes, because I just want to fly."

Similar to the complaint about doctrine, we often hear "the letter kills" as a protest against intense concern over Scripture. The expression comes from, "The letter kills, but the Spirit gives life" (2 Cor. 3:6b). The protest simply misinterprets Scripture. The verse is preceded by a contrast associating the Old Covenant with the letter and the New Covenant with the Spirit. The passage thus contrasts the Old and New Covenants. The Old Covenant leads to death while the Spirit's ministry of the New Covenant brings life.[5] Moreover, the unqualified notion that words kill cannot be aligned with Jesus' proclamation that, "The words that I speak to you are spirit, and they are life" (John 6:63).

A related charge is that the Scriptures should not be thought of as the word of God, because Jesus is the living Word. The title "Word of God" is a title for Jesus, used only by John in two passages (John 1 and Rev 19:13). In the New Testament, the expression "word of God" more commonly refers to the apostolic message.[6] We ought not to be troubled that the expression was used for both Jesus and the apostolic message. Neither should we feel a need to defend one usage over another. To oppose "living Word" with "written word" is a misguided enterprise.

This chapter will attempt to lay the foundation for how Scripture

---

[4] Timothy Ward, *Words of Life*, InterVarsity Press (2009), p. 10.

[5] Ben Witherington III, *Conflict and Community in Corinth*, Eerdmans (1995), pp. 378-379.

[6] 1 Thess. 2:13; Acts 4:31, 6:2, 8:14, 11:1, 13:5, 13:7, 13:44, 18:11; and Rev. 1:2.

should be used in relating to God. The questions to be examined are: "Why is it the case that, in order to worship God faithfully, we need to pay close attention to the Bible? Why is it the case that, in order to be a faithful disciple of the Word-made-flesh, I need to base my life on the words of Scripture? Why is it the case that, in order to walk in step with the Spirit, I need to trust and obey what Scripture says? And how can we do all of this without beginning to worship a book instead of the Lord?"[7]

God's words, actions, and personhood

Throughout Scripture, God's actions are closely tied to His speech. Similarly, His speech is closely bound to His action. "To say of God that he spoke, and to say of God that he did something, is often one and the same thing."[8] In the creation account in Genesis, God's speech is described as the means of His creative power. When God spoke, matter came into being. When God spoke, the heavenly bodies appeared. When God spoke, animals and man were created. The great covenants forged with Abraham and Moses could be construed as merely words, but these words form the backbone of God's attendant actions in the Old Testament.

Not only are God's actions closely associated with His words, but His very personhood is associated with His words:

> When Adam and Eve disobey God's *spoken command*, they fracture their relationship with *God himself*...To disobey the words God speaks is simply to disobey God himself, and to refuse to submit to the commands God utters is simply to break one's relationship with him. Thus (we may say) God has *invested* himself in his words, or we could say that God has so *identified* himself with his words that whatever someone does to God's words (whether it is to obey or to disobey) they do directly to God himself.[9]

[7] Ward, pp. 11-12. I draw extensively from Ward's book in this chapter. Several questions will not be touched in this chapter, including canonicity and inerrancy. For a superb defense of the New Testament canon, see Michael Kruger's *Canon Revisited: Establishing the Origins and Authority of the New Testament Books*, Crossway (2012). Ward's *Words of Life*, InterVarsity Press (2009) is an excellent introduction to Scripture and contains a defense of inerrancy, as well as a valuable trinitarian grounding to understand Scripture. Finally, John Wenham's *Christ and the Bible*, Wipf & Stock (2009) is a classic and helpful work on the authority of the Scripture.

[8] Ward, p. 20.

[9] Ward, p. 27.

When the Old Testament prophets delivered the "word of the LORD," the people's response to those words was treated as a response to God Himself. When Jehoiakim burns Jeremiah's scroll (Jer. 36), God punishes Jehoiakim for how he treated the *written* word of the LORD. Jehoiakim's relationship to God had been violated because Jehoiakim violated God's words.

A beautiful illustration of God being invested in His words comes from the ark of the covenant. God commanded that the stone tablets reside in the ark, as a symbol of His presence among them. As the ark was found in the heart of the tabernacle, so God's words were found in the heart of the ark. "This was a powerful illustration of all God's covenant-based relationships with his people. His words, literally written in stone, represented the place where he met with the leader of his people, at the centre of their encampment (and later at the centre of their city, Jerusalem). This spoke powerfully of the fact that God's words were in some sense the mode in which he had chosen to be present among his people."[10]

Jesus also associates His person with His words, "Abide in Me, and I in you…If you abide in Me, and My words abide in you" (John 15:4, 7). The parallel between "I" and "My words" is unmistakable. Jesus identifies His words with His personhood. He does the same for His disciples: "And whoever will not receive you nor hear your words, when you depart from that house or city, shake off the dust from your feet. Assuredly, I say to you, it will be more tolerable for the land of Sodom and Gomorrah in the day of judgment than for that city!" (Matt. 10:14-15) Again we see the parallel, "will not receive *you* nor hear *your words*." Just as with the ancient prophets, to reject the words of an apostle is to reject the apostle himself. And the one who rejects an apostle rejects Jesus Himself (Luke 10:16).

The book of Hebrews personifies the word of God, blurring the lines of division between God's word and His personhood. "For the word of God is living and powerful, and sharper than any two-edged sword, piercing even to the division of soul and spirit, and of joints and marrow, and is a discerner of the thoughts and intents of the heart. And there is no creature hidden from His sight, but all things are naked and open to the eyes of Him to whom we must give account" (Heb. 4:12-13). God's word is described as alive and discerning, supporting the intimate relationship between word and person. Other New Testament passages further illustrate how Jesus and the apostles viewed the Scriptures. Paul writes, "For the Scripture says to the Pharaoh, 'For this

[10] Ward, p. 29.

very purpose I have raised you up, that I may show My power in you, and that My name may be declared in all the earth' " (Rom. 9:17). The quote is from Exodus 9:16, where it is God speaking. Paul's language is striking: *The Scripture is personified as speaking to Pharaoh*, when the actual person speaking was God through Moses. Jesus demonstrates an equally astonishing insight: "Have you not read that He who made them at the beginning 'made them male and female,' and said, 'For this reason a man shall leave his father and mother and be joined to his wife, and the two shall become one flesh'?" (Matt. 19:4-5). Jesus describes that God "said" that a man shall leave his father and mother to join his wife. The quote directly comes from Genesis 2:24, and Moses is the speaker, not God. Jesus, however, attributes Moses' words to God. Other similar examples reinforce this point.[11] In Galatians 3:8, the Scripture "foresees" the justification of the Gentiles by faith. "When we take the two classes of passages together, in the one of which the Scriptures are spoken of as God, while in the other God is spoken of as if He were the Scriptures, we may perceive how close the identification of the two was in the minds of the writers of the New Testament."[12] We should not hesitate to refer to both Old and New Testament as the word of God. As it has been said, "what Scripture says, God says."[13]

Today, people tend to disdain words in favor of experience. Such a disposition is shared by the mystically oriented. Given the scriptural patterns we have briefly surveyed, this impulse should be held in check. God's creative activity, His covenants, and His very personhood are all closely connected to His words. Far from disdaining God's words, we should therefore cherish them as closely identified with Him. Indeed, a person's love for God can be measured by his love for God's words.

In summary, how we respond to God's word is how we respond to God Himself. "When we encounter certain *human words* (e.g. the words of an Old Testament prophet), we are in direct contact with *God's words*. This is itself a direct encounter with *God's activity* (since God's speech is one form in which he regularly acts), especially with his *covenant-making* activity. And an encounter with God's covenant-making communicative activity is *itself an encounter with God*."[14]

---

[11] See Heb. 3:7-11, quoting Ps. 95:7-11; Acts 4:25, quoting Ps. 2:1; and Acts 13:34, quoting Isa. 55:3.

[12] B. B. Warfield, quoted in Fred Zaspel, *The Theology of B. B. Warfield*, Crossway (2010), p. 132.

[13] B. B. Warfield's well-known expression, but originally found in Augustine's *Confessions*, xiii, 29: "O man, that which My Scripture says, I say."

[14] Ward, p. 36.

Speech-act theory

Another discipline for understanding Scripture has been brought to the foreground in recent years. The discipline is called *speech-act theory*. "It begins by rejecting the widespread notion that language is primarily a logical system for the conveying of bits of information, rather in the way one computer sends data to another. This model of language is commonly assumed to be the correct one whenever human beings are conceived of primarily in terms of their minds and rationality, as they have often been in Western philosophy since the Enlightenment. By contrast, speech-act theory thinks of language as at root a means by which one person performs actions in relation to another."[15]

We have all had experiences where we have believed someone's word, only to be dismayed by a broken promise. Speech-act theory focuses on the ability of speech to influence others, and also for persons to use speech to incur trust, rights, and responsibilities—or their violations.[16] "That natural conclusion reveals that language exchange between people, while of course including the communication of propositions, is fundamentally to do with something different and much more profound. It is to do with active relationships of trust and obligation between us...For you to say, 'I trust you to keep your promise' or 'I trust your promise' or 'I trust your words' is in effect to say the same thing in regard to me. For you to distrust the words of my promise is simply to distrust *me*."[17]

When thought of in this way, rather than communicating bare facts, Scripture becomes a much richer interplay of personhood. In that way, speech-act theory sheds light on how the word of God can be "living and active." Speech-act theory also helps us understand how God's personhood and ours have a contact point in Scripture. Through Scripture, we can draw close to God.

Avoiding bibliolatry and a Pharisaical spirit

Given the close relationship of God's actions, personhood, and word, there may be a temptation to exalt the written word to a status beyond what is proper. These accusations have been leveled against various groups for centuries.[18] Other concerns include making aca-

---

[15] Ward, p. 57.

[16] Nicholas Wolterstorff, *Divine Discourse*, Cambridge University Press (1995), p. 93.

[17] Ward, pp. 58-59.

[18] One example includes Charles Briggs' charge that B. B. Warfield held an "idolatrous" view of inspiration. See Zaspel, p. 122.

demic knowledge of the Scriptures equivalent to personal knowledge of God—the Pharisaical trap. Still worse, mastery of the Scriptures can be taken as mastery over God, a grave sin indeed.[19]

Several correctives can be given to the serious charge of bibliolatry. First, as described in chapter 2, the Bible is fundamentally the Book of Covenants. Covenants are the instruments by which kings relate to their people. Hence the Scriptures are in a sense the perfect *instrument* of God the King. Just as no one should bow to the sword or chariot of a King, so no one should worship the covenant that God ordains.

A second corrective concerns the transience of Scripture. The description of the new heavens and the new earth (Rev. 21) notably lacks mention of Scripture. The personal presence of the Father, Son, and Spirit may therefore obviate the need for Scripture. If this view is correct (though it must be held as speculative), this should check the tendency to divinize the Bible. This view of Scriptures stands therefore quite unlike the Islamic view of the Qur'an, which Muslims regard as eternal.

Third, Jesus teaches that the Scriptures play a role of testimony. When rightly used, they testify to the Son of God: "You search the Scriptures, for in them you think you have eternal life; and these are they which testify of Me. But you are not willing to come to Me that you may have life" (John 5:39-40). Scripture ultimately plays the role of pointing to King Jesus. Thus Scripture is in a sense a servant of God, not God Himself.

Some worry that a high of view of Scripture tends to produce Pharisees. As mentioned earlier, critics have a concern (often a caricature) that by holding such a high view of Scripture people will tend to obsess over gnats, usually doctrines the critics have little patience for, and ignore weightier matters such as love and justice. Jesus rebuked the scribes and Pharisees for exactly this: "Woe to you, scribes and Pharisees, hypocrites! For you pay tithe of mint and anise and cummin, and have neglected the weightier matters of the law: justice and mercy and faith. These you ought to have done, without leaving the others undone. Blind guides, who strain out a gnat and swallow a camel!" (Matt. 23:23-24)

Yet it is Jesus' response that we should emulate. He challenged the Pharisees to re-read Scripture and correctly understand it. He challenged their error with a new reading of Scripture, never by dissuading them from its study. "The right way forward is rather to pay more attention to the content, form and aims of Scripture as God has in fact

[19] Karl Barth's fear. Ward, pp. 61-63 addresses this concern.

given it to us. It was just in this way that Christ challenged the Pharisees in their dangerously short-sighted reading of their Scriptures...He urged them to read their Scriptures again, but this time more fully and wisely. He is recorded on a number of occasions asking them, and others of his devout Jewish opponents, 'Haven't you read...?' (Matt. 12:3, 4; 19:4; 21:16, 42; 22:31). Paying full and wise attention to Scripture as the written Word of God is crucial if we wish to worship and follow the Word-made-flesh, the Son of God, rightly."[20]

Toward a trinitarian view of Scripture

One of the most welcome developments in recent years has been a new appraisal of Scripture in light of the Trinity. The conventional theology book begins with a doctrine of Scripture using language like perspicuity or infallibility and subsequently moves to the doctrines like God and the church. In such a linear approach, a doctrine of Scripture feels detached from much of the substance of theology, including the Trinity, salvation, and the church. Such approaches appear to leave the Scriptures as little more than a container, useful to convey important facts, but with little additional value. We have already seen that speech-act theory counters such a "container" view, but more can be said.

If the Scriptures truly are God's word, then His character and nature should be stamped upon it. As we gain insights about God, especially the Trinity, we can then revisit our understanding of Scripture. This mutual reinforcement enlivens our study of both. For example, the church has long recognized that the beauty of the created world reflects God's wisdom and majesty from passages like: "The heavens declare the glory of God, and the sky above proclaims his handiwork" (Ps. 19:1). The New Testament affirms that creation bears divine attributes, "For his invisible attributes, namely, his eternal power and divine nature, have been clearly perceived, ever since the creation of the world, in the things that have been made" (Rom. 1:20). Just as creation reflects God's wisdom and majesty, we should expect the God-breathed Scriptures to bear divine beauty. "If the created world (general revelation) is able to speak clearly that it is from God, then how much more so would the canon of Scripture (special revelation) speak clearly that it is from God?"[21]

Revisiting the doctrine of Scripture with such themes and divine attributes is far more satisfying and rich approach than leaving it be-

[20] Ward, p. 74.

[21] Kruger, p. 99.

hind as if it were merely an introduction. For example, Abraham's offering Isaac on Mount Moriah is widely regarded as a foreshadowing of God the Father offering His Son on Mount Calvary. While this foreshadow is nowhere mentioned in the New Testament, it was almost certainly intended by the Holy Spirit as a beautiful testimony of the Father sacrificing the Son. Similarly, the story of Daniel and the lions' den foreshadows Jesus' death and resurrection. For example, Daniel prayed three times before being thrown into a cavernous underground structure covered by a large stone.[22] God's rule over history, the beauty and creativity of the Holy Spirit's inspiration of Scripture, and the Son's activity in Scripture form a breathtaking gem. "Holy Scripture should be thought of as God *preaching*—God preaching to me every time I read or hear any part of it—God the Father preaching God the Son in the power of God the Holy Spirit. God the Father is the giver of Holy Scripture; God the Son is the theme of Holy Scripture; and God the Spirit, as the Father's appointed agent in witnessing to the Son, is the author, authenticator, and interpreter, of Holy Scripture."[23]

---

[22] Charles Pike, "Seeing Christ in Daniel," audio lecture, Scroll Publishing (2012). Pike gives many more instances of foreshadowing from the book of Daniel in this message.

[23] J. I. Packer, *God Has Spoken*, third edition, Baker (1993), p. 91.

Chapter 7

Church history: the spadework of biblical interpretation

For inquire, please, of bygone ages,
and consider what the fathers have searched out.
For we are but of yesterday and know nothing,
for our days on earth are a shadow.
Will they not teach you and tell you
and utter words out of their understanding?
(Job 8:8-10)

In Jesus' high priestly prayer, He prays for unity. He declares that unity will be what convinces the world that He was sent by God (John 17:20-21). Tragically, however, the world would never describe the church as united. The world sees hundreds of denominations and points of division. Unbelief's reign should then come as no surprise. Countless fractures and divisions have marred the witness of the church, leaving most bewildered or cynical.

The most obvious divisions within the church concern interpretations of the Bible. If fundamental differences persist around how to interpret Scripture, there naturally cannot be biblical unity. Hence the discipline of how we interpret Scripture takes on vital importance in fulfilling Jesus' prayer.

As has been said, church history is the history of biblical interpretation. Church history has been described as one very long Bible study, with diverse participants over the centuries weighing in on the true meaning of Scripture. All of us now take part in that Bible study that has lasted for nearly two thousand years. Because few, if any, views we might hear are truly original, there is great value in studying church history to gain insights on the most important questions of biblical interpretation.

Cohesive packages

Biblical interpretation need not be daunting. Interpretative systems are in fact packages, and history has shown that there are only two or three significant interpretive systems (the identities to be discussed later). Thus one of the first comforts in the enterprise of biblical interpretation is its cohesiveness. The main reason for this cohesion is that only a few assumptions produce a broad set of attendant consequences.

When I studied quantum mechanics in college, I was deeply impressed by the beauty of the subject. One makes only five postulates, which can be written on just one page, and an entire system spanning many books necessarily derives from these five postulates. The essence of electronics, nuclear reactors, X-rays, cell phones, microwave ovens, and rainbows, resides in these five postulates. Quantum mechanics is a cohesive discipline such that if you can merely assent to these five postulates, then you are in a sense "done." All the rest of the theorems, consequences, and applications naturally follow.

Of course a person can say that they assent to the five postulates but disagree with some later consequence. But this is simply inconsistency. They may like aspects of quantum mechanics and be impressed with the genius of the minds that developed the system, but disbelieve certain conclusions. Many find it hard to believe that objects like baseballs have wavelengths. I remember being stunned while studying the "particle in a box" that an object could pass through a wall, even lacking enough energy to surmount the height of the wall. Albert Einstein's genius in the field of relativity was that he took just a handful of truths and pressed them to their logical conclusions. Very surprising conclusions emerged, such as the passage of time slowing at high speed travel relative to a stationary observer. One may choose to disbelieve this conclusion because of bias or lack of primary experience, but that would be only irrationality and inconsistency.

Cohesive systems exist in virtually every domain and subject area. In United States politics, those who vote for higher taxes tend to be those who vote pro-choice with respect to abortion. Why would views correlate on such disparate subjects as taxes and abortion? The answer is that an underlying worldview produces both. The underlying worldview could be summarized on one page, and it produces a broad set of consequences that travel together. As before, people may be contradictory. In politics, some may argue vehemently for small government and deficit cutting but want the milk in *their* grocery store to be subsidized. Staunchly pro-life advocates found their position on the grounds that an embryo or fetus should be regarded as human life. But they then say that this innocent human life can be terminated in the case of rape that someone else perpetrated. At the root of these inconsistencies is simply unwillingness to accept the consequences. Few people want to experience the sticker-shock of the true price of milk at the grocery store. Few people want to press forward the pro-life stance into urging a traumatized rape victim to carry the baby to term. Politicians who are actually consistent are virtually assured to get voted out of office. Overstating the challenge of consistency is difficult.

In the same way, only a few principles undergird biblical interpretation. If one agrees to these foundational principles, one should carry them to their logical conclusion. Very few actually do. We balk at the radical conclusions. We do not want to accept the costs.

Perhaps the best preparatory activity, or spadework, of biblical interpretation is to survey church history. While history does not repeat, it rhymes, and we should learn the tune. Like Bunyan's traveler Christian, great value can be obtained in meditating on the successes and failures of those who have gone before us. In this chapter we will inquire of a "bygone age" to "consider what the fathers have searched out" (Job 8:8-10). Unfortunately most have not labored at this exercise, dooming themselves to divisiveness and a loop of rhyming errors.

For reasons of space, we will focus this chapter exclusively on the sixteenth-century Reformation. The period of the Reformation was a time in which two competing interpretive systems were clearly articulated. History itself was shaken by these hermeneutical wars. Partly because the printing press had just made books more accessible, people of the sixteenth century grappled with the interpretation of texts like no generation before. The early church fathers made passing statements on their interpretative methods in various writings but did not develop the discipline nearly to the degree seen in the Reformation.

Sixteenth century keys

The 1520s may be the most remarkable decade to occur since the first century. Sparked by Luther's writings, the Reformation worked its way across Europe. William Tyndale completed his translation of the New

Testament into English in 1525. The Anabaptist movement, or Radical Reformation, began that same decade. On January 21, 1525, Conrad Grebel baptized George Blaurock and Blaurock baptized Felix Manz in bold acts of believer's baptism—as opposed to the infant baptism that the Roman Catholic and Protestant churches taught.[1] Manz and Blaurock were martyred in 1527 and 1529, respectively. Michael Sattler, the former Benedictine monk, emerged as another leader of the fledgling Anabaptists and penned the Schleitheim Confession. Only months later, he was put on trial for heresy and found guilty. On May 20, 1527, his tongue was cut out, his flesh torn out four times with hot tongs, and he was burned at the stake. By the thousands, the Anabaptists were martyred by both the Roman Catholic and Protestant authorities, about a quarter of them in Luther's territory of Saxony.[2] Melanchthon, Luther, and Calvin gave their approval.

Understanding the relationship between the Protestants and Anabaptists pays tremendous rewards for the discipline of biblical interpretation.[3] This is generally untrodden ground and is fraught with pitfalls. To this day, Protestant writers pour acid on the Anabaptists by attacking caricatures, hurling insults, and consistently displaying poor understanding of their views.[4] By mostly quoting each other through secondary and tertiary sources as opposed to interacting with primary

[1] The name Anabaptist simply means "baptized again." Since virtually all sixteenth-century Europeans were baptized as infants, the Anabaptists believed they needed to undergo a second baptism as consenting believers. The name itself does not accurately capture the substance of the movement. The Anabaptist vision principally concerned ecclesiology: they understood the church to be a visible and pure group of disciples free from the control of the state. In contrast, Luther, Calvin, and Zwingli supported a state church.

[2] Gottfried Seebaß, referenced by John D. Roth, "A Historical and Theological Context for Mennonite-Lutheran Dialogue" *Mennonite Quarterly Review*, Vol. LXXVI, No. 3 (2002), p. 274f. Roth notes, "Indeed, one of the very few points where Protestants and Catholics found themselves in agreement during the course of the sixteenth century was their mutual antagonism to the Anabaptist movement" (p. 264).

[3] One work stands out as especially profitable: Stuart Murray's *Biblical Interpretation in the Anabaptist Tradition*, Pandora Press, co-published with Herald Press (2000).

[4] John Oyer has pointed out that the early Protestants developed a basket of insulting titles: Fanatics (*Schwarmer*), Corner-preachers (*Winkelprediger*), Mob-spirited factionalists (*Rottengeister*), Donatists, Revolutionaries (*Aufrüherer*). Oyer notes, "English translations of these terms cannot quite convey the degree of contempt or hatred of their sixteenth-century German originals; even present-day German dictionaries have succeeded in domesticating and taming some of these unruly names." Ironically, Luther probably only met one Anabaptist, and that person was on the spiritualist fringe. In modern times, Protestant writers who are normally very capable scholars often make belittling statements that are demonstrably untrue.

sources, Protestant writings offer little value on this subject. Most Anabaptist writers, perhaps wary from historical persecution, have little desire to interact with Protestant hermeneutics. Names like Luther and Calvin have decidedly negative connotations in such circles, and there has been little meaningful effort on the part of Anabaptists to understand similarities and differences in approach.[5]

This background may seem like unnecessary digression away from biblical interpretation. It is most certainly not! At the risk of overstatement, contained within the Protestant and Anabaptist movements are the keys to unified biblical interpretation—the principles that form the cohesive system of scriptural understanding. The equivalent of the five postulates of quantum mechanics can be found here. While it may take some work to uncover the keys, the effort will pay handsomely.

We first must understand where each group made wrong turns. As Burke's famous saying goes, if we choose not to understand history, we will repeat it.

The Protestants lose their nerve

The opening years of the Reformation were dynamic and reactive:

> For Luther, the early years of the Reformation were decisively shaped by a series of battles that unfolded on two fronts. Luther's struggle against the ecclesiastical authority of the Roman Catholic Church is well known; and certainly this consumed the greatest part of his energies. But at the same time that Luther was trying to articulate an 'evangelical' theology against the established consensus of medieval Catholicism, he was also forced to define his emerging theology against those *within* his camp who were pushing his central ideas in ways more radical than he had intended or foreseen. This latter group became the seedbed for the Anabaptist movement.
>
> In 1521, shortly after his dramatic break with the temporal and ecclesiastical authorities of the Holy Roman Empire at the Diet of Worms, Luther was confident that the power of the gospel—unleashed from bonds of tradition in the form of the pure and unfettered Word of God—would persuade all Christian believers to affirm an understanding of salvation grounded solely in the outworking of God's grace. Al-

[5] The last two decades have showed encouraging signs of progress, however.

most immediately, however, it became clear to Luther that the principles of *sola Scriptura* and *sola gratia* upon which he had grounded his new movement could work themselves out in a disturbing variety of ways. Already in 1522, Luther looked on in dismay from the Wartburg, where he was being held in protective custody, at the preaching of his colleague and fellow Wittenberg theologian Andreas von Karlstadt. Taking to heart Luther's conviction that salvation was an inward act of grace, completely separate from any external rituals or forms, Karlstadt had roused the evangelical believers in Wittenberg to frenzied acts of iconoclasm in which books were burned, religious statuary destroyed, paintings defaced and altars overturned. Shortly thereafter, Thomas Müntzer—whom Luther had recommended for a pastorate at Zwickau in 1520—began to spread teachings concerning the End Times and to gather around him a group of armed peasants to help inaugurate the reign of the righteous and, eventually, the Second Coming of Christ. In 1524 such teachings, combined with Luther's own insistence that the true Christian is 'free from the law,' helped to spark the so-called Peasants' War of 1525. Armed with pitchforks and scythes, thousands of artisans and peasants throughout the German territories demanded a series of dramatic economic, political and religious reforms, basing their claims (as had Luther!) on the authority of scripture over that of tradition.

Like many other reformers, Luther looked on with horror as the 'law of unintended consequences' began to unfold. He quickly wrested control of the Reformation in Wittenberg away from Karlstadt, denounced Müntzer as a 'scourge of Satan' and angrily dismissed the peasants who were using his arguments on Christian liberty to justify their insurrection against feudal lords. In the spring of 1525 Luther wrote a pamphlet *Against the Robbing and Murdering Hordes of Peasants* in which he fulminated against political sedition and called on the princes to spare no violence in restoring order. Shortly thereafter some 5000 peasants were killed at the Battle of Frankenhausen, and the uprising was soundly defeated.

In the historiography of the Radical Reformation, Luther's response proved to be a decisive moment for the future

> direction of the Reformation. In the aftermath of the tumultuous events of 1525, the Reformation ceased to be a popular reform movement and, instead, came fully under the political control of the German princes and Imperial City councils. Within a decade the conservative nature of Protestantism became increasingly evident. In Lutheran territories the prince emerged as the *summus episcopus* of the church—a kind of secularized version of the Catholic pope—with the right to determine the nature and form of religious life within his territory. A new Protestant clerical estate emerged, claiming a monopoly on the interpretation of scripture. And the sacrament of infant baptism continued to fuse membership in a religious community with the political obligations and allegiances to a territorial lord.
>
> The Anabaptist movement emerged within this dynamic, highly charged context. Sharing fully with Protestant reformers in the complex mix of theological zeal, anticlerical frustration, apocalyptic fears and the struggle for survival, most Anabaptist leaders would have described themselves as embracing all of the essential convictions of the early Reformation. It was not that they had suddenly become 'radical,' but rather that Luther, Zwingli and the other so-called 'magisterial reformers' had lost their theological nerve in 1525 and had capitulated to political interests and the desire for self-preservation.[6]

The Protestants and Anabaptists shared a similar approach to biblical interpretation. The breaking point between the two groups concerned hermeneutical consistency. While the Anabaptists desired to carry out biblical interpretation to its consistent and logical end, the Protestants chose to stop short, thus keeping the radical message of the New Testament within more comfortable bounds of their culture's power structures.

The inconsistencies of the Protestants were a major driver of the Anabaptists' beginnings. The three early leaders—Grebel, Blaurock, and Manz—were disappointed by their mentor Zwingli's deference and compromise to the Zurich city council on matters pertaining to the church.[7] The Protestants failed to accept the consequences of the

---

[6] Roth, pp. 266-267.

[7] For a more detailed history, see Harold S. Bender, *Conrad Grebel: The Founder of the Swiss Brethren*, Wipf and Stock (1998), pp. 76-110.

hermeneutics they advocated. "A key factor in the development of Anabaptist thinking was their experience of the Reformers' handling of Scripture. Anabaptists were disappointed, impatient, and at times outraged by the Reformers' unwillingness to teach and practise what was crystal clear."[8] Menno Simons wrote, "Here Luther and Melanchthon have rightly expressed themselves according to the Scripture, although alas, they did not practice upon it."[9] The Anabaptists wanted to press the principles of the Reformers beyond doctrine into a comprehensive reform of ethics and church life, steps that the Reformers generally hesitated to take. From this vantage point, the Reformers were but half-Reformers and the Anabaptists were the true Reformers.

A related reason the Protestants went awry was their approach of gradualism. When the Anabaptists saw a truth in Scripture, they would separate from existing structures if they believed the structures were antithetical to the practice of Scripture. The Protestants, however, chose to try to operate within the confines of existing structures. This choice partly explains why the Protestants adopted the Roman Catholic fusion of church and state. From Luther's Saxony to Calvin's Geneva, the Protestants embraced a close union between church and state, an element of *status quo* the Anabaptists were sure was unbiblical.

The consequences of these divergent choices bore immediate fruit. The Protestants and the Catholics would grudgingly admit that the congregations of the Anabaptists surpassed their own regarding discipleship and purity of life. In 1527, Wolfgang Capito, the Reformed leader of Strasbourg, marveled at their "piety and consecration and indeed a zeal which is beyond any suspicion of sincerity." Franz Agricola, a Roman Catholic, would write in 1582, "As concerns their outward public life they are irreproachable. No lying, deception, swearing, strife, harsh language, no intemperate eating and drinking, no outward personal display, is found among them, but humility, patience, uprightness, neatness, honesty, temperance, straightforwardness in such measure that one would suppose that they had the Holy Spirit of God."[10]

---

[8] Murray, p. 53.

[9] Menno Simons in "Infant Baptism," *The Complete Works of Menno Simons*, John F. Funk and Brother (1871, reprint by Pathway Publishers in 1983), Second Part, p. 269.

[10] Quotes taken from Harold S. Bender, *The Anabaptist Vision*, Herald Press (1944), pp. 23-24.

The Anabaptists lose course

One of the greatest problems to befall the early Anabaptists was the loss of their bright young leaders. Not only were they strong leaders, but they were learned men able to clearly articulate the faith from Scripture. Skilled in Greek and Latin, Conrad Grebel was a well respected scholar of classical literature before his conversion. These skills served him well as a prominent expositor of the movement's bold conclusions. He constantly fled persecution and died of an unidentified illness at a young age. The martyrdoms of Felix Manz, George Blaurock, and Michael Sattler were heavy blows for the burgeoning movement. Also learned men, Manz and Sattler were knowledgeable in Hebrew, Greek, and Latin. Sattler was learned enough to give his trial defense in Latin.

Often whole groups were executed at a time, in public settings, beginning with the men and then moving to their wives. They were designed to strike fear into Anabaptist adherents and provoke recantation. Sattler's trial involved twenty-one prisoners. Two recanted after the charges were read. Then, "Following Sattler's death by fire, four of his brethren, including Matthias Hiller, were beheaded; Margaretha Sattler [Michael Sattler's wife] was drowned two days later. The remaining prisoners, with the possible exception of Veit Veriner, recanted."[11] The persecution was effective: of the twenty-one prisoners, six were martyred and fifteen recanted. These campaigns did not snuff out the movement, but they severely weakened it from the top down.

More importantly, intense persecution distanced the Anabaptists from the interpretive principles they had shared with the Protestants. While the early Anabaptists shared substantially similar hermeneutics with the Protestants, indeed being more faithful to these principles than the Protestants themselves, later Anabaptists failed to grasp these principles. Because the Protestants continued their inconsistent applications, the interpretative principles themselves became tarnished. And without their early leaders who worked through these principles, in an ironic twist, the Anabaptists would partly return to Roman Catholic views (as we will see). In addition, they grew suspicious of learning and favored survival instead of advance. The grand dreams of Grebel and his co-workers for total church renewal shrank to a defensive congregationalism.

Most tragically, later Anabaptists failed to grasp the foundation of interpretative principles laid by its pioneers: "Because [the Anabaptists] did not carefully examine their assumptions on scriptural interpreta-

[11] C. Arnold Snyder, *The Life and Thought of Michael Sattler*, Herald Press (1984), p. 104.

tions, they at times failed to understand each other and often lacked sympathetic appreciation for any interpretation other than the one which they proposed. The fragmentation into smaller and intolerant groups in the second generation was partially a consequence of this weakness."[12]

And so the world was left without a consistent application of these great principles *by any group*. With this short exercise of spadework complete, we can turn to an exposition of what these interpretative principles actually are in the next chapter. The world has been waiting to see a consistent, vibrant application of these principles by a living group.

[12] William Keeney, quoted in Murray, p. 56.

Chapter 8

Principles of faithful biblical interpretation

Be diligent to present yourself approved to God, a worker who does not need to be ashamed, rightly dividing the word of truth. (2 Timothy 2:15)

Hold in your mind this image from John Bunyan's *Pilgrim's Progress*: the path to the Celestial City. The central figure of the story, Christian, is summoned to leave the City of Destruction and sojourn upon this difficult path. The path is straight, but fraught with peril. If Christian can faithfully walk this path, avoiding snares like the House of Legality, Vanity Fair, and Doubting Castle, he will arrive at his destination safely. Bunyan reminds us that we do not travel alone: just as Christian had Faithful, Hopeful, and Great-heart, so we too walk in the company of other saints.

God's word is described as a lamp to our feet in this journey (Ps. 119:105). Without properly interpreting the word, the church will fall into cavernous ruin. In this chapter, we will examine seven principles of faithful biblical interpretation. Some of these principles reinforce one another, while others balance each other. All of these principles interlock. If we get these principles right, our churches will thrive. If we get them wrong, our churches will wither. The costs of failure are immeasurably large; the rewards of success are unimaginably great. So we cry out with the Psalmist, "Give me life according to your word!" (Ps. 119:25) With that prayer, we will begin examination of the following seven principles:

1. The clarity of Scripture
2. The necessity of the Spirit

3. Christocentric exegesis
4. A New Covenant perspective
5. *Sola scriptura*
6. The sufficiency of Scripture
7. The testimony of the persecuted cloud of witnesses

The clarity of Scripture

The clarity of Scripture—sometimes called by an older expression, the "perspicuity" of Scripture—serves as a foundational interpretative key. Yet this doctrine is as challenging as it is foundational. "No confession concerning Scripture is more disturbing to the church than the confession of its perspicuity."[1]

Once over dinner with a graduate student at Harvard University, we came to discuss 1 Timothy 2:8-10 where Paul prohibits wearing gold and expensive clothes. My friend agreed that taking such a passage at face value had demanding implications for the church. But he went on to insist that someone at Princeton was about to publish a dissertation on why the straightforward reading was incorrect. He himself did not know the argument, but he was sure that it would be right. He never did report on what that argument was, but I could not help but sigh in dismay at the acrobatics sinful humanity will undertake to avoid obedience to God's word. In this case, the strategy involved a tacit subversion of the clarity of Scripture.

The clarity of Scripture challenges us precisely because Scripture is demanding and our wills are bent against God's. In the face of a demand to repent, we would rather engage in contemplative reflection, discussion, or debate, than respond with simple obedience. The fallen human mind will spin every manner of controversy and blow fog over the matter, asking "Did God really say?"

While the clarity of Scripture may be demanding, the church withers in its absence. Without the clarity of Scripture, Christian boldness and confidence evaporate. In fact, "yielding to the word is premised upon its clarity."[2] We live in an age where certainty is a rare commodity, largely because clarity has been undermined. Scholars of every stripe offer a parade of conflicting views, furnishing the doubt-filled Christian with the excuse to defy God's clear command on the grounds that nobody can agree on what the passage even says.

---

[1] G. C. Berkouwer quoted in Mark Thompson, *A Clear and Present Word: The Clarity of Scripture*, InterVarsity Press (2006), p. 19.

[2] James Callahan, *The Clarity of Scripture*, InterVarsity Press (2001), p. 268.

Many passages attest to Scripture's clarity (Deut. 30:11-14; Ps. 19:7-9, 119:105; Matt. 22:31; John 7:17). In fact, most passages in Scripture presuppose their own clarity as well as the clarity of referent passages.[3]

Yet perhaps the best grounding for the clarity of Scripture comes from God's nature. As was discussed in chapter 6, our study of Scripture should lead us to God, and then our doctrine of Scripture should be informed by the nature of God as the author of Scripture. Because God is light and desires to illuminate our minds and hearts, Scripture as His word reflects His character:

> These words are themselves God's self-revelation in the world. In them *he* presents his Son to us. By them *he* gathers his people and brings about his ancient intention. God's self-communication is no more distorted by its expression in human words than his compassion is distorted by its expression in human flesh. To put this another way, the ultimate guarantee that God's word will be heard and understood, that it will achieve the purpose for which it was spoken and written, is the power and goodness of God himself. In this sense, a conviction that Scripture is clear is something believers bring *to* their reading of the Bible. Yet...this is not an alien imposition on the text. It just as powerfully arises *from* the pages of Scripture. In the Gospels, Jesus exhibits precisely this confidence as he quotes from and alludes to passages of the Old Testament.[4]

Childlike faith leads to clarity better than education or privilege (Luke 10:21). After all, Jesus prayed, "I thank you, Father, Lord of heaven and earth, that you have hidden these things from the wise and understanding and revealed them to little children" (Matt. 11:25). As was the case in Jesus' day, a true understanding of Scripture will not generally be found in the famous seminaries or universities—but among those with childlike faith and obedience.

Another facet of the clarity of Scripture, stressed in the sixteenth century by Protestant and Anabaptist alike, is summarized by the Latin phrase, *scriptura sui ipsius interpres*: Scripture is its own interpreter. The passages of the Bible interpret one another. To understand the whole of Scripture, one must understand the parts. To understand the parts, one must understand the whole. This naturally implies that reading and re-reading Scripture are required for proper understanding. Diligence is therefore required to understand Scripture (2 Tim. 2:15).

---

[3] Thompson gives a helpful overview in pp. 81-110.

[4] Thompson, p. 111.

Clarity does not imply that the Scriptures are clear to all persons alike, or even that the clarity is easily obtained. Neither does the clarity of Scripture imply that all of Scripture is equally easy to understand, or that certain parts will not be difficult. "Clarity is not the same thing as simplicity or uniform transparency."[5] The Bible itself says that certain domains of knowledge are reserved for God (Deut. 29:29). In fact, the Bible itself repeatedly teaches that the Spirit's illumination is required to understand the Scriptures. "Open my eyes, that I may see wondrous things from Your law" (Ps. 119:18). The Ethiopian eunuch required instruction to understand the passage from Isaiah (Acts 8:26-40). Even the disciples could not understand the Scriptures without Jesus' illumination. The clarity of Scripture, similar to salvation, is a gift premised on faith: "The clarity of Scripture is that quality of the biblical text that, as God's communicative act, ensures its meaning is accessible to all who come to it in faith."[6]

Many have objected to the clarity of Scripture on the grounds that there are so many divisive interpretations of the Bible. Yet these objections do not appropriately weigh the effects of the Fall and human disobedience. Jesus Himself, the incarnate Word of God, was misunderstood and a source of division. These divisions say little about His luminous and simple speech. In the same way, objecting to the clarity of Scripture because sinful humanity misunderstands the Bible says more about humanity than the Bible:

> Holy Scripture is clear; but because its matter is that to which we must be reconciled, readers can only discern its clarity if *their* darkness is illuminated...Interpretation of the clear Word of God is therefore not first of all an act of clarification but the event of being clarified. Reading, therefore, always includes a humbling of the reader, the breaking of the will in which there is acted out the struggle to detach our apprehension of the text from the idolatrous schemas which we inevitably take to it, and by which we seek to command or suppress it or render it convenient to us.[7]

[5] Thompson, p. 112.
[6] Thompson, pp. 169-170.
[7] J. B. Webster, quoted in Thompson, p. 141.

The necessity of the Spirit

The clarity of Scripture depends on the second principle of biblical interpretation, which is the necessity of the Spirit. Scripture attests that the Spirit is required to understand the things of God: "And we impart this in words not taught by human wisdom but taught by the Spirit, interpreting spiritual truths to those who are spiritual. The natural person does not accept the things of the Spirit of God, for they are folly to him, and he is not able to understand them because they are spiritually discerned" (1 Cor. 2:13-14 ESV). Yet, one author has lamented, "when it comes to scholarly methods of interpreting the Bible, the Holy Spirit may as well be dead."[8] This ought to provide caution in receiving the scholarly consensus as the proper interpretation of the word of God.

While the Spirit's work should never justify laziness (He in fact commands diligence in 2 Tim. 2:15), human cleverness or ingenuity cannot command the Spirit's instruction. The Spirit empowers a person to obey God; obedience thus is a more important mark of a person's ability to interpret the Scriptures than education or skill with languages.

Study of the Bible should therefore never be divorced from prayer, fasting, obedience, worship, and humility. Jesus' Sermon on the Mount, with its blessings pronounced on the poor, meek, and persecuted, naturally implies that such persons, being blessed of God, would be the most suited to understand God's revelation through Scripture. This mantle was claimed by the persecuted churches throughout history, including the early Anabaptists: "Anabaptists saw themselves as the true heirs of the persecuted early churches and believed this gave them insights hidden from state theologians who were comfortable, had vested interests, and were persecutors rather than the persecuted. Menno, for example, identified sufferings as one of the marks of a true church. This suffering brought the believer into deep fellowship with Christ and this fellowship was a key to understanding Scripture."[9]

When looking for truth, one ought to search out the persons and groups most radically committed to follow the Lord, despite the consequences. Tragically, most people select churches based on the aesthetics of the worship, the beauty of a building, the charisma of the preacher, the intelligence of the ministry, or the demographics of the membership. Holy living typically weighs little in this selection. The interrogation of the Anabaptist Claes de Praet by the Dean of Ronse brings out Claes' concerns for faithful obedience in contrast with his interrogator

[8] James B. De Young in "The Holy Spirit—The Divine Exegete."

[9] Stuart Murray, *Biblical Interpretation in the Anabaptist Tradition*, Pandora Press, co-published with Herald Press (2000), p. 198.

who values education and official status:

> Dean: "You think you have the faith, but you have departed from it. And that you people are so bold and of good cheer even unto death, is all owing to the devil, who can transform himself into an angel of light. Hence, when you read the Scriptures, you were instructed by some poor, simple tradesman, who taught you the same according to his reason; therefore you are now deceived. You should have let those teach you, who have received the true doctrine, the ministers of the holy church, that is, the pastors."
>
> Claes: "Are they the ones that have received the true doctrine?"
>
> Dean: "Yes."
>
> Claes: "Why, then, do they live the life of devils; as may be seen?"
>
> Dean: "What does that concern you? It is written, Matt. 23: 'Do after their commandments, but not after their works.' "
>
> Claes: "Are you, then, the scribes and Pharisees, of whom Matthew has written?"
>
> Dean: "Yes."
>
> Claes: "Then all the woes come upon you, that follow further on, in said chapter."
>
> Dean: "No, they do not."[10]

Claes would be burned at the stake in 1556.

The person not bearing the fruit of the Spirit—love, joy, peace, patience, kindness, goodness, and self-control—is unlikely to hold true interpretations from the Spirit. Reprobate people will almost of necessity twist the Scriptures to fit their designs. In contrast, the obedient follower of Jesus would be granted the Spirit of understanding. "Pneumatic exegesis" thus involves "a reciprocal experience of understanding and obedience, obedience and understanding."[11]

---

[10] *Martyr's Mirror*, Herald Press (1938), thirty-third printing, p. 556.

[11] Dyck, quoted in Murray, p. 138 and 194.

Christocentric exegesis

While nearly everyone claims Christocentric exegesis, very few put this interpretative principle into practice. There are two ideas behind Christocentricity: order and focus. To understand the concept of order, the scriptural description of Jesus as the cornerstone proves useful. The cornerstone is the very first stone set in a building, which all subsequent stones are set in reference to. If the cornerstone is set later, it cannot be a cornerstone.

This cornerstone concept bears resemblance to a non-commutative operation in mathematics. A commutative operation, such as multiplication, is something in which the order does not matter. Two times three gives the same result as three times two. Division, however, is non-commutative: the order matters. Two divided by three is not the same as three divided by two.

The interpretation of Scripture is a non-commutative operation: order matters. A somewhat technical example illustrates the importance of sequence. In dispensational eschatology, the Old Testament promises to Abraham and Israel are fixed as the starting point. Dispensationalists thus believe that ethnic Israel will receive the promised land at a future date. Jesus' and the apostles' teachings are *subsequently* aligned with those promises. This order generates a vastly different eschatology than classical amillenial theology, which begins with the words of Jesus on the two ages.[12] By starting with the Old Testament, one arrives at a different conclusion than starting with Jesus' words.

The apostles themselves begin with Jesus in their reading of the Old Testament. Many people have struggled with how quotations from the Old Testament are carried into the New in ways that appear not to square with the original context. A well known example is Matthew's citation from Hosea, "Out of Egypt I called My Son" (Matt. 2:15). While some have argued that Matthew was drawing from Hosea in a way that violated the Old Testament context, this fails to account for the radically Christocentric way that the apostles read the Old Testament. "Christ as the centre of history is the *key to interpreting the earlier portions of the Old Testament and its promises.*"[13]

Order effectively dictates what is a fixed point (that is, the cor-

[12] K. Riddlebarger, *The Case for Amillenialism*, Baker (2003) makes this point quite effectively.

[13] G. K. Beale, "Did Jesus and His Followers Preach the Right Doctrine from the Wrong Texts? An Examination of the Presuppositions of Jesus' and the Apostles' Exegetical Method," in *The Right Doctrine from the Wrong Texts?*, G. K. Beale (ed.), Baker (1994), p. 392.

nerstone), and what will be cast in reference to that point. With this background, the contrast between the Anabaptist and Protestant understandings of Scripture is more easily understood. Anabaptists have generally begun with the Gospel accounts—Jesus' teachings and examples—while Protestants have generally begun with the epistles, particularly the book of Romans. Neither side claims one set of books to be less inspired, but vastly different theologies emerge because of differing starting points, different cornerstones.

The impact of Romans on Luther's theology is well known. Calvin was similarly affected, as illustrated in his *magnum opus*. One of Calvin's translators into English has noted that his *Institutes of the Christian Religion* "may be thought of as an extended commentary on Romans."[14]

The early Anabaptists viewed Paul's letters as an infallible exposition of Jesus' words and deeds. But they preferred to begin at the Gospel accounts themselves. This manner of reading more appropriately uses canonical and covenantal structure as a hermeneutical lens. Using the covenantal language described in chapter 2, Anabaptists "begin at the beginning" of the covenant (preamble, history, and stipulations) rather than the later "prosecution of God's covenant lawsuit" found in the epistles. They also distrusted some of the conclusions arrived at by the Protestants on the meaning of Romans. They recognized that the book had multiple interpretations. "It is common to list saints and Christian leaders whose lives have been changed by reading [Romans]; the catalog could be balanced by a similar number who have radically misunderstood it. Troublingly, the lists would overlap."[15]

Christocentric interpretation involves focus as well as order. Jacobus Arminius, who trained in Geneva at Calvin's academy under Theodore Beza, rejected Calvinism because it was not adequately Christocentric.[16] He and the Remonstrants felt that for the sake of their theological system, the Calvinists had lost Christ-centered exegesis.[17]

The distinction between the Anabaptists and Protestant thinking has been characterized as Christocentric (Anabaptist) versus Christo-

[14] Ford Lewis Battles, in his introduction to John Calvin's *Institutes of the Christian Religion*, 1536 edition, Eerdmans (1986), p. xxvii. The book of Romans was the most cited book of the 1559 edition as well.

[15] N. T. Wright in "The Letter to the Romans" *New Interpreter's Bible: Volume X*, Abingdon Press (2002), p. 395.

[16] Robert Picirilli, *Grace, Faith, and Free Will*, Randall House Publications (2002), p. 49.

[17] Besides Picirilli's excellent work, which is somewhat technical, see Roger Olson's *Against Calvinism*, Zondervan (2011).

logical (Protestant).[18] For the Protestants, the doctrine of salvation, especially justification by faith, provided the starting point for their theology, and formed the lens through which the rest of Scripture was read. "Anabaptist hermeneutics, however, were not only Christological but *Christocentric* in the sense of focusing on Jesus himself instead of a doctrine describing the effects of his redeeming work."[19]

The Protestants spent a great deal of time on the historic creeds of the church. Calvin's *Institutes of the Christian Religion* is organized around the structure of the Apostle's Creed. In contrast, the "Anabaptists acknowledged the Christ of the creeds, but they were captivated by the Jesus of the Gospels."[20]

Consistent with a Christocentric approach, simple obedience to the Sermon on the Mount characterized persecuted churches like the ante-Nicene church, the Waldensians, and the Anabaptists. In contrast, because of their prior commitment to the church-state union, the Protestants severely weakened obedience to Jesus' teachings on matters such as war, oaths, and wealth: "In Protestantism we meet with a celestial Christ, a cosmic figure who through his self-sacrifice makes possible the salvation of the soul. In Catholicism Jesus is frequently and boldly encountered in the Mass, where he is constantly offered up again for the sins of man. In Anabaptism...Jesus is all that the historic creeds claim for him but he is also more. For he is also the example for the Christian...He is not only the centre of a theological system to which one gives assent. Rather he is the centre of a way of life."[21]

Protestant churches have greatly suffered without a Christocentric interpretation to ethics:

> That Christ alone is Lord and Saviour was, although it is the most precious insight of the Reformation, limited by the Reformers to one field of application. In soteriology and church order, Christ's uniqueness enabled a polemic against the mass, against hagiolatry and the hierarchy. Yet Christ's authority remained strangely circumscribed; He could not be normative for ethics. Christ's perfect obedience is, for orthodox Protestantism, no criterion for the obedience of the believer, but merely the prerequisite to an innocent and therefore vicariously valid death. The guide for ethics for the Reformers was neither Christ himself,

---

[18] Murray, p. 84.
[19] Murray, p. 84.
[20] Murray, p. 78.
[21] Klaassen, quoted in Murray, p. 86.

> nor the New Testament, but the 'Rule of Love.' 'Love' in this usage signified for them not that quality of God's Being which is seen in Christ, but rather whatever seemed to them to be required by the best interests of the social order. They assumed with touching naiveté, that the precise requirements of the Rule of Love were self-evident, and could be doubted only by the willfully recalcitrant ... [For the Protestants], giving immediate *ethical* relevance to the human obedience of Christ, so that the Christian should love as He loved, be persecuted as He was persecuted, was at the best pride, and at the worst blasphemy. The Reformers were so fully conditioned by their anti-Catholic polemic that they fell prey to the temptation to affirm simply the opposite of what the Roman Church has taught. Against Catholic immanence they leaned toward an almost Docetic transcendentalism; against Catholic legalism they tended toward antinomianism. They were far too close to the Gospel to be frankly antinomian; but they had enormous difficulty in finding a place to attach ethics to the rest of their doctrine. Having thus thrown out the baby with the bath, they condemned Protestantism to a centuries-long pendulum movement between ethical liberalism and nonethical orthodoxy. There being no essential structural connection between Christ and ethics, except the negative one that we are saved by Christ instead of by works, Protestants have had to choose between a high Christology and a high ethic. The Anabaptist claim that Christ is authoritative in ethics in the same way as for soteriology, so that only the disciple can really *know* him..., avoided such a posing of alternatives, and perceived that a high ethic and a high Christology are possible only together.[22]

A New Covenant Perspective

Understanding the relationship between the Old Testament and the New Testament is best achieved by examining how Jesus and the apostles used the Old Testament. Several themes emerge from a disciplined

[22] John H. Yoder in "The Prophetic Dissent of the Anabaptists," *Recovery of the Anabaptist Vision*, Guy Hershberger (ed.), Herald Press (1957, reprint by the Baptist Standard Bearer), pp. 99-100.

examination of how Jesus and the apostles handled the Old Testament.

First, Jesus teaches that His commands supersede those of the Old Testament, most notably in the Sermon on the Mount. In founding His own nation, Jesus stressed that the governance of His nation was different from that of Israel. This was done by saying, "You have heard that it was said" followed by citing an Old Testament teaching. Immediately following the citation Jesus would say, "But I say to you …"; Jesus then supersedes the Old Testament teaching, sometimes intensifying it and sometimes modifying it. One of the best examples of this "you have heard…but I say" formula concerns oaths:

> Again you have heard that it was said to those of old, "You shall not swear falsely, but shall perform your oaths to the Lord." But I say to you, do not swear at all: neither by heaven, for it is God's throne; nor by the earth, for it is His footstool; nor by Jerusalem, for it is the city of the great King. Nor shall you swear by your head, because you cannot make one hair white or black. But let your "Yes" be "Yes," and your "No," "No." For whatever is more than these is from the evil one. (Matt. 5:33-37)

In this passage, Jesus makes a reference to Leviticus 19:12, "You shall not swear by my name falsely." Yet He astonishes his hearers by banning oaths altogether, "But I say to you, do not swear at all" (Matt. 5:34). Jesus' prohibition of all oaths is striking because in the Old Testament only false oath taking was condemned. Oath taking was approved and even *commanded.*[23] Moreover, Israel's godly leaders like Abraham, Moses, and David swore oaths.[24] Even a righteous angel could be found swearing by God in the Old Testament (Dan. 12:7).

This command against oaths serves then as a powerful example of the New Covenant marking Christ's nation, because here the New must supersede the Old. One cannot observe both Old Testament and New Testament practices simultaneously. The argument can be made simpler still: since we are under the New Covenant and not the Old, the New Covenant must take primacy.

A second theme is that without Jesus' instruction, the Old Testament cannot be understood (Luke 24:44-45). The disciples, while familiar with traditional Jewish understanding of the Old Testament, needed their eyes opened by Jesus and required His instruction to correctly understand the Old Testament. Harmonizing well with the Christocentric

[23] Exod. 22:10-13; Num. 5:19; Deut. 6:13, 10:20; Jer. 12:16.

[24] See Gen. 21:31, 24:8-9, 31:53, 47:31; Josh. 2:16-17, 6:26, 9:15, 14:9; 1 Sam. 24:22; 2 Sam. 3:35; 1 Kings 1:17, 2:8; Ezra 10:5; Neh. 13:25; Ps. 119:106, 132:2; and Isa. 65:16.

method of exegesis discussed earlier, this points to the requirement of the New Testament to properly understand the Old.

Scripture develops the relationship of the covenants in several passages:

- When the New Covenant is promised in the Old Testament, it is described as, "not like the covenant that I made with their fathers" (Jer. 31:33). Difference is emphasized more than similarity in Jeremiah 31:31-34 as well as Ezekiel 36:24-38.
- In Galatians 3, Paul expounds a careful argument that the Old Covenant law served as a guardian, the term used for those who protected children,[25] for the people of God until Jesus came. To follow the Old Testament view of circumcision would be like an adult going back to a childish state. The motif of bondage is closely related to this unnatural condition (Gal. 4).
- A contrast is drawn between the ends of the covenants (see 2 Cor. 3:6). "The ministry of the letter, that is, the Law [Mosaic Covenant], kills fallen people (cf. Rom. 6-7), while the ministry of the Spirit [through the New Covenant] gives them life."[26]
- When Paul describes being "not under the law" (for example in Rom. 6:14), this is a reference to the Old Covenant—the Mosaic law. "As in all these references, *nomos* [law] here must be the Mosaic law, the torah."[27]
- A major theme of the book of Hebrews concerns the relationship between the Old and New Covenants. The author calls the Old Covenant "obsolete" (Heb. 8:13).
- Balancing what might be construed as negative views, the Old Testament is described as being written for our instruction (1 Cor. 10:11), filled with models of faith (Heb. 11). Moreover, the Old Testament is filled with portraits of Jesus, serving to validate His Messiahship and inspire His followers. This makes the Old Testament extremely profitable for study and meditation.

The Anabaptist view attempts to balance these tensions: "They taught both continuity and discontinuity. They were not arguing for the rejection of the Old Testament, nor for the complete divorce of the Testaments. But most were convinced that the New Testament was radically new and could not be seen as being in unbroken continuity with the Old. It was not that the New Testament revoked the Old and made

[25] N. T. Wright uses the more vivid word, "babysitter," to translate *paidogogos*.

[26] Ben Witherington III, *Conflict and Community in Corinth*, Eerdmans (1995), p. 379.

[27] Douglas Moo, *The Epistle to the Romans*, Eerdmans (1996), pp. 387-388.

it worthless, but that the Old was subsumed in the New and could not function in isolation from it."[28]

A helpful contrast of how the Protestants and Anabaptists understood Scripture is in how false prophets were treated. Citing Old Testament passages, Luther, Melanchthon, and Calvin advocated that such men be executed.[29] In contrast, the Anabaptists noted that the New Testament mentions that false teachers should be neither greeted nor received.[30] While not explicitly overturning Old Testament teaching, the New Testament paradigm was sufficient to cause the Anabaptists to advocate rebuke and separation as opposed to execution.

On matters such as war, oaths, wealth, and baptism, the Protestants relied heavily or even primarily on the Old Testament while the Anabaptists drew their views primarily from the New Testament. The Anabaptists continued to press the charge of inconsistency. For example, they believed that the Protestants compromised on salvation by faith by maintaining the Roman Catholic, state-church position of infant baptism as the entry point into the covenant, despite the absence of the infant's faith. The Anabaptists held that believer's baptism reinforced salvation by faith. Arminius and the Remonstrants made the case that the Protestants, while using the words "salvation by faith" in fact denied that truth at the core of their theology.[31]

Sola scriptura

Sola scriptura is one of the most misunderstood and maligned slogans from the Reformation. Today's opponents of the doctrine mistakenly attack positions that bear little resemblance to the original doctrine as articulated in the sixteenth century. Being richer and more complex

---

28 Murray, p. 100.

29 For more on Calvin's views, see Bruce Gordon, *Calvin*, Yale University Press (2009), pp. 217-232. Luther's views changed over time, generally growing more intolerant. He advocated killing Jews, prostitutes, and occasionally Anabaptists. "Luther called for the punishment for blasphemy found in the Mosaic Law." in John S. Oyer, *Lutheran Reformers Against Anabaptists*, Baptist Standard Bearer (1964), p. 138. Philip Melanchthon taught that all Anabaptists who did not recant should be killed. See Oyer, pp. 155-158.

30 For example, Dirk Philips wrote that anything more than exclusion was neither Christian nor apostolic. See *The Writings of Dirk Philips*, Cornelius Dyck, William Keeney, and Alvin Beachy (translators and editors), Herald Press (1992), p. 375.

31 Picirilli, pp. 160-182, gives a helpful overview. While Calvinists affirm the language of salvation or justification by faith, they wince at the logical inference that election must be by faith. But then, "If election is not by faith, then neither is salvation" (p. 169).

than most doctrines, we will build up a definition slowly, drawing heavily on church history.

With the Protestants, the early Anabaptists cherished *sola scriptura*. The Anabaptists "followed rigorously the principle of *sola scriptura*: only the Bible is to be followed."[32] The prominent Anabaptist leader Menno Simons supported *sola scriptura*: "I dare not go higher nor lower, more stringent nor lenient than the Scriptures and the Holy Spirit teach me; and that out of great fear and anxiety of my conscience, lest I again burden the godfearing hearts who now have renounced the commandments of men, with those commandments. Self-conceit and human opinions I hate, nor do I desire them; for I know what tribulation and affliction they have caused me for many years."[33]

Most contentious with the doctrine of *sola scriptura* is the relationship of Scripture to tradition. Several views can be found in church history in understanding this relationship. The oldest, called Tradition I, states that tradition describes the church's understanding of Scripture.[34] Tradition is not an addition to Scripture; Scripture and tradition "coinhere" and are "coextensive" with each other.[35] Tradition is essentially the church's exegesis of Scripture. "Tradition I, then, represents the sufficiency of Holy Scripture as understood by the Fathers and doctors of the Church. In the case of disagreement between these interpreters, Holy Scripture has the final authority."[36] As a corollary to the Tradition I viewpoint, extrabiblical tradition is rejected by Tradition I advocates. The earliest post-apostolic church leaders affirm a Tradition I view. Irenaeus and Tertullian, "deny most decidedly the existence of extra-scriptural tradition."[37] Other advocates of the classical Tradition I position include Clement of Alexandria, Cyprian, John Wycliffe, John Huss, and the sixteenth century Protestants.

In contrast to the early Tradition I view, a second view known as

---

[32] J. C. Wenger in "Biblicism of the Anabaptists," *Recovery of the Anabaptist Vision*, Guy Hershberger (ed.), Herald Press (1957, reprint by the Baptist Standard Bearer), pp. 170-171. Murray, p. 19., notes that the early Anabaptists "fully shared" a commitment to *sola scriptura* with the Protestants. Harold S. Bender affirms the early Anabaptist commitment to *sola scriptura* in *The Mennonite Encyclopedia: Volume I*, Mennonite Brethren Publishing House (1955), pp. 322-323.

[33] Menno Simons in *The Complete Works of Menno Simons*, John F. Funk and Brother (1871, reprint by Pathway Publishers in 1983), Second Part, p. 281.

[34] This nomenclature comes from Heiko Oberman, *The Harvest of Medieval Theology*, Harvard University Press (1963, reprint by Baker Academic in 2000), pp. 365-390.

[35] Oberman, pp. 366-367.

[36] Oberman, p. 372.

[37] Flesseman-van Leer, quoted in R. P. C. Hanson, *Tradition in the Early Church*, SCM Press (1962, reprint by Wipf and Stock in 2009), p. 25f.

Tradition II crept into the church after 325 AD. Tradition II teaches that tradition contains material beyond the interpretation of Scripture, representing a distinct source of revelation. Tradition becomes an *addition* to Scripture. Tradition II also endows tradition with co-equal authority to Scripture. "Ecclesiastical traditions, including canon law, are invested with the same degree of authority as that of Holy Scripture."[38] Tradition II thinking is quite similar to rabbinic Judaism's view that "oral Torah" was given at Sinai, apart from written Torah, and that it represents a distinct body of revelation. Rabbinic Judaism spent centuries debating and elaborating the contents of oral Torah, such as details concerning Sabbath observance, washings, and dietary laws.

Within Christianity, while faintly emerging in the fourth century, Tradition II advocates clearly blossomed by the late middle ages, typified by William of Occam.[39] At the time of the Reformation, in reacting against the Protestants, the Roman Catholic church clung to Tradition II, despite its historic novelty. For this reason, a substantial amount of the Protestant polemic against the Roman Catholic church amounted to citations of the church fathers, demonstrating that Protestant doctrines were original and that the Roman Catholic church was the innovator: "Within this historical context, the Reformers saw themselves not as introducing some new teaching about 'Scripture alone', but as overturning the dangerous innovation brought in by the growth of Tradition II, and recovering for the church as a whole the early church's 'Tradition I' position. For the Reformers, *sola scriptura* meant a return to Tradition I. In other words, the Reformers had a high regard for the authority of inherited traditions of biblical interpretation, and of the views of earlier generations of widely respected theologians, as well as for the church's role in providing a context in which Scripture can properly be understood."[40]

In distinguishing between Tradition I and Tradition II, one must be clear that *sola scriptura* does not teach that Scripture is the only authority, but that it is the only *infallible* authority.[41] Other authority does exist, such as the received wisdom of the early church, but such authority is subordinate to Scripture. Another way of framing this distinction draws on an analogy to faith and works. While we are saved by faith alone, we are not saved by a faith that is alone—that is, true faith always produces works. Similarly, "our final authority is Scripture alone,

[38] Oberman, p. 373.

[39] Oberman gives a helpful survey of the evidence in pp. 365-390.

[40] Timothy Ward, *Words of Life*, InterVarsity Press (2009), p. 146.

[41] Ward, p. 147.

but not a Scripture that is alone."[42] Other subordinate authorities are useful aids in comprehending and obeying the only infallible authority of Scripture.

Another view concerning the relationship between Scripture and tradition, popular in modern evangelical churches, states that Scripture is not only the sole infallible authority, it is the *only* authority. This "Bible and me" doctrine has largely flourished because of the rise of individualism and weak-group thinking and is radically different from Tradition I thinking. This view has been termed Tradition 0, because it allows for no room for tradition.[43] Being so different from *sola scriptura*, Tradition 0 has been called solo *scriptura*.[44] Solo *scriptura*, in contrast to *sola scriptura*, exalts the individual's private judgment over the corporate judgment of the church. Solo *scriptura*, by encouraging the autonomy of the individual, lays the groundwork for church division. Weak-group churches go hand-in-hand with solo *scriptura*. Besides promoting division, another serious flaw of solo *scriptura* is that it does not adequately confront the prejudice and bias which all readers naturally have:

> Everyone who reads the Bible does so with a set of expectations and assumptions, some consciously held and some subconscious, that have been handed on to them. It is dangerous, of course, if these are misleading expectations and assumptions. What is often equally dangerous is to deny that one has them at all. Indeed, in practice, communities that espouse Tradition 0 cannot usually avoid adhering to some kind of tradition, in order to provide coherence in faith across the community, and to avoid falling into an anarchy in which each one does and believes simply what is right in his own eyes. They therefore smuggle 'tradition' in, without identifying it as such, in the form of a senior position in the community given to one or more individuals judged to be especially gifted in discerning the voice of the Spirit in Scripture.[45]

Not surprisingly, then, solo *scriptura* can supply the fertile soil for the growth of charismatic (sometimes abusive) leaders.

---

[42] Keith Mathison, *The Shape of* Sola Scriptura, Canon Press (2001), p. 259.

[43] Alistair McGrath is credited with this term, building on Oberman's nomenclature. Cited in Mathison, p. 126.

[44] A term coined by Douglas Jones. Cited in Mathison, p. 238.

[45] Ward, p. 150.

Some are uncomfortable with saying that Scripture is the only infallible authority—should not that be reserved for God? To answer that question, we recall the presentation from chapter 6, where we saw that God's word and God Himself are closely bound, and that God's word is invested with God's very authority. Scripture's status as being the sole infallible authority comes directly from its status as God-breathed.

By now, it should also be clear how poorly misunderstood *sola scriptura* generally is. "It does not deny the necessity of traditions of biblical interpretation, creedal formulations of biblical faith, and inherited church practices that help to express and pass on the faith. Rather it ensures that all those traditions serve Scripture, the supreme authority, rather than compete with it. *Sola scriptura* means 'Scripture supreme'."[46] *Sola scriptura* can be defined in a single sentence: the Scriptures are the only infallible authority, in a Tradition I sense. This interpretative principle has a powerful binding effect upon the church, promoting the unity that Jesus earnestly sought. *Sola scriptura* combats against the divisiveness of unchecked individualism (Tradition 0) as well as autonomous and corrupt institutions (Tradition II).

Sufficiency of Scripture

The sufficiency of Scripture is closely related to *sola scriptura*, but has a different emphasis. The sufficiency of Scripture means, "Scripture contained all the words of God he intended his people to have at each stage of redemptive history, and that it now contains all the words of God we need for salvation, for trusting him perfectly, and for obeying him perfectly."[47] Several biblical passages attest to the sufficiency of Scripture.

In the Old Testament, both taking away from or adding to the Scriptures were prohibited, implying a doctrine of sufficiency: "You shall not add to the word which I command you, nor take from it, that you may keep the commandments of the Lord your God which I command you" (Deut. 4:2; see also 12:32 and Prov. 30:5-6). Confirming the law's sufficiency, the Psalms attest that God's word tells us *everything* needed to live a blameless life, "Blessed are those whose way is blameless, who walk in the law of the LORD!" (Ps. 119:1) The New Testament attests to the sufficiency of Scripture with respect to salvation: "From childhood you have known the Holy Scriptures, which are able to make you wise for salvation through faith which is in Christ Jesus" (2 Tim. 3:15). The Scriptures "complete" a person, equipping him or her for every good

[46] Ward, p. 151.

[47] Wayne Grudem, *Systematic Theology*, Zondervan (1994), p. 127.

work: "All Scripture is given by inspiration of God, and is profitable for doctrine, for reproof, for correction, for instruction in righteousness, that the man of God may be complete, thoroughly equipped for every good work." (2 Tim. 3:16-17). In Jesus' parable about the rich man and Lazarus, He affirms that nothing outside of the Scriptures is required for salvation: "They have Moses and the prophets; let them hear them" (Luke 16:29).

The New Testament prohibits the addition of new commandments (Col. 2:20-23) and speaks of a closure to the faith (Jude 1:3). The book of Revelation closes the New Testament canon with a warning similar to that given in Deuteronomy (the close of the Torah): "For I testify to everyone who hears the words of the prophecy of this book: If anyone adds to these things, God will add to him the plagues that are written in this book; and if anyone takes away from the words of the book of this prophecy, God shall take away his part from the Book of Life, from the holy city, and from the things which are written in this book" (Rev. 22:18-19).

The implications of the sufficiency of Scripture are manifold. First, the doctrine reinforces *sola scriptura*, by confirming that our sole infallible authority is also complete. Second, sufficiency speaks against adding to Scripture any extrabiblical requirements or prohibitions. Proper commands or prohibitions must be found in Scripture or be necessary inferences from Scripture. Third, the sufficiency of Scripture should drive us to Scripture for meditation, study, memorization, and prayer, as we seek to be the "complete" people that God wills. Fourth, we should never elevate other documents to the level of Scripture, nominally or practically. Some churches recite creeds, confessions, or disciplines during their gatherings or discuss them so often that they functionally become Scripture. Such distorting practices set the stage for reading Scripture through the lens of other documents, rather than on Scripture's own terms.

The testimony of the persecuted cloud of witnesses

Early in church history, divergent interpretations of Scripture were recognized and judged as problematic. One powerful tool to find the correct interpretation was proposed by the church fathers. Irenaeus and Vincent of Lérins proposed that the true teaching of Scripture would be found in the church across time (*semper*), across persons (*ab omnibus*), and across distance (*ubique*).[48] While remarkably simple, this

[48] See Irenaeus, *Against Heresies*, IV.33.8 and Vincent, *Commonitorium*, II.5.

tool offers remarkable power and precision.

The principle weighs the consensus biblical interpretation of the "cloud of witnesses." Hebrews 11 portrays how we can learn from those who have gone before us, especially those who were mistreated, persecuted, and shunned by the world. The Scriptures promise that the godly will suffer persecution (2 Tim. 3:12). The godly, being endowed with the Holy Spirit, will naturally be able to interpret the Scriptures best.

It must be clear that this principle is not an exercise of simple "nose-counting" to ascertain what Scripture truly says. That would approach blasphemy, as if the word of God depended on some kind of majority vote. The Scriptures caution against such an approach by warning us that in the last days, men will go from bad to worse, and that teachers will tickle ears to gain a greater audience. Paul warns that teachers will arise to twist the word in order to gain followers after themselves. We must be cognizant that even at the close of the New Testament canon, Jesus rebukes five out of seven churches in Revelation. Today, false churches and teachers abound to an even greater degree.

While the Scriptures describe that heretics live lustful lives (2 Pet. 2:13-14), the true church will experience suffering and persecution (John 15:20). Jesus promises that a faithful remnant will never be extinguished but will resist the gates of Hades (Matt. 16:18). Integrating these insights, faithful biblical interpretation will be associated with a fivefold norm:

1. Diffusion: across distance
2. Endurance: across time
3. Breadth: across persons
4. Purity: with holiness
5. Suffering: with adversity

By weighing more heavily the persecuted, faithful "cloud of witnesses" there is much to be gained. It breaks us out of a solo *scriptura* mentality, which tends to fracture the church and exalt autonomy. It in fact represents an aspect of Tradition I thinking and helps us to eliminate bias and blind spots. Every generation is susceptible to "groupthink," and by studying believers outside of one's culture and time period, we may more clearly see timeless truth. This exercise requires humility, acknowledging that God has worked through saints outside of our limited circle.

Examples of the "cloud of witnesses" principle in action best illustrate its use. By the end of the second century, the church had developed the *regula fidei*, or rule of faith, similar to the Apostle's creed of the fourth century. Useful in combating anti-trinitarian and gnostic heresies, the rule was affirmed by the persecuted church and thoughtfully drawn from Scriptures. The contents of the *regula fidei* were affirmed by the medieval church, the Anabaptists, and the Protestants. Given such a broad reception, especially from the early church and persecuted church, this interpretative principle would strongly suggest that the contents of the *regula fidei* are a faithful interpretation of Scriptures.

The persecuted groups include the ante-Nicene church, the Waldensians, the Lollards (followers of John Wycliffe), and the Anabaptists.[49] In contrast, the Roman Catholic church and the Protestant churches, allied to the state, have been persecuting churches at many points in their history.

The persecuted churches are typically those that hold the clarity of Scripture most dearly: they tend to take the Bible at face value and not allow clear teachings to be accommodated to culture or prevalent expectations. When the word of God confronts a structure or institution, the suffering churches tend to modify or withdraw from the structure or institution. The Roman Catholic and Protestant churches instead tend to employ the "principle of accommodation," modifying the teaching in some way to fit existing structures and institutions. Again, the Sermon on the Mount serves as the classic litmus test. The persecuted churches have usually obeyed Jesus' prohibition to not swear oaths at all and to love their enemies, that is, to reject the taking of human life, even in war. They have also embraced the plain readings of Jesus' teachings on divorce and wealth found in the Sermon on the Mount. Conversely, the Roman Catholic and Protestant churches have been much more lenient about divorce and wealth, have supported participation in state warfare, and have allowed their members to take oaths.[50]

The Protestants employed the "cloud of witnesses" interpretative principle in certain areas but generally avoided it in wide swaths of ecclesiology and ethics. On the positive side, Calvin took great pains to show that doctrines such as salvation by faith were the doctrines of the church fathers. His careful argument implied that the Roman Catholic church had left the historic faith, innovating in this departure. Sadly, however, Calvin and the other Protestants ignored or rejected a great

[49] For more on these groups, see Leonard Verduin's *The Anatomy of a Hybrid*, Eerdmans (1976) and John W. Kennedy's *The Torch of the Testimony*, Christian Books Publishing (1965, reprint 1983).

[50] The Westminster Confession tries to justify oaths at length, despite the Sermon on the Mount. One cannot help but wonder from the length if the authors' consciences were pricked by Jesus' plain words. As Bruner puts it, the WCF "protesteth too much."

deal of the early church's teachings on other matters. On matters of oaths, war, infant baptism, and separation from the world, they chose to adopt Roman Catholic views and reject the early church's position.

In contrast, the early Anabaptists much more consistently adopted the positions of the early church regarding ethics and ecclesiology. They affirmed the *regula fidei* and the historic creeds, but also chose to obey Jesus' teachings in ways very close to the early church.

In the last chapter we saw that interpretative systems are like packages where seemingly divergent subjects are bundled together. Regarding areas like jewelry, fashion, entertainment, the headcovering, home life, education, separation from the world, oaths, war, government involvement, remarriage, and infant baptism—the cloud of witnesses offers strong testimony. The suffering, persecuted church—beginning with the church described in Acts and progressing through the centuries—therefore offers illumination, conviction, and encouragement. On the other side are the churches that have embraced the power of temporal government, the fashions and entertainments of the world, "just war," beautiful cathedrals, and prestigious institutions. Those churches will mock the persecuted churches, disparage their doctrines, and even kill their members, imagining that they do service to God. The period of the Reformation illustrates this story in microcosm as the Roman Catholic and Protestant churches turned violent against the Anabaptists and Waldensians.

Employing the principles

In this chapter, seven principles of biblical interpretation have been offered. Those principles are: the clarity of Scripture, the necessity of the Spirit, Christocentric exegesis, a New Covenant perspective, *sola scriptura*, the sufficiency of Scripture, and the testimony of the persecuted cloud of witnesses.

If one assents to these principles and agrees to be consistent, then the exercise of biblical interpretation is, in some sense, finished. A cohesive set of conclusions naturally follows. As the book progresses, we will employ these principles in the context of specific issues.

Chapter 9

Against cultural relativism

Let God be true but every man a liar. (Romans 3:4)

Having examined the principles of faithful biblical interpretation, we turn our attention to how *not* to read Scripture. While there are many ways to twist God's words, one especially pernicious error has invaded the modern churches.

When encountering difficult commands in the Bible, a commonly expressed sentiment when softening or even avoiding the same application for today is something like, "That was a cultural practice, so we are not obligated to follow such a teaching." Such a sentiment may be termed *cultural relativism*, since it communicates a belief that certain commands or patterns may lose their relevance due to changes in the culture. This approach has been used so often that many people in modern churches assume that any teaching of the New Testament must be subjected to the "culture test." Sexual behavior (especially homosexuality), the nature of the church meeting, standards of dress, women's silence, and headcoverings are seemingly unrelated topics that are all united by the assault of cultural relativism. The original and historic position on each of these issues has been forcefully and repeatedly challenged by the charge of cultural relativism.

The rise of cultural relativism is closely related to one of the long running "scandals," or stumbling blocks, of evangelism. That stumbling block is usually called the *scandal of particularity*. The scandal of particularity concerns the apparently arbitrary choice of having the Son of God manifest as Jesus of Nazareth two thousand years ago. Why should the Savior of the *whole* world come as a solitary man in an obscure location at one moment in time thousands of years ago? The notion that the God of the universe would reveal Himself in such a *particular* way has been repugnant to intellectuals for generations. Those who have reacted against the scandal of particularity often take refuge in atheism, deism, agnosticism, or unitarianism.

Ironically, however, many professing Christians continue to stumble at the scandal of particularity *after* declaring faith in Jesus. While embracing a particular Savior, they reject His particular teachings. Doctrines like the Lord's Supper, feet washing, the holy kiss, and the head-covering are modified or explained away using the same logic employed by anti-Christian intellectuals. They feel that God simply *could not* have meant that such a particular behavior or command would be relevant for Christians at all times and everywhere.

Several books in the New Testament, particularly 1 Corinthians, shed light on the question of whether culture can abrogate scriptural commands. Two case studies serve as fruitful starting points.

Case study 1: Seating arrangements in church

> When you come together in one place, it is not to eat the Lord's Supper. For in eating, each one takes his own supper ahead of others; and one is hungry and another is drunk. What! Do you not have houses to eat and drink in? Or do you despise the church of God and shame those who have nothing? What shall I say to you? Shall I praise you in this? I do not praise you...Therefore, my brethren, when you come together to eat, wait for one another. (1 Cor. 11:20-22, 33)

> My brethren, do not hold the faith of our Lord Jesus Christ, the Lord of glory, with partiality. For if there should come into your assembly a man with gold rings, in fine apparel, and there should also come in a poor man in filthy clothes, and you pay attention to the one wearing the fine clothes and say to him, "You sit here in a good place," and say to the poor man, "You stand there," or, "Sit here at my footstool," have you not shown partiality among yourselves, and become judges with evil thoughts? (James 2:1-4)

These passages can mystify modern readers for two reasons. First, these letters were written to house-churches that met around the Lord's Supper, which involved a full meal. The host, in whose house the church met, instructed guests to sit at varying positions around the table. This practice resembles visiting a home for dinner and waiting for the host to tell you where to sit around the table. It does not resemble going to a typical modern church where people generally sit wherever they like. In addition, because the early church typically met around an evening meal, some people might have arrived late, especially the slaves or the poor detained by work.

Second, it was considered proper decorum in the Greco-Roman world to determine seating and fare by social status.[1] These situations described in 1 Corinthians and James arose because some people in these early churches assumed that church should function like the world around it, following these customs:

> Ancient society provided a number of special benefits to those of high class and status. Those with the highest status in a locale could claim the front seat at shows, they had the right to wear and display certain symbols of their status, and when the state distributed money, food, or wine, they were entitled to a bigger portion than were the poor...A person's place at table and the quality of food served depended on the person's status. This was true both of private dinner parties to which a rich patron invited some clients and of public banquets given by an aristocrat for fellow citizens. The dispute at Corinth that Paul takes up may reflect this practice: the host at a Christian agape feast is acting like a patron at a banquet, making distinctions between the guests with higher status and those with lower status (1 Corinthians 11:17-34). The Epistle of James depicts a similar situation in which a stranger with a gold ring and fine clothes is given a seat of honor while a poor stranger is given a place of dishonor.[2]

Strong internal and external pressures therefore influenced the believers at Corinth to function as they were conditioned by the culture. In looking at the passages in historical context, our conclusion is this: Paul and James are exhorting their readers: "Do not allow the cultural customs of how to seat and feed people to encroach upon the practice of the church. You must be different."

---

[1] For example, Pliny the Younger (writing around 100 AD) describes how the best food and wine were given to the host and a select few, while the other guests received scraps. Another second-century writer, Lucian, complains that he does not eat the same dinner as his host. The host enjoys oysters, mushrooms, and turtledove, while Lucian receives mussel, hog funguses, and a magpie that died in its cage.

[2] James Jeffers, *The Greco-Roman World of the New Testament Era: Exploring the Background of Early Christianity*, InterVarsity Press (1999), pp. 191-192.

Case study 2: Headcoverings

In 1 Corinthians 11:2-16, Paul's insistence on the headcovering includes some of the strongest language that he uses anywhere in his writings: "We have no other practice, nor do the churches of God" (v. 16).[3] He employs multiple arguments rooted in the nature of God, the creation of humankind, and angelic activity. Lastly he appeals to the universality of this practice in the churches.

While essentially all the churches practiced the headcovering for nearly two thousand years, few churches in today's world do, especially in the West). Those who do not typically cite the cultural relativism argument, saying something like, "Paul is commanding the Corinthian church not to violate cultural standards, which would cause offense. Because people today are not offended by a woman's head being uncovered, we are allowed to pass over this command."

Such an argument bears an appearance of plausibility, but fails under examination. Nowhere in the text does Paul cite reasons relating to offending others or keeping cultural practices—something he does concerning other issues in Romans 14:13, 1 Corinthians 8:9-13, 9:19-23, and 10:23-33. Given that he does so elsewhere, and is thus in full possession of the vocabulary and thought paradigm to have potentially offered an argument of cultural offense, it defies plausibility that such reasons are being advanced in this text. Instead, Paul decisively refers to the nature of the Godhead (clearly not cultural), the creation of man and woman (which would encompass all cultures), and angelic activity (also not cultural).

Cultural relativists instead say that Paul is drawing out a universal principle of not offending others that might have specific cultural application. Again, the principle of not offending others is nowhere to be found in his argument, so this inference would seem to be reading into the text. However, for the sake of argument, let us grant that it is merely a command to fit the cultural norms of the day and lacks absolute, timeless instruction. This interpretation falls under its own weight. The interpretation crucially ignores the fact that this text is also addressed to men, who were instructed to keep their heads uncovered. Yet we know that in the Corinthian culture (which was Roman, not Greek), men were supposed to keep their heads covered in worship or pious acts. Evidence from archeology demonstrates "the widespread use of male liturgical head coverings in the city of Rome, in Italy, and in numerous cities in the Roman East...on coins, statues, and architec-

[3] Author's translation.

tural monuments from around the Mediterranean Basin."[4] In addition, "The practice of men covering their heads in a context of prayer and prophecy was a common pattern of Roman piety and widespread during the late Republic and early Empire."[5] A statue of Augustus found at Corinth itself revealed that even Caesar covered his head when sacrificing to the gods.[6] The apostolic practice therefore clashed with society's expectations for men: "In view of the argument about both men and women and head-coverings, it is likely that both, not just women, were creating the disorder in Christian worship. In light of Roman practice, it is very believable that some Christian Roman males were covering their heads when they were about to pray or prophesy. Paul is not interested in baptizing the *status quo* or normal Roman practice. He is setting up new customs for a new community, and these customs are deeply grounded in his theological understanding."[7]

Hence we conclude that Paul's instruction to the men in this passage is profoundly countercultural—interestingly, for the women, it is less so! Women normally covered their heads as a sign of modesty and respectability.[8] Taken as a whole, we are confronted with the fact that Paul was not merely accommodating cultural expectations—he was overturning them. This is corroborated by the universality of the practice; Paul informs his hearers that in all churches men are to uncover their heads and women are to cover them. Given the diversity of locales and cultures represented by churches at the time of Paul's writing (Rome, Asia minor, Macedonia, Achaea, Cyprus, Syria, Judea, Samaria, etc.), the unity of this practice is astonishing. Moreover, 1 Corinthians opens with, "To the church of God which is at Corinth, to those who are sanctified in Christ Jesus, called to be saints, *with all who in every place* call on the name of Jesus Christ our Lord" (1 Cor. 1:2). The addressees are explicitly named as all believers everywhere. To bind its commands and patterns to one group in one place does injustice to the entire letter. "Paul is not simply endorsing standard Roman or even Greco-Roman customs in Corinth. Paul was about the business of reforming his converts' social assumptions and conventions in the context of Christian community. They were to model new Christian customs, common to the assemblies of God but uncommon in the culture, thus staking out

[4] R. E. Oster, quoted in Anthony Thiselton, *The First Epistle to the Corinthians: A Commentary on the Greek Text*, Eerdmans (2000), p. 805.

[5] David Garland, *1 Corinthians*, Baker Academic (2003), p. 517.

[6] The statue, the *Via Labicana Augustus*, is exhibited in the Palazzo Massimo alle Terme at the National Museum of Rome.

[7] Ben Witherington III, *Conflict & Community in Corinth*, Eerdmans (1995), p. 238.

[8] Garland, pp. 520-521.

their own sense of unique identity."[9] If Paul was being countercultural in this text, how can we discard the headcovering for cultural reasons?

Application

After appreciating that the Corinthians were conforming to cultural patterns in these cases of the Lord's Supper and headcoverings—and that Paul was giving countercultural commands—many other instances of this same phenomenon leap out throughout the book. Another example is the issue of eating food in the temples of idols, something that was a mainstay of social life. Paul attacks this practice (1 Cor. 8 and 10:1-22), along with the other apostles (Acts 15:20) and even Jesus Himself (Rev. 2:14, 2:20).

This theme of God's truth over and against human and cultural wisdom includes still more examples: tolerating sin (1 Cor. 5), something pervasive in the culture; rallying around certain leaders in personality cults (1 Cor. 1:10-17), a well-known trait of Greco-Roman society; glorifying celibacy and denigrating marriage (1 Cor. 7), also widespread in the often ascetic Roman empire; denying or having strange views on the resurrection (1 Cor. 15), which would naturally have flowed from the views common in paganism. In a fascinating statement that might seem out of place, while rebuking their views on the resurrection, Paul writes, "Bad company ruins good morals" (1 Cor. 15:33 ESV). Unless one understands that even their doctrinal problems were absorbed from the wider culture, this statement could seem unrelated. Thus perhaps it is not overstatement to say: *cultural conformity was the primary problem of the church in Corinth.*

New Testament eschatology provides another basis for questioning cultural relativism. Frequently, the New Testament authors write that they are in the last days, or even in the last hour (Acts 2:17; 2 Tim. 3:1; Heb. 1:2; James 5:3; 1 John 2:18; 2 Pet. 3:3). From God's perspective, the time gap between the first century and our era is vanishingly small. Imagine if a professing Christian in AD 90 protested against the headcovering because of a cultural gap. While most of us might think that was foolish, that same manner of error is upon us. Jesus did not forecast another age wherein His particular commands would lose relevance. Rather we ought to see ourselves in continuity with first-century Christians, as if our ages are telescoped. Set in this light, the apostles' objective of thoroughgoing resocialization must also be our objective.

[9] Witherington, p. 234.

Modern church leaders have been advancing imagery that assists cultural relativism. Some have said that church history should be like a five act play, with the first four acts being creation, fall, Israel, and Jesus. Looking at the first four acts, we "improvise" then on what the fifth act should be like.[10] Others speak of a trajectory or arc of revelation. Perhaps not surprisingly, these proponents propose a fifth act or final leg of the arc that is quite acceptable to our cultural norms. Proponents of these analogies tend to have permissive stances on women's ordination and homosexuality and to shudder at commands like the headcovering. These analogies help detach us from Jesus' and the apostles' hardest commands, and "liberate" us to our twisted and people-pleasing ways.

Those stumbling over the scandal of particularity have fallen into other errors. Most professing Christians effectively live an ethic indistinguishable from moral Jews, Hindus, Mormons, or agnostics. Indeed, outside of mental beliefs, the teachings of the modern evangelical churches could hardly be distinguished from those in any other religious setting. The scandal of particularity has led to the scandal of indistinguishability.

Paul was not simply trying to create unity amongst individuals in the sense of creating a group of people who merely "got along." The apostles sought to create a unique and separate *Christian* nation: "Come out from among them and be separate" (2 Cor. 6:17). "Paul works also for the transformation of the multiplicity of different social and ethnic/cultural value systems into a unity," that is, "a new social order."[11]

The church today should stop conforming to the world. The church must be distinguished biblically in many areas including nonresistance, sexual behavior, headcoverings, the holy kiss, feet-washing, manner of dress, entertainment, and the very way that it meets. The church should be a new social order, with a wholly new identity. For when the scales fall from our eyes, cultural relativism will be seen as nothing more than a repetition of the Enemy's tactic in the garden, "Did God really say?"

[10] N. T. Wright's unfortunate analogy.
[11] W. Wuellner, quoted in Witherington, p. 274.

Chapter 10

The law of the King

Fulfill the law of Christ. (Galatians 6:2)

All nations have a constitution, a body of laws that defines how citizens must behave. A constitution grants privileges and liberties to citizens of good standing and also declares punishments for those who violate the law. The New Testament, more properly called the New Covenant, is similar to the constitution of a nation. As we saw in chapter 2, the New Covenant is organized similarly to ancient covenants that kings established with their subjects. The New Covenant contains preamble, history, stipulations, document clause, witnesses, and sanctions. The political dimensions of the New Testament are confirmed by the very word *Christ*, which can be translated as *God's anointed King*. The New Testament describes King Jesus' coming to announce that His kingdom is finally invading this hostile world.

Like other covenants, the New Covenant contains stipulations, also called commandments or laws. The Gospel accounts contain these commandments, and the epistles elaborate upon them. Yet two great commands undergird all the laws of the King. Jesus succinctly described these fundamental commandments of His nation: " 'You shall love the Lord your God with all your heart, with all your soul, and with all your mind.' This is the first and great commandment. And the second is like it: 'You shall love your neighbor as yourself.' On these two commandments hang all the Law and the Prophets" (Matt. 22:37-40). The common word between these two commandments is *love*. So it may be properly said that the law of King Jesus is simply the law of love. That only one word, *love*, captures the essence of God's commandments highlights a beautiful feature of Christ's nation—its simplicity. From "love God" and "love your neighbor" flow the commandments of Scriptures.

But love has been cheapened. "The problem is, most people today have a sentimentalized view of love: love as being made to feel special. Or they have a romanticized view of love: love as being allowed to express yourself without judgment. Or they have a consumeristic view: love as finding the perfect fit for you. In the popular mind, love has little to do with truth and holiness and authority."[1] These various views degrade the meaning of love.

Christian love, which is Christ-like love, represents a choice and is less about feelings. While feelings may be present, biblical love is first and foremost a choice and an orientation of the will. In fact, it is possible for someone to show love to another person, while being displeased with or repulsed by that person (Matt. 5:43-48, Rom. 5:6-8, 1 Cor. 13). Hence the popular notion of "falling in love," or "falling out of love," because it implies an involuntary act (which falling usually is), shares no resemblance with Christian love.

One useful definition of Christian love is: *choosing the highest good of another, even at one's own expense.* The famous Good Samaritan is praised by Jesus precisely for this quality (Luke 10:29-37). Love is putting another's interests ahead of one's own, a recurrent teaching in Scripture (for example, see 1 Cor. 10:24).

The total demand of love

One of the corollaries of the law of love is that in seeking another's good, there will be cost to secure that interest. Put another way, if one makes it his end to advance others' interests, then he must embrace the means to achieve that end. Loving God and loving one's neighbor will be costly, and only those who consider the cost and remain willing to pay it can be said to love God and love their neighbor. Jesus taught:

> For which of you, intending to build a tower, does not sit down first and count the cost, whether he has enough to finish it —lest, after he has laid the foundation, and is not able to finish, all who see it begin to mock him, saying, "This man began to build and was not able to finish"? Or what king, going to make war against another king, does not sit down first and consider whether he is able with ten thousand to meet him who comes against him with twenty thousand? Or else, while the other is still a great way off, he

[1] Jonathan Leeman, *Church Discipline*, Crossway (2012), p. 131.

> sends a delegation and asks conditions of peace. So likewise, whoever of you does not forsake all that he has cannot be My disciple. (Luke 14:28-33)

Jesus teaches that following Him costs everything—each citizen of His nation must "forsake all that he has" (Luke 14:33). If love demands a certain cost, then it must be paid to be genuine love.

Sadly, many today conflate *desiring* to follow Jesus with *choosing* to follow Jesus. Desire and choice are entirely different matters. Suppose that you stood on a street corner in a busy city and asked passersby how many would like to have a house on the beach. Practically everyone would say "yes." Yet how many of those same people were saving for that goal and looking at actual properties? Probably almost none. While many *desired* a house on the beach, few were *choosing* a house on the beach.

So it is today that many desire to follow Jesus, but few choose to follow Jesus. Choosing to follow Jesus necessarily involves forsaking all that one has. That is a high cost that few are willing to pay.

Obedience cannot be partial

Imagine a man telling his wife, "I love you" but then saying, "I will be faithful to you six days out of a week, but not the seventh." This man does not truly love his wife, but rather loves himself and is using his wife for his own pleasures. So if a man tells God, "I love you, but will obey all of your commands except this one," he does not love God. By choosing which commands to obey and which to reject, he puts himself above God. There can be no compromise: one either chooses to follow God in every way, or not at all.

Love and sin are therefore opposite states of the heart, without middle ground. Scripture states this truth in strong language:

> Whoever shall keep the whole law, and yet stumble in one point, he is guilty of all. (James 2:10)

> No one can serve two masters; for either he will hate the one and love the other, or else he will be loyal to the one and despise the other. (Matt. 6:24)

> Does a spring send forth fresh water and bitter from the same opening? Can a fig tree, my brethren, bear olives,

> or a grapevine bear figs? Thus no spring yields both salt water and fresh. (James 3:11-12)

A person either follows Jesus, or follows his own desires—one cannot do both. We either choose to love God and others or we choose our own selfishness. Thinking that obedience can be partial has many dire implications:

1. It falsely makes standards very low by conveying the notion that one can be acceptable before God while consciously accepting present sin.
2. It makes believers complacent, by not encouraging them to search out the whole counsel of God.
3. It can cause someone who struggles with obedience and then disobeys to wrongly think themselves somewhat holy because they at least seriously considered obedience. (This confounds desire with choice.)
4. It instills false security in those who are living in sin by making them think they are still acceptable before God.
5. It makes believers think that in their best, most sincere and holy acts, they still necessarily sin.

Understanding that obedience (or love) and sin are opposite states, without middle ground, is a both a terrifying and liberating truth.

Law and liberty in the New Testament

Many have been confused by the use of the word "law" in the New Testament. Often the word refers to the Torah, the law of Moses. In this sense, the word can carry negative connotations (for example, Rom. 6:14, 8:3; Gal. 2:21, 3:20, 5:18), being shorthand for the failure of the Old Covenant to cultivate a faithful Israel. In contrast, the epistles are dotted with positive statements about a different law, the "law of Christ" (Gal. 6:2). Elsewhere it is called the law of faith (Rom. 3:27), the law of the Spirit (Rom. 8:2), the royal law of love (James 2:8), and the law of liberty (James 2:12). Many texts speak favorably of this new law of Christ (Rom. 2:13, 3:31, 8:4, 8:7, 13:8, 13:10, 1 Cor. 9:21, Gal. 5:14, 1 Tim. 1:8, and James 2:8, 2:12). Too often professing Christians conflate these two senses of law, and allow the negative connotations of the former to overpower the latter. This mistake leads to derision of the law of Christ and an attendant lack of obedience. This error can be traced back to early misunderstandings of the Protestants:

> The New Testament use of the word "law" (*nomos*) is decisively conditioned by the Old Testament background and the Jewish milieu in which it was written. The word therefore almost always denotes not "law" in general, but the Mosaic law, the *Torah (tora)* As a result the New Testament Law-"Gospel" tension is not, as in Luther, primarily static and theological, but historical. "Law" (*tora*) came into history at a specific point in time (430 years after the promise, according to Gal. 3:17). In the New Testament, therefore, Law and "Gospel" primarily denote, not two constant aspects of God's word to us, but two successive eras in salvation history.[2]

Given this understanding of law as an era, it follows that we are not under the Mosaic law. Thus we are not bound by Old Testament dietary laws—"thus [Jesus] declared all foods clean" (Mark 7:19 ESV, see also Rom. 14:2), circumcision laws (Acts 15:24-29, 1 Cor. 7:19, Gal. 5:2-11, 6:15), or Sabbath laws (Col. 2:16, Rom. 14:5). Sabbath serves as a particularly important case study because the New Testament explicitly describes it as an issue of liberty (Col. 2:16, Rom. 14:5), having been fulfilled in Jesus' work (Heb. 4:1-8). Of course, our physical constitutions have not changed across the covenants. Thus we should still partake in Sabbath-like rest, but not necessarily in the precise way demanded by Moses.

Obedience to the law of Christ is possible

Throughout history, one of the most common attacks on those who have emphasized total obedience to the King is to say that true obedience is not even possible.[3] Martin Luther's sentiment (possibly apocryphal, though the idea can be found throughout his writings) that believers are like "snow-covered dung" continues to dominate Protestant discourse. In this thinking, Jesus' righteousness covers us while we remain sinful and disobedient. While sounding pious and humble, such statements flatly deny the biblical witness and undermine essential Christian doctrine. Even under the Old Covenant, God anticipated this charge:

---

[2] Douglas Moo in *Five Views of Law and Gospel*, Stanley Gundry (ed.), Zondervan (1996), p. 322.

[3] John Wesley was frequently attacked on these grounds. Protestant groups have historically leveled these charges the loudest. Their charges are an excellent example of reading Scripture through the lens of various unbiblical confessions.

> For this commandment that I command you today is not too hard for you, neither is it far off. It is not in heaven, that you should say, "Who will ascend to heaven for us and bring it to us, that we may hear it and do it?" Neither is it beyond the sea, that you should say, "Who will go over the sea for us and bring it to us, that we may hear it and do it?" But the word is very near you. It is in your mouth and in your heart, so that you can do it. (Deut. 30:11-14)

The promise of the New Covenant is accompanied with a promise of obedience (see Jer. 31:31-33; Ezek. 36:35-37). To deny that Christians can obey God is therefore to deny the heart of the New Covenant and the Spirit-given power to obey. Consistent with the promise of the New Covenant, Jesus' birth is connected with salvation from sin: "You shall call His name Jesus, for He will save His people from their sins" (Matt. 1:21). Jesus is not described as the one who will save His people from hell (which He of course does), but from sins.

Jesus' own teachings affirm that we can obey. To a person whom He healed, Jesus said, "See, you have been made well. Sin no more, lest a worse thing come upon you" (John 5:14). To the woman caught in adultery, Jesus sends her away with the words, "Neither do I condemn you; go and sin no more" (John 8:11). In that same chapter, Jesus says, "Most assuredly, I say to you, whoever commits sin is a slave of sin…Therefore if the Son makes you free, you shall be free indeed" (John 8:34, 36). In the Great Commission, Jesus tells His disciples to teach the world "to observe *all things* that I have commanded you" (Matt. 28:20).

The New Testament commends obedience to the law of Christ. The author of Hebrews exhorts believers to purse "holiness, without which no one will see the Lord" (Heb. 12:14). John stresses the necessity of obedience. "Whoever abides in Him does not sin. Whoever sins has neither seen Him nor known Him…Whoever has been born of God does not sin, for His seed remains in him; and he cannot sin, because he has been born of God" (1 John 3:6, 9; see also 1 John 5:18). Could there be more clear language? Christians are marked by their obedience, and sin is the exception. This obedience is not some Pelagian heresy; it is biblically the unmerited gift of God. But grace is not opposed to effort or obedience—it is opposed to earning. Jesus' followers are marked by their obedience to the law of love. Following this law does not *earn* citizenship in the King's nation, but it *marks* the true citizen.

Why is this doctrine so important? For while we are saved by faith alone through grace alone (Eph. 2:8-9), obedience demonstrates the presence of saving faith. Ongoing defeat by sin demonstrates a lack of saving faith. "Now by this we know that we know Him, if we keep His commandments" (1 John 2:3).

The very litmus test given by Scripture for assessing whether we are truly Christians is to look at our own obedience. This also makes intelligible the concept of church discipline (1 Cor. 5:11). The ongoing presence of sin demands expulsion from a pure body. Modern churches of the West have historically been weak or highly selective with church discipline (typically restricted to sexual sins), largely because of a fatalistic belief that Christians will continue to live in sin.

The great heresy of the last days

The greatest heresy raging *within* the church is one of which most are unaware. This ignorance should not be a surprise; destructive heresies are prophesied to enter the church secretly: "But there were also false prophets among the people, even as there will be false teachers among you, who will secretly bring in destructive heresies, even denying the Lord who bought them, and bring on themselves swift destruction. And many will follow their destructive ways, because of whom the way of truth will be blasphemed. By covetousness they will exploit you with deceptive words" (2 Pet. 2:1-3).

The technical name for the heresy is *antinomianism*. Antinomianism comes from the Greek word *anomos*, which means to be without or against the law. The word and its cognates are used twenty-five times in the New Testament. *Antinomianism can be defined as selective or partial obedience.* The antinomian typically finds certain commands unpalatable or too difficult; those commands are ignored or explained away. Despite the selective obedience, the antinomian still professes allegiance to Jesus. They are convinced they are Jesus' followers.

Near the close of Jesus' longest sermon, the Sermon on the Mount, Jesus makes a chilling prophesy that many who think they are His followers will be condemned because they are antinomians: "Not everyone who says to Me, 'Lord, Lord,' shall enter the kingdom of heaven, but he who does the will of My Father in heaven. Many will say to Me in that day, 'Lord, Lord, have we not prophesied in Your name, cast out demons in Your name, and done many wonders in Your name?' And then I will declare to them, 'I never knew you; depart from Me, you who practice lawlessness! [literally, antinomians]' " (Matt. 7:21-23).

The context is extremely important. Jesus had just finished teaching on a number of hard subjects, pronouncing new laws for His nation (including on anger, divorce and remarriage, oaths, love toward enemies, and storing up earthly treasures). At the close of this sermon, He impresses His listeners with four warnings: first, the necessity of traveling the narrow road that only a few find (Matt. 7:13-14); second, vigilance for false prophets (Matt. 7:15-20); third, forewarning about professing followers to be condemned because of disobedience to Jesus' law (Matt. 7:21-23); and fourth, the importance of building on Jesus' teachings to avoid destruction (Matt. 7:24-27). Jesus seems to anticipate the obstinacy of the human heart toward the Sermon on the Mount and thus gives a fourfold warning to heed His words with the highest care.

Those who are sent away from Jesus are the antinomians, those who have rejected portions of His law. *Selectivity and delusion are the hallmarks of antinomianism.* Another portrayal of judgment, the parable of the wheat and the tares, highlights the presence of the antinomians within the church and their subsequent destruction: "The Son of Man will send out His angels, and they will gather out of His kingdom all things that offend, and those who practice lawlessness [literally, antinomians]" (Matt. 13:41).

While perhaps counterintuitive, even though the Pharisees set up many man-made laws, they denied God's laws and were called antinomian (Matt. 23:28). Legalism may be defined as either: believing that one earns salvation by good works; or adding humanly devised commands and doctrines in order to gain God's favor. Either posture is dangerous. Legalism is no defense against antinomianism; legalism paradoxically fosters it.

Jesus prophesies that antinomianism will strengthen in the last days: "Then many false prophets will rise up and deceive many. And because lawlessness [antinomianism] will abound, the love of many will grow cold" (Matt. 24:11-12). Remarkably, the final antichrist is literally called the man of antinomianism, usually translated as man of lawlessness (2 Thess. 2:3). Antinomianism is the final great heresy of humanity, as it shakes its fist against Jesus' reign. Because antinomianism opposes Jesus' kingship, antinomianism opposes the gospel itself.

Despite these repeated warnings, the largest Christian denominations tragically depart from Jesus' instructions in the very areas that the Sermon on the Mount dwells upon: divorce and remarriage, oaths, loving one's enemies (nonresistance), and wealth. These denominations and churches will also hurl stones at those exhorting total obedience to the law of the King. The heresy gains force by the day. Yet surely the church stands without excuse.

New Covenant power to obey

God made a breathtaking promise with the New Covenant: "I will sprinkle clean water on you, and you shall be clean from all your uncleannesses, and from all your idols I will cleanse you. And I will give you a new heart, and a new spirit I will put within you. And I will remove the heart of stone from your flesh and give you a heart of flesh. And I will put my Spirit within you, and cause you to walk in my statutes and be careful to obey my rules" (Ezek. 36:25-27). God Himself will put His Spirit into His people, enabling them to obey. New Covenant obedience is no bootstrapped effort; it is divine power at work. This message of God's action generating human faithfulness is portrayed in multiple ways. Believers are said to be "in Christ," united to His death and resurrection. The death Jesus died enables us to die to sin. His resurrection power gives us victory over sin (see Rom. 6:6-18). This new life is captured by language as dramatic as God's first creation of the universe. "Therefore, if anyone is in Christ, he is a new creation; old things have passed away; behold, all things have become new" (2 Cor. 5:17). The very action of grace provides a power to obey (Rom. 1:5, 5:21, 2 Cor. 9:8; Titus 2:11-14). Paul described God's grace as energizing him to work: "I worked harder than any of them, though it was not I, but the grace of God that is with me" (1 Cor. 15:10 ESV). God's promise in the New Covenant is that we may become "partakers of the divine nature" (2 Pet. 1:4), and therefore become His children. This waterfall of ideas should invigorate and refresh any believer.

If we understand the power to obey as fundamentally about the divine nature transforming us into God's children rather than naked human effort, then our lives should naturally be structured around opportunities to receive this grace and unite ourselves to God. We nourish ourselves with the words of the Father. We cry out in prayer for the Spirit. We join faithful saints and commune with Jesus through the Lord's Supper. These actions take on renewed importance in striving for the holiness required to see the Lord.

Chapter 11

The propaganda of disobedience and the war of words

Death and life are in the power of the tongue. (Proverbs 18:21)

As soon as Jesus inaugurated the new nation of God, its advance was met with opposition. The Gospel accounts and book of Acts narrate the struggles and triumphs of this burgeoning nation. The struggles of the nation included temptation, misunderstanding, slander, persecution, and martyrdom. All of these challenges have persisted through history, though some with comparatively greater strength than others.

When Satan tempted Jesus in the desert, the temptations were not directed at obvious areas like lust or anger, but came in more subtle fashion. Satan twice challenged Jesus' *understanding* of "Son of God" (Matt. 4:3, 5). The Enemy selected backdoor, subtle attacks of challenging Jesus' definitions as opposed to direct assault. Similar tactics can be found elsewhere. The false apostles of Corinth, called "deceitful workers" and "ministers" of Satan (2 Cor. 11:13-15), were said to preach "another Jesus" and a "different gospel" (2 Cor. 11:4). While these false apostles used the same vocabulary, the meanings poured into these words were radically different from those used by Paul.

At a larger scale, when definitions are challenged and new meanings are poured into words for the purpose of influencing others toward an agenda, this manipulation is a form of *propaganda*.

Propaganda and influence

Propaganda is among the most ancient techniques of political warfare. Employed by figures like Darius the Great of Persia and Livy of Rome, propaganda has been used for millenia for the purpose of influence and control. Since the beginning of the twentieth century, propaganda has grown more pervasive and effective, even as warfare between soldiers on open battlefields has diminished in frequency. Propaganda is one of the most potent instruments by which nations exert influence over their subjects, as well as their enemies. It should be no surprise that Satan and his ministers use a political tool, propaganda, to destabilize and hinder God's nation.

Christians should be vigilant because the Enemy is clever and because "the whole world lies under the sway of the wicked one" (1 John 5:19). Soldiers of King Jesus are in enemy territory, surrounded by the propaganda through which Satan enslaves humanity and tries to win back rebels. "Be sober, be vigilant; because your adversary the devil walks about like a roaring lion, seeking whom he may devour" (1 Pet. 5:8). In the same letter that Paul warns about the false apostles who were twisting biblical terms for their own ends, he writes that "we are not ignorant of his devices" (2 Cor. 2:11). Understanding one of Satan's favorite devices, propaganda, should thus be an element of preparation for warfare. Yet most Christians are unaware of the significance and techniques of propaganda.[1]

As we observed in the last chapter, antinomianism is the great heresy of the last days. Not surprisingly then, most propaganda has antinomian tendencies. This propaganda of disobedience helps fulfill what Jesus described, "because lawlessness [literally, antinomianism] will abound, the love of many will grow cold" (Matt. 24:12). Such propaganda helps rob the church of its vitality and provides false security to those who are deceived (Matt. 7:21-23).

Propaganda involves an array of techniques. The thesis of this chapter is that virulent forms of propaganda have infected the church. We begin by looking at broader trends in society.

Competing visions: Orwell versus Huxley

Convulsed with change unlike ever seen before, the twentieth century inspired authors to extrapolate trends in government, culture, and tech-

[1] An introduction to the subject of propaganda was penned by Jacques Ellul in *Propaganda: The Formation of Men's Attitudes*, Random House (1965).

nology. George Orwell's book *1984* prophesied a heavy-handed government that would control its citizens with an iron fist. But the year 1984 came and went, and Western civilization never succumbed to the Orwellian horror.

> But we had forgotten that alongside Orwell's dark vision, there was another—slightly older, slightly less well known, equally chilling: Aldous Huxley's *Brave New World.* Contrary to common belief even among the educated, Huxley and Orwell did not prophesy the same thing. Orwell warns that we will be overcome by an externally imposed oppression. But in Huxley's vision, no Big Brother is required to deprive people of their autonomy, maturity and history. As he saw it, people will come to love their oppression, to adore the technologies that undo their capacities to think.
>
> What Orwell feared were those who would ban books. What Huxley feared was that there would be no reason to ban a book, for there would be no one who wanted to read one. Orwell feared those who would deprive us of information. Huxley feared those who would give us so much that we would be reduced to passivity and egoism. Orwell feared that the truth would be concealed from us. Huxley feared the truth would be drowned in a sea of irrelevance. Orwell feared we would become a captive culture. Huxley feared we would become a trivial culture ...As Huxley remarked in *Brave New World Revisited*, the civil libertarians and rationalists who are ever on the alert to oppose tyranny 'failed to take into account man's almost infinite appetite for distractions'. In *1984*, Huxley added, people are controlled by inflicting pain. In *Brave New World*, they are controlled by inflicting pleasure. In short, Orwell feared that what we hate will ruin us. Huxley feared that what we love will ruin us.[2]

History has proven that Huxley's vision was closer to the mark. This realization has significant implications for the advance of the gospel and the state of the church. We will briefly explore some implications concerning the relationship of propaganda to technology and media, the effect of technology on our minds, and the role of education in the spread of propaganda.

---

[2] From Neil Postman's foreword to *Amusing Ourselves to Death: Public Discourse in the Age of Show Business*, Penguin (1985).

Huxley's vision materialized partly through advances in technology. Television, film, computers, the internet, and mobile phones occupy a large portion of our attention. Most have had the truth "drowned in a sea of irrelevance." We live in a world of triviality, where people rush between activities of inconsequence. Meaningful engagement of the mind has become more difficult and rare. The addictive qualities of television, the internet, mobile phones, and video gaming are widely known. Thus modern propaganda overwhelms its subjects with so much information, visual stimulation, and addictive distraction that there will be little felt need or time left for serious matters. So long as society is entertained or "busy," truth can be buried. Not just the content but dominant *forms* of technology have themselves influenced how we think. "The medium is the message."[3] Not only is the *form* of technology damaging, its *content* synergizes to impair clear thinking.[4] Oversimplification and superficiality reign in our world. Partly because of the media, influence is attained in today's world primarily through images and soundbites, not through sustained argumentation. Debates with actual content between knowledgeable participants are rare or looked down upon as impolite, antiquated, or boring. Few people engage in vigorous, rational, and respectful dialogue.

Modern education, instead of countering propaganda's force, actually facilitates its spread.[5] Modern education imparts a vast amount of information through secondary and tertiary sources and encourages students to take superficial positions on virtually all issues. Catchphrases and "things everyone knows" are introduced to minds at a very young age. Tremendous deference is given to "scholarly consensus" without critically evaluating the evidence. Unaware of their own biases and vulnerabilities, the intelligentsia is in fact the primary means by which propaganda spreads. Paradoxically, educational propaganda leads to beliefs that often produce the strongest feelings and opinions in those who have the least primary knowledge of the subject. I can remember a fellow physician once blustering into a room complaining about how "Paul founded religion, not that good person Jesus." With great emotion he bellowed, yet when questioned, he could cite nothing to prove his argument. Eventually he admitted that he had no acquaintance with the Bible. Educational propaganda makes minds foolish by breeding overconfidence and superficiality. This warfare thus requires prudence: "Let a man meet a bear robbed of her cubs, rather than a fool

[3] Marshall McLuhan's insightful expression.

[4] Postman elaborates on both facets in *Amusing Ourselves to Death.*

[5] This is a major theme of Ellul's work and John Gatto's *Weapons of Mass Instruction*, New Society (2010).

in his folly" (Prov. 17:12).

Leadership training and the decline of the church

A minister today is typically expected to have graduated from seminary and ideally hold degrees from prestigious institutions. Yet often these qualifications can undermine biblical faith. The modern training of church leaders has failed for several reasons.

First, most theological training does not start with the right definition of success. Professors are incentivized to publish research articles and books. At some institutions they are incentivized to teach effectively as judged by student feedback. But the ultimate "report card" for theological training should be the vibrancy of the church. Jesus' test of fruits (Matt. 7:16-20) should apply to theological training since the purpose of education should be to foster discipleship. We should be using a test proposed by the early church: "In their discipline we have an index of their doctrine."[6] But for structural reasons, the connections between seminary and church life are often weak, especially in the West. Even in seminaries that are explicitly denominational, the report card of the seminary is hardly dependent upon the life of its affiliate churches. Theological training has generally neglected the measurement of how its efforts lead to benefits in church life. Let us contrast this with a distantly related field. In cell biology, for example, the goal is to describe how the cell functions. Scrutiny and challenge expose shaky hypotheses and establish theories that better explain the data. The acid test of laboratory experimentation validates or disproves a scientific hypothesis. This winnowing process usually leaves only one or two plausible theories in a given area. Because of the power to falsify, laboratory experiments generate confidence in the theories that survive. Society's confidence in the disciplines of science, such as cell biology or quantum mechanics, has grown stronger with time.

But in modern theology, the situation is almost the complete opposite. Most surveys show that churches are weakening in America and Europe.[7] The "lab results" are clear. This should have sent convulsive change through our leadership training process. But because there is little emphasis on falsifying doctrine by looking at the practical life of the church, little has changed. The field is littered with multiple, contradictory theologies. No one is able to clean up the mess; in fact, some in academics almost revel in it. Much of the problem comes from not

[6] Tertullian, *The Prescription Against Heretics*, chapter XLIII.

[7] George Barna's findings are a good example.

applying a scriptural acid test (the equivalent of the scientific laboratory experiment) to weed out truth from error. This will be discussed at greater length in the next chapter.

Second, the critical methods of academia have generally led to a decline in confidence in a host of truths, not least of which is the divine nature of the Scriptures. There is something gravely wrong about this picture. By exposing the weaknesses of competing theories, critical methods should increase our confidence in the truth. (In our cell biology example, critical thinking and experiments have generated tremendous confidence in the truth.) While some useful insights from critical scholarship have been obtained, they have come at a heavy cost. For example, most modern commentaries give so many viewpoints that they leave readers more bewildered than before they started. Demanding or controversial applications from the "respected" commentaries are rare. Meanwhile, the congregation looks to its pastor with deference and for guidance. He in turn gives his congregants a lighter version of what he learned in seminary. Scarcely able to comprehend all the viewpoints that theologians debate, churchgoers are ultimately left with the sense that Scripture is very uncertain. With such educated people disagreeing, how could the ordinary person hope to sort it out? By leaving its mark on the pastors, the academic world has led to the obfuscation of Scripture and a consequent destruction of confidence in the word of God. "Having escaped the clutches of the priests, to some it seems as if today the Bible is being sequestered by the academic guild under the guise of hermeneutical sophistication."[8]

Because academia's postmodern bent has been transmitted to professing Christians through the ministry, the pendulum has swung much too far to the side of skepticism, subjectivity, and antinomianism. The end result of this uncertainty is lukewarmness. "The love of many shall grow cold" (Matt. 24:12). The church lacks passionate zeal. Meanwhile, there are scarcely martyrs to be found. No one chooses to be martyred over a dialectic tension. Christians die for clear truth.

Third, we have not fully appreciated the sway of eloquence. Many popular ministers today are skilled writers and speakers who are sowing antinomian destruction (see previous chapter). Listeners and readers are enamored by these men's flashing brilliance as they tear down hard biblical truths with the blade of rhetoric. The problem is that most people do not have "immunity to eloquence," as it has been called. Most people are moved more by rhetorical style, vocabulary, erudite citations, and reputation than by the actual content of an argu-

[8] Mark Thompson, *A Clear and Present Word: The Clarity of Scripture*, InterVarsity Press (2006), p. 132.

ment. (Such people often care a great deal for sophisticated art, refined music, exquisite dining, glamorous fashions, witty erudition, and academic prestige.) The seductive powers of aesthetics strengthen the propaganda of disobedience and has already drawn millions of young people into unbelief and antinomianism. Groupthink (a major component of propaganda) begins to take over when a small number of eloquent men articulate a belief system; the herd quickly follows. Calvinism is an excellent example of a theology developed by eloquent writers that has gained a following far disproportionate to the merits of the system. Very few appreciate how dominant Calvinism is at modern seminaries and churches, largely because of beautiful writing, eloquent speaking, and scholarly groupthink. Tragically, Calvinism has served as a large pipe for the propaganda of disobedience into modern churches.

The seduction of eloquence and aesthetics was a major problem of the Corinthians. Paul did not come to them with "excellence of speech or of wisdom" (1 Cor. 2:1). "My speech and my preaching were not with persuasive words of human wisdom, but in demonstration of the Spirit and of power, that your faith should not be in the wisdom of men but in the power of God" (1 Cor. 2:4). Because of this lack of eloquence, Paul's opponents said that his speech was "contemptible" (2 Cor. 10:10). Paul's response was to boast about his sufferings. Paul boasts of his lashings, beatings, sleepless nights, hunger, thirst, and dangerous travels (2 Cor. 11:22-33). This argument fits exactly the seventh principle of biblical interpretation from a prior chapter (chapter 8, "Principles of faithful biblical interpretation"): the persecuted, suffering church carries the truth of God.

The war of words

Society's penchant for soundbites has given catchphrases inordinate power. Forming an important component of the propaganda of disobedience, many catchphrases are weapons against Jesus' kingship. When urging obedience to the Scriptures, a common retort is, "But it's the heart that matters." Muddled and sin-serving thinking lurk behind such responses. Just as well could someone speak vulgarities and say, "But it's the heart that matters."[9] If the heart is right, then outward actions follow. Nevertheless, the sway of such statements can undo hours of sound instruction.

The ultimate soundbite is a single word. In this way, the meanings of words are an important battlefield, worthy of Christian defense. Trans-

[9] Charles Finney, *Lectures to Professing Christians*, Lecture VIII (1836).

formations of the definitions of important words often occur right under our noses. Commenting on this phenomenon in politics, George Orwell noted, "It will be seen that, as used, the word 'Fascism' is almost entirely meaningless. In conversation, of course, it is used even more wildly than in print. I have heard it applied to farmers, shopkeepers, Social Credit, corporal punishment, fox-hunting, bull-fighting, the 1922 Committee, the 1941 Committee, Kipling, Gandhi, Chiang Kai-Shek, homosexuality, Priestley's broadcasts, Youth Hostels, astrology, women, dogs and I do not know what else."[10] In less than 30 years, the word fascism, once denoting a political system headed by Mussolini, was evacuated of meaning. We have even more cause to be circumspect with spiritually significant words that the Enemy would love to commandeer. With these words being used for hundreds, even thousands of years, there has been ample opportunity for Satan, the world, and false prophets to twist their meanings for self-serving purposes.

We noted in chapter 2 how the word "religion" has been co-opted to become a dirty word. Sadly, this has been done by pastors and theologians within the church, under antinomian influence. We also saw that the words *Christ* and *gospel* have been altered to oppose Jesus' kingship.

Another important example is the word *faith* or *belief*. Imagine that a friend asks you, "Do you believe in God?" Most people would take such a question as, "Do you believe that God *exists*?" But consider how differently we understand each of the following three questions:

- Do you believe that God exists?
- Do you have faith in God?
- Are you faithful to God?

In the Greek of the New Testament, all three senses are captured by the word translated as "faith." The word "faith" is a translation of the Greek word *pistis*. The Septuagint, New Testament, and first-century Greek literature often use the word *pistis* and its cognates in the sense of being faithful, loyal, and reliable.[11] The first definition of *pistis* from a prominent Greek lexicon is: "the state of being someone in whom confidence can be placed, faithfulness, reliability, fidelity, commitment."[12] A few examples illustrate this point.

[10] George Orwell, "What is Fascism?", *Tribune* (1944).

[11] The majority of instances of *pistis* in the Septuagint correspond to this sense. Josephus also uses *pistis* in the sense of faithfulness. See *Antiquities of the Jews*, 15.6.5, 15.10.4; *The Wars of the Jews*, 2.16.2, 3.7.33.

[12] *A Greek-English Lexicon of the New Testament and other Early Christian Literature*, third edition (BDAG), Frederick Danker (ed.), Univ. of Chicago Press (2000), p. 818.

When the disciples ask Jesus to increase their faith, He responds with a story about a servant who dutifully does his master's bidding (Luke 17:5-12). When Jesus describes the persistent widow, He closes the parable by asking if the Son of Man will really find faith on the earth (Luke 18:1-8). *Pistos*, the adjectival form of *pistis*, is nearly always translated as faithful in the New Testament.[13] Just as in English, the adjective form of a word provides valuable insight to what the cognate noun means; for example, the relationship of strong to strength. "Faithful" captures an important dimension of what the word "faith" means.[14]

The meaning of the word faith cannot be restricted to just one sense; its semantic range is broad and different contexts will highlight different senses. But we must be careful not to be overpowered by Protestant sensibilities where faith is nearly always contrasted to works. The New Testament sometimes contrasts faith to *disobedience* (for example John 3:36; Heb. 3:18-19; 1 Pet. 2:7). By setting up faith as a contrast to faithful *obedience*, the propaganda of disobedience gains a major victory.

A final cautionary example is the word *conservative*. The Enemy would love to break Christians into docile, tame creatures who are loathe to rattle *status quo*. Consequently, care should be used when using expressions like "conservative Christian" or "liberal Christian." The term conservative has three liabilities: first, it is not found in Scripture; second, it is allied to political parties; third, it is associated with preserving the existing state of affairs. The latter liability has especially important implications for young people. "One of the greatest injustices we do to our young people is to ask them to be conservative. Christianity is not conservative, but revolutionary."[15] Jesus' kingdom is at war; we need bold, courageous warriors —not timid, conservative bystanders. We need young people in a resistance movement against the world's powers. The need for boldness is well aligned with the natural impulse of youth. Some of the greatest feats in the church age have been done by young people. Conrad Grebel, William Tyndale, Michael Sattler, John Wesley, David Brainerd, Adoniram Judson, and Amy Carmichael are but a handful of noteworthy believers who accomplished great things in the Lord while in their twenties or thirties.

Of course, many people use conservative as shorthand for adherence to traditional doctrines like the Trinity or a willingness to obey

---

[13] See Matt. 24:45, 25:23; Luke 16:10; 1 Cor. 1:9, 4:2, 10:13; 2 Cor. 1:18; Eph. 6:21; Col. 1:7; 1 Thess. 5:24; 1 Tim. 1:15, 3:1, 4:9; Heb. 2:17, 3:5; 1 John 1:19; Rev. 1:5, 2:10, 3:14, 19:11 for passages containing *pistos*.

[14] David deSilva, *Honor, Patronage, Kinship, & Purity*, IVP Academic (2000), p. 115.

[15] Francis Schaeffer, *The Church at the End of the Twentieth Century*, second edition, Crossway (1994), p. 78.

plain Scripture. But perhaps better language exists. The expression "kingdom Christian" works somewhat better because it capture a sense of fidelity to Scripture and traditional doctrine (in a Tradition I sense), without the connotations of earthly politics or *status quo*. It also seizes the word *kingdom*, a word used often in the New Testament. Other terms could certainly be used. No matter what, we must remember that the early Christians were called those "who turned the world upside down" (Acts 17:6). Unfortunately, today's conservative people are not typically referred to in such terms. Our language must remind us that we are not to be comfortable vacationers, but active soldiers. "The kingdom of heaven suffers violence, and the violent take it by force" (Matt. 11:12).

Chapter 12

Recognizing enemies from allies

You shall know the truth and the truth shall set you free. (John 8:32)

If you were in battle and could not recognize enemies from allies, you would surely be in a dangerous position. You would either wield your weapons indiscriminately or not wield your weapons at all. You would have no sense of when to be on guard or when to be trusting. Such an ignorant state would virtually ensure defeat.

Jesus wanted His followers to have the power to discern friends from foes. So He taught His disciples how to apply a test that separates allies from enemies. Tragically, most professing Christians do not apply this test. This failure leaves them vulnerable to deception—one important reason why the church has experienced such stinging defeats. Jesus gave the test in plain language: "Beware of false prophets, who come to you in sheep's clothing, but inwardly they are ravenous wolves. You will know them by their fruits. Do men gather grapes from thornbushes or figs from thistles? Even so, every good tree bears good fruit, but a bad tree bears bad fruit. A good tree cannot bear bad fruit, nor can a bad tree bear good fruit. Every tree that does not bear good fruit is cut down and thrown into the fire. Therefore by their fruits you will know them" (Matt. 7:15-20). Twice in this passage Jesus says that we can know false prophets by their fruits (vv. 16 and 20). Leaders must be carefully scrutinized, not for their scholarship or their degrees, but for their fruit.

The meaning of "fruits" is given earlier in the book, "Therefore bear fruits worthy of repentance" (Matt. 3:8). Fruits thus represent the outworking of repentance in a holy life. This meaning is confirmed later in the book: Matthew 12:33-37 connects fruit to speech; Matthew 21:33-

43 portrays fruit as a group's loyalty and obedience. Paul uses the term similarly in the book of Galatians in reference to godly character (Gal. 5:22-23).

While fruits exhibit the quality of a tree, they are also the means and result of reproduction. The word *fruits* is used in this second sense later in the Gospel according to Matthew. Jesus teaches that fruits represent spiritual offspring (Matt. 13:8, 23). He also chides the Pharisees for bearing wicked fruit: "Woe to you, scribes and Pharisees, hypocrites! For you travel land and sea to win one proselyte, and when he is won, you make him twice as much a son of hell as yourselves" (Matt. 23:15). Thus the fruit of which Jesus speaks has two primary meanings:

- The outworking of repentance in a holy life, manifesting in godly character, especially to be examined in the prophets and leaders of a group.
- The quality of the spiritual life of the "offspring" of the group or person. This would naturally include long-standing members, new converts, and children.

Jesus adjures that we be "fruit inspectors" for the sake of our souls. He places this admonition after His teaching on the straight and narrow road and before His teaching on the condemnation of the antinomians. This positioning underscores the importance of the test.

Putting the test to work

Jesus charges us to look at the fruits of a leader or prophet. The early Protestants challenged the legitimacy of the Roman Catholic church on the grounds of reprobate behavior among its leaders.[1] Centuries of debauchery, greed, and aggressive war made the Roman Catholic church an easy target. The debauchery was especially prominent in the late medieval church, typified by popes like Alexander VI.

The early Protestant leaders, however, left themselves vulnerable to the same form of criticism. They demonstrated arrogance and murderous behavior that would match the Roman Catholic church. Luther's bellicosity, short-temper, and anti-Semitism are well known. While not leaving behind as embarrassing a paper trail, Calvin also had a sinister reputation: "The trial and execution of Michael Servetus made Calvin an international figure for all the wrong reasons. For his opponents, he had come to represent the failure of the Reformation, demonstrating

[1] See Calvin's *The Institutes of the Christian Religion*, Book IV, chapter 5.

the extent to which the Protestant churches, once founded on the principle of scripture alone and justification by faith, had degenerated into institutions of power and vested interests that served the state."[2]

Sadly, similar fruits have sprung from the modern churches of the West. The leadership of the Roman Catholic church has been tarnished with vile sexual sins. Protestant and evangelical leaders have also been badly devastated by sexual sins, including many high profile casualties. About 40% of evangelical pastors report a problem with pornography.[3] Charismatic churches and televangelists often have leaders and prophets who indulge in lavish lifestyles. This is hardly the fruit of the Spirit described in the book of Galatians.

Besides recognizing enemies, The New Testament teaches the test can be used to identify allies, "Now by this we know that we know Him, if we keep His commandments" (1 John 2:3). Paul's appeals to the churches frequently rode on his claims of upright character (Acts 20:17-35; 1 Cor. 11:1; 1 Thess. 2:5-12; 2 Tim. 3:10-11). He also used his sufferings as a badge of authenticity (2 Cor. 6:4-10). Godly character that leads to suffering should therefore be our test as well. The early church, the Waldensians, the Lollards, and the early Anabaptists could point to their sufferings as corroboration of having a biblical message. Highlighting this truth, the apostles actually rejoiced in their suffering. "So they departed from the presence of the council, rejoicing that they were counted worthy to suffer shame for His name" (Acts 5:41). Both forms of fruit—godly character that leads to suffering and the offspring of the group—are revealing.

We must not be blind to the reality around us today: by applying Jesus' test, contemporary churches can be seen as filled with false prophets. The groups that modern prophets and pastors oversee unfortunately have shown similarly bad fruit. There are approximately 220 denominations in the United States that call themselves Christian.[4] Because of their large numbers, these groups can be subjected to the test of fruits with statistical rigor.

Jesus' test gives clear results. Diverse behavioral metrics like divorce rates, financial giving, and horoscope reading show disappointing re-

---

[2] Bruce Gordon, *Calvin*, Yale University Press (2009), p. 232.

[3] *Christianity Today* leadership survey, December 2000. In a separate survey of 1351 pastors in 2002, a Rick Warren affiliate organization, Pastor.com, reported that 54% of pastors visited a pornography website in the last year and 30% within the last 30 days. Among youth leadership in campus fellowships, the statistics are much worse.

[4] Unless otherwise indicated, all subsequent statistics in this chapter are from George Barna, *Futurecast: What Today's Trends Mean for Tomorrow's World*, Tyndale House (2011).

sults. In America, about 33% of all married couples have been divorced. Among the born again, this number is 32%, an insignificant difference. Regarding giving, those who call themselves Christian donate less than 2% of their income to their church. No differences could be found in reading horoscopes or viewing adult-only material in the born again versus non-born again populations.[5]

Beliefs cannot be separated from behavior and thus should also be considered while testing fruits. Surveys of beliefs in the modern churches show similarly tragic results. Belief that Jesus was sinless can be found in less than 50% of Lutherans, Presbyterians, Methodists, and Catholics.[6] Belief in Satan's existence is even lower in prevalence, being held by less than 20% of Roman Catholics.

The absence of suffering and persecution is striking among the modern churches of the West. Their lives are marked with comfort and ease; "their bodies are fat and sleek" (Ps. 73:4). Those who earnestly fast and pray can be scarcely found. From several perspectives, the test results are clear. The real question is, "What will we do about it?"

Application

If professing Christians would decide to heed Jesus' instruction regarding this test of fruits, there would be an earthquake in the landscape of churches.

My mother recently had surgery to replace the lenses of both her eyes. She selected a physician who had done hundreds of cases, without a single poor outcome. Who would entrust their eyes to a doctor who had a history of blinding his patients? How much more caution should we take with our very souls and the souls of our families! Sadly, people give more care to purchasing a home or selecting a barber than to identifying the shepherds of their souls.

To sweep the sinful behavior of leaders and groups away is to spit upon the Savior's admonition to judge prophets by their fruits. While some will try to undercut the test by throwing around expressions like "We all sin anyway" or "Do not judge, lest you be judged," such sloganeering has an inescapable end—it robs the church of the very tool Jesus gives us to save ourselves from the broad path of destruction. Those who advocate such careless behavior effectively make Jesus' admonition meaningless. They open the door to the antinomian influence of

[5] "Survey shows faith impacts some behaviors but not others," October 2002, www.barna.org.

[6] "Religious Beliefs Vary by Denomination," June 2001, www.barna.org.

today's false prophets, leading to condemnation at the last day.

Like the proverbial exercise in futility, many recognize this tragic situation, but then do nothing about it. They remain stationary like sheep about to be devoured by wolves rather than fleeing as we are commanded (Matt. 7:15; 2 John 10-11). They remain in their groups, preserving *status quo*, contributing to the rotten fruit. While most people rationalize that their churches are somehow different, they nearly always ignore contradictory evidence.

We must open our eyes and recognize reality; "many false prophets have gone out into the world" (1 John 4:1). Until their presence is recognized by this test of fruits, the Enemy can have free course among the people of God.

In the previous chapter, we discussed how society's confidence in the conclusions of science has grown with time as objective laboratory experiments have provided validation. However in the realm of theology and the church, society's confidence has withered. This is because the church has given little thought to what "laboratory validation" would look like. Jesus has given us clear instruction with this test of fruits, but we have not heeded it. Should the church have diligently applied Jesus' test, the world would have long ago put its trust in the King.

But there is good news: we must not despair as Elijah did, thinking that he was the only true prophet of the land. True churches and prophets can be found, though they are not well known. Discouraged by the hypocrisy and disobedience to Scripture in the churches in America, I went on a search for groups that strove to unashamedly obey the Lord, without explaining away the hard commands of Scripture. As I discovered, they can be found. There are churches and groups that actually obey the Sermon on the Mount, have near-zero divorce rates, forsake the entertainment and fashions of the world, speak with grace, and love sacrificially. They are gathering strength and advancing. King Jesus is claiming His church.

Chapter 13

Spiritual gifts

Now concerning spiritual gifts, brothers, I do not want you to be uninformed. (1 Corinthians 12:1 ESV)

The protection and growth of the church depends on the power of the Spirit. After the resurrection, Jesus told His disciples, "You shall receive power when the Holy Spirit has come upon you; and you shall be witnesses to Me in Jerusalem, and in all Judea and Samaria, and to the end of the earth" (Acts 1:8). Jesus connects the power of the Spirit to the witness of the church. The book of Acts describes how this little band of Spirit-empowered disciples launched an offensive within the Roman Empire.

But instead of attracting unbelievers, the gifts of the Spirit have too often become stumbling blocks to the world. Televangelists have made a circus of the gifts, often using them as cover to solicit money. The flock has frequently been fleeced by the ones who say they embrace the gifts the most. The gifts have led to pride and focus on the gifts themselves rather than the Giver. This in turn has pressured people to fake spiritual gifts, especially tongues. Spiritual gifts have been taken to such extremes that many are simply embarrassed to be associated with "charismatic" groups. The abuse has prompted many denominations to follow the so-called eleventh commandment: "Thou shalt not do at all what others do poorly."[1] But despite the abuse of the gifts at Corinth, Paul does not want to see the gifts stifled. He encourages the Corinthians to pursue the spiritual gifts, especially prophecy (1 Cor. 14:1). The apostle wants the church to experience the Spirit's power, but subject to order and disciplined constraints. Just as dangerous as abuse of the gifts is, "not to pant after God at all, and to be satisfied with a merely

[1] C. Samuel Storms, *Are Miraculous Gifts for Today?*, Zondervan (1996), p. 204.

creedal Christianity that is kosher but complacent, orthodox but ossified, sound but soundly asleep."[2]

Indeed, Peter's sermon at Pentecost proclaims that the last days will be marked by supernatural activity from the Spirit. The Holy Spirit's power should *characterize* the church age. Prophesying, visions, dreams, and wonders will accompany the servants of the King (Acts 2:17-21). The church will be impoverished if it rejects these gifts.

A defense of the continuation of the gifts

Christians should see themselves in continuity with the people of the New Testament. The apostles believed that they were in the last days, even the last hour. There is no biblical warrant to interpose another age between the first century and the return of the King. The eschatological structure taught in the New Testament supports the Spirit's gifts being sustained through the entire church age.[3] On these grounds alone, we should doubt the claim that the spiritual gifts have passed away.

Those who oppose the doctrine of the miraculous gifts of the Spirit for the church age are often called *cessationists*. Cessationists correctly observe that miraculous gifts served a role of attestation to Jesus and the apostles' unique authority (John 10:38), but this was not the sole function of the gifts. The gifts testified *to an age* that Jesus and the apostles inaugurated, the one in which we live (Acts 2:17-21). Moreover, the Spirit's power and His gifts are associated with two related goals: the advance of the church and the building of the body. Neither of these goals has been reached, so on pragmatic grounds, the gifts are just as needed today as in the first century. Moreover, the distribution of the gifts among non-apostles undermines the cessationist's claims. Stephen, Agabus, and Philip's daughters all had spiritual gifts. Paul also encourages all the Corinthians to prophesy.

While not definitive, passages in the New Testament seem to imply when the spiritual gifts come to an end. First consider: "And He Himself gave some to be apostles, some prophets, some evangelists, and some pastors and teachers, for the equipping of the saints for the work of ministry, for the edifying of the body of Christ, *till we all come to the unity of the faith and of the knowledge of the Son of God, to a perfect man, to the measure of the stature of the fullness of Christ*" (Eph. 4:11-13). Next, "You were enriched in everything by Him in all utterance and all knowledge, even as the testimony of Christ was confirmed in

[2] D. A. Carson, *Showing the Spirit*, Baker Academic (1996), p. 160.

[3] Carson unpacks this theme in greater detail in his book.

you, *so that you come short in no gift, eagerly waiting for the revelation of our Lord Jesus Christ, who will also confirm you to the end*, that you may be blameless in the day of our Lord Jesus Christ" (1 Cor. 1:5-8). Both passages suggest that prophets and the gifts are intended to last until the Lord comes.

Another powerful argument for the continuation of the spiritual gifts comes from the recorded testimony of trustworthy Christians. There are hundreds, if not thousands, of well documented cases of miracles and supernatural gifts. Simply because a person may not have direct experience with such gifts does not mean they have not occurred elsewhere. One example comes from Charles Spurgeon, a well-known Baptist preacher from London. He writes:

> There were many instances of remarkable conversions at the Music Hall; one especially was so singular that I have often related it as a proof that God sometimes guides His servants to say what they would themselves never have thought of uttering, in order that He may bless the hearer for whom the message is personally intended. When preaching in the hall, on one occasion, I deliberately pointed to a man in the midst of the crowd, and said, "There is a man sitting there, who is a shoemaker; he keeps his shop open on Sundays, it was open last Sabbath morning, he took nine-pence, and there was fourpence profit out of it; his soul is sold to Satan for fourpence!" A city missionary, when going his rounds, met with this man, and seeing that he was reading one of my sermons, he asked the question, "Do you know Mr. Spurgeon?" "Yes," replied the man, "I have every reason to know him, I have been to hear him; and under his preaching, by God's grace I have become a new creature in Christ Jesus. Shall I tell you how it happened? I went to the Music Hall, and took my seat in the middle of the place; Mr. Spurgeon looked at me as if he knew me, and in his sermon he pointed to me, and told the congregation that I was a shoemaker, and that I kept my shop open on Sundays; and I did, sir. I should not have minded that; but he also said that I took ninepence the Sunday before, and that there was fourpence profit; but how he should know that, I could not tell. Then it struck me that it was God who had spoken to my soul through him, so I shut up my shop the next Sunday. At first, I was afraid to go again to hear him, lest he should tell the people more

> about me; but afterwards I went, and the Lord met with me, and saved my soul."
>
> I could tell *as many as a dozen similar cases* in which I pointed at somebody in the hall without having the slightest knowledge of the person, or any idea that what I said was right, except that I believed I was moved by the Spirit to say it; and so striking has been my description that the persons have gone away, and said to their friends, "Come, see a man that told me all things that ever I did; beyond a doubt, he must have been sent of God to my soul, or else he could not have described me so exactly." And not only so, but I have known many instances in which the thoughts of men have been revealed from the pulpit. I have sometimes seen persons nudge their neighbours with their elbow, because they had got a smart hit, and they have been heard to say, when they were going out, "The preacher told us just what we said to one another when we went in at the door."[4]

Spurgeon was no unsteady soul prone to exaggeration. Such an account from a man as credible as Spurgeon should weaken the cessationist argument. Other respected Christians have documented the activity of supernatural gifts.[5] An even more astonishing report comes from Pilgram Marpeck, an early Anabaptist leader. "One also marvels when one sees how the faithful God (who, after all, overflows with goodness) raises from the dead several such brothers and sisters of Christ after they were hanged, drowned, or killed in other ways. Even today, they are found alive and we can hear their own testimony."[6] Marpeck attests to *several* resurrections in his age. Hundreds of accounts across denominations, centuries, and geographies provide a compelling historic case that miraculous gifts have been present throughout the church age.

Baptism in the spirit

Some have argued that there is a second blessing, a second experience, called "baptism in the Spirit" to which Christians should aspire. Ad-

[4] *The Autobiography of Charles H. Spurgeon: Volume II, 1854-1860*, Fleming Revell Company (1899), pp. 226-227, emphasis added.

[5] Some have been compiled by Jack Deere in *Surprised by the Voice of God*, Zondervan (1996), chapters 5 and 6.

[6] *The Writings of Pilgram Marpeck*, translated and edited by William Klassen and Walter Klaassen, Herald Press (1978, Wipf and Stock reprint 1999), p. 50.

vocates teach that this second blessing is normally accompanied with the gift of tongues, and carries the believer to new heights of spiritual power. This teaching is sometimes called the doctrine of subsequence. In contrast, the historic view of the church is that Spirit-baptism happens to all at conversion, but that subsequent and multiple (as opposed to one-time) fillings of the Spirit are normative and to be encouraged.

One key text in this debate is 1 Corinthians 12:3. "For in one Spirit we were all baptized into one body—Jews or Greeks, slaves or free—and all were made to drink of one Spirit" (1 Cor. 12:3 ESV). Unfortunately some translations read, "for *by* one Spirit we were all baptized…" Advocates of the doctrine of subsequence say that in this baptism the Spirit baptizes the Christian into the church, but at another event, Jesus baptizes the believer into the Spirit. These overly fine distinctions largely come from poor English translations and weak exegesis.[7]

At the same time, the New Testament affirms that Christians should be filled with the Spirit (Eph. 5:18).[8] Rather than highlight one grand postconversion filling, the New Testament affirms continually being filled. The New Testament texts "dispel the concept of a singular, once-for-all deposit of the Spirit that supposedly renders superfluous the need for subsequent, postconversion anointings. The Spirit, who was once given and now indwells each believer, is continually given to enhance and intensify our relationship with Christ and to empower our efforts in ministry."[9]

Prophecy in the New Testament

"Earnestly desire to prophesy" (1 Cor. 14:39). Of all the gifts, more time is devoted to extolling prophecy than the others. We are commanded to desire to prophesy. But there is much confusion today on the meaning of prophecy in the New Testament.

Two incorrect views of prophecy are in wide circulation. One view is that New Testament prophecy is the human report, possibly fallible,

---

[7] Careful exegesis requires examination of the Greek pronouns *eis* and *en* which have often been poorly rendered into English. John Stott in *Baptism and Fullness*, second edition, InterVarsity Press (1975), pp. 36-46 and C. Samuel Storms in *Are Miraculous Gifts for Today?*, Zondervan (1996), pp. 176-185 present exegetical cases against the doctrine of subsequence.

[8] Carson agrees and wryly notes, "Although I find no biblical support for a second-blessing theology, I do find support for a second-, third-, fourth-, or fifth-blessing theology" (p. 160).

[9] Storms, p. 185.

of divine revelation.[10] Advocates of this view believe there are irreconcilable differences in how prophecy is portrayed across the Old and New Testaments. They see Old Testament prophecy as canonical and infallible, while they believe New Testament prophecy can be fallible. One problem with this "human report" view is that it is based on far too narrow of an understanding of prophecy in both Testaments.[11]

Another view regards prophecy as infallible speech given by God, on par with canonical books like Isaiah and Ezekiel. Here adherents argue that the gift of prophecy has ceased, just as the canon has closed. They fear that allowing prophecy today would functionally destabilize the authority of the canon. One problem with this view is that it fails to fully appreciate how, even in the Old Testament, prophecy was not always associated with infallible speech intended for the canon. For example, prophecy sometimes meant ecstatic worship (1 Chron. 25:1-2; 1 Sam. 19:20-24). This ecstatic worship was hardly some canonical revelation. In the New Testament, prophecy exposed the secrets of unbelievers (1 Cor. 14:24-25). It is hard to imagine an unbeliever's secret sins being special revelation associated with the canon or some great truth on which the church would be built. Prophesy in the New Testament involves more than the writing of the canon.

While today's two prevailing views miss the mark, a better starting point is to identify the nature of prophecy and the prophets in the Old and New Testaments:

1. Absent from most discussion is consideration of the *covenantal* role of prophets in Scripture. Prophets prosecuted God's covenant lawsuit to a wayward people. This could defensibly be called the main activity of the Old Testament prophets. They applied the Torah to the situations of their day. In applying the law to personal and corporate behavior, the prophets gave a thundering call for repentance.
2. Prophets understand the principles that undergird the letter of the law. When prophets hear Scripture, they listen for the determinative principles *behind* the pronouncements and narratives. These principles touch on aspects of life that the letter may not address. While many people tend to overly restrict Scripture into the past or restrict its application to comfortable and socially ac-

[10] This has most notably been championed by Wayne Grudem in *The Gift of Prophecy in the New Testament and Today*, Crossway (2000). Many evangelicals have expressed support for this position.

[11] While beyond the scope of this chapter, this view also wrongly imputes error to New Testament prophets like Agabus.

ceptable boxes, the prophets preach contemporary and demanding applications that incur society's wrath. Because of their clear vision, prophets rise above the errors of popular wisdom.

3. Consistent with the first two characteristics, prophets have a great sensitivity to sin. Prophets are indignant at what most people believe to be trivial issues or matters of indifference. Because the prophets can see what most cannot, their bones burn (Jer. 20:9). They cannot compromise. They see danger where others perceive safety. They have the passion of a person watching a house burn, while its inhabitants slumber.
4. Prophets provide the vision that leads to obedience. "Where there is no prophetic vision the people cast off restraint, but blessed is he who keeps the law" (Prov. 29:18). Prophets are able to portray a broad vision that wins the heart and leads to keeping the law. Prophets do not have a lone hobby horse: they paint an inspiring, wide-angle portrait of the Spirit-filled life.
5. The speech of a true prophet can be recognized (1 Sam. 3:1, 3:19-20). Prophets utter powerful speech that cannot be imitated (Matt. 7:26; Luke 4:36). The force of their words grips the hearer and authenticates that their words are from God.
6. God gives the prophets supernatural knowledge. While widely appreciated as a gift of Old Testament prophets (such as Joseph and Daniel), this pattern continues in the New. When Jesus' feet were anointed with oil and washed with the tears of a sinful woman, the host says to himself, "If He were a prophet, He would know who and what manner of woman this is who is touching Him, for she is a sinner" (Luke 7:39; see also John 4:19).
7. Ecstatic worship was called prophecy in the Old Testament (1 Sam. 10:11, 19:20-24; 1 Chron. 25:1-2). The New Testament also describes prophecy as worshipping God. Note Luke's parallel expression: "speak with tongues and magnify God" (Acts 10:46) compared to "spoke with tongues and prophesied" (Acts 19:6).

The term is clearly multifacted, and different contexts highlight different meanings.[12] What unites the above elements? *Being under the influence of God's Spirit* marks prophecy, and that may be as narrow as we can go. Under the Spirit's influence, the fear of man evaporates. Through the Spirit, God directly teaches His prophets.

[12] Our basic thesis is that the New Testament's usage is similar to how the Old Testament employs the term. Students of Hebrew will be familiar with the very broad semantic range that Hebrew verbs cover. This can be frustrating for English speakers, but we must not allow reductionism to crush a multifacted jewel.

The early Anabaptists used the term prophecy in a sense quite close to the first meaning in the list above. In this sense, prophecy is applying Scripture to current situations. This dimension of prophecy—not the only one, as demonstrated above—closely relates to biblical interpretation. The hermeneutical significance of the prophet has escaped the attention of most: "What is required for restoring such a connection to present-day hermeneutics is recovery of the ministry of the prophet and recognition that prophecy has hermeneutical significance…As both Testaments amply demonstrate, the prophet can function as contextualizer, applying Scripture to specific cultural, social, and ecclesiological contexts. The prophetic interpreter listens to the Spirit, is sensitive to cultural perspectives, but remains submitted to the normative authority of Scripture."[13]

With prophecy connected to biblical interpretation, we can recognize examples of prophecy that have received little attention. When the Jerusalem council met to discuss the role of circumcision in the present age, they applied Scripture to a new situation under the Spirit's guidance. This was prophecy. Supporting that this act was prophetic, the biblical account notes that the summary letter would also be carried by prophets. "Judas and Silas, *themselves being prophets also*, exhorted and strengthened the brethren with many words" (Acts 15:32). When the early Anabaptists burst onto the scene, they called for the church to come out from control of the state and assemble as a pure brotherhood, starting with believer's baptism. They prophesied: through their keen and penetrating interpretation of Scripture they eclipsed the dominant wisdom of the age. Because of the need for these kinds of transcendent insights throughout the church age, "apostles and prophets" are foundational to the church's life.

Part II of this book has been presenting the great battle of God's nation as being in the arena of biblical interpretation. Seen in this light, prophets are the warriors who lead the assault on the forces of evil that twist the Scriptures. Prophecy, more than any other gift, helps anchor the church in accurate doctrine and holy living. We desperately need more prophets today.

---

[13] Stuart Murray, *Biblical Interpretation in the Anabaptist Tradition*, Pandora Press, co-published with Herald Press (2000), pp. 244-246.

Chapter 14

The commandments of men

In vain do they worship me, teaching as doctrines the commandments of men. (Mark 7:7)

The church has a tendency to fall into extremes. More commonly, it falls into the error of presuming that it can decide which of God's commandments are to be obeyed—the antinomian heresy coming through arguments of cultural relativism. Using worldly wisdom, church leaders decide that some commands are "essential" and other commands are "non-essential." This partitioning usually depends upon prevailing cultural expectations. And so the world exerts great influence over church doctrine and practice. Commands concerning the headcovering, jewelry, nonresistance, and homosexuality are but three examples that many church leaders have decided are "non-essential."

The other extreme, less common but also dangerous, occurs when church leaders use their own wisdom to add to God's commands. This practice flourished among Jewish leaders during the intertestamental period and came to be known as "fence around the Torah." The motivating impulse is to avoid breaking the commands of the Torah; thus extra laws would be put into place to avoid *getting close* to breaking the Torah. For example, observant Jews today are taught not to eat meat and dairy in the same meal. This comes from the verse that states, "You shall not boil a young goat in its mother's milk" (Deut. 14:21).

Presumably this command was given to prevent a cruel death to an animal where the soothing milk of its mother became the means of its death. To "fence in" this law, rabbinic teaching stated that meat and milk should not be consumed in the same meal, even if they were from different animals. (After all, it might not always be apparent if two animals were mother and grown child.) Some rabbis expanded the fence further by specifying how many hours needed to elapse between meals to prevent meat and milk from being "cooked" together in one's digestive tract. Still other rabbis commanded that dishes be reserved separately for meat and dairy products.

While this progression might seem strange to the outsider, similar practices have occurred in Christian groups wherein very particular details (for example, of dress or facial hair) that were not commanded in Scripture became taught as doctrines to "fence in" scriptural teachings of modesty or separation. These groups would scarcely recognize this practice as a modern form of "fence around the Torah," a Pharisaical practice that Jesus condemns:

> Then the Pharisees and some of the scribes came together to Him, having come from Jerusalem. Now when they saw some of His disciples eat bread with defiled, that is, with unwashed hands, they found fault. For the Pharisees and all the Jews do not eat unless they wash their hands in a special way, holding the tradition of the elders. When they come from the marketplace, they do not eat unless they wash. And there are many other things which they have received and hold, like the washing of cups, pitchers, copper vessels, and couches. Then the Pharisees and scribes asked Him, "Why do Your disciples not walk according to the tradition of the elders, but eat bread with unwashed hands?" He answered and said to them, "Well did Isaiah prophesy of you hypocrites, as it is written: 'This people honors Me with their lips, But their heart is far from Me. And in vain they worship Me, Teaching as doctrines the commandments of men.' For laying aside the commandment of God, you hold the tradition of men." (Mark 7:1-8)

While washings were a part of Old Testament priestly practice (Exod. 29:4; Lev. 16:4, 24), the Pharisees began to *command* that this be done before all meals for all people, an example of "fence around the Torah." Jesus harshly rebukes this as an unnecessary command that actually caused adherents to "leave the commandment of God." Adding to God's commands must therefore be taken very seriously.

The Scriptures give four reasons not to add human commandments to our churches. First, Scripture affirms that either adding or subtracting to the Lord's commandments hinders obedience: "You shall not add to the word which I command you, nor take from it, that you may keep the commandments of the LORD your God which I command you" (Deut. 4:2). Note that *either* adding or taking away hinders keeping the commandments of the Lord. Hence the first reason to avoid adding to the commandments of God is that *it hinders biblical obedience.*

Second, the commandments of men represent a form of slavery: "If with Christ you died to the elemental spirits of the world, why, as if you were still alive in the world, do you submit to regulations—'Do not handle, Do not taste, Do not touch' (referring to things that all perish as they are used)—according to human precepts and teachings? These have indeed an appearance of wisdom in promoting self-made religion and asceticism and severity to the body, but they are of no value in stopping the indulgence of the flesh" (Col. 2:20-23 ESV). Adding extrabiblical commandments like "Do not handle, do not taste, do not touch" are in fact associated with the elemental spirits of the world.[1] The elemental spirits are enslaving false gods that, among other activities, divide humanity and hinder unity in the body. Representing a form of slavery, adding commandments therefore opposes the unity that ought to be in the Lord.

Third, the commandments of men are stumbling blocks that hinder others from entering the kingdom of God. Jesus denounced the Pharisees for putting burdens upon the people's backs: "For [the scribes and Pharisees] bind heavy burdens, hard to bear, and lay them on men's shoulders...But woe to you, scribes and Pharisees, hypocrites! For you shut up the kingdom of heaven against men; for you neither go in yourselves, nor do you allow those who are entering to go in." (Matt. 23:4, 13) The commandments of men are a heavy burden that cause sincere seekers to stumble. They also move the church's focus from weightier matters to trivial matters. "Therefore rebuke them sharply, that they may be sound in the faith, not giving heed to Jewish fables and *commandments of men* who turn from the truth" (Titus 1:13-14).

The final reason to avoid adding to God's commandments is that it undermines the common faith, the sufficiency of Scripture (the sixth principle of faithful biblical interpretation, see chapter 8), and the wisdom of King Jesus. "Beloved, although I was very eager to write to you about our common salvation, I found it necessary to write appealing to you to contend for the faith that was *once for all* delivered to the saints" (Jude 1:3). The faith has *already* been delivered—past tense—implying

[1] This expression, "elemental spirits of the world" (Greek: *stoicheia tou kosmou*), remains one of the most studied expressions in the Pauline corpus. Used three times (Col. 2:8, 20 and Gal. 4:3), it is sometimes translated "rudiments" or "elemental principles." However, the fact that the stoicheia have the ability to enslave (Gal. 4:3) and are referred to as false gods that are "weak and beggarly" (Gal 4:8-9) makes "elemental spirits of this world" the better translation. In Galatians, the elemental spirits of this world were dividing Jewish from Gentile believers.

there is no need for men to layer upon their own novel commands. If Jesus wanted a particular command, He would have already given it. Hubris enables fallen man to suppose that he should command where God has not. Numerous Scriptures reinforce this principle (Deut. 12:32; Prov. 30:5-6; Rev. 22:18-19). Notably, the faith is "common"—the faith that a believer in Judea holds should be the same as that held in China or Peru or Mozambique. Additional commands perturb the commonality of the true Christian faith, often culturally dividing those who are supposed to be one.

We saw in chapter 8 that Tradition II involves adherence to tradition that is outside of Scripture. Tradition II thinking is central to rabbinic Judaism and Roman Catholicism but cannot be found among the early Protestants or early Anabaptists. While human commandments are generally accepted today in conservative Anabaptist groups, this is a departure from their historic foundation. The earliest Anabaptist leaders advocated for *sola scriptura* and the sufficiency of Scripture in order to reject the commandments of men. Conrad Grebel, the "father of Anabaptism," employed the principle that, "Everything must be tested by the New Testament, and what is not found therein as the teaching of Christ and the apostles or as an apostolic practice must be abandoned."[2] Menno Simons protested extrabiblical standards: "I dare not go higher nor lower, more stringent nor lenient than the Scriptures and the Holy Spirit teach me; and that out of great fear and anxiety of my conscience, lest I again burden the godfearing hearts who now have renounced the commandments of men, with those commandments. Self-conceit and human opinions I hate, nor do I desire them; for I know what tribulation and affliction they have caused me for many years."[3] Dirk Philips wrote in a similar fashion, "The holy divine Scripture teaches us everywhere that we should neither accept nor believe nor observe anything except God's Word and command alone, and that we should neither add to nor subtract from God's Word."[4]

In summary, we must not embrace the commandments of men for four reasons:

1. Despite the good intentions behind building a "fence around the Torah," Jesus prohibits this practice. He teaches that it promotes "leaving the commandments of God" (Mark 7:1-8; Deut. 4:2).

[2] This summary of Grebel's methodology is from Harold S. Bender, *Conrad Grebel: The Founder of the Swiss Brethren*, Wipf and Stock (1998), p. 175.

[3] Menno Simons in *The Complete Works of Menno Simons*, John F. Funk and Brother (1871, reprint by Pathway Publishers in 1983), Second Part, p. 281.

[4] *The Writings of Dirk Philips*, Cornelius Dyck, William Keeney, and Alvin Beachy (translators and editors), Herald Press (1992), pp. 83-84.

2. Adding commands leads to enslavement to the elemental spirits of this world, which divide the brotherhood (Col. 2:20-23; Gal. 4:1-11).
3. The commandments of men are stumbling blocks that hinder others from entering the kingdom. (Matt. 23:4,13; Titus 1:14)
4. Adding commands beyond Scripture is antithetical to the faith that has been once for all delivered to the saints, the sufficiency of Scripture, and the wisdom of King Jesus (Jude 1:3; 2 Tim. 3:15-17). Additions represent Tradition II thinking, cherished by rabbinic Judaism and Roman Catholicism, but rejected by the early Anabaptists and Protestants.

Chapter 15

Biblical standards

For it has seemed good to the Holy Spirit and to us to lay on you no greater burden than these requirements. (Acts 15:28)

The faithful church must walk with careful balance. It should not relax the teaching or practice of *any* commands, yet it also must not *add* to God's commands, thereby engaging in "fence around the Torah" (see prior chapter). Yet articulating what biblical obedience represents in today's world is made difficult because of the diversity of new situations that could not possibly be addressed in the first century. Questions like the morality of cable television or public school were not *directly* addressed in the New Testament and hence require more than pointing to a "proof-text."

Thankfully, the Holy Spirit provided in Scripture a paradigm of how to grapple with new issues. The particular issue was the necessity of circumcision for the Gentiles, which Jesus did not directly address. And so a council was convened, the so-called Jerusalem council, to discuss the matter and pronounce judgment on the issue (Acts 15:1-29). While detailed exegesis of the passage is beyond the scope of this chapter, several observations should be made:

1. The church sought clarity on this issue, not wanting it to languish in a vague, undefined state that could remain a point of contention among individuals or congregations.
2. There was extensive discussion and debate on the matter, where both sides of the issue were heard (15:6-12).
3. An argument derived from Scripture proved decisive in settling the matter (15:15-17).
4. After the scriptural argument was presented, the leadership and church came to "one accord" (15:22-25). Since the "whole

church" heard James speak (v. 22), the council was obviously not restricted to the leaders.

5. As the outcome attests, the council weighed not only circumcision, but the broader issues at hand (15:19-21). By considering these broader issues, the council wisely sought to preemptively address areas of potential future conflict.
6. The council was very specific and practical in its decision. While the headline issue of circumcision was determined to be a matter of liberty, other issues raised at the council were deemed to be matters requiring obedience: not eating meat offered to idols, not drinking blood, not eating what was strangled, and avoiding sexual immorality. (While at first glance these four matters might seem to be an unusual grouping of issues, they actually represent the set of activities that occurred in pagan temple feasts.[1]) These pronouncements were practical and specific.
7. The conclusions were *put into writing* and circulated among the churches (15:22-29). Approved messengers carried the letter to bring an additional personal dimension that led the recipients to "rejoice" and be "encouraged and strengthened" (15:31-32).

Using the Jerusalem council as the template, this same sevenfold process should be the process by which the church today wrestles with new issues. The Jerusalem council thus forms the model of how church standards are to be birthed, and gives a biblical basis for the nature of church standards.

The term *church standard* is often used in certain churches, but should be clarified. The term describes a set of issues which the church (or larger denomination) has pronounced to be a test of membership. These are often associated with Anabaptist churches. For example, one standard that some churches have is "Members are expected to avoid worldly entertainment, such as television." Standards often have a negative connotation in Protestant circles because they tend to have a negative "do not" character.

Before proceeding further, we must draw a careful distinction: *certain church standards are biblical, while others are extrabiblical.* Extrabiblical standards have the following characteristics:

1. Their proponents cannot stitch together an argument from Scripture *requiring* the standard. Examples include requiring church members to avoid facial hair or requiring members to wear suspenders. It is difficult, if not impossible, to point to Scripture to

[1] See Ben Witherington III, *The Acts of the Apostles*, Eerdmans (1997), p. 462.

support such requirements. While these practices may be compatible with Scripture, they are not demanded by Scripture.
2. The origin of an extrabiblical standard is typically historic in nature and not biblical. Often a group will have split off from another and desire to keep certain distinctives in relation to the other group. Even decades or generations later, the distinctives will be rigidly held.
3. Extrabiblical standards are often rooted in a particular culture. For example, requiring women in Africa to wear a *particular style* of headcovering common in Pennsylvania would be imposing an extrabiblical standard.
4. Extrabiblical standards often have precise numbers or colors in them, having a somewhat arbitrary character. Examples include a certain dollar amount that a bank account cannot exceed, or a certain car color that must be maintained.

Perhaps not surprisingly, extrabiblical standards can be a stumbling block. They oppose the sufficiency of Scripture (chapter 8), forming a "fence around the Torah" (see previous chapter). Biblical standards, in contrast, have the following characteristics:

1. They are either restatements of Scripture or logical deductions from Scripture. When questioned, the proponent of the biblical standard turns to the Bible and not to a church document.
2. Biblical standards are not bound by culture or by time. They could as well be implemented in Kenya or Canada. Regarding the headcovering, a biblical standard would allow for differing cultural expressions for the woman's headcovering.
3. Biblical standards lack precise numbers or colors, but involve principles that will require a searching of the heart to implement. Hence biblical standards are not as easy to quickly pronounce judgment upon, because they will of necessity require discussion, prayer, and careful consideration of the factors involved.

Most Protestant and evangelical churches lack standards altogether, and prefer a saying like, "We use only the Bible." Yet this saying, while apparently in line with *sola scriptura*, falls short. *Sola scriptura* does imply Scripture alone as final authority, but not a Scripture that is alone (see chapter 8). It is hypocritical to accept the wisdom of the church on matters like the Trinity or Apostles' Creed with respect to doctrine (in a Tradition I sense, where these teachings are derived from Scripture), but then reject such wisdom for practice and holy living.

For example, the New Testament forbids gold, pearls, and expensive clothes in very plain language (1 Tim. 2:9-10). A church standard understands these to be examples and thus interprets the verse in its larger context to forbid jewelry and other displays of fashion. (This was also how the early church understood this passage.) But most Protestant and evangelical churches refuse to go this far and either say the command is "non-essential" or quietly ignore it. By not enumerating modern applications, pastors leave the gate open for antinomianism, individualistic autonomy, and a weakening of Scripture.

Ironically, those same churches will typically have a creed or "statement of faith" that affirms, for example, the Trinity or virgin birth. Their ministers acknowledge that Mormons and Jehovah's Witnesses also say "I believe the Bible" but mean something quite different by that statement. Wanting to differentiate themselves from such heresies, churches employ a "statement of faith" so that visitors and members know what the group believes. *The statement of faith clarifies how the group understands Scripture with respect to doctrine. In the same way, biblical standards clarify how the group understands Scripture with respect to practice.* Orthopraxy cannot be separated from orthodoxy. Biblical standards thus seek to interpret Scripture holistically, in a Tradition I sense. Biblical standards have several other benefits:

1. History teaches that unless a group defines its stance on an issue, or explicitly says that a matter is one of liberty, the vacuum often causes a subsequent split. This consideration seemed to be a factor in motivating the Jerusalem council. To avoid needless divisions, a group should articulate its beliefs on disputed points. If that point is an issue of liberty, it should be stated as such.
2. An important reason to hold standards is because of the fallen nature of our minds. While it would be ideal if everyone could read Scripture and come to the same conclusions, the tragic reality is that sin has blinded humanity to the truth. Sin hinders us from seeing spiritual matters clearly. Standards are useful to unpack Scripture into the practicalities of daily life, especially for those who may not have had a background wherein a particular truth was lived out.
3. Standards promote unity. Scripture asks the rhetorical question "Can two walk together, unless they are agreed?" (Amos 3:3). The implied answer is no. Agreement is a vital element in being able to walk together peacefully. Standards serve as a useful tool in attaining that harmony.
4. Scripture commands us to be of the same mind and in full accord:

> "Therefore if there is any consolation in Christ, if any comfort of love, if any fellowship of the Spirit, if any affection and mercy, fulfill my joy by being like-minded, having the same love, being of one accord, of one mind" (Phil. 2:1-2). Standards are an *expedient* way to test and attain unity of mind.

For the above reasons, a church should reasonably strive for a set of biblical standards. The process of expressing standards should train members to point back to Scripture and not to a church document. The final "rule" will have little intrinsic power to motivate or convince a person on the validity of a particular truth—but the exposition of the rule should be a well-reasoned "pointer" to Scripture, using clear logic to show the necessity of a given practice in light of Scripture. Because of the hardening nature of "do not" lists, it is dangerous to circulate naked lists of rules devoid from their biblical underpinnings.

The process of wrestling, studying, discussing, and praying to reach unity around standards will challenge our fallen minds on how to reason biblically. But the standard by itself should not be intended to change hearts. Only the Holy Spirit can change hearts, and to use standards to try to change the heart is folly. Seeing a healthy, biblical group live out a particular standard with joy and good fruit is probably the most powerful means that the Spirit uses to change hearts.

A positive feature of healthy, biblical standards is that the resulting unity enables strong evangelism: "Only let your manner of life be worthy of the gospel of Christ, so that whether I come and see you or am absent, I may hear of you that you are standing firm in one spirit, with one mind striving side by side for the faith of the gospel, and not frightened in anything by your opponents" (Phil. 1:27-28). Jesus' prayer to the Father was along similar lines: "[May] they all may be one, as You, Father, are in Me, and I in You; that they also may be one in Us, that the world may believe that You sent Me" (John 17:20-21).

Imagine if churches were not known for splitting but for unity! Biblical standards, as a tool in attaining that noble goal, should be counted worthy of great diligence.

Answering common questions

Is there room for local standards?

The New Testament never describes local standards. The Jerusalem council was an international body that sought biblical standards for the whole church, not one local body. Having elders from a diversity of backgrounds and cultures would naturally defend against blind spots or idiosyncratic prejudices. While a conscience-binding *local standard* lacks biblical warrant, there is clearly room and even biblical precedent for *local wisdom*. For example, in a Hindu area, it may be wise to refrain from purchasing or eating beef. But that should never be elevated to the level of a standard, as if to eat beef were always a sin.

What about the binding and loosing that Jesus described?

Taken in context, this passage concerns putting people out of the church. It will be addressed in more detail in a later chapter (chapter 28, "The local church and membership").

How do you differentiate between biblical and extrabiblical standards?

Many people raised in churches with numerous extrabiblical standards struggle with this question. Partly because of years of church indoctrination, their mental acuity is especially dull in this area. The litmus test is the following: does the particular standard *necessarily* follow from Scripture? The question is not if a particular practice is *compatible* with Scripture, but rather if it is logically *demanded*. Two examples illustrate this test. For a man to wear suspenders is compatible with Scripture as they serve a useful role. But one should not *insist* that men wear suspenders, because Scripture does not demand it. This should be an issue of liberty. Second, the cape dress is a modest form of dress, compatible with scriptural principles. But Scripture nowhere demands that women everywhere around the world wear the cape dress. The church can only bind the conscience to Scripture, not to human wisdom or preferences. Binding the conscience to human wisdom violates the sufficiency of Scripture, puts stumbling blocks before others, and builds the "fence around the Torah" that Jesus spoke so strongly against.

Can you provide an example of how to use Scripture to form a biblical standard?

A good portion of the remainder of this book will contend for specific standards and provide scriptural support for those standards.

Part III

The Governance of the Nation

Chapter 16

Inward holiness

Having these promises, beloved, let us cleanse ourselves from all filthiness of the flesh and spirit, perfecting holiness in the fear of God.
(2 Corinthians 7:1)

When I was a boy, I remember speaking with a man who had recently become a Christian. He described how his mind no longer raced and that he could genuinely be at peace. His tranquil and loving demeanor confirmed his words. I remember another young man who met the Lord and was transformed overnight from a person who was cynical and apathetic to inspiring and passionate. He began to preach with a wisdom and power obviously from the Spirit. In both of these true stories, something at the core of their inward being changed. Instead of incremental improvement, there was metamorphosis.

God intends to transform one's inward person at salvation, to provide a change of heart. God wants to obliterate sin from our hearts. For this reason He sent His Son into the world: "You shall call His name Jesus, for He will save His people *from their sins*" (Matt. 1:21).

God wants our hearts. When Jesus gave the Sermon on the Mount, He emphasized the heart. Jesus understood that the heart was what really mattered. Consider the example of a person enflamed with lust. Perhaps he is about to buy an inappropriate magazine at the store, but at the last minute he sees someone outside the window that he knows. He refrains from making the purchase, for fear of damaging his reputation. In this case, one selfish impulse, the desire for a good reputation, impeded another selfish impulse, his lust. While outwardly it may appear as if he did well, his heart did not act from virtue.

This was the genius pervading Jesus' Sermon on the Mount: the centrality of the heart. Inward lust is essentially the same sin as outward adultery or fornication. Inward anger is essentially the same sin as outwardly injuring a person. When we hear in the news of a murder, many people look down upon the murderer as if they would never do such a thing. But in reality, only another selfish impulse, such as the desire to avoid punishment, checks their anger from lashing out in a similar way. For this reason, our hearts manifest themselves most clearly when there is little chance of punishment or damage to reputation. When no one can see you, your heart can be most easily seen.

From transactional to relational

The selfish heart is always looking out for itself. It always murmurs, "What's in it for me?" Tragically, some portray the Christian faith as a transaction. They say that as a way to maximize your happiness, you should pray this prayer or live in such and such a way. While people do of course find the greatest happiness in following the Lord, this happiness comes because they are not seeking their own advantage. True salvation is found in not seeking one's own gain.

Consider the jaw-dropping example of Moses who placed his own salvation after that of Israel: "Alas, this people has sinned a great sin. They have made for themselves gods of gold. But now, if You will forgive their sin—but if not, please blot me out of Your book that You have written" (Exod. 32:31-32). Paul makes a similar statement, "For I could wish that I myself were accursed from Christ for my brethren, my countrymen according to the flesh" (Rom. 9:3). How could Paul say such a thing? Both Moses and Paul could say such things because they had God's heart. Their inward being was transformed. The essence of the heart of God is to give without concern of getting back. Moses and Paul's ultimate goal in life was not to achieve salvation, but to promote God's glory. Meditate carefully on the following passages:

> For whoever desires to save his life will lose it, but whoever loses his life for My sake will save it. (Luke 9:24)

> Let no one seek his own, but each one the other's well-being. (1 Cor. 10:24)

> Seek first the kingdom of God and His righteousness. (Matt. 6:33)

> Incline my heart to your testimonies, and not to selfish gain. (Ps. 119:36)

> Greater love has no one than this, than to lay down one's life for his friends. (John 15:13)

> You ask and do not receive, because you ask amiss, that you may spend it on your pleasures. (James 4:3)

> He died for all, that those who live should live no longer for themselves, but for Him who died for them and rose again. (2 Cor. 5:15)

This self-giving love is the very heart of Jesus. While of course one receives the greatest happiness and fulfillment by following the King, the one who desires to save his life will lose it (Luke 9:24). Biblical happiness comes by not pursuing your own happiness. This is one of the great paradoxes of the plan of salvation. The essence of the Christian faith is a covenantal relationship with God, not a transaction.

The manifestations of inward holiness

Those who have true inward holiness cannot be missed. They have a desire to follow God that comes from within; it is no burden. All of us have experiences of working with those who are motivated versus those who are apathetic. In my years teaching at universities, I could easily recognize students who cared about the subject versus those who were there because it was a requirement. Only a fraction were truly motivated, but they made teaching a pleasure. Those who have God's Spirit are a pleasure to God. When a person has God's Spirit in them, they are driven. Just as Jesus was "driven" into the wilderness by the Spirit (Mark 1:12), so a person with inward holiness is driven by the Spirit. Without being told, they seek out the word, pray, proclaim the gospel, and strive for holiness. God's word is like a fire in their bones that cannot be extinguished (Jer. 20:9).

Those with God's holiness are consistent. Because they have a new nature and are not papering over an old nature, their new nature organically expresses itself. Their new nature dominates their thoughts and actions. This is why John can write, "Everyone who abides in Him does not sin" (1 John 3:6).[1] Those who do not have new hearts are constantly falling into sin and ride on a roller-coaster of emotions. They seek the next revival meeting, worship experience, or exciting technique to fix

[1] Author's translation.

their problems. Those with inward holiness steadily walk the long road of obedience.

Those with inward holiness have so united themselves to King Jesus that sin breaks their heart. They would rather lose their health, fail at work, not find a spouse, and lose their money rather than sin against God. With the divine nature filling them, their joy is found only in right relationship to God. With such a disposition, pride is crushed. Such people do not try to project images. They are not afraid to confess their sins. Those around them sense their humility.

Those with inward holiness speak every word with honesty. How rare this attribute is in the church today! Many bend the truth for the sake of an argument, humor, money, or reputation. Few today in the church have commendable honesty. They deceive others, and then deceive themselves that they have acted acceptably. They can no longer determine right from wrong because God has given them over to a spirit of delusion. From their tax returns to their interactions with co-workers, "little white lies" pepper their dealings. But, "there is no such thing as a minor lapse in integrity."[2] Those who have God's holiness can be trusted to keep their word, no matter the burden.

Those with inward holiness are not jealous. When one lives before an audience of One, only His approval matters. Earthly possessions, money, and human approval are trivialities before the throne of heaven. With God as their Father, fear is cast out. A calmness and tranquility rules the hearts and minds of those who are the children of God.

Inward holiness manifests in tender, loving speech. Instead of harsh words, there is gentleness and meekness. Meekness is not weakness, for a "soft tongue will break a bone" (Prov. 25:15). To the man's wife, children, and friends, he is known for gentleness and strength. From the overflow of the heart, the mouth speaks. Because his heart is fixed on the Lord, the divine nature marks his speech.

Obtaining inward holiness

True inward holiness cannot be bootstrapped; it comes from God. Yet Scripture exhorts us to strive for the holiness without which we cannot see the Lord (Heb. 12:14). "Sanctification is not by surrender, but by divinely enabled toil and effort."[3] How do we understand this tension? Holiness is a gift, an aspect of the grace found in Jesus. But it is also something that we strive for, by God's grace and in His power. We

[2] Attributed to Tom Peters.

[3] Kevin DeYoung, *The Hole in Our Holiness*, Crossway (2012), p. 90.

appropriate that holiness in several ways. First, through prayer. Prayer exemplifies the tension discussed above. In prayer we can do nothing but receive from God. Yet the very act of persevering in prayer requires significant effort. If our prayer lives are shallow and impoverished, we cannot have God's holiness. We must call out for the Spirit and for deeper union with the King. Only the power of the Spirit, which is Jesus' resurrection power, can crush our sins and induce real transformation. Let a person cry out to the Lord for His holiness—God will be faithful.

Second, the sword by which the Spirit tears out our old hearts is the word of God (Eph. 6:17). We must place the word of God deeply in our hearts so that we will not sin against Him (Ps. 119:11). God's word has a power to change our lives that human words do not. We must read it, meditate on it, study it, discuss it, and pray over it. Third, we find God's holiness by obeying the light that we already have. We must separate ourselves from what we know to be wicked. God will reward those steps with a fuller revelation of Himself. Fourth, we should bind ourselves to a faithful congregation for accountability, exhortation, and the fellowship of the Lord's Supper. These elements synergize to produce inward holiness. Sometimes the Lord acts quickly to change a person's heart; sometimes it takes longer. But we may confidently declare to the Lord that "none who wait for You shall be put to shame" (Ps. 25:3).

The priority of inward holiness

The remainder of Part III of the book will focus on issues that have been controversial for centuries. They are surely very important and even impact inward holiness. But let us never forget how significant the non-controversial issues are. Everyone within the church has always agreed that pride, lying, vanity, lust, ingratitude, unkindness, and hatred are wrong. If we forget these basics, there is no point in moving on to controversial topics. The first mark of the Spirit is that within ourselves, we manifest "love, joy, peace, longsuffering, kindness, goodness, faithfulness, gentleness, self-control" (Gal. 5:22). Would others describe you in such terms? Do you dare to ask? More importantly, do you dare ask God to purify yourself from any evil, no matter what the cost?

Chapter 17

Peacemaking and nonresistance

Blessed are the peacemakers,
For they shall be called sons of God.
(Matthew 5:9)

The nations of this world employ physical weapons of offense and defense. When Jesus announced His new nation, He needed to clarify the character of His nation with respect to the use of force. Would the new nation be similar to Old Testament Israel? Would this new nation throw off Roman oppression with violence? In the Sermon on the Mount, Jesus devotes considerable time to the subject of how enemies should be treated (Matt. 5:38-48).

Instead of fighting against their enemies, Jesus' followers are to love their enemies, bless them, and generously serve them. Peacemaking and loving one's enemies are revolutionary concepts, difficult to overstate in importance. Jesus taught and modeled peacemaking and nonresistance, showing humanity a new way. As described in the Sermon on the Mount, the term *nonresistance* (from Matt. 5:39) encompasses the peaceful, non-retaliatory, and loving disposition toward a person's enemies:

> You have heard that it was said, "An eye for an eye and a tooth for a tooth." But I tell you not to resist an evil person. But whoever slaps you on your right cheek, turn the other to him also. If anyone wants to sue you and take away your tunic, let him have your cloak also. And whoever compels you to go one mile, go with him two. Give to him who asks you, and from him who wants to borrow from you do not

> turn away. You have heard that it was said, "You shall love your neighbor and hate your enemy." But I say to you, love your enemies, bless those who curse you, do good to those who hate you, and pray for those who spitefully use you and persecute you, that you may be sons of your Father in heaven; for He makes His sun rise on the evil and on the good, and sends rain on the just and on the unjust. For if you love those who love you, what reward have you? Do not even the tax collectors do the same? And if you greet your brethren only, what do you do more than others? Do not even the tax collectors do so? Therefore you shall be perfect, just as your Father in heaven is perfect. (Matt. 5:38-48)

Nonresistance should never be confused with cowardice or fleeing from danger. Jesus does not say that when slapped on one cheek, we are to run away. We are called to stand and actively offer the other cheek—a brave deed no doubt! When a disciple is sued for his tunic (inner shirt), he is not to cry, fall to the ground, or shrink away. Jesus asks His disciple to offer his cloak (outer coat), leaving him with effectively nothing. To walk with a person an extra mile is the very opposite of cowardice or fleeing from danger. These three examples involve a wrong to the body (slapping the cheek), wrong to one's property (lawsuit for a tunic), and wrong to one's liberty (being compelled to walk).[1] Nonresistance is a bold, daring position. "Our Peacemaking Command is the command to be a Surprising Person."[2]

Jesus' lengthy teaching on loving one's enemies is preceded by the Beatitudes, which declare that those who are peacemakers will be called sons of God. Contrast the following groups of people:

- Peacebreakers: those who stir up controversy, dissension, and violence.
- Peacefakers: those who ignore the dissension, unrest, and violence in the world around them, selfishly choosing to attend to their own interests or respond with "an eye for an eye."
- Peacemakers: those who identify unrest and strife, and respond with surprising nonresistance. Peacemakers sacrifice their own comfort by loving their enemy.

Outside the Sermon on the Mount, the doctrine of nonresistance is implied or affirmed in several locations:

---

[1] Matthew Henry's insightful observation.

[2] F. D. Bruner, *Matthew: A Commentary, Volume 1*, Eerdmans (2007), p. 252.

> Behold, I send you out as sheep in the midst of wolves. Therefore be wise as serpents and harmless as doves. (Matt. 10:16)

> But Jesus said to him, "Put your sword in its place, for all who take the sword will perish by the sword." (Matt. 26:52)

> Repay no one evil for evil. Have regard for good things in the sight of all men. If it is possible, as much as depends on you, live peaceably with all men. Beloved, do not avenge yourselves, but rather give place to wrath; for it is written, "Vengeance is Mine, I will repay," says the Lord. Therefore "If your enemy is hungry, feed him; If he is thirsty, give him a drink; For in so doing you will heap coals of fire on his head." Do not be overcome by evil, but overcome evil with good. (Rom. 12:17-21)

> For the weapons of our warfare are not of the flesh. (2 Cor. 10:4 ESV)

> See that no one renders evil for evil to anyone, but always pursue what is good both for yourselves and for all. (1 Thess. 5:15)

> For to this you were called, because Christ also suffered for us, leaving us an example, that you should follow His steps: "Who committed no sin, Nor was deceit found in His mouth"; who, when He was reviled, did not revile in return; when He suffered, He did not threaten, but committed Himself to Him who judges righteously. (1 Pet. 2:21-23)

> He who kills with the sword must be killed with the sword. Here is the patience and the faith of the saints. (Rev. 13:10)

After the horrific loss of life through the wars of the twentieth century, much reflection has occurred on Jesus' teachings in the Sermon on the Mount. George Zabelka, the Roman Catholic chaplain of the Hiroshima and Nagasaki World War II airmen, gave the following interview:[3]

> Q: You said the atomic bombing of Nagasaki happened to a Church that "had asked for it." What do you mean by that?
>
> Zabelka: For the first three centuries, the three centuries closest to Christ, the Church was a pacifist Church. With Constantine the church accepted the pagan Roman ethic of a just war and slowly began to involve its membership in mass slaughter, first for the state and later for the faith.
>
> Catholics, Orthodox, and Protestants, whatever other differences they may have had on theological esoterica, all agreed that Jesus' clear and unambiguous teaching on the rejection of violence and on love of enemies was not to be taken seriously. And so each of the major branches of Christianity by different theological methods modified our Lord's teaching in these matters until all three were able to do what Jesus rejected, that is, take an eye for an eye, slaughter, maim, torture.
>
> It seems a "sign" to me that seventeen hundred years of Christian terror and slaughter should arrive at August 9, 1945 when Catholics dropped the A-Bomb on top of the largest and first Catholic city in Japan. One would have thought that I, as a Catholic priest, would have spoken out against the atomic bombing of nuns. (Three orders of Catholic sisters were destroyed in Nagasaki that day.) One would have thought that I would have suggested that as a minimal standard of Catholic morality, Catholics shouldn't bomb Catholic children. I didn't.
>
> I, like that Catholic pilot of the Nagasaki plane, was heir to a Christianity that had for seventeen hundred years engaged in revenge, murder, torture, the pursuit of power and prerogative and violence, all in the name of our Lord.
>
> I walked through the ruins of Nagasaki right after the war and visited the place where once stood the Urakami Cathedral. I picked up a piece of a censer from the rubble. When I look at it today I pray God forgives us for how we have distorted Christ's teaching and destroyed His world by the

[3] A complete transcript of the interview entitled "Fr. George Zabelka: A Military Chaplain Repents" is available from www.centerforchristiannonviolence.org.

> distortion of that teaching. I was the Catholic chaplain who was there when this grotesque process, which began with Constantine, reached its lowest point—so far.
>
> Q: What do you mean by "so far"?
>
> Zabelka: Briefly, what I mean is that I do not see that the moral climate in relation to war inside or outside the Church has dramatically changed much since 1945. The mainline Christian Churches still teach something that Christ never taught or even hinted at, namely the Just War Theory, a theory that to me has been completely discredited theologically, historically, and psychologically.
>
> So as I see it, until the various churches within Christianity repent and begin to proclaim by word and deed what Jesus proclaimed in relation to violence and enemies, there is no hope for anything other than ever-escalating violence and destruction.

A Protestant commentator on the book of Matthew, after mentioning Timothy McVeigh's training with the army (involving a chant of "Kill! Kill! Kill! Blood makes the grass grow!"), Christian-Muslim strife in Indonesia, and the Vietnam war, writes with remarkable humility and candor:

> If these samples give the realities of war, can Christians conscientiously participate? The first three Christian centuries answered with a ringing 'No.' From the fourth-century Constantinian settlement to the present the overwhelming majority, including my own Reformation heritage, has answered with an almost equally unanimous 'Yes.' Matthew's Gospel forces me to question this tradition. I am a new student of the pacifist position and, if I should adopt it, I do not yet know how to answer all the uncomfortable questions (such as, 'Do we leave all the dirty work to others?' 'Do you just let a Hitler invade you?'). I intend to study the issue more thoroughly and to come to a more settled position. Our decisions on this issue are full of consequences. Jesus' Political Commands (5:33-48) are as difficult as they are timely.[4]

[4] Bruner, p. 265.

Nonresistance and peacemaking historically serve as the bright dividing line separating the peace churches from the state churches.[5] The principles of faithful biblical interpretation (see chapter 8) give laser-like convergence to the position of nonresistance. The modern evangelical church errs in its general position that Christians should be peaceful in their personal lives, but are freed from this obligation insofar as they are employed by the state. Such a division between personal life and work life is alien to Scripture. In fact, the necessary inference is that disciples cannot serve in positions that involve the use of violence, such as police or military work. Notably, this passage on loving one's enemies follows Jesus' prohibition on oath-taking, which has been part of government service for millenia. Jesus' prohibition of oaths thus practically prevents Christians from serving in government roles.

Besides Jesus' direct teachings, a strong argument against Christian participation in war comes from the larger theme of Jesus' founding a nation (see chapter 1). If Jesus' founded a nation, then to join in the squabbles of other nations comes close to treason. In a very real sense, a Christian American is closer to a Christian Iraqi than he or she is to a pagan American. They are brother or sister in the Lord, an eternal bond. Should they kill one another?

Peacemaking and nonresistance are broader than refraining from physical violence. As noted above, this is an active, benevolent, comprehensive, and demanding position. Nonresistance touches virtually every area of life (body, property, and liberty, not to mention pride). Jesus gave examples of walking with a person an extra mile, or giving more than asked when sued. Paul offers the example of not engaging in lawsuits (1 Cor. 6:1-11). Jesus' example of silence when reviled is an example of nonresistance in speech. While the focus of nonresistance and peacemaking is often toward war (for good reason), nonresistance touches virtually all aspects of life.

---

[5] For more on the rejection of war by the early church, see John Cadoux's *The Early Christian Attitude to War* (1919).

Answering Objections

What if someone breaks into your home—would you not harm the intruder?

A thoughtful and helpful response has been prepared elsewhere.[6] Before answering the objection, a true story offers helpful perspective.[7] Several years ago, Pablo Yoder and his family moved to Nicaragua, a nation known for its violence. On *dozens* of occasions the family has been robbed at gunpoint in their home. Women have even been molested. Yet they have chosen to respond with love to these assailants, including offering them food and drink—excellent examples of the active and surprising elements of nonresistance. Remarkably, their nonresistant behavior has broken the cycle of violence; most of these robbers have not returned, out of shame to harm such loving people. If the Yoder family chose to defend themselves with arms, they themselves might have been killed in a gunfight and their Christian testimony would have been lost.

Returning to the objection, its main flaw is that it poses a *counterfactual*. It depicts future circumstances as if one knew the outcome in advance. In reality, it is impossible to have this perfect foreknowledge. The situation is posed as an oversimplistic either/or: you shoot an assailant *or* he harms your family. However, this counterfactual quickly breaks down. A defender might shoot and miss, enraging the attacker, causing the invader to shoot and kill when he was not so intending. The counterfactual in fact is statistically misleading. In the United States, persons with guns in the home are twice as likely *themselves* to be killed as those without guns.[8]

The question also covertly challenges one's manhood. "Of course, you would protect your family wouldn't you?" as if to say "no" would be to deny your masculinity and honor. Contrast the world's shame in answering "no" to defending your home with arms to how Ezra found shame: "For I was ashamed to ask the king for a band of soldiers and horsemen to protect us against the enemy on our way, since we had told the king, 'The hand of our God is for good on all who seek him, and the power of his wrath is against all who forsake him' " (Ezra 8:22).

---

6 John Howard Yoder, *What Would You Do? (If a Violent Person Threatened to Harm a Loved One)*, Herald Press (1992).

7 Pablo Yoder, Philip Cohen, and Nate Yoder, *Angels Over Waslala: God Had Sent Us Into Nicaragua's War-Ravaged Interior*, Harbor Lights Publishing (1998).

8 Linda Dahlberg, Robin Ikeda, and Marcie-jo Kresnow, "Guns in the Home and Risk of a Violent Death in the Home: Findings from a National Study," *American Journal of Epidemiology*, 160:929-936 (2004).

What is the difference between nonresistance and pacifism?

Nonresistance is a term used by Christians who are following Jesus' teachings. Nonresistance is practiced by those who hold to a "two kingdoms" doctrine, and they practice nonresistance because Jesus commanded it, not for political purposes. Nonresistance is also a broader term that encompasses not using violence in defending the home, not suing another person, and not verbally retaliating.

In contrast, *pacifism* is a term often used by non-Christians or by those who do not see themselves as citizens of another nation. They use pacifism as a political tool for changing the laws of an earthly nation. They will often stage rowdy protests against the government to accomplish their goals. Pacifists will use arms in defending their homes. Pacifism therefore is not biblical nonresistance. Because Christians are citizens of another nation, and their goals are different than those of the world, the term nonresistance is preferred.

Didn't soldiers like Cornelius become Christians? Doesn't that speak against nonresistance?

If this argument is valid, then prostitution and adultery are biblically sanctioned as well. Prostitutes and adulterers came to Jesus and were forgiven (see John 8:1-11). Though the Bible does not specifically follow their repentance and later lives, we can safely assume that they forsook their prior lifestyles. Similarly, with Cornelius, we can only assume that repentance and a change of occupation occurred. Indeed, the fact that New Testament authors go out of their way to describe those ostensibly furthest away from the kingdom—adulterers (John 8:1-11), cheaters (Luke 19:8), demon-possessed (Mark 5:15) and fortune-tellers (Acts 16:16)—delivered from bondage and turning to Jesus, makes it probable that the soldier's story was chosen *because* his profession was so opposed to Jesus' teaching.

What about men like David who served in war?

The Old Testament is filled with men of faith who engaged in physical combat. David is but one example. Like practices of polygamy or animal sacrifice, physical war pertains to the Old Covenant but not to the New. Jesus often supersedes Old Testament practices in the Sermon on the Mount. A Christocentric, New Covenant perspective demands that Jesus' followers obey His teaching rather than follow Old Testament examples (see chapter 8).

Didn't Paul approve of the sword in Romans 13:1-7?

The governments of this world have been given the sword to preserve order. In Romans 13:1-7, Paul refers to the authorities in the third person (they) and to Christians in the second person (you). The different choice of pronouns for Christians and those bearing the sword is remarkable. Yes, earthly governments have been given the sword. But Paul did not use language consistent with Christians being in government or the military. In fact, in the same book, Paul affirms nonresistance (Rom. 12:19-21). Jesus also affirms that the Gentiles have their way of conducting themselves, but it shall not be so among His followers (Matt. 20:26).

Isn't it wrong to benefit when others are sacrificing, letting them do the dirty work?

God has given the state the authority of the sword to maintain order. This is necessary in a world where so many do not follow Jesus' new way for humanity. But if everyone were to follow Jesus' ways, there would be no need for the sword. In fact, swords will be destroyed when Jesus' kingdom comes in fullness (Isa. 2:4; Micah 4:3; Joel 3:10). Christians in fact render a still greater benefit to the world by proclaiming Jesus' kingship and by inviting others to submit to His peaceful reign. While Christians should look upon the state with gratitude for maintaining order, Christians also usher in another state that has perfect order. And as described earlier, nonresistance is sacrificial, messy work that requires as much or more bravery than using physical arms.

What about Hitler? Would you have let him invade?

This question represents another example of posing a counterfactual. The counterfactual being posed is, "If Christians were nonresistant, Hitler would have won World War II and the world would be living in the nightmare of the Third Reich." The question fails to acknowledge the tremendous Protestant and Roman Catholic support that Hitler received to gain power. Perhaps if Christians were nonresistant, Hitler would never have come to power in the first place. This would have prevented the Holocaust altogether. (Just War theorists do not pose *that* counterfactual and take responsibility for those deaths.) The question also minimizes the active power of nonresistance. The term nonresistance can be misunderstood: while Christians should not use weapons of the flesh to oppose evil, they are called to oppose evil through spiritual warfare, especially through prayer and preaching the gospel. "Do not be overcome by evil, but overcome evil with good" (Rom. 12:21). If there is any lesson to be gained from Old Testament wars, it is that God can intervene supernaturally and rout armies without the aid of a superior military. Finally, Christians are simply called to obedience, not to disobey Jesus' teachings because of pragmatic forecasts of what might occur in the future. This is precisely the meaning of *trust*. "Some trust in chariots and some in horses, but we trust in the name of the LORD our God" (Ps. 20:7).

Chapter 18

Government entanglement

For our citizenship is in heaven. (Philippians 3:20)

Because Jesus proclaimed the coming of a new nation, an important question arises as to how His disciples should relate to earthly governments. For example, can a disciple hold government positions? In previous centuries, one often finds this question posed as "Can a Christian serve as a magistrate?"

A question that we have skirted so far must finally be addressed. If there are two kingdoms at war, who reigns over the kingdom that is opposed to God's? That is, if Jesus proclaimed a new nation, with Himself as its king, who reigns over all the other nations of the world?

When the question is posed in such a way, the answer is obvious. All other nations must in some sense be under Satan's dominion. While there is a tension in understanding governments as under God yet as evil (the theme of the book of Habakkuk), the modern church has failed to appreciate the evil spiritual forces behind the world's governments. The Satanic side of this tension is perhaps difficult to bear but carries strong biblical support. Several passages depict Satan as the ruler of the world (John 12:31, 14:30, 16:11; 2 Cor. 4:4; Eph. 2:2; 1 John 5:19). Satan offers Jesus all the nations of the world in one of the desert temptations (Matt. 4:8-9). Jesus does not contest the premise. Elswhere, Jesus affirms that Satan has his own kingdom (Matt. 12:26). The obvious inference is that Satan's kingdom consists of the nations of the world. This inference finds substantiation in a fascinating but chilling set of passages:

1. After being visited by an angel, Daniel is told that the angel's journey involved warfare with the Prince of Persia and the Prince of

Greece (Daniel 10:13, 20). Apparently, demonic powers are associated with earthly nations and make war against God and his angels.

2. While denouncing the king of Babylon, Isaiah uses language for the king that applies to Satan (Isa. 14:12-15). Isaiah calls the king Lucifer. He describes how the king wanted to be like God yet was cast down. Isaiah was evidently speaking to the power that lay behind the king.
3. While denouncing the king of Tyre, Ezekiel also speaks to the king as if he were Satan (Ezek. 28:12-17). He says the king lived in Eden, was once a beautiful cherub, but became proud and was cast down—language impossible to apply to any mortal.
4. The famous beasts of Revelation 13 are "none other than the governing and political and economic powers of the earth."[1] "When we are shown a beast whose power is…of government ('diadems' and a 'throne'), who combines all the powers of Daniel 7, and whose authority is worldwide (verse 7), we see in him the principle of power politics: in a word, the state."[2]

This understanding should permanently change how followers of Jesus view the earthly nations of the world. Some find this conclusion counterintuitive because some nations of this world do not seem very bad. Many of them even claim to follow God. Yet this veneer of righteousness covers a trapdoor. "For Satan himself transforms himself into an angel of light. Therefore it is no great thing if his ministers also transform themselves into ministers of righteousness, whose end will be according to their works" (2 Cor. 11:14-15). Appearing righteous is precisely the deception of the dragon, the beast, and the false prophet. These three attempt to mimic the holy Trinity and exalt virtue. But the righteousness of Satan and his ministers is filled with compromise and licentiousness; this false righteousness advances the antinomian insurrection against Jesus' kingship.

Understanding the Satanic power behind earthly nations should precede attempts to answer questions about government involvement. With that conviction, it should be obvious that Christians should play no part in serving these hostile powers. Christians belong to another

---

[1] G. K. Beale, *The Book of Revelation: A Commentary on the Greek Text*, Eerdmans (1999), p. 680. Beale notes, "The dragon in Revelation 12 was seen as the ultimate force behind the kingdoms of the world" (p. 683). Also, "The 'blasphemies' written on the beast's heads represent his blasphemous claims to earthly, divine kingship, in feeble imitation of Christ's true kingship" (p. 684).

[2] Michael Wilcock, *The Message of Revelation*, InterVarsity Press (1975), pp. 123-124.

nation and cannot serve in competing governments. Other arguments can be marshaled:

1. Jesus' example was to decline positions of office. The people tried to make Jesus king, but He withdrew (John 6:15). Furthermore, He had numerous opportunities to weigh into politics, particularly given the conflict between Israel and Rome but always refrained.
2. Christians are called citizens of heaven (Phil. 3:20), "ambassadors" (2 Cor. 5:20; Eph. 6:20), and "strangers and pilgrims" (Heb. 11:12). Can a foreign ambassador stand for election in an alien country? Should a citizen of one nation meddle in the affairs of another government? Strangers and pilgrims are those who respectfully pass through, not those who try to govern.
3. In Romans 13:1-7, Paul refers to the authorities in the third person (they) and to Christians in the second person (you). Evidently, Paul did not envision that Christians would be authorities in government.
4. Particularly in a democracy, no true Christian could ever be sufficiently popular to win the majority vote. Those who desire to live a godly life will suffer persecution (2 Tim. 3:12) and will be hated by all for Jesus' sake (Matt. 10:22). Speaking Christian truth would eliminate the possibility of success in an election. Any victor in a democratic election must have compromised.
5. The entire model of the world's leadership is opposed to what Jesus taught. "You know that the rulers of the Gentiles lord it over them, and those who are great exercise authority over them. *Yet it shall not be so among you*; but whoever desires to become great among you, let him be your servant." (Matt. 20:25-26)
6. To serve in worldly governments will inevitably lead to compromise and sin. A discerning eye will see much sin in every government, enshrined in its laws and in its practices. Consider abortion, divorce and remarriage, war, and state education. No faithful disciple could endorse or preside over these ways.
7. No government in history has been nonresistant. The sword is ordained for governments (Rom. 13:4) but not for Christians (Matt. 26:52, John 18:11). Serving as a police officer or government official thus involves breaking the Sermon on the Mount's teaching on nonresistance (see previous chapter). A disciple should not compromise Jesus' teaching by participating in the governments of this world.
8. Jesus' prohibition against oaths naturally prevents Christians

from serving in government offices. Jesus prohibits swearing "at all" (Matt. 5:34). His command is reinforced by James: "But above all, my brethren, do not swear, either by heaven or by earth or with any other oath. But let your 'Yes,' be 'Yes,' and your 'No,' 'No,' lest you fall into judgment" (James 5:12). These strong commands demand our attention. "Did Jesus realize that not to swear *at all* would constantly put disciples in unavoidable and unenviable tension with governments all of which have historically required oaths?"[3] For this reason, Jesus' teachings concerning oaths and nonresistance (Matt. 5:33-42) have been called the political commands of the Sermon on the Mount.

9. Followers of Jesus have a higher calling than to serve earthly nations. Christians are called to serve Jesus' nation, the church, and so bless the world.

This stance accords with the testimony of persecuted, suffering people of God. The early church taught that it was impermissible to serve in government.[4] This stance has always been an emphasis of the Anabaptists.

The most common objection to this position is a pragmatic one. Many say, "It is a noble calling to serve in government and be a light for the Lord, potentially influencing policy and helping millions of people." This objection relies heavily on a counterfactual, "Unless the church sends people into government, the world will descend into sin." But what if Christians had put as much time, energy, and money into building up the church and caring for the poor as into earthly politics? Is it possible that the world might be a vastly better place? The objection does not address the fact that since Constantine, professing Christians have served in government, and it has consistently marred the church's witness. Rather than bring light to the world, this choice has too often darkened the church. To all these pragmatic objections Jesus says, "What is that to you? You follow Me" (John 21:22).

Another intriguing line of thought merits consideration. Might it be that God intended for Christians to be purified through persecution and hardship? To then seek government office and lobby against such trials would fight against God's intentions. Despite the hardship and persecution that the apostles endured, they did not seek positions of power or advise Christians to do so. Perhaps one reason that the church is spoiled and weak today is that we have run from the chastisement that

---

[3] F. D. Bruner, *Matthew: A Commentary, Volume 1*, Eerdmans (2007), pp. 237-238.

[4] See entry under "Public office" in *A Dictionary of Early Christian Beliefs*, David Bercot (ed.), Hendrickson (1998).

our loving Father intends (Heb. 12:6).

The implications for voting are similar. Voting is a smaller example of government involvement. Advocates of voting offer pragmatic arguments, and Christians are advised to vote for "the lesser of two evils." Yet the spirit of compromise infiltrates these arguments and their adherents. A professor at an evangelical seminary has said, "There is no vote cast that does not require some measure of forgiveness."[5] While most Protestants and evangelicals acknowledge that all candidates and parties advocate sinful positions, they tend to overweight the importance of certain sins and underweight others. Such selectivity is founded upon antinomian thinking.

The lesser of two evils is in fact a tacit acceptance of sin under the cover of an "ends justify the means" argument. Yet when Jesus was tempted by Satan to worship him, Jesus showed by His actions that the ends do not justify the means. Jesus could never accept sin, even if it could spare Himself and others a great deal of misery and suffering. The church needs to recover Jesus' uncompromising stance.

[5] J. Daniel Kirk of Fuller Seminary, www.jrdkirk.com.

Chapter 19

The principle of separation

Adulterers and adulteresses! Do you not know that friendship with the world is enmity with God? Whoever therefore wants to be a friend of the world makes himself an enemy of God. (James 4:4)

Surrounding the practical teachings of Jesus, there are two bookends of kingdom faith. The bookends are nonresistance and separation from the world. These teachings distinguish kingdom churches from most modern churches. But there is an important difference between nonresistance and separation. Nonresistance is often admired by the world while separation is despised. Many figures in history have been admired for their stance on pacifism and nonviolence. They include Henry David Thoreau, Albert Einstein, Mohandas Gandhi, Leo Tolstoy, Martin Luther King Jr., and Aung San Suu Kyi. While both nonresistance and separation are countercultural stances, separation from the world more often incurs the contempt of the world. For example, those affiliated with liberal political positions tend to admire nonresistance but look down on separation.

The pressures to conform to the world, the pressures not to separate, are inestimably high. The real barriers to the church to living separate from the world are social and psychological, not theological. Few people even understand their own hearts well enough to perceive how powerful these pressures are. Crossing the bridge of separation from the world means losing the approval of friends, colleagues, and family members. It means not being "cool" or fashionable. It means being accused of being narrow-minded or a Pharisee. For many, this is too heavy a cross to bear.

Losing separation is historically the first chink in a church's armor. This loss blinds the church from seeing the antinomian trapdoor toward *status quo*. Mark it well: every church that fails with separation will eventually be swallowed up by the worldly churches, or even by the world itself. Churches that fail to practice separation lose the qualities that mark a nation. They become more like social clubs. People come and go, denomination and church hopping, and weak-group behavior prevails.

The modern evangelical church trumpets a desire for community. But without strong separation from the world, community is impossible. Churches and individuals are not willing to pay the cost. Sometimes a man sees separation in Scripture and recognizes its truth. But because of a relationship with a woman who loves fashion, jewelry, or something else in the world, the man quietly sheds his convictions. Sometimes a woman sees separation in Scripture and is ready to obey. But because her husband or boyfriend loves his sports, television, or a worldly career, she will regress to the lukewarmness of the apostate church. For some, the family tension is too great to bear. For others, it is the pull of friends or coworkers. Biblical separation is demanding. But genuine community, durable vibrancy, and sustainable growth are predicated upon it.

Biblical perspectives on separation

Separation from the world is a recurrent teaching of the Old and New Testaments. Old Testament Israel was often plagued with sins that came from close contact with other nations. This contact led them to sexual immorality, a desire for a human king, idolatry, child sacrifice, and false doctrine. Lack of separation from the world was perhaps Israel's primary problem. God commanded His people to drive out the inhabitants of Canaan, which Israel failed to do. The remaining Canaanites snared Israel into sin patterns from which they would never escape. But hope punctuated this bleak situation. The heroes and prophets of Israel affirmed the blessing and virtue of separation: Abraham's separation is contrasted with Lot's mingling with the world; Daniel refuses to eat the king's table and is blessed; Ezra opposes pagan intermarriage and rescues the nation.

The word *holiness* means "to be set apart." "Separation" and being "set apart" are closely related, making separation a key dimension of holiness. While many Scriptures affirm separation from the world (John 15:19; Rom. 12:2; Eph. 5:11; 1 John 2:15-17; Rev. 18:4), the most commonly cited passage on separation is: " 'Come out from among them and be separate, says the Lord. Do not touch what is unclean, and I will receive you.' 'I will be a Father to you, and you shall be My sons and daughters, says the Lord Almighty' " (2 Cor. 6:17-18). The context of this passage is involvement in pagan temple practices (2 Cor. 6:15-16). During the first century, the temple was the city's center of social activity. Temples functioned almost like restaurants. They served as locations for birthday celebrations, special occasions, and stimulating conversation.[1] The Corinthians were participating in temple feasts and eating meat offered to idols, rationalizing this practice on the basis that idols were "nothing in the world" (1 Cor. 8:4). Paul responds by explaining that the temple practices had real spiritual power and that to eat at temple feasts was to join oneself to the demonic (1 Cor. 10:20-22). Paul also reminds them that, "Bad company ruins good morals" (1 Cor. 15:33 ESV). Because so much of life revolved around temples in the first century, the sin of eating meat sacrificed to idols had to be repeatedly rebuked (Acts 15:29, 21:25; 1 Cor. 8-10; Rev. 2:14, 2:20). The Corinthian Christians struggled to extricate themselves from these patterns. As we noted in chapter 9, cultural conformity and cultural relativism were the primary problems of the church in Corinth. This conformity led them to lawsuits, sexual immorality, wrong views of marriage, participation in idol feasts, defilement of the Lord's Supper, false doctrine, and a tol erance of sin.

Because this issue of separation from the world has been such an area of failure of the people of God in both the Old and New Testaments, we must be especially vigilant. Surely we are not immune from this same area of temptation. Indeed, one of the greatest problems of churches today is lack of separation from the world.

Separation from the world is closely related to being part of a strong-group church and practicing discipleship as intensive companionship (chapters 3 and 4). These are different facets of the same jewel. Separation stakes out a biblical culture, forging a Christian social order with a unique identity and distinctive practices. Separation is required because there are two opposing kingdoms at war—a person is either on one side or the other. "No one can serve two masters" (Matt. 6:24). To be allied with the world is to be opposed to God (James 4:4; 1 John 2:15). This polarity should naturally drive each person to choose his or her side.

While it is easy to make separation only about outward practices, these are the outworking of something more fundamental. Separation begins in the heart and mind: "If then you were raised with Christ, seek those things which are above, where Christ is, sitting at the right hand of God. Set your mind on things above, not on things on the earth. For

[1] Ben Witherington III, *Conflict and Community in Corinth*, Eerdmans (1995), pp. 188-195.

you died, and your life is hidden with Christ in God" (Col. 3:1-3). A good starting point to ascertain one's degree of separation from the world is to ask:

- What do I think of when I go to bed at night?
- What are the first thoughts of my mind when I wake up?
- What does my mind drift to during the meetings of the church?
- What is my pleasure reading?
- What activities bring me the greatest joy?

No one may answer these questions for another person, because they involve searching the heart. If your answers are not centered on the Lord, then you should question your heart. Layering on outwardly separate actions cannot change the heart.

Biblical separation is not physical or geographic separation. This has been the error of various monastic communities and other groups that remove themselves from society. Paul in fact speaks against that practice (1 Cor. 5:10). The church at Corinth was situated in a densely populated, urban area. Nowhere are they charged to move to another location and live in isolation. Rather they are to preach the gospel in their city in word and action, demonstrating the power of Jesus working through the holy, separate people of God. They are to be in the world—evangelizing and ministering to unbelievers. But they are not to be of the world—engaging in the same pleasures and practices.

If one's thoughts and heart are with King Jesus seated in heaven above, everything changes. Because separation begins in the heart and mind, it radiates out and touches all aspects of life. It certainly touches fashion, but this is a small portion of what separation involves. It affects one's speech, associations, hobbies, occupation, courtship, marriage, home life, recreation, and worship.

Historic arguments for separation

Two historic arguments support a case for separation from the world: the testimony of those who have gone before us, and the trajectories of churches that neglect separation. Regarding those who have gone before us, successful evangelists have lamented their failure to teach separation. Near the end of his life, John Wesley wrote:

> I am distressed. I know not what to do. I see what I might have done once. I might have said peremptorily and expressly, "Here I am; I and my Bible. I will not, I dare not

> vary from this Book either in great things or small. I have no power to dispense with one jot or tittle of what is contained therein. I am determined to be a Bible Christian, not almost, but altogether. Who will meet me on this ground? Join me on this, or not at all." With regard to dress in particular, I might have been as firm (and I now see it would have been far better,) as either the people called Quakers, or the Moravian brethren. I might have said, "This is our manner of dress which we know is both scriptural and rational. If you join with us, you are to dress as we do; but you need not join us unless you please." But, alas! The time is now past; and what I can do now, I cannot tell.[2]

Charles Finney expressed a similar sentiment:

> The question now regards fashion, in dress, [ornaments], and so on. And here I will confess that I was formerly myself in error. I believed, and I taught, that the best way for Christians to pursue, was to dress so as not to be noticed, to follow the fashions and changes so as not to appear singular, and that nobody would be led to think of their being different from others in these particulars. But I have seen my error, and now wonder greatly at my former blindness. It is your duty to dress so plain as to show to the world, that you place no sort of reliance in the things of fashion, and set no value at all on them, but despise and neglect them altogether. But unless you are singular, unless you separate yourselves from the fashions of the world, you show that you do value them. There is no way in which you can bear a proper testimony by your lives against the fashions of the world, but by dressing plain.[3]

The trajectories of churches over time are instructive. Protestant and modern evangelical churches have traditionally not emphasized separation from the world, so there is little trajectory to follow. But among the churches that have taught separation from the world there is much to be learned. The ante-Nicene church generally taught separation in matters of fashion, entertainment, and government involve-

[2] John Wesley, "Inefficacy of Christianity," (Sermon CXX) in *The Works of the Reverend John Wesley: Volume II*, J. Emory and B. Waugh (1831), p. 439.

[3] Charles Finney, *Lectures to Professing Christians*, Brick Church Chapel (1837), p. 107.

ment.[4] The early church's ruin came partly from bringing the state into the church (see chapter 17). Other groups that taught separation include the Waldensians, Lollards, and Anabaptists. For each of these groups, losing separation has been the first step down the slope toward laxity and worldliness.[5] Sadly, most modern Anabaptist groups have lost the separation from the world that their spiritual predecessors held and only hold vestiges of nonresistance.

Besides the arguments of cultural relativism, churches justify blending with the world on the grounds of being "seeker-sensitive" or being ecumenical in order to learn from others. (As stated above, the actual reasons are nearly always social and psychological, but these are the stated reasons.) The poisonous compromise with sin does not lead to a violent, convulsive death, but rather a slow, sleepy death. We must be vigilant.

[4] This is a major theme of David Bercot's corpus. His lectures and books on the subject are available from Scroll Publishing.

[5] For a historic survey, see J. C. Wenger, *Separated Unto God*, Sword and Trumpet (1979), pp. 47-88.

Chapter 20

Separation in fashion

Do not be conformed to this world. (Romans 12:2)

Because of pride, the Pharisees loved attention and admiration (Matt. 23:5-7). Because of pride, the Pharisees sought outward adornment (Matt. 23:6). Because of pride, just like the Pharisees, millions of people have sought attention and admiration through fashion, jewelry, and cosmetics. Indeed, the goddesses of fashion and jewelry have snared more devotees into false worship than all the idols of wood and stone of history combined. Despite clear teachings on this subject in the New Testament, the ministers and pastors of today shrink from declaring the whole counsel of God. And the more the sin is practiced, the more professing Christians rationalize away Scripture, thinking, "But it just *can't* mean that." As separation from the world has dimmed, the temptation to dress like the world has strengthened.

Because this topic has suffered from so much neglect, we will approach it from three different perspectives. First, we will read one of the most remarkable letters ever written on the subject, penned by Adoniram Judson. Second, we will meditate on the heart principle behind the New Testament commands and draw out contemporary applications. Finally, we will answer objections made to the historic interpretation of Scripture.

An earnest plea

(This section reproduces a letter written by Adoniram Judson, the first person to leave American soil as a missionary.[1] *At the age of twenty-five,*

[1] Text from Francis Wayland, *A Memoir of the Life and Labors of the Rev. Adoniram Judson: Volume II*, Philips, Sampson, and Company (1853), pp. 476-485.

Judson left for Burma, now Myanmar, where he served as a missionary for almost 40 years.)

Dear Sisters in Christ: Excuse my publicly addressing you. The necessity of the case is my only apology. Whether you will consider it a sufficient apology for the sentiments of this letter,—unfashionable, I confess, and perhaps unpalatable,—I know not. We are sometimes obliged to encounter the hazard of offending those whom of all others we desire to please. Let me throw myself at once on your mercy, dear sisters, allied by national consanguinity, professors of the same holy religion, fellow-pilgrims to the same happy world. Pleading these endearing ties, let me beg you to regard me as a brother, and to listen with candor and forbearance to my honest tale.

In raising up a church of Christ in this heathen land, and in laboring to elevate the minds of the female converts to the standard of the Gospel, we have always found one chief obstacle in that principle of vanity, that love of dress and display,—I beg you will bear with me,—which has, in every age and in all countries, been a ruling passion of the fair sex, as the love of riches, power, and fame has characterized the other. That obstacle lately became more formidable, through the admission of two or three fashionable females into the church, and the arrival of several missionary sisters, dressed and adorned in that manner which is too prevalent in our beloved native land. On my meeting the church, after a year's absence, I beheld an appalling profusion of ornaments, and saw that the demon of vanity was laying waste the female department. At that time I had not maturely considered the subject, and did not feel sure what ground I ought to take. I apprehended, also, that I should be unsupported, and perhaps opposed, by some of my coadjutors. I confined my efforts, therefore, to private exhortation, and with but little effect. Some of the ladies, out of regard to their pastor's feelings, took off their necklaces and ear ornaments before they entered the chapel, tied them up in a corner of their handkerchiefs, and on returning, as soon as they were out of sight of the mission house, stopped in the middle of the street to array themselves anew.

In the meantime, I was called to visit the Karens, a wild people, several days' journey to the north of Maulmain. Little did I expect there to encounter the same enemy, in those "wilds, horrid and dark with o'ershadowing trees." But I found that he had been there before me, and reigned with a peculiar sway from time immemorial. On one Karen woman I counted between twelve and fifteen necklaces, of all colors, sizes, and materials. Three was the average. Brass belts above the ankles; neat braids of black hair tied below the knees; rings of all sorts on the fingers; bracelets on the wrists and arms, long instruments of some metal, perforating the lower part of the ear, by an immense aperture, and reaching nearly to the shoulders; fancifully-constructed bags enclosing the hair, and suspended from the back part of the head; not to speak of the ornamental parts of their clothing,—constituted the fashions and the ton of the fair Karenesses. The dress of the female converts was not essentially different from that of their countrywomen. I saw that I was brought into a situation that precluded all retreat—that I must fight or die.

For a few nights, I spent some sleepless hours, distressed by this and other subjects, which will always press upon the heart of a missionary in a new place. I considered the spirit of the religion of Jesus Christ. I opened to 1 Tim. ii. 9, and read those words of the inspired apostle: "I will, also, that women adorn themselves in modest apparel, with shamefacedness and sobriety; *not with broidered hair, or gold, or pearls, or costly array.*" I asked myself, Can I baptize a Karen woman in her present attire? No. Can I administer the Lord's Supper to one of the baptized in that attire? No. Can I refrain from enforcing the prohibition of the apostle? Not without betraying the trust which I have received from him. Again: I considered that the question concerned not the Karens only, but the whole Christian world; that its decision would involve a train of unknown consequences; that a single step would lead me into a long and perilous way. I considered Maulmain and the other stations; I considered the state of the public mind at home. But "what is that to thee? Follow thou me," was the continual response, and weighed more than all. I renewedly offered myself to Christ, and prayed for strength to go forward in the path of duty, come life or death, come praise or reproach, supported or deserted, successful or defeated in the ultimate issue.

Soon after coming to this conclusion, a Karen woman offered herself for baptism. After the usual examination, I inquired whether she could give up her ornaments for Christ. It was an unexpected blow! I explained the spirit of the gospel. I appealed to her own consciousness of vanity. I read her the apostle's prohibition. She looked again and again at her handsome necklace,—she wore but one, —and then, with an air of modest decision that would adorn, beyond all outward ornaments, any of my sisters whom I have the honour of addressing, she took it off, saying, *I love Christ more than this.* The news began to spread. The Christian women made but little hesitation. A few others opposed, but the work went on.

At length the evil which I most dreaded came on me. Some of the Karen men had been to Maulmain, and seen what I wished they had not; and one day, when we were discussing the subject of ornaments, one of the Christians came forward, and declared that at Maulmain he had actually seen one of the great female teachers wearing a string of gold beads around her neck.

Lay down this paper, dear sisters, and sympathize a moment with your fallen missionary. Was it not a hard case? However, though cast down, I was not destroyed; I endeavored to maintain the warfare as well as I could, and when I left those parts, the female converts were, generally speaking, arrayed in modest apparel.

On arriving at Maulmain, Burma and partially recovering from a fever, which I had contracted in the Karen woods, the first thing I did was to crawl out to the house of the patroness of the gold necklace. To her I related my adventures, and described my grief. With what ease, and truth too, could that sister say, "I dress more plainly than most ministers' wives, and professors of religion in our native land! This necklace is the only ornament I wear; it was given me when quite a child, by a dear mother, whom I never expect to see again, (another hard case,) and she begged me never to part with it as long as I lived, but to wear it as a memorial of her." Oh, ye Christian mothers, what a lesson you have before you! Can you, dare you, give injunctions to your daughters, directly contrary to apostolic commands? But, to the honor of my sister, be it recorded, that, as soon as she understood the merits of the case, and the mischief done by such an example, off went the gold necklace, and she gave decisive proof that she loved Christ more than father or mother. Her example, united with the efforts of the rest of us at this station, is beginning to exercise a redeeming influence in the female department of the church.

But, notwithstanding these favorable signs, nothing, really nothing, is yet done! And why? This mission and all others must necessarily be sustained by continual supplies of missionaries, male and female, from the mother country. Your sisters and daughters will continually come out, to take the place of those who are removed by death, and to occupy numberless stations, still unoccupied. And when they arrive they will be dressed in their usual way, as Christian women at home are dressed. And the female converts will run around them, and gaze upon them with the most prying curiosity, regarding them as the freshest representations of the Christian religion from that land where it flourishes in all its purity and glory. And when they see the gold and jewels pendent from their ears, the beads and chains encircling their necks, the finger rings set with diamonds and rubies, the rich variety of ornamental hair dress, "the mantles and the wimples and the crisping pins," (see Is. iii. 19,23,) they will cast a reproachful, triumphant glance at their old teachers, and spring with fresh avidity, to repurchase and resume their long-neglected elegancies; the cheering news will fly up to the Dah-gyne, the Laing-bwai, and the Salwen; the Karenesses will reload their necks, and ears, and arms, and ankles; and when, after another year's absence, I return, and take my seat before the Burmese or the Karen church, I shall behold the demon of vanity enthroned in the centre of the assembly, more firmly than ever, grinning defiance to the prohibitions of apostles, and the exhortations of us who would fain be their humble followers. And thus you, my dear sisters, sitting quietly by your firesides, or repairing devoutly to your places of worship, do, by your example, spread the poison of vanity through all the rivers, and mountains, and wilds of this far distant land; and, while you are sincerely and fervently praying for the upbuilding of the Redeemer's kingdom, are inadvertently building up that of the devil. If, on the other hand, you divest yourselves of all meretricious ornaments, your sisters and daughters, who come hither will be divested of course; the further supplies of vanity and pride will be cut off, and the churches at home being kept pure, the churches here will be pure also.

Dear sisters: Having finished my tale, and therein exhibited the necessity under which I lay of addressing you, I beg leave to submit a few topics to your candid and prayerful consideration.

1. Let me appeal to conscience, and inquire, What is the real motive for wearing ornamental and costly apparel? Is it not the desire of setting off one's person to the best advantage, and of exciting the love and admiration of others? Is not such dress calculated to gratify self-love, and cherish sentiments of vanity and pride? And is it not the nature of those sentiments to acquire strength from indulgence? Do such motives and sentiments comport with the meek, humble, self-denying religion of Jesus Christ? I would here respectfully suggest, that these questions will not be answered so faithfully in the midst of company as when quite alone, kneeling before God.

2. Consider the words of the apostle quoted above from 1. Tim. ii 9; "I will also that women adorn themselves in modest apparel, with shamefacedness and sobriety, *not with broidered hair, or gold, or pearls, or costly array.*" I do not quote a similar command recorded in 1 Pet. iii. 3, because the verbal construction is not quite so definite, though the import of the two passages is the same. But cannot the force of these passages be evaded? Yes, and nearly every command in Scripture can be evaded, and every doctrinal assertion perverted, plausibly and handsomely too, if we set about it in good earnest. But preserving the posture above alluded to, with the inspired volume spread open at the passage in question, ask your hearts, in simplicity and godly sincerity, whether

the meaning is not just as plain as the sun at noonday. Shall we then bow to the authority of an inspired apostle, or shall we not? From that authority, shall we appeal to the prevailing usages and fashions of the age? If so, please to recall the missionaries you have sent to the heathen; for the heathen can vindicate all their superstitions on the same ground.

3. In the posture you have assumed, look up and behold the eye of your benignant Saviour ever gazing upon you, with the tenderest love—upon you, his daughters, his spouse, wishing above all things, that you would yield your hearts entirely to him, and become holy as he is holy, rejoicing when he sees one after another accepting his pressing invitation, and entering the more perfect way.

4. Anticipate the happy moment, "hastening on all the wings of time," when your joyful spirits will be welcomed into the assembly of the spirits of the just made perfect. You appear before the throne of Jehovah; the approving smile of Jesus fixes your everlasting happy destiny; and you are plunging into "the sea of life and love unknown; without a bottom or a shore." Stop a moment; look back on yonder dark and miserable world that you have left; fix your eye on the meagre, vain, contemptible articles of ornamental dress, which you once hesitated to give up for Christ, the King of glory; and on that glance decide the question instantly and forever.

Surely, you can hold out no longer. You cannot rise from your knees in your present attire. Thanks be to God, I see you taking off your necklaces and earrings, tearing away your ribbons, and ruffles, and superfluities of headdress, and I hear you exclaim, What shall we do next?—an important question, deserving serious consideration. The ornaments you are removing, though useless, and worse than useless, in their present state, can be so disposed of as to feed the hungry, clothe the naked, relieve the sick, enlighten the dark minded, disseminate the Holy Scriptures, spread the glorious gospel throughout the world. Little do the inhabitants of a free Christian country know of the want and distress endured by the greater part of the inhabitants of the earth. Still less idea can they form of the awful darkness which rests upon the great mass of mankind in regard to spiritual things. During the years that you have been wearing these useless ornaments, how many poor creatures have been pining in want! How many have languished and groaned on beds of abject wretchedness! How many children have been bred up in the blackest ignorance, hardened in all manner of iniquity! How many immortal souls have gone down to hell, with a lie in their right hand, having never heard of the true God and the only Savior! Some of these miseries might have been mitigated; some poor wretch have felt his pain relieved; some widow's heart been made to sing for joy; some helpless orphan have been taught in the Sabbath school, and trained up for a happy life here and hereafter. The Holy Bible and valuable tracts might have been far more extensively circulated in heathen lands had you not been afraid of being thought unfashionable, and not "like other folks;" had you not preferred adorning your persons, and cherishing the sweet seductive feelings of vanity and pride.

O Christian sisters, believers in God, in Christ, in an eternal heaven, and an eternal hell, can you hesitate, and ask what you shall do? Bedew those ornaments with the tears of contrition; consecrate them to the cause of charity; hang them on the cross of your dying Lord. Delay not an instant. Hasten with all your might, if not to make reparation for the past, at least to prevent a continuance of the evil in future.

And for your guidance allow me to suggest two fundamental principles —the one based on 1 Tim. ii. 9—*all ornaments and costly dress to be disused*; the other on the law of general benevolence —*the avails of such articles, and the savings resulting from the plain dress system, to be devoted to purposes of charity*. Some general rules in regard to dress, and some general objects of charity, may be easily ascertained, and free discussion will throw light on many points at first obscure. Be not deterred by the suggestion, that in such discussions you are conversant about *small* things. Great things depend on small; and, in that case, things which appear small to shortsighted man are great in the sight of God. Many there are who praise the principle of self-denial in general, and condemn it in all its particular applications, as too minute, scrupulous, and severe. The enemy is well aware, that if he can secure the minute units, the sum total will be his own. Think not anything small, which may have a bearing upon the kingdom of Christ, and upon the destinies of eternity. How easy to conceive, from many known events, that the single fact of a lady's divesting herself of a necklace for Christ's sake may involve consequences which shall be felt in the remotest parts of the earth, and in all future generations to the end of time—yea, stretch away into a boundless eternity, and be a subject of praise millions of ages after this world and all its ornaments are burned up.

Beware of another suggestion made by weak and erring souls, who will tell you that there is more danger of being proud of plain dress and other modes of self-denial, than of fashionable attire and self indulgence. Be not in-snared by this last, most finished, most insidious device of the great enemy. Rather believe that He who enables you to make a sacrifice is able to keep you from being proud of it. Believe that he will kindly permit such occasions of mortification and shame as will preserve you from the evil threatened. *The severest part of self-denial consists in encountering the disapprobation, the envy, the hatred, of one's dearest friends.* All who enter the strait and narrow path in good earnest soon find themselves in a climate extremely uncongenial to the growth of pride.

The gay and fashionable will, in many cases, be the last to engage in this holy undertaking. But let none be discouraged on that account. Christ has seldom honored the leaders of worldly fashion, by appointing them leaders in his cause. Fix it in your hearts that in this warfare *the Lord Jesus Christ expects every woman to do her duty.* There is probably not one in the humblest walks of life but would, on strict examination, find some article which *might* be dispensed with for purposes of charity, and *ought* to be dispensed with in compliance with the apostolic command.

Wait not, therefore, for the fashionable to set an example; wait not for one another; listen not to the news from the next town; but *let every individual go forward*, regardless of reproach, fearless of consequences. The eye of Christ is upon you. Death is hastening to strip you of your ornaments, and to turn your fair forms into corruption and dust. Many of those for whom this letter is designed will be laid in the grave before it can ever reach their eyes. We shall all soon appear before the judgment seat of Christ, to be tried for our conduct, and to receive the things done in the body. When placed before that awful bar, in the presence of that Being, whose eyes are as a flame of fire, and whose irrevocable fiat will fix you forever in heaven or in hell, and mete out the measure of your everlasting pleasures and pains, what course will you wish you had taken? Will you then wish that, in defiance of his authority, you had adorned your mortal bodies with gold, and precious stones, and costly attire, cherishing self-love, vanity, and pride? Or, will you wish that you had chosen a life of self-denial, renounced the world, taken up the cross *daily* and followed him? *And as you will then wish you had done*, do now.

Dear Sisters, your affectionate brother in Christ,

A. Judson
Maulmain, October, 1831.

Biblical reflections

Two New Testament passages speak directly to the issue of fashion:

> Women should adorn themselves in respectable apparel, with modesty and self-control, not with braided hair and

> gold or pearls or costly attire, but with what is proper for women who profess godliness—with good works. (1 Tim. 2:9-10 ESV)
>
> Do not let your adorning be external—the braiding of hair and the putting on of gold jewelry, or the clothing you wear—but let your adorning be the hidden person of the heart with the imperishable beauty of a gentle and quiet spirit, which in God's sight is very precious. (1 Pet. 3:3-4 ESV)

These passages share obvious similarities, including the order that various items are mentioned—first hair, then gold, then clothing. Paul and Peter were speaking against elaborate hairstyles, jewelry, expensive clothing, or other similar ornaments. This plain understanding was held by the early church.[2]

Lest we fall into a legalistic mentality in understanding these passage, three things should be stated. First, this must not only apply to women, but also to men. Men often seek attention through clothing and jewelry just like women, and sometimes even in other ways, such as through the muscular build of their bodies. Second, the teaching must apply to *anything that is outward that is used to gain attention.* Besides gold, pearls, and expensive clothes, we must include styling the hair, dyeing the hair, seeking excessively thin bodies, "painting the eyes" (made famous by Jezebel in 2 Kings 9:30 and practiced by the two prostitutes of Ezek. 23:40), cosmetics, extravagant watches, fashionable eyeglasses, necklaces, bracelets, earrings, piercings, tattoos (also see Lev. 19:28), tight clothing, nail painting, high heels, and showing midriff, provocative skin, or chest. For are these not all various manifestations of seeking external beauty? These are the pursuits of the modern Pharisees. While the letter of 1 Tim. 2:9-10 and 1 Pet. 3:3-4 does not address these manifestations, the spirit surely does. Third, it is most important to remember that this teaching flows from a principle, a heart-attitude of not seeking to gain the admiration of others. The foundational principle is simply, *do not seek approval, attention, or admiration through fashion or outward adornment.*

The apostle calls for modesty in 1 Timothy 2:9-10. But how do we define modesty? There are three witnesses as to what constitutes mod-

[2] David Bercot has an audio lecture on this topic entitled "What the Early Christians taught about Modest Dress and Cosmetics," available from Scroll Publishing. Or see my essay, "Views from Church History on Fashion, Adornment, and Jewelry" on www.anchorcross.org.

esty: first, the Scriptures; second, "nature itself" (1 Cor. 11:14), which includes the received wisdom throughout the ages; third, understanding what is sexually provocative. Integrating these sources, the Bible consistently teaches that baring the legs is associated with shame (Exod. 20:26, Isa. 47:1-4, Jer. 13:22-26). Because God regards exposure of the legs to be nakedness, shorts (men's or women's), short skirts, or short dresses are not appropriate for the Christian. Jesus gives us His example that his robe extends down to his feet.[3] There can be no better standard than Jesus' example. Even in much of the Eastern non-Christian world, such as India or China, this has been the standard for centuries. Only comparatively recently has the West descended into shame. Next, clothes should not be form fitting or transparent. Clothing should cover and not reveal. A descending neckline, very common in Western clothing for women, must be avoided as it serves to expose and draw attention to the chest. Covering the shoulders has been judged to be modest by the witness of "nature itself" and understanding what is sexually provocative.

Deuteronomy 22:5 commands that women and men wear distinct clothing and that to violate this is an abomination. There are time-honored expressions of these distinctions in varying regions, and these boundaries should be respected. In America, dresses or skirts for women and slacks for men represents a traditional distinction that nicely serves this purpose. History also should inform our practice. American women began to wear pants in the early twentieth century as expressions of new workplace status, rebellion, lesbian behavior, or androgynous fashion. The Christian should avoid practices rooted in rebellion or paganism.

Believers should model Christian simplicity, with clothes that are economical and subdued in color, pattern, and design, showing that they are dead to the world and the world is dead to them (Gal. 6:14). Young people often aim for a "cool" appearance that is designed to project a certain image. Many are so accustomed to pursuing stylishness they have lost self-awareness of their motivations. Often professing Christians seek admiration by wearing torn clothes or having a disheveled appearance. "Random" logos and designs are also often thought to be fashionable. Believers are called to be ambassadors of King Jesus—not of a worldly clothing or shoe company, a university, a city, or an earthly nation. Of course, there may be situations of abject poverty where the only available clothing is handed down and may not fit this description. But whenever possible Christians should be known

[3] See Rev. 1:13. Unfortunately, many translations do not render the literal sense, "a garment down to the feet."

for their separation from the world.

The wedding ring

My wife and I exchanged rings as part of our wedding vows and wore simple gold bands after our marriage (acknowledging that some may call "simple gold" an oxymoron). We had "I am my beloved's and my beloved is mine" inscribed in Hebrew letters on our bands. We wore our rings as a symbol of fidelity and a public sign of exclusive commitment. But we eventually felt compelled to remove them for several reasons. First, the Bible speaks against wearing gold (1 Tim. 2:9-10; 1 Pet. 3:3-4), and offers no exception. We were forced to ask if we would follow culture or the Scriptures.

Again, historical considerations offer insight. Nowhere mentioned in Scripture, they originate from pagan practices.[4] Indeed, rings have been bound up with magical thinking since their origins. They were used in Egypt in the second millennium BC and drawn into Greco-Roman practice. Evidence of the use of rings in betrothal can be found by the second century BC.[5] The first betrothal rings were iron, but by the second century AD these rings were generally gold. The fourth finger was chosen because of an ancient belief that a nerve or vein coursed from that finger directly to the heart.[6]

The custom of the diamond ring took root in the early twentieth century when diamond giant DeBeers experienced languishing sales. The company contracted with an American advertising firm, N. W. Ayer, which unleashed one of the most effective media campaigns the world has ever seen. They gave diamonds to movie icons and had magazines run glamorous stories and photographs linking diamonds to romance and high society. In a 1948 strategy paper, N. W. Ayer wrote, "We spread the word of diamonds worn by stars of screen and stage, by wives and daughters of political leaders, by any woman who can make the grocer's wife and the mechanic's sweetheart say 'I wish I had what she has.' "[7] In a memo to DeBeers, the agency described targeting young girls through lectures at high schools: "All of these lectures revolve around the diamond engagement ring, and are reaching thousands of girls in their assemblies, classes and informal meetings in

---

[4] For a history of the finger ring, see George Kunz's *Rings for the Finger*, J. B. Lippincott (1917).

[5] Kunz, p. 199.

[6] Referenced in Macrobius' *Saturnalia*, book VII, chap 13. See Kunz, p. 194.

[7] Edward Jay Epstein, "Have You Ever Tried to Sell a Diamond," *The Atlantic* (1982).

our leading educational institutions."[8] After twenty years of effort, N. W. Ayer declared victory in the late 1950s. They reported to DeBeers, "Since 1939 an entirely new generation of young people has grown to marriageable age...To this new generation a diamond ring is considered a necessity to engagements by virtually everyone."[9] The firm would next take aim at Japan and introduce the diamond engagement ring as a posh Western custom. The firm succeeded: from 1967 to 1981 the percentage of Japanese brides wearing diamond rings went from less than 5% to about 60%.[10] It is a sickening story of corporate greed preying upon weakness, lust, and pride.

In the Bible, married couples did not have wedding rings and were able to remain faithful. Do we need something that they lacked? The statement "with this ring, I thee wed" is alien to scriptural example and thought. As we have seen, our practices concerning rings come more from pagan culture or the media than from Scripture or thoughtful contemplation. We should not deceive ourselves as to the power of the ring. Wedding rings protect against infidelity as much as belts do against overeating. The real protection comes from a couple's hearts and actions, not an outward object.

Wedding rings are also part of a culture that devalues singleness. Our society makes the wedding ring a status symbol that can even inadvertently make those who are single envious or dejected. Rather than participate in such a system, we should reject the symbols that stratify society into classes. Today's churches often look down on those who remain single; wedding rings propagate this unhealthy stratification.

The combination of the biblical remarks against gold, the pagan origins of the wedding ring, and the attendant devaluation of singleness proved decisive for my wife and me. Forgoing the wedding ring has generally been the testimony of kingdom Christians. Such a testimony generally makes a deep impression: professing Christians and the world understand that such a person is serious about following God's word despite the consequences.

Answering objections

(This section is excerpted and edited from Charles Finney, Lectures to Professing Christians, *Lecture VIII, given in 1836.)*

[8] Ibid.

[9] Ibid.

[10] Ibid.

Objection: With this strictness, you carry Christianity too far away from the people. It is better not to set up an artificial distinction between the church and the world.

The direct reverse of this is true. The nearer you bring the church to the world, the more you annihilate the reasons that should stand out in view of the world, for their changing sides and coming over to the church. Unless you show that you are not like them, and carry the church so far as to have a broad gap between saints and sinners, how can you make the ungodly feel that so great a change is necessary?

Objection: But the change that is necessary is a change of heart.

True—but will not a change of heart produce a change of life?

Objection: You will throw obstacles in the way of people becoming Christians. Many respectable people will become disgusted, and if they cannot be allowed to dress fashionably and be Christians, they will become completely worldly.

This is just about as reasonable as it would be for a sober man to think he must get drunk now and then, to avoid disgusting the drunken, and to retain his influence over them. The truth is, that persons should know, and should see in the lives of professing Christians, that if they embrace God, they must be weaned from the world, and must give up the love of the world, and its pride and show and folly, and live a holy life, in watchfulness and self-denial and active benevolence.

Objection: It does not matter how we dress, if our hearts are right.

Your heart right! Then your heart may be right when your conduct is all wrong. Just as well might the vulgar person say, "It does not matter what words I speak, if my heart is right." No, your heart is not right, unless your conduct is right. What is outward conduct, but the acting out of the heart? If your heart was right, you would not wish to follow the fashions of the world.

Objection: We may be proud of a plain dress as well as of a fashionable dress.

So may any good thing be abused. But that is no reason why it should not be used, if it can be shown to be good. I put it back to the objector:

is that any reason why a Christian female, who fears God and loves the human souls, should neglect the means which may make an impression that she is separated from the world, and pour contempt on the fashions of the ungodly, in which they are moving their way to hell?

Objection: This is a small thing, and ought not to take up so much of a minister's time.

This is an objection often heard from worldly professing Christians. But the minister that fears God will not be deterred by it. He will pursue the subject, until such professing Christians are cut off from their conformity to the world or cut off from the church. It is not merely the dress, as dress, but it is the conformity to the world in dress and fashion, that is the great stumbling block in the way of sinners. How can the world be converted, while professing Christians are conformed to the world? What good will it do to give money to send the gospel to the lost, when Christians live the way they do at home? Well might non-Christians ask, "What profit will it be to become Christians, when those who are Christians are pursuing the world with all the zeal of the ungodly?" The great thing necessary for the church is to break off from conformity to the world, and then they will have power with God in prayer, and the Holy Spirit will descend and bless their efforts, and the world will be saved.

Objection: But if we dress like this, we shall be called fanatics.

Whatever the ungodly may call you, fanatics or anything else, you will be known as Christians, and in their secret consciences will be acknowledged as such. How was it with the early Christians? They lived separate from the world, and it made such an impression, that even hostile writers say of them, "These people win the hearts of the masses, because they give themselves up to deeds of charity, and pour contempt on the world." Depend upon it, if Christians would live so now, the last effort of hell would soon be expended in vain to defeat the spread of the gospel. Wave after wave would flow abroad, until the highest mountain tops were covered with the waters of life.

Chapter 21

The headcovering

We have no other practice, nor do the churches of God.
(1 Corinthians 11:16[1]*)*

For almost two thousand years, nearly every church agreed on the issue of the headcovering. But in the twentieth century, the church bowed to culture. The teaching on the woman's headcovering represents a powerful test of a person's willingness to follow the Scriptures, despite the prevailing cultural influences. Professing Christians verbally declare that Jesus is their Lord, and say they will follow him despite the consequences. Yet most stumble at this teaching. The crucial passage in this discussion is 1 Corinthians 11:1-16. While detailed exegesis is beyond our scope, several questions will be addressed.

What was the cultural background?

During the first century, women's practices were mixed. Jewish women generally covered their heads, but Greco-Roman art and literature indicates that non-Jewish women often did not keep their heads covered. The public portraits from Corinth, "often show them bareheaded."[2] The lack of a uniform practice fits the diversity of a metropolitan trading port like Corinth.

Men's practices were similarly mixed, although during religious observations and sacrifice, their heads would typically be covered.[3] In the Old Testament, priests wore a turban (Exod. 28:39, 29:6, 39:31, Lev. 8:9,

---

[1] Author's translation.

[2] Ben Witherington III, *Conflict & Community in Corinth*, Eerdmans (1995), p. 234.

[3] Witherington, pp. 231-240.

16:4, Ezek. 24:17, Zech. 3:5). Even in pagan society, men would cover their heads when offering sacrifice. Caesar Augustus himself covered his head when offering a sacrifice to a pagan god.[4]

What was the command being given?

Two commands are being given. The men are instructed to keep their heads uncovered (11:4). Such instruction would have been surprising to both Jewish and pagan audiences, given its countercultural nature. Because of Old Testament laws, Jews would have been accustomed to priests covering their heads. Pagan men covered their heads out of respect to their gods.

Most likely, the believing women were likely confused by the men's countercultural practices, which prompted some of them to remove their headcoverings as well—motivating Paul to lay out a comprehensive theology in 1 Corinthians 11:1-16 for both genders. Women are told to cover their heads (with an imperative verb in v. 6) while praying or prophesying. While the exact nature of the covering is not specified, early Jewish and Christian literature and art demonstrate that it was typically an opaque cloth drawn over the head.

Is 1 Corinthians 11 about long hair?

Paul does make an analogy with long hair in 11:14-15. But as is always the case with analogies, the analogy is not the same as the thing itself. Long hair is being appealed to in order to show that the natural state of women is to be covered.

Paul uses two expressions to describe the headcovering.[5] Both expressions were consistently used in Greek literature for an external covering. For example, the first was used by Philo: "[The priest] shall take away from her the head-dress on her head, that she may be judged with her head bare...the woman with her head uncovered."[6] The *Shepherd of Hermas* uses the expression similarly: "her head was covered by a hood."[7] The second expression was used in Greek literature to mean a cloth covering. Plutarch describes Scipio traveling covertly in Alexandria: "As he came to Alexandria and landed, he went with his head cov-

[4] Illustrated by the statue (circa BC 12), the *Via Labicana Augustus*, which is held in exhibition in the Palazzo Massimo alle Terme at the National Museum of Rome.

[5] In Greek, *katakalytpos*, "covered," and *kata kephales*, "down from the head."

[6] Philo, *De Specialibus Legibus* 3:56,60. The word for "uncovered" is *akatakalypto*.

[7] *Shepherd of Hermas*, Vision 4, 2:1.

ered [*kata kephales*, identically to 1 Cor. 11:4], and the Alexandrians running about him entreated he would gratify them by uncovering and showing them his desirable face. When he uncovered his head, they clapped their hands with a loud acclamation."[8]

Both expressions are clearly about external coverings. The interpretation of the early church confirms that 11:1-16 is about a cloth covering.[9] Being closer in time, geography, language and culture to the apostles, these witnesses are especially important. Attempts to make 1 Corinthians 11:1-16 about hair instead of a headcovering thus violate the Greek and are illogical (especially in light of v. 6, which would implausibly read "if a woman will not have long hair, let her cut her hair").

1 Corinthians 11:6 implies that shorn hair for women is "shameful." Christian women should heed this remark, and maintain long hair. (The practice of short, styled hair is a relatively recent phenomenon in history, notably popularized in America during the 1920s.)

Could this be a temporary cultural command?

Many modern Bible teachers try to dismiss this passage by saying that it was merely "cultural" practice, which we are no longer obliged to follow. Yet these teachers greatly err because *scriptural headcovering practices were countercultural in the first century as well.* As seen above, uncovering the head represented a countercultural practice *for the men.* This teaching violated both Greco-Roman culture and Old Testament law. Since it was countercultural in the first century, we cannot cry "culture" in an attempt to avoid the application.

Honestly examining our motives will reveal that we are looking for excuses for women not to wear the headcovering because it is such a countercultural practice. Hence modern professing Christians are liable to follow the flimsiest of arguments that relieve them from following Scripture. Such a biased state warrants great caution.

Other arguments show that the commandment cannot be cultural:

- Men uncovered and women covered reflects the God-Christ relationship (11:3-7), which surely is not cultural.

[8] Plutarch, *Regum et Imperatorum Apophthegmata (Sayings of Kings and Commanders)*, 82. Translation by William Goodwin. Supporting the overall thesis, Witherington, pp. 233-234, cites Plutarch in *Aetia Romana* 267C, *Vitae Decem Oratorae* 842B, *Pyrrhus* 399B, *Pompeius* 640C, *Caesar 739D*; Varro in *De Lingua Latina* 5.29.130; and Juvenal in *Sat.* 6.390-392.

[9] If there is any doubt, Tertullian's survey of second-century church practices in *De Virginibus Velandis (On the Veiling of Virgins)* puts the matter to rest.

- 11:11-12 offers arguments rooted in creation to support the headcovering, which also transcend culture.
- Angels are offered as a third reason for women keeping covered (11:10), also not a cultural reason.
- Paul nowhere says that culture was the motivation for the headcovering. Crying "culture" profanes the text.

When should the headcovering be worn?

Many people wrongly believe that 1 Corinthians 11:1-16 is about public worship. This false conclusion is derived from its proximity to a passage on the Lord's Supper (11:17-34). We must remember that the chapter and verse divisions in our Bible are from the Middle Ages and are not part of the original text. Since the passage on the Lord's Supper follows, many infer that the headcovering passage must be about church gatherings as well. Several arguments dispel that notion.

First, the immediate context of the headcovering passage involves eating meals in private homes (10:27-33). This preceding passage has nothing to do with the meetings of believers. Second, after the passage on headcovering, a sharp break follows in verse 17, in which Paul introduces a new topic. Behavior during public worship is introduced in 11:17-18, for Paul writes, "when you come together as a church" (again repeated in verse 20). This crucial breakpoint marks a division in the text. This *subsequent* language of "coming together" confirms that 11:1-16 is not about public worship.

Third, an apparent contradiction dissolves when one sees that 11:1-16 is not about public worship. In 14:34, women are instructed to be completely silent in the churches, so people have asked, "How can they be praying or prophesying in 11:1-16?" The contradiction disappears when one sees that the headcovering is about ordinary life; this passage is not about the public gathering of the church. Women were not publicly praying or prophesying during the Lord's day gathering, but they were silent, consistent with the prohibition in 14:34. However, outside the Lord's day gathering, in the home, women were praying and prophesying. (Acts 21:9 illustrates this with Philip's daughters.)

Given that 11:1-16 is not primarily about the Lord's day gathering, when should the headcovering be worn? The passage answers: a woman is to be covered when she "prays or prophesies." This is a literary device known as a *merism*. A merism is a device where the parts represent the whole. Through a merism, a totality is referenced by its parts or poles. Merisms are common in the Bible. Psalm 139:2 is a good example, "You know when I sit down and when I rise up." By this the Psalmist means that the Lord knows all of his life. Clues to the presence of a merism include poetic devices and context. "When I sit down" is poetically parallel to "when I rise up." Jesus uses three merisms in a cluster to describe Himself, "I am the Alpha and the Omega, the Beginning and the End, the First and the Last" (Rev. 22:13). When Jesus says "Beginning and End," He also means everything in between. 1 Corinthians 11 uses the merism, "prayer and prophesy," which are the representative parts of a person's spiritual life. Prayer represents our spiritual life in relationship to God, and prophecy represents our spiritual life in relationship to others (the latter described in 14:1-25). Even in Greek, both of these words begin with a "p" sound,[10] further supporting that this is a poetic expression undergirding a merism. So the exhortation that Paul offers encompasses more than isolated periods of praying and prophesying.

In addition to the literary device, Scripture teaches that we are to pray without ceasing (1 Thess. 5:17). Praying should be an activity we participate in throughout the day, informing our understanding of duration of practice. While the headcovering should not be treated in a superstitious way (for example while bathing), the evidence supports that it should be worn throughout the wakeful hours.

Because Paul describes the reasons for wearing the headcovering, we should also use common sense and let those reasons help answer the question of when to wear the covering. Neither the God-Christ relationship nor the creation order are transient, hence it is logical that our witness to those orders would be persistent and public. Moreover, the God-Christ, man-woman analogy places the woman in the position of imitating Jesus. Just as the Son of God veiled His glory, so the woman veils her glory, which is her hair. With rare exception (such as the Mount of Transfiguration), Jesus kept His glory concealed.

Finally, two more reasons should be given that are not described in the passage. The first involves modesty. Many are not conscious of the allure of women's long hair, but this ignorance belies reality. Exploiting this allure, contemporary magazine covers typically show women with their hair down, long and flowing. In contrast, covering the hair represents modest behavior and helps restore our God-given sensibilities. Second, the headcovering preserves the distinctions between male and female. Such logic pervades 11:1-16. These distinctions are badly needed in the modern world. The Christian woman's testimony through the headcovering testifies to these gender distinctions.

---

[10] *proseuchomenos* and *propheteuon.*

To whom does this text apply?

The passage applies to both men and women. Men ought not to cover their heads in spiritual acts and should avoid a headcovering unless the weather demands it. That many professing Christian men (especially priests, ministers, bishops, and popes) cover their head during their religious ceremonies simply demonstrates their forsaking of God's word.

Women should cover their head in the range of spiritual exercises. The age at which a woman would begin this would sensibly correspond to the age at which she properly begins to be able to make spiritual exercises such as prayer and prophecy. Parents may choose an earlier age for their daughters for the sake of modesty.

What about the angels?

While Paul offers several reasons why men's heads are to be uncovered and women's covered, the most terse explanation offered is "because of the angels" (11:10). There are two ways to understand this reason, both of which have scriptural support.

First, the church is called to demonstrate the manifold wisdom of God to the principalities and powers in the heavenly places (Eph. 3:10). When a woman covers her head, she demonstrates a willingness to take her position within the created order. This action demonstrates her submission, not merely to people around her, but also to the angels. The evil angels rebelled because they wanted to be exalted beyond their appointed station. The righteous angels submit to God and His Son, covering themselves in God's presence (Isa. 6:2). Hence the woman testifies of God's wisdom to both righteous and evil angels.

Another explanation of this phrase, not necessarily incompatible with the first, was offered by the early church.[11] When evil spirits saw women in Genesis 6:2, they apparently were attracted to them and took them as wives, which in turn provoked the Lord to anger.[12] Evil spirits were apparently attracted to the beauty of women in Genesis.[13] The headcovering may thus offer a protection from the influence of these evil angels.

---

[11] See Tertullian, *De Virginibus Velandis (On the Veiling of Virgins)*, chapter 7.

[12] This interpretation of Gen. 6:2 was favored by the early church. It was also offered in the *Book of Enoch* which is approvingly quoted in the New Testament (Jude 14-15). Angels often took human form in the Old Testament, such as those who rescued Lot.

[13] *The Book of Enoch*, cited in the book of Jude, describes that demons taught women the arts of jewelry-making and the painting of the eyelids.

Chapter 22

Worldly entertainment

I will not set before my eyes anything that is worthless. (Psalm 101:3)

The Scriptures often describe disease as related to sin. Leprosy, for example, is described as an analogy to sin. By understanding disease, particularly infections, we may learn a great deal about Satan's schemes and the mechanism by which sin operates.

Viruses, particularly the herpes virus family, are among the most common infections in the world. The herpes virus family is responsible for chicken pox, cold sores, and venereal disease. The virus is transmitted through close physical contact and then enters the bloodstream. Chicken pox in particular causes skin lesions, fever, and fatigue for about a week, and then the symptoms normally subside. *But the virus is never actually cleared.* Instead, it inserts itself into the DNA of the infected person and waits. The person will carry this virus in their DNA to the grave. Over the lifetime of the individual, the virus patiently waits in tissues like the spinal cord. It waits until the immune system is depressed and then surges back into activity again, this time in a different form known as shingles. Shingles is an extraordinarily painful disease because of its origins in the spinal cord. Skin lesions erupt on a portion of the body, and until the immune system can gain the upper hand again, the virus rages.

Worldly entertainment is much like this virus. The images, videos, and music of this world enter a person's soul and cause a first wave of disease: skin lesions, fatigue, and fever, one could say. But those images, videos, and music never really leave. Yes, a person can be forgiven for viewing worldly entertainment, but the consequences remain. David was forgiven for his sin with Bathsheba, but God demanded that he bear the consequence of his sin. The entertainment of the world—its television, its movies, its novels, its magazines, its music—infect the person ingesting the material and permanently alter that person's memory and sensibilities, introducing vulnerabilities. Even years later, at times of weakness, the spiritual virus will emerge, perhaps by stirring up thrill seeking or recalling a pornographic image, thoughts of violence, foolishness, or vulgarity. Through this temptation, the virus may inflict a second round of pain, crippling the person into spiritual lethargy or even death.

If we could see the world with spiritual glasses, the majority of people would be covered in oozing sores and pustules, repeatedly being infected by the world's entertainment. Even people in the church would carry these wounds. Though the viruses may be dormant, they will have permanently introduced weaknesses and vulnerabilities.

And yet to the world, being entertained is part of being human. Relaxing in front of the television after dinner, browsing fashion magazines, rooting for the local sports team, watching movies, reading novels, and dancing at nightclubs are not exceptional activities—they are the norm. Scripture provides several reasons why worldly entertainment should be rejected:

1. Worldly entertainment violates Scripture by filling the recipient's minds with material that is not "true, noble, just, pure, lovely, and praiseworthy" (Phil. 4:8). Psalms 101:3 teaches that we should not place before our eyes any worthless thing.
2. Entertainment is prized by the world, making it an abomination before God. Professional sports and Hollywood's movies fall into this category. "For what is highly esteemed among men is an abomination in the sight of God" (Luke 16:15). From the exorbitant money given to athletes and movie stars to the time spent on the world's entertainment, no person could deny that the world highly esteems its entertainment. See also 1 John 2:15 and James 1:27.
3. The world's entertainment enslaves people into the bondage of addiction (John 8:34; Rom. 6:20; 1 Cor. 6:12). Television, movies, and novels can addict a person as much as tobacco or drugs.
4. The media warps a person's sensibilities. It twists an individual's sense of humor and beauty. One can hardly overstate the magnitude of the effects of entertainment. Often a man's sense of beauty becomes so acclimated to the faces and figures of models that he hardly will show interest in marrying the "ordinary" young woman that should have captured his heart, or still worse, he strains to love his own wife. Another example would be the

world's depiction of the incompetence and foolishness of fathers, which has undermined God's design for the household and respect for the father. A final example involves how homemaking is portrayed; heroines are not those who serve in their home, but are off voyaging on some adventure.

5. Worldly entertainment violates separation (2 Cor. 6:14-18).
6. The world's entertainment is a gateway to other sins such as pornography and blasphemy. Even children's entertainment displays women's bodies in subtle ways to make boys crave for more. Television serves as a gateway to pornography, as well as manners of speech or humor that are blasphemous.
7. The mixture of good and evil seduces the masses of humanity. While sometimes virtue is depicted in a positive light, such depictions enter a person with a "Trojan horse" of sins. The careful observer will note that even in "family-friendly" entertainment, much error and sin is portrayed positively, which deceives most people by imprinting worldly thinking into their hearts and twisting their sensibilities.
8. Much entertainment involves patronage, which propagates the world's sins and helps enslave others. For example, cable television involves paying a monthly fee which is distributed among various channels. (Those who pay for cable television are paying monthly fees to MTV, for example.) This patronage effectively asks for more worldly material and puts God's money in the service of evil. Professing Christians thus give their money to help fund music videos, professional sports, movies, soap operas, and reality television. By patronizing such an evil system, great bloodguilt comes upon their heads. Let any with a conscience forsake such wickedness.
9. It robs God of His time.

Scripture promises many blessings for those who keep themselves unspotted by the world. Jesus says that those who are pure in heart will see God (Matt. 5:8). Without being twisted from continual exposure to sin, believers are able to have a clear mind. Disciples of the Lord can steward their time, money, and energy much more effectively, enabling them to better serve the Lord and give to those in need.

By forsaking the world's entertainment, Christians taste the isolation and exclusion from the world which strengthens their faith. "For we have spent enough of our past lifetime in doing the will of the Gentiles—when we walked in lewdness, lusts, drunkenness, revelries, drinking parties, and abominable idolatries. In regard to these, they think it strange that you do not run with them in the same flood of dissipation, speaking evil of you." (1 Pet. 4:3-4; see also Matt. 5:11-12). Because entertainment is so woven into the world's life, when Christians avoid these activities, they put into practice what it is to be "aliens and strangers." They cannot participate in the same conversations or go to the same events. They then begin to taste the hostility of the world, which sharpens them and reminds them that true Christians are soldiers, not of this world.

Chapter 23

Care of the physical body

Do you not know that your body is the temple of the Holy Spirit who is in you, whom you have from God, and you are not your own? (1 Corinthians 6:19)

When unbelievers walk into the midst of a gathering of the saints, are they impressed at how disciples treat their bodies as not their own, but as temples of the Holy Spirit? Do they see a people that honor Jesus' words of pronouncing a blessing on the hungry and woe to the full (Luke 6:21, 25)? Do they see a people whose God is the Lord or whose god is their belly (Phil. 3:19)? Sadly, many visitors are repulsed at the overweight members and lack of discipline among professing Christians. Scripture has much to say about the appetite and treatment of the body:

> Be not among drunkards or among gluttonous eaters of meat. (Prov. 23:20)
>
> Their [those who are enemies of the cross] end is destruction, their god is their belly, and they glory in their shame, with minds set on earthly things. (Phil. 3:19 ESV)
>
> And put a knife to your throat if you are given to appetite. (Prov. 23:2)
>
> So when the woman saw that the tree was good for food, and that it was a delight to the eyes, and that the tree was to be desired to make one wise, she took of its fruit and ate, and she also gave some to her husband who was with her, and he ate. (Gen. 3:6)

They tested God in their heart by demanding the food they craved. (Ps. 78:18)

Happy are you, O land, when your king is the son of the nobility, and your princes feast at the proper time, for strength, and not for drunkenness! (Eccles. 10:17)

I beseech you therefore, brethren, by the mercies of God, that you present your bodies a living sacrifice, holy, acceptable to God, which is your reasonable service. (Rom. 12:1)

Put on the Lord Jesus Christ, and make no provision for the flesh, to fulfill its lusts. (Rom. 13:14)

Now the rabble that was among them had a strong craving. And the people of Israel also wept again and said, "Oh that we had meat to eat!" (Num. 11:4)

And God said, "Behold, I have given you every plant yielding seed that is on the face of all the earth, and every tree with seed in its fruit. You shall have them for food." (Gen. 1:29)

See to it…that no one is sexually immoral or unholy like Esau, who sold his birthright for a single meal. (Heb. 12:15-16 ESV)

But Daniel resolved that he would not defile himself with the king's food. (Dan. 1:8)

By faith Moses, when he became of age, refused to be called the son of Pharaoh's daughter, choosing rather to suffer affliction with the people of God than to enjoy the passing pleasures of sin, esteeming the reproach of Christ greater riches than the treasures in Egypt; for he looked to the reward. (Heb. 11:24-26)

Behold, this was the guilt of your sister Sodom: she and her daughters had pride, excess of food, and prosperous ease, but did not aid the poor and needy. They were haughty and did an abomination before me. So I removed them, when I saw it. (Ezek. 16:49-50)

We remember the fish we ate in Egypt that cost nothing, the cucumbers, the melons, the leeks, the onions, and the garlic. But now our strength is dried up, and there is nothing at all but this manna to look at. (Num. 11:5-6)

While the meat was yet between their teeth, before it was consumed, the anger of the Lord was kindled against the people, and the Lord struck down the people with a very great plague. (Num. 11:33)

Now the sons of Eli were worthless men. They did not know the Lord…This is what they did at Shiloh to all the Israelites who came there…[Their servant] would say, "No, you must give [the meat] now, and if not, I will take it by force." (1 Sam. 2:12-17)

When you reap the harvest of your land, you shall not reap your field right up to its edge, neither shall you gather the gleanings after your harvest. And you shall not strip your vineyard bare, neither shall you gather the fallen grapes of your vineyard. You shall leave them for the poor and for the sojourner: I am the Lord your God. (Lev. 19:9-10)

All things are lawful for me, but all things are not helpful. All things are lawful for me, but I will not be brought under the power of any. (1 Cor. 6:12)

And do not become idolaters as were some of them. As it is written, "The people sat down to eat and drink, and rose up to play." (1 Cor. 10:7)

"And I will say to my soul, 'Soul, you have many goods laid up for many years; take your ease; eat, drink, and be merry.' " But God said to him, "Fool! This night your soul will be required of you; then whose will those things be which you have provided?" So is he who lays up treasure for himself, and is not rich toward God. (Luke 12:19-21)

> Whether you eat or drink, or whatever you do, do all to the glory of God. (1 Cor. 10:31)

Working in hospitals gave me a new perspective on life. Most people do not regularly encounter death and disease much until they are much older. While I was in my twenties working in hospitals, I felt like I was being artificially aged into the realm of the elderly. I saw firsthand the top three causes of death in the United States (tobacco, poor diet, and alcohol) rob patients of life.[1] All three causes of death are preventable. Smoking was already obvious, but I had failed to appreciate the significance of eating.

The human race fell into sin through food. Food is often associated in the Scriptures with sin and idolatry. Yet Christians rarely treat gluttony as a sin, like lying, hatred, or lust. The church's general neglect of this topic and fixation on other sins are partly because so many are guilty of gluttony, including church leaders. It is easier to rail against problems one does not have, rather than those which one does have. While one hears about church discipline over sexual sins, one hardly hears of discipline over gluttony. Some people are obese because of genuine medical conditions. We should be compassionate and slow to judge. Yet we should be aware of prevailing trends. To use the example of lung cancer, approximately 90% is smoking-related. We should never automatically assume that a lung cancer patient is in the 90%. But we should be aware of what is most likely and seek to address what is preventable. With food, the obesity epidemic has escalated with the church playing virtually no constructive role. Those who should be leading by example sadly are at the rear. Yet surely God's word offers insights and help.

Satan loves to steal, kill, and destroy; food is a powerful weapon in his arsenal. Wisely does the proverb ring, "You dig your grave with your teeth." The rise of obesity, heart disease, and strokes are part of Satan's domination of the world system to promote his agenda of sickness and death. In contrast, the Lord desires that we live abundant lives. Healthy eating promotes a longer life far beyond what pills can do. One study showed a lifespan benefit of thirteen years due to healthy eating alone.[2] Though Paul noted that to die is gain, he said that it was better that he remain alive to serve the church (Phil. 1:23-24). A healthy diet dramat-

---

[1] A. H. Mokdad et al., "Actual Causes of Death in the United States," *JAMA*, 291:1238-1245 (2004).

[2] Joel Fuhrman, *Eat to Live*, Little, Brown and Co. (2011), p. 92. Similar results were more recently published in *JAMA Internal Medicine*, 173:1230-8 (2013).

ically lowers the risks of certain diseases, especially heart disease—the greatest killer in the Western world. Well-respected physicians have noted that heart disease is preventable.[3] The incidences of other diseases such as cancer and osteoporosis are markedly reduced by healthy eating.[4] A life free from disease enables disciples to more energetically serve the Lord and the church. A person's lifetime medical bills will be significantly reduced, enabling disciples to additionally help the brotherhood.

But especially in the West, we have become a soft, weak people with little self-control. The lack of self-control with food spills over other aspects of life. This problem is compounded by the food industry and media that seeks to turn people into addicts who provide recurring revenue streams. The industry promotes foods that have an addictive quality, especially chocolates, ice creams, cheeses, meats, and coffees.[5] Fast-food chains such as McDonald's design their foods to be addictive. Yet the believer should say, "I will not be enslaved by anything" (1 Cor. 6:12).

The world and the media exert considerable force on our minds. Unless we are consciously resisting its pull, we will be prey. The world promotes stimulation and thrill-seeking through the palate. The world chases after a new delicacy and flavor with nearly every meal, fostering the lust of the flesh. Thus while all foods are clean and to be received with thanksgiving (Mark 7:19; 1 Tim. 4:4), believers should be content to eat simple and repetitive meals. This battle is more easily won if addressed early; one's tastes are developed in childhood. Insofar as possible, parents should provide simple, nutritious meals that emphasize vegetables, legumes, and whole grains, rather than fats, meats, and sweets. Restaurant patronage should be minimized to teach children contentment with simple home cooking. Few people think of these disciplines as connected to spiritual victory, but they surely are.

By enslaving the church to food, Satan gains an important victory: the loss of fasting and prayer. By not fasting, we lose considerable power in our spiritual battle (to be discussed in chapter 33). The connections between food, self-discipline, and spiritual power are profound.

The love feast (part of the Lord's Supper) should reflect the simplicity of the Lord, not the decadence of the world. The Schleitheim confession says, "All gluttony shall be avoided among the brothers who are

---

[3] Caldwell Esselstyn, *Prevent and Reverse Heart Disease*, Avery Trade (2008).

[4] T. Colin Campbell and Thomas Campbell II, *The China Study*, BenBella (2006).

[5] See Neal Barnard, *Breaking the Food Seduction*, St. Martin's Press (2003) for a medically informed presentation on the neglected but important topic of addiction and diet.

gathered in the congregation; serve a soup or a minimum of vegetable and meat, for eating and drinking are not the kingdom of heaven."

Common sense would imply that other activities that harm the body, such as smoking, are similarly sins against the Holy Spirit. While not specifically addressed in the Bible, sometimes young women seek excessively thin bodies, through anorexia and bulimia, as a means to gain admiration. This sin has become more frequent, largely due to the media and internet. Anorexia is rooted in pride and can be as unhealthy as gluttony.

While duly acknowledging that most consider the subject of care for the physical body to be beneath the dignity of the pulpit, or even impolite, what we do not speak about is as instructive as what we do. May the Lord give us wisdom and strength to live as disciplined soldiers for the King.

Chapter 24

Technology

The LORD said, "Behold, they are one people, and they have all one language, and this is only the beginning of what they will do. And nothing that they propose to do will now be impossible for them. Come, let us go down and there confuse their language, so that they may not understand one another's speech." (Genesis 11:6-7)

Themes concerning knowledge and technology figure prominently in the first half of the book of Genesis. The pivotal tree in Eden is described as the "tree of the knowledge of good and evil." This expression is a merism,[1] implying that the tree stands for all knowledge. When Adam and Eve partake of the tree, God declares that "man has become like one of us," meaning that man now has access to boundless knowledge. This knowledge first involves understanding nakedness, which brings shame upon the man and woman. No longer child-like, man and woman are plunged into a new world, even without leaving Eden, as their minds gain access to truths to which they were previously oblivious. God declares that they must be driven out lest they consume fruit from another tree, the tree of life, and gain immortality.

After eating from the tree of knowledge of good and evil, humans became morally fallen creatures with intellectual and imaginative abilities exceeding their moral capacity to control them. Like a little boy behind the wheel of a truck with the ignition turned on, humanity now

[1] This term was discussed in chapter 21. A merism is an expression where something is referenced by one or more of its parts. Psalms 139 describes how God knows David's sitting and rising—meaning that God knows all of David's actions. Another example is the old English expression that describes looking in every "nook and cranny," meaning to look everywhere. Or "lock, stock, and barrel" to describe a gun. Regarding the tree in Eden, "good and evil" are the poles of knowledge and constitute a poetic expression to represent the totality of knowledge.

wielded powers that it could not handle. Much of the rest of Genesis describes the consequences.

The effects of the first tree are bestowed to posterity. Two genealogies are followed: the line of wicked Cain (Gen. 4:17-24) and the line of godly Seth (Gen. 4:25-5:32). The descendants of Cain embark upon a spree of technologic innovation. They invent musical instruments and instruments of bronze and iron (Gen. 4:21-22). Notably, the seventh son through Cain is Lamech, a murderer and the first person to practice polygamy. The righteous line of Seth, in contrast, lacks men with these exploits, and the seventh son in this lineage is Enoch, who walked with God (Gen. 5:22). The line of Seth also produces Noah, an exemplar of faithfulness. The contrasting depiction of these two lines serves as a harbinger of the conflict between the kingdom of righteousness and the kingdom of evil. Moreover, one cannot escape the negative connotations of technology given the character of its inventors.

This theme of innovation in technology crescendos with the account of the tower of Babel where mankind attempts to build a tower to the heavens. God recognizes that when society is coordinated, there will be no limit to its accomplishments. "Nothing they propose to do will now be impossible for them" (Gen. 11:7). So God throws their enterprise into confusion and halts their progress.

Babel returns in the New Testament, under its other name of Babylon. The Bible closes with a description of Babylon's rich web of commerce that is ultimately destroyed on judgment day (Rev. 18). While disciples are both persecuted and poor, worldly society thrives with commerce and industry. Both in Genesis and Revelation, God judges Babel with its innovation and commerce—an ominous portrait indeed.

Thinking about technology

The temptation is to think of technology as whatever has been invented after you were born.[2] But that will not do. The wheel, the pen, and the phone were novel at some point in history, and despite society's perception, each is an authentic form of technology. There are two primary ways to think about technology.[3] On the one side is *instrumentalism*, which regards technology as basically neutral. In this view, the human will chooses to wield technology for good or for evil. On the other side is *technological determinism*, which ascribes power to technology to change society. In this view, technology is a quasi-autonomous force

[2] Paraphrased from Alan Kay.

[3] John Dyer, *From the Garden to the City*, Kregel (2011), chapter 6.

that shapes society, usually in a negative manner. While it is beyond the scope of this chapter to explore this debate, both sides make valid points and the truth is somewhere in between.

Another important axis of thought concerns how technology affects our "ecosystem," the totality of our activities and abilities.[4] Just as pythons let loose in the Florida everglades have changed the distribution of species in that area, so technology changes our world in complex ways. While technology may extend or magnify a person's abilities to do a task, it also reduces or eliminates other practices and abilities. We usually focus on what technology adds to our lives, but it virtually always eliminates other things as well. Email has made communication easier and more rapid, but it has reduced the composition of handwritten letters. Calculators have eroded our ability to hold numbers in our minds and work out math. Light bulbs illuminate our rooms to facilitate activities at night; but they have scattered the family away from the hearth, partitioning parents and children into their own rooms and weakening the family unit. Understanding how technology impacts our ecosystem is a challenging and important task.

Responding to technology

So how should the church interact with technology? The New Testament gives no general command on technology. But in assessing technology's value and danger, we can use Jesus' principle that "wisdom is proved by her children" (Matt. 11:19; Luke 7:35). By examining the fruits of technology, the church can make a better assessment of the role it should play in the lives of disciples today.

We should not have too fatalistic or negative a view of technology. Noah used the technology of his day to build an ark. Advanced technology of a later era was used in building Solomon's temple. In the New Testament, the gospel traveled via roads and ships that were the product of Roman technology. As a physician, I have often seen the power of technology to save lives. The invention of the needle with a hollow bore, enabling delivery of intravenous fluids, has saved millions of lives. A similar story could be told with antibiotics, anesthesia, and hundreds of medications. Likewise there many simple devices, which were once novel technologies, that pose little or no danger and are universally accepted: the wheel, the shovel, and the rake are just a few examples.

On the other side, we have noted that in Genesis evil men were the inventors of their day. This should signal caution in hastily embracing

[4] Dyer, pp. 87-92.

innovation. So-called "high technologies," such as television and the internet, tend to disrupt our ecosystems in more profound ways. The harmful fruits of technology, especially high technology, have become increasingly apparent over the last three decades:

1. Superficiality and foolishness tend to afflict users of high technology.[5] While it promises connectivity, technology actually produces stress, isolation, and depression.[6] These forces have generally led people away from God.
2. Television and the internet deliver all kinds of lewdness and evil, causing an unquenchable thirst for violence and sexual immorality.
3. High technology enslaves into addiction. The flicker of the screen, the constant stimulation, and the novelty all combine to offer a "rush" not unlike stimulants such as cocaine. Heavy use of high technology is associated with gluttony, addiction to drugs or alcohol, and pornography.
4. Countless hours have been wasted on foolish and unprofitable activities such as video games or social networking.
5. By facilitating socialization outside of the family through inventions like the phone, car, and internet, family communication has been hollowed. This naturally harms the family unit.
6. Hospitality is weakened. Not uncommonly, when a guest arrives at a home, the children are distracted or annoyed at the guest because of disruptions to their video games or favorite television shows. Adults tinker with their smartphones even while speaking to each other, denigrating their presence.
7. By more easily supplying needs like food, water, clothing, and shelter, technology has made people more independent, fostering arrogance and self-sufficiency that undermine trust in God. By making society vastly richer in a material sense, technology has brought the curse of wealth upon us. "Give me neither poverty nor riches; feed me with the food that is needful for me, lest I be full and deny you and say, 'Who is the LORD?' " (Prov. 30:8-9).

[5] See Neil Postman's *Amusing Ourselves to Death: Public Discourse in the Age of Show Business*, Penguin (1985, revised 2005) and Nicholas Carr's *The Shallows: What the Internet is Doing to Our Brains*, W. W. Norton (2011).

[6] For example, the work of C. Morrison and colleagues in *Psychopathology*, 43:121-6 (2010). They and dozens of other studies have found a strong association between depression and internet use. Arthur Boers' *Living into Focus: Choosing What Matters in an Age of Distractions*, Brazos (2012) presents thoughtful remedies.

8. Technology enables people to spend their time and emotions on matters that should be of no concern. "The discerning sets his face toward wisdom, but the eyes of a fool are on the ends of the earth" (Prov. 17:24).
9. Much money and effort are wasted in the pursuit of technology and gadgets. This money would be far better spent on serving the brotherhood and the poor.
10. By fostering distraction, much of high technology has hurt the education process. Students today are generally less diligent and disciplined than those a hundred years ago.
11. Staring at a screen, particularly at night, alters one's natural circadian rhythms. Many suffer from poor sleeping. The normal cadence of the created order is thus subverted by machines.

Considering these fruits, a wise response is to use technology (especially high technology) *as little as possible, and only as much as necessary*. Necessary examples include medical treatments, proper communication with family and friends, business purposes, and transportation between spiritually profitable locations. Unnecessary examples include video games, entertainment through technology, television, and surfing the internet for pleasure.

Parents play a large role in forming their children's habits and attitudes toward technology. Parents should instill in their children a healthy sense of caution toward technology. After all, parents seek to instill a healthy fear and respect into their children around many objects: knives, flames, plastic bags, etc. because they understand that children do not have the abilities to handle these objects that can lead to their harm. Similarly, believers generally underestimate their own sinfulness by believing that they can handle any technology they choose. Because technology changes quickly, we all need accountability from our brothers and sisters. We need a spirit of humility and transparency as we may be handling that which we are unable to properly wield. The issues are complex and rapidly changing; carefully assessing the heart and examining fruit are more likely to be profitable than trying to chase technology with standards that are all too soon obsolete.

The thesis of this chapter has been that the church enters into a deceptive bargain with a generally uncritical adoption of technology—in exchange for receiving a little good, God's people often lose much more than they gain. Wisdom, transparency, accountability, and humility should be integral to working out these issues in everyday life. In this way, the church can interact with technology in a godly and responsible manner.

Chapter 25

Divorce and remarriage

Everyone who divorces his wife and marries another commits adultery, and he who marries a woman divorced from her husband commits adultery. (Luke 16:18)

The church in a sense is a family of families. Rightly understanding the centerpiece of a family, the husband-wife union, is thus crucial to having a strong church. The problems of divorce and broken families have been greatly weakening the church in the last century. Yet most churches do not possess a biblical theology of the husband-wife relationship, which is so closely linked to the Christ-church relationship.

Divorce is perhaps the most painful wound a family can experience. After the initial trauma, its scars run deep and wide. Many have friends who have gone through a divorce, even while in their twenties or thirties. The question for examination at present is whether remarriage to another person is biblically permissible after divorce, while the former spouse is living. After surveying the question from historical and biblical perspectives, pastoral implications will be explored.

Historical perspectives

In most professing Christian churches today, the question of "Can remarriage be biblically allowed after divorce?" is met with an overwhelming "Yes." In fact, few have heard or considered the alternative view that remarriage is biblically prohibited after divorce while the former spouse lives. Because of the dominance of this view today, the historic views of the church surprise those who have not studied this subject. In the first five centuries of church history, there was essential unanimity of the Greek (Eastern) and Latin (Western) church fathers in viewing remarriage as adultery.[1] Such writers include early Greek fathers such as Hermas, Justin Martyr, Athenagoras, Theophilus of Antioch, Irenaeus, Clement of Alexandria, and Origen and later Greek writers such as Basil, Gregory Nazianzus, Appollinarius, Theodore of Mopsuestia, and John Chrysostom. The early Greek writers should be heavily weighed since they knew Koine Greek as their mother tongue and thus understood the nuances of the New Testament language better than anyone could today. Of the early church writers who wrote in Latin, a similar picture exists: Tertullian, Ambrose, Innocent, Jerome, and Augustine concurred that remarriage after divorce is biblically forbidden. The witness of the early church is clear. "In all, twenty-five individual writers and two early councils forbid remarriage after divorce."[2]

The contrast in views on remarriage between the early church and most modern churches is therefore stark. Anytime there is a clear disagreement between the views of the modern and early church, we should not casually dismiss the early church. Rather we should study the matter with humility, acknowledging that we live in a period of laxity and disobedience as "evil men go from bad to worse." Of course, the biblical witness stands as the final arbiter of truth.

Biblical texts

Most of the verses contained in the New Testament appear to be quite plainly opposed to remarriage after divorce. These passages merit careful reading:

> Whoever divorces his wife and marries another commits adultery against her. And if a woman divorces her husband and marries another, she commits adultery. (Mark 10:11-12)

> Whoever divorces his wife and marries another commits adultery; and whoever marries her who is divorced from her husband commits adultery. (Luke 16:18)

> Now to the married I command, yet not I but the Lord: A wife is not to depart from her husband. But even if she does depart, let her remain unmarried or be reconciled to her husband. And a husband is not to divorce his wife. (1 Cor. 7:10-11)

[1] A historical overview is presented in Wenham and Heth, *Jesus and Divorce*, Paternoster press (2002).

[2] Wenham and Heth, p. 38.

> For the woman who has a husband is bound by the law to her husband as long as he lives. But if the husband dies, she is released from the law of her husband. So then if, while her husband lives, she marries another man, she will be called an adulteress; but if her husband dies, she is free from that law, so that she is no adulteress, though she has married another man. (Rom. 7:2-3)

Looking at these passages in turn, Mark records a saying of Jesus that is perfectly symmetric: if either the husband or wife divorce and remarry, he or she is guilty of adultery. No qualification is given concerning the reason for divorce. Luke records a saying with the same first half as Mark, but the saying goes on to note that whoever marries the divorced woman is also guilty of adultery. Luke's additional recording (16:18b) implies that neither spouse may remarry after divorce, neither the "guilty" nor "innocent" party. Both Mark's and Luke's Gospel accounts were written for a predominantly Gentile audience that would have been familiar with Greco-Roman laws. Such laws were quite permissive about divorce: either the husband or wife could initiate divorce for any reason, including sexual immorality. The words against divorce and remarriage from either Gospel thus would have been heard as profoundly countercultural. It even surprised the Jewish disciples: "In the house His disciples also asked Him again about the same matter" (Mark 10:10).[3]

Paul, in 1 Corinthians 7:10-11, notes that neither the wife nor husband should initiate divorce or separation. If it had already occurred, the Christian should remain "unmarried or be reconciled" (v. 11). This is entirely consistent with Mark and Luke, in that all three passages forbid remarriage to another person. The fourth passage in Romans teaches that unless a spouse dies, the marital bond persists.

Matthew records Jesus' teachings on this issue in two separate locations:

> But I say to you that whoever divorces his wife for any reason except sexual immorality causes her to commit adultery; and whoever marries a woman who is divorced commits adultery. (Matt. 5:32)

> And I say to you, whoever divorces his wife, except for sexual immorality, and marries another, commits adultery;

[3] While beyond the scope of this chapter, views of prominent rabbis like Hillel and Shammai were considerably more permissive than Jesus' commands.

> and whoever marries her who is divorced commits adultery. (Matt. 19:9)

The passage from Matthew 5 is taken from the Sermon on the Mount, a passage where Jesus intensifies the Mosaic law (for example, by saying that being angry is to be guilty of murder) or gives a law that supersedes Moses (such as with oath taking). In Matthew 5:32, two slight variants on the teachings in Mark and Luke are presented. In Matthew 5:32a, if the man divorces his wife, then this makes *her* commit adultery. While not initially obvious why this would be true, this statement almost certainly flows from the assumption that social and economic forces would pressure the woman to be remarried. In this case, the man is culpable for the woman's sin by practically forcing her into this adulterous situation. Next, an "exception clause" is introduced, not found in Mark or Luke, "except for sexual immorality." Divorce is allowed (though not required) in the case of "sexual immorality" (Greek: *porneia*). Before elaborating on the exception clause, an important observation must be made. Just as in Mark and Luke, Matthew 5:32b clearly teaches that remarriage is not permitted. In this case, whoever marries the apparently innocent woman is guilty of adultery. The entire passage (Matt. 5:27-32) thus progresses through a crescendo of events: lust in the mind, looking lustfully, sinning with the hands, divorce, adultery by proxy, and finally actual adultery.

What about this phrase, "except for sexual immorality," that Mark and Luke lack? An important detail of Matthew 5:32 and 19:9 revolves around the Greek word *porneia*, an umbrella term for sexual immorality and rarely used just for adultery.[4] *Porneia* includes premarital sexual relations, prostitution, homosexuality, incest, and adultery. *Porneia* is used by Paul in 1 Corinthians 5:1 where a man is described to be sleeping with his father's wife. The specific term for adultery, *moicheia*, was not chosen there or in Matthew 5:32 or 19:9.

Jesus allows for divorce in the case of *porneia* but forbids remarriage. Examples of permissible divorce come directly from Matthew's gospel. "And her husband Joseph, being a just man and unwilling to

---

[4] The word porneia is translated "sexual immorality" (ESV, NASB, NKJV, HCSB), unchastity (RSV, NRSV), or fornication (KJV). Of these, "sexual immorality" is closest to the accepted lexical range of the word. "Unchastity" and "fornication" are not far off the mark, but are a bit unclear. The NIV, however, translates *porneia* as "marital unfaithfulness," a somewhat misleading interpretation. This has been corrected in the TNIV to be "sexual immorality." Related to this point, for any study on marriage it is best not to rely on the NIV due to some faulty translation decisions that the NIV committee made (also in Matt. 19:12 and 1 Cor. 7:1).

put her to shame, resolved to divorce her quietly." (Matt. 1:19, ESV) Because Joseph felt that Mary was guilty of premarital relations, such a divorce was permitted (though not required). Second, in Matthew 14:3-4, John the Baptist tells Herod to put away his wife, because she had been married to his brother Philip. In such a case, divorce was not merely permitted but demanded (see Lev. 18:16 and 20:21).

In Matthew 19:9, the verse that could be construed as the most permissive of all Jesus' teachings, the exception clause in Greek modifies "divorce" and *not the entire clause* which contains "marries another." Hence Jesus statement here is perfectly consistent with his other teachings: remarriage is not permitted, but divorce may be allowed due to *porneia*.

The disciples' astonishment at Jesus' reply makes the case for taking Mark 10:11-12, Luke 16:18, 1 Corinthians 7:10-11, and Romans 7:2-3 at face value: marriage is binding for life. The disciples' incredulous reply of "it is better not to marry" makes perfect sense with this context. Jesus was teaching that a person's marital status persisted despite the other spouse's behavior—a seemingly precarious situation. Jesus appears to undercut the Pharisees' question altogether by arguing that divorce goes against something far more fundamental, the one flesh union that God Himself has forged (19:5-6).

There is one last passage that must be addressed before claiming complete coherence among texts in the New Testament, the so-called "Pauline privilege" text: "But if the unbelieving partner separates, let it be so. In such cases the brother or sister is not enslaved. God has called you to peace" (1 Cor. 7:15). In context, it appears that Paul is saying that a believer is not held captive to the demands of the unbeliever after abandonment. Earlier in the chapter Paul argued that normally in marriage the body of either spouse belonged to the other (1 Cor. 7:4), language very similar to mutual "slavery." 1 Corinthians 7:15 thus implies that when the unbelieving spouse leaves, he or she forfeits conjugal rights or other claims over the abandoned spouse. In contrast, while married, the believing spouse is supposed to submit, precisely as a means to win the unbelieving spouse to the Lord (see 1 Pet. 3:1-2). But after abandonment, a believer should not endure conflict and subjugation but rather live in "peace." The underlying Greek word for "enslaved" is never used in the New Testament to describe a marriage bond, so it is exegetically unwarranted to claim that by being "not enslaved" Paul is not saying that the person is now free to remarry. Paul would have surely used another word in that case, or explicitly stated the freedom to remarry. Especially in the light of verses 10 and 11 where Paul requires either celibacy or reconciliation, this view makes the best sense of the passage. Thus this verse should be taken as a comfort to those who have been abandoned: they should not despair but realize that they are no longer "under bondage." It is not, however, license to remarry.

Putting all the pieces together, we have coherence across all the New Testament texts. To summarize thus far:

- Marriage is a covenantal relationship that is binding until the death of one of the marriage partners (Rom. 7:2-3).
- Remarriage after divorce is tantamount to adultery for either spouse (Matt. 5:32, Matt. 19:9; Mark 10:11-12; Luke 16:18).
- Matthew's exception clause refers to *porneia*, a broad term that encompasses immorality during betrothal, unlawful marriages, and adultery (Matt. 1:19, 5:32, 14:3-4, 19:9). The exception clause, however, does not allow for subsequent remarriage (Matt. 5:32b; Mark 10:11-12; Luke 16:18).
- In the event of separation, the Christian should remain celibate or be reconciled (1 Cor. 7:10-11). If an unbelieving spouse leaves, the Christian is not obligated to submit again to the departing spouse (1 Cor. 7:15).

These truths are tightly woven together in most Christian wedding vows, where each spouse promises fidelity until death. Most spouses take a vow of commitment "as long as we both shall live" or "until death do us part." We should not treat this language as flighty romantic language (few who utter those words do anyway) but as covenantal, weighty language. Those who have taken this vow before God and before man should honor their word.

Critique of the modern view

The prevailing view that remarriage is biblically permitted if adultery has occurred originated near the time of the Renaissance and is sometimes called the Erasmian view since Erasmus was the first major writer to advocate the view. Erasmus was responding to excesses in the Catholic understanding of marriage, and many figures of the Reformation adopted this understanding. This view has percolated down to most modern churches.[5]

The modern view, however, is fraught with problems and inconsistencies. The first major problem is that "he who marries a woman di-

[5] Chapters 3 and 4 of Wenham and Heth contain a historical summary.

vorced from her husband commits adultery" (Luke 16:18b) and "whoever marries a divorced woman commits adultery" (Matt. 5:32b) say, at a bare minimum, that remarriage for at least some people is wrong. This is typically handled by saying that the "guilty" party can never remarry, but that the "innocent" party can. (Sometimes the distinction between guilty and innocent is blurry or disputed, but this remains another issue.) Allowing the innocent party to remarry contradicts the evidence in Matthew 5:27-32 that the man is the guilty party and not the divorced woman. In addition, the modern view has another major inconsistency. If the guilty party cannot remarry without being adulterous because he or she is still united to the former spouse (the only way to plausibly interpret the word *adultery*), then the former spouse must also still be connected to the guilty spouse. If the innocent spouse is free to remarry, then he or she becomes a bigamist after remarriage, because of the persistent bond with the guilty party.

In the New Testament, we learn that that the "two becoming one flesh" represents Christ and the church (Eph. 5:22-33). The husband, like Christ, represents the head, and the wife, like the church, represents the body. Husbands are called to "love their wives as their own bodies" (Eph. 5:28), and wives are called to regard their husbands as "head" (Eph. 5:22). The bond between husband and wife may be dissolved legally (as Moses permitted), but not in essence. The husband who is unfaithful to his wife is sinning precisely because the martial bond persists. If adultery dissolved the marital bond, then it could not be called adultery since adultery implies violation of an existing marital relationship. The true marital bond can be dissolved as easily as the head can be removed from the body. Can the head find a new body or the body a new head? The marital union is humanly unbreakable—only God can sovereignly break it by the death of one of the spouses (Rom. 7:2-3). This was precisely why Jesus answered the question of the Pharisees in the manner that He did; they entirely misunderstood the issue. Those who teach and practice that the marital bond can be humanly broken contradict the witness of Jesus' love for His church and the resulting permanent union: Jesus in the church, and the church in Him.

Thus we are left with the typical modern interpretation of these passages as being slippery, illogical, and out of step with individual verses as well as larger themes of the Bible. Only the early church's interpretation of these verses remains viable: remarriage for either spouse is biblically prohibited while the other spouse lives.

Pastoral application

Based on the biblical witness, those who have experienced a divorce should be counseled to remain single or be reconciled with their former spouse, assuming that the former spouse is still unmarried. This counsel merely follows 1 Corinthians 7:10-11. Should reconciliation fail (or be inadvisable as in the case of persistent abuse or if the former spouse has remarried), lifelong singleness is the only option. This may seem like a bitter pill. But when wedded to the Lord, it should be a fruitful and joyful time to be in undivided ministry.

The thorniest question involves counseling a person who is already in a second marriage (while the former spouse lives) or married to a divorced person.[6] In the fourth century, Jerome counseled a woman named Fabiola to leave a subsequent marriage because he understood it to be adulterous.[7] Many modern advocates of the "no remarriage" view advocate expressing sorrow for the remarriage but then counsel to remain in the subsequent marriage. This view is certainly more humanly palatable than the alternative counsel to view the subsequent marriage as adulterous. But such an application betrays the very heart of the argument for not remarrying. If the subsequent marriage is truly adulterous, it should not persist.

Some reject this application because it seems too extreme and too hard to ask any family to face. But God's word must not be rejected because of harsh implications, particularly when devout people across diverse traditions throughout church history have practiced those very implications. Our hearts should sorrow in contemplating the ramifications but at the same time be stirred to action: "Do you not know that the unrighteous will not inherit the kingdom of God? Do not be deceived: neither the sexually immoral, nor idolaters, *nor adulterers*, nor men who practice homosexuality, nor thieves, nor the greedy, nor drunkards, nor revilers, nor swindlers will inherit the kingdom of God" (1 Cor. 6:9-10 ESV).

A person is obligated to keep their promises insofar as they are not sinful. Similarly with marriage, uniting with another person while a former spouse lives is a violation of another promise and another union. This would imply that the subsequent marriage should be dissolved. This principle was apparent to Ezra, the great scribe who reformed the

---

[6] For a deeper treatment, see Roger Hertzler's *Dear Pastor* (2008), available at www.watchmangospelsigns.com. Hertzler's book is perhaps the best introductory book on the subject of divorce and remarriage. His treatment of subsequent marriages is especially helpful.

[7] Jerome, *To Amandus*, Letter 55.

Jewish people who returned to Jerusalem after exile. "For Ezra had set his heart to study the Law of the LORD, and to do it and to teach his statutes and rules in Israel" (Ezra 7:10). In Ezra 9-10, he takes part in dissolving the marriages of those Jews who had married with non-Jews. Ezra did not believe those were valid marriages:

> The situation described in Ezra 9 and 10 is often set forth as the classic example of one in which the lesser of two evils had to be chosen: divorce is a lesser evil than the destruction of the Jewish people. This can only be said, however, if Ezra looked upon these connections as real marriages. All the evidence indicates that he did not. As early as 1890, George Rawlinson observed:
>
> > It is quite clear that [Ezra] read the Law as absolutely prohibitive of mixed marriages (Ezra ix. 10-14)—i.e., as not only forbidding their inception, but their continuance. Strictly speaking, he probably looked upon them as unreal marriages, and so as no better than ordinary illicit connections. For the evils which flow from such unions, those who make them, and not those who break them, are responsible.
>
> In Ezra's eyes this was not a question of breaking up legitimate marriages but of nullifying those which were contrary to the law. This is further suggested by the two Hebrew words Ezra chose to describe these "marriages" (*nasa* and *yasab*) and the "divorce" terminology he employs. Ezra "was a scribe skilled in the law of Moses" (Ezra 7:6). He studied, practiced, and taught it in Israel (v. 10). Yet he employs out-of-the-ordinary terminology to describe the "marrying" ("taking") and the "divorcing" ("sending away") of these women. Furthermore, how could these Israelites have made a covenant with God (Ezra 10:3) to put away their legal "wives" if it is true that Scripture portrays marriage as a covenant made between husband and wife in the presence of God? Ezra's prayer seems to indicate further that "intermarriage" had not yet actually taken place (cf. Ezra 9:2 with 9:14).[8]

[8] Wenham and Heth, p. 163.

Ezra led the people of God into a repentance that was more than mere words. He saw this as necessary to restore the Jewish people into right standing with God (see his prayer in Ezra 9:6-15). This type of dramatic action was not confined to the Old Testament. John the Baptist, who according to Jesus was the greatest man of the Old Testament era, advocates the dissolution of Herod's marriage (Matt. 11:11, 14:3-4). The actions of Ezra and John the Baptist, as well as the logical inference from Scripture perfectly harmonize. As one author notes:

> There is, to be sure, forgiveness for those who have committed adultery, wickedly divorced, and remarried. But there is forgiveness only in the way of repentance. And true repentance never goes on happily in the sin repented of (e.g. sleeping with another man's wife) but rather breaks with the sin, whatever the cost...Grace calls and empowers the forgiven sinner to walk in holiness of life. The divorced man may not remarry. Grace will enable him to live a single life. Grace calls those who are already remarried to stop living in that state that Jesus describes in Matthew 19:9, Mark 10:11, 12 and Luke 16:18 as continual adultery. Grace will enable the repentant, pardoned adulterer and adulteress to do this. It is the very nature of the grace of repentance itself that the sinner breaks with the sin that he sorrows over and confesses. The penitent brings forth works worthy of repentance. Only this repentance is genuine. Only this repentance finds forgiveness with God, regardless of what the churches may say.[9]

The application of this teaching may be the single most difficult expression of repentance in the entire Bible. Jesus warned that the cost of following Him would be high: "He who loves father or mother more than Me is not worthy of Me. And he who loves son or daughter more than Me is not worthy of Me. And he who does not take his cross and follow after Me is not worthy of Me" (Matt. 10:37-38).

God has lovingly given a special grace to those who have been through a divorce. Jesus draws attention to this grace: "For there are eunuchs who were born thus from their mother's womb, and there are eunuchs who were made eunuchs by men, and there are eunuchs who have made themselves eunuchs for the kingdom of heaven's sake" (Matt. 19:12). Some "have made themselves eunuchs for the kingdom

[9] David Engelsma, *Marriage: The Mystery of Christ and the Church*, Reformed Free Publishing Association (1998), p. 206 and 228.

of heaven's sake," possibly in reference to those who had experienced divorce (v. 10) and then chose to remain celibate. God can be a husband to the lonely woman, and the source of consolation to the lonely man. Children are often implicated in such a situation, and thinking of them may present the greatest temptation to abandon this position. But God provides the grace to meet any situation in which we sacrifice in order to obey His word. If done with God's grace, then could this not give children a deeper understanding of the binding nature of marital commitment and God's love for His church? Moreover, in Christian community and service, the advantages of being single can come to fruition, expressed in a life wedded to the Lord. Ultimately all earthly marriage is transitory (Matt. 22:30), and only the marriage of the King to His bride endures. May the church conduct herself in this world in light of that enduring union.

Chapter 26

Servant-leadership and the offices

When the righteous are in authority, the people rejoice; But when a wicked man rules, the people groan. (Proverbs 29:2)

Many spiritual movements have had great potential, but were undermined by unbiblical leadership. Some movements have waned because the movement was built on a man's charismatic personality or domineering leadership. When such men fail, the movement goes with it. Such a movement also has the tendency for imbalance, because it reflects the imbalances and quirks of its charismatic leader.

Other movements have failed because they were too opposed to structure. Perhaps their members have been wounded from previous experiences, and they are now content to languish without real leadership of any kind, or with a makeshift leadership derived from human wisdom rather than the word of God.

Leadership is a subject worthy of special care. In the Old Testament, God specified with great detail the nature of His desired leadership, beginning with Moses. Despite the clarity that God had provided, the Israelites struggled with leadership throughout the Old Testament. These problems included:

- An "anti-structure" leadership model. Korah said to Moses, "All the congregation is holy, every one of them, and the LORD is among them. Why then do you exalt yourselves above the assembly of the LORD?" (Num. 16:3)
- Leaders striving for authority out of jealousy and a desire for power. Aaron and Miriam's challenge of Moses exemplifies this pattern (Num. 12:1-2).

- A desire to copy pagan leadership models. The Israelites were dissatisfied with having God as their leader and asked Samuel for a king, to copy the nations around them (1 Sam. 8:19-20).
- Falling prey to charisma and eloquence rather than valuing righteous character. Absalom used charm and false promises to usurp the kingship (2 Sam. 15:1-6).

Whenever the people challenged God's model for leadership, they brought ruin upon themselves. The failures seen in Scripture should signal the church to tread carefully when considering leadership models. The New Testament provides another reason for caution. Immediately after specifying the qualifications of elders and deacons, Paul writes, "I write so that you may know how you ought to conduct yourself in the house of God, which is the church of the living God, the pillar and ground of the truth" (1 Tim. 3:15). Because the church is God's house, dare we deviate from His directions concerning its order and governance?

The New Testament offices

Much confusion has arisen as to the number and character of the New Testament offices of leadership. It is instructive first to lay out the relevant terms from the New Testament, and how various translations render those words.

Greek word	English translation
presbyteros	elder or presbyter
episkopos	overseer or bishop
poimen	pastor or shepherd
diakonos	deacon or servant

The New Testament uses the first three words, *presbyteros*, *episkopos*, and *poimen* interchangeably. This implies that there are only two offices of leadership: elders (also called overseers, bishops, shepherds, or pastors) and deacons. The interchangeability of elders, bishops, and pastors is found in three places in the New Testament. First, "For this reason I left you in Crete, that you should set in order the things that are lacking, and appoint elders in every city as I commanded you—if a man is blameless, the husband of one wife, having faithful children not accused of dissipation or insubordination. For a bishop [or overseer] must be blameless, as a steward of God, not self-willed, not quick-tempered..." (Titus 1:5-7). While elaborating on the qualifications of elders, Paul then refers to them as bishops. The connecting "for" is a grammatical construction of elaboration, making these terms functionally equivalent. The account of Paul's farewell address to the Ephesian elders bolsters the argument: "From Miletus [Paul] sent to Ephesus and called for the elders of the church. And when they had come to him, he said to them…, 'Therefore take heed to yourselves and to all the flock, among which the Holy Spirit has made you overseers, to shepherd the church of God which He purchased with His own blood.' " (Acts 20:17-18, 28). Here Paul calls the elders together, then refers to them as "overseers" and tells them to shepherd (or pastor) the church of God. Hence the three terms are seamlessly woven together in this passage. The final passage on this topic comes from Peter: "The elders who are among you I exhort, I who am a fellow elder and a witness of the sufferings of Christ, and also a partaker of the glory that will be revealed: Shepherd the flock of God which is among you, serving as overseers, not by compulsion but willingly, not for dishonest gain but eagerly; nor as being lords over those entrusted to you, but being examples to the flock; and when the Chief Shepherd appears, you will receive the crown of glory that does not fade away" (1 Pet. 5:1-4). Peter exhorts the "elders," commands them to "shepherd" (or pastor) the flock of God, and calls them to serve as "overseers." This beautiful passage further illustrates how all three terms are used interchangeably. The two-office model is also supported by Philippians 1:1, where Paul greets the "overseers and deacons"—if elders were a distinct group, one would expect that greetings would be offered to them also.

The simplicity of the two office model contrasts most starkly with the hierarchy of the Roman Catholic church. The pioneers of Bible translation into English, John Wycliffe (1324-1384 AD) and William Tyndale (1492-1536 AD), staunchly advocated the two-office model. The Roman Catholic church had Wycliffe's bones exhumed and burned. Several articles of offense were raised against him, one point being: "In the time of St. Paul, only two orders of clerks did suffice in the church."[1] Tyndale's position was similar: "Wherefore the apostles following and obeying the rule, doctrine, and commandment of our Saviour Jesus Christ, their master, ordained in his kingdom and congregation two officers; one called, after the Greek word, bishop, in English an overseer…Another officer they chose, and called him deacon after the Greek."[2] The men of faith who translated the Scriptures into

---

[1] George Townsend, *The Acts and Monuments of John Foxe: Volume III*, Stephen Cattley (ed.), R. B Seeley and W. Burnside (1837), p. 63.

[2] *The Works of the English Reformers: William Tyndale and John Frith (Volume I)*, Thomas Russell (ed.), Ebenezer Palmer (1831), pp. 400-401.

English saw how far the church had drifted and called for a return to the New Testament model.

The qualifications and duties of elders

Twice the qualifications of elders (also known as overseers) are presented in the New Testament (1 Tim. 3:1-7; Titus 1:5-9). When elders are appointed, great care must be taken in weighing these qualifications. A period of testing is referenced for both elders and deacons (1 Tim. 3:10), to see if they can be found "blameless." The congregation should measure candidates according to this list of qualifications, with sobriety and careful scrutiny. Three items from these lists merit expansion.

First, elders must be men (1 Tim. 3:1). Elders cannot be women, since women are forbidden to teach the congregation (1 Tim. 2:11-13). The prohibition of women teaching immediately precedes the qualification list of elders; this is surely no accident. Second, the children of any man reflect his character—magnifying both his faults and strengths—and so represent a powerful lens into the character of a man. Having children "in submission with all reverence" (1 Tim 3:4-5) is thus an acid test. Third, elders should normally be *older* men. The word *presbyteros* literally means older man, and this word choice cannot be ignored. (The test of having children obedient to the faith implies that his children would be able to be assessed for their submissiveness and reverence, so they should at least be teenagers, and ideally adults.) The elders' advanced age confers a sense of stability, maturity, and wisdom to the local congregation. Stability was particularly important in the first century when the apostles were mostly itinerant.

The duties of elders are specified:

1. They are to provide a living example of faith, worthy of imitation by the congregation (Heb. 13:7).
2. Elders are to teach the word (1 Tim. 3:2, 5:17).
3. They are to keep watch over the souls in the church (Heb. 13:17).
4. They are to be vigilant for false teachers (Acts 20:30-31).
5. Elders are to support the weak (Acts 20:35).
6. They are to resolve disputes and help apply Scripture to new circumstances (Acts 15:6-29).
7. Elders pray for the sick and anoint with oil (James 5:14).

In view of the responsibilities that elders bear, they will give an account for the souls under their watch (Heb. 13:7). This entails a stricter judgment (James 3:1).

On the number of elders

Throughout the book of Acts, the word *elders* is used in the plural and never in the singular (Acts 11:30, 14:23, 15:2, 15:4, 15:6, 15:22, 15:23, 16:4, 20:17, 20:18, 24:1). The epistles bear similar witness (1 Tim. 5:17; Titus 1:5; James 5:14; 1 Pet. 5:1, 5:5). Despite this overwhelming witness, many churches follow a model where there is a singular minister, often called the "senior pastor," who is placed in charge of a congregation.

The expression "senior pastor" should be abolished from a Christian's vocabulary as a title for a man. The term actually is used once in Scripture, but as a title for Jesus! "When the Chief Shepherd appears, you will receive the crown of glory that does not fade away" (1 Pet. 5:4). Remembering that pastor is equivalent to shepherd (both translated from the Greek word *poimen*), Jesus is the only "Chief Shepherd" or "Chief Pastor" spoken of Scripture. To apply that title to a man approaches blasphemy. In contrast, a plurality of elders offers great practical value:

1. Plural elders better reflect Jesus as the church's true leader.
2. The imbalances or quirks of any single individual can be counterbalanced in group leadership.
3. Leaders need accountability even more than others. Plural eldership offers that provision.
4. Strong-groups are more susceptible to cult-like leadership that can damage the group. A group of men reduces that risk.
5. Some members will respond best to certain leaders and their teaching, while others respond well to different leaders. A diversity of leaders best meets the needs of a diverse group.

The qualities and duties of deacons

The word *deacon* means "servant." Jesus said, "If anyone desires to be first, he shall be last of all and servant of all" (Mark 9:35). This could as well have been translated "last of all and deacon of all," because *deacon* and *servant* are English translations of the same word in Greek.

Deacons require similar qualifications as elders, except they do not need the ability to teach. They also require a period of testing (1 Tim. 3:10), given the importance of the office. While not specified in great detail, deacons appear to inherit the duties of the original seven "proto-deacons" (Acts 6:1-6), among whom was Stephen. The original seven assisted in serving the widows in food distribution. While elders have the responsibility for teaching, deacons have the responsibility of material service. Because of the biblical importance of providing for "the least of these My brethren," the office of deacon requires men of no less moral stature than the elders. Hence they also must be "blameless" men (1 Tim. 3:10).

The nature of New Testament leadership

Jesus draws a contrast between Gentile leadership and Christian leadership: "You know that the rulers of the Gentiles lord it over them, and those who are great exercise authority over them. Yet it shall not be so among you; but whoever desires to become great among you, let him be your servant. And whoever desires to be first among you, let him be your slave—just as the Son of Man did not come to be served, but to serve, and to give His life a ransom for many" (Matt. 20:25-28).

Both elders and deacons should be appointed because they prove to be servants. Servants are those who do not seek power or acclaim but find satisfaction when others are blessed. The qualification of a man's wife and children being reverent and submissive (1 Tim. 3:4, 11-12) exposes whether or not a man has labored to serve his wife and children, out of public view. Submissive children learn by example from men who have served their families.

Prospective elders or deacons should be examined as to whether they have labored to serve *individuals*, out of the public eye. Many men covet leadership because they love to speak to crowds. Those who are genuine servants labor to serve individuals, often those who are overlooked. They are those who clean toilets, disciple individuals, and selflessly provide for others' needs—activities not in the spotlight.

All titles such as "Reverend" or "Pastor" or "Father" should be eschewed. Special garb, elevated seating, or lofty pulpits fall into the same category. For Jesus said, "Do not be called 'Rabbi'; for One is your Teacher, the Christ, and you are all brethren. Do not call anyone on earth your father; for One is your Father, He who is in heaven. And do not be called teachers; for One is your Teacher, the Christ. But he who is greatest among you shall be your servant. And whoever exalts himself will be humbled, and he who humbles himself will be exalted" (Matt. 23:8-12).

The elder also knows every person and family in the flock—he knows their names, their spiritual state, and their struggles. Is this not implied from Jesus' teaching on the lost sheep? This limitation naturally restricts the size of any local congregation. Jesus' parable contained a flock of a hundred sheep; while we should not become legalistic with numerical limits, something of that range is a sensible limit on the elders' capacity. Smaller sized congregations also deter leadership-seeking among those whose goal is to draw large numbers after themselves. The mega-church model where the supposed elders do not even know the names of those in attendance can hardly be called a biblical church.

Decision-making vested in the body

Corinth was a church plagued with problems. Divided leadership, sexual immorality, lawsuits, prostitution, loss of the women's headcovering, drunkenness at the Lord's Supper, and disorderly meetings were some of the problems addressed by the apostle Paul. In the book of 1 Corinthians, he had numerous opportunities to address the elders and say, "Make sure those people obey you! Put in stricter standards!" Yet remarkably, *the word elder or overseer is not used even once in the entire book.* Paul appeals directly to the body, instructing them as to the significance of their condition and appeals *directly to the congregation.* The silence of address to the leaders is deafening. The body, the individual members, were ultimately the ones who held responsibility for their church—hence appeal was made directly to them.

When Paul pleads for the man in sexual immorality to be removed from the body, he addresses the body (not the elders) to make this decision. When the time comes for restoration, he says that the punishment inflicted *by the majority* (2 Cor. 2:6) was sufficient. Perfect unity is the goal, but decisions of significance require the backing of the majority of the congregation. Much prayer, fasting, study, and discussion should be a part of any deliberation, with the goal of reaching "one spirit, with one mind" (Phil. 1:27).

How leaders are appointed

When Paul planted churches, he did not immediately recognize any local leadership. Instead, *after* the church had functioned for a period of time, he would have elders appointed (Acts 14:21-23; Titus 1:5). Why was there a period of time without local leadership?

The delay in appointing leaders exists because elders are *recognized,* not determined or manufactured. Elders are recognized by their service to the flock and their character. Time and adversity are necessary elements to reveal the character of any man—so the period of testing described in 1 Timothy 3:10 (which applies to both elders and deacons) reveals to the congregation who the true elders are. So when the time comes for appointing elders, the congregation is merely declaring what is already true. Thus Paul could say, “the Holy Spirit has made you overseers” (Acts 20:28), and not men.

Part IV

The Gatherings of the Nation

Chapter 27

Sacraments and ordinances

When He was at table with them, He took the bread and blessed and broke it and gave it to them. And their eyes were opened, and they recognized Him. (Luke 24:30-31 ESV*)*

Word choices expose a person's beliefs. "Housewife" versus "homemaker" communicates a different understanding of a woman's vocation. The subtle difference between saying that one is "grateful" versus "happy" can communicate a belief in God's goodness versus blind luck.

Within the church, some choose to describe the Lord's Supper as a *sacrament* while others choose the term *ordinance*. These word choices reflect particular theological beliefs that have been debated through the centuries. Sacramental advocates maintain that something *actually* happens in the spiritual realm as participants partake in certain acts. "The term 'sacrament' suggests the power of symbols to link us to the depths of reality, and points us to the use by God of material means to mediate His saving action."[1] Sacramental advocates hold that God uses rites, ceremonies, and physical elements as a means of pouring out His grace.

Partly because of a concern of becoming superstitious, ordinance advocates believe that rites like the Lord's Supper are simply acts of obedience. While God certainly blesses and rewards obedience, they believe there is no intrinsic spiritual power that is communicated through a particular outward act. Ordinance advocates remember the historic abuses of the Roman Catholic church and the associated quasi-pagan thinking that resembles magic more than biblical faithfulness.

---

[1] Christopher Ellis in "Baptism and the Sacramental Freedom of God" in *Reflections on the Water*, Paul Fiddes (ed.), Smyth & Helwys (1996), p. 36.

With that brief introduction, each position will be laid out in slightly more detail. We will conclude this chapter by advocating for a biblically faithful, mediating position.

The sacramental view

The term *sacrament* was used in the Latin translation of the New Testament, and means *mystery*. "This is a great mystery [sacramentum], but I speak concerning Christ and the church" (Eph. 5:32). Sacraments are mysterious because a deeper spiritual reality accompanies what may appear to be merely physical.

The resolution to the sacrament-ordinance debate partly comes from having more clarity as to what precisely is under discussion. Often sacramentalists narrow the discussion by focusing on baptism and the Lord's Supper. But this is too restricted. After all, marriage itself is sacramental: it is the very topic that Paul presents as a *sacramentum* in Ephesians. It is mysterious because it represents the relationship of Jesus to His church. It is also mysterious because the two become one (Eph. 5:31). This mystery eludes modern society's understanding of human marriage. Society defers or rejects marriage while engaging in sexual relationships. They cannot understand why someone else's words that pronounce them "man and wife" matter. They say, "Aren't those merely words? Isn't the reality the relationship?" They do not understand the hidden spiritual reality behind marriage.

Similarly, when some Corinthians were having relations with prostitutes, Paul does not reprimand them for exposing themselves to a sexually transmitted disease or for frittering their money away. He reprimands them because they have united Jesus to a prostitute. The sexual union represents something much more than physical: it entails a spiritual union. Even if the Corinthians did not understand that they were uniting Jesus to a prostitute through their sin, it was happening irrespective of intent. A mysterious unifying power is at work in any sexual union.

The sacramental view harmonizes well with several teachings concerning the Lord's Supper. Scripture teaches that the Lord's Supper carries the power to spiritually unify believers (1 Cor. 10:17) and slay careless participants (1 Cor. 11:29-30). A divine power infuses this holy meal.

The ordinance view

The word ordinance simply means law. The word has come to represent "special" teachings of Jesus, which may not be obvious from just "love God" and "love your neighbor." Ordinance advocates generally name two ordinances: baptism and the Lord's Supper. Others describe as many as seven. Ordinance advocates are wary of the sacramental view for three main reasons. First, they are wary of grace or spiritual power being associated with an outward work. They believe that grace comes through faith only, as an inner disposition.

Second, advocates of the ordinance view highlight a passage worthy of careful study: 1 Corinthians 10:1-13. In this passage, Paul rebukes a view in which baptism and the Lord's Supper automatically and permanently place a person into a secure relationship with God. In an argument by analogy, Paul reminds his hearers that the Israelites shared a baptism into Moses. They also ate the same food and drank from the Rock of Jesus Himself. But in the Old Testament, many of these same people were judged and their bodies scattered in the wilderness (1 Cor. 10:1-5). Israel's common experiences of "baptism into Moses" and "eating and drinking," which prefigure New Testament baptism and the Lord's Supper, were not sufficient to secure salvation for all. The analogy has obvious implications for complacency among the baptized and partakers of the Lord's Supper. The Corinthians (and we) should take heed.

Third, ordinance advocates also point out the tendencies of sacramental thinking to promote superstition and magical thinking. For centuries, the Roman Catholic church has fostered antinomianism and false security. While its members are baptized as infants and share the Mass together, many live deplorable and sinful lives. Yet they cling to these rites and ceremonies in a manner similar to what Paul rebukes in 1 Corinthians. Ordinance advocates are wary of sacramental thinking because of this kind of abuse.

A mediating biblical position

Ordinance advocates are of course correct in their assertion that baptism and the Lord's Supper do not ensure salvation. Neither is there an automatic grace associated with these practices. Faith in King Jesus is essential. Without faith, no one can please God (Heb. 11:6). Any view in which rites effect grace or salvation apart from faith must be vigorously rejected.[2]

The crowning application of 1 Corinthians 10:1-13 is a command to flee idolatry, specifically the feasts of the pagan temples. By partaking in pagan feasts alongside the Lord's Supper, the Corinthians risk provoking God's judgment because of their fellowship with demons. Far from nullifying the sacramental viewpoint, this passage actually strengthens it. Both the Lord's Supper and the temple feasts have real spiritual power. The Corinthians simply failed to recognize the power of the pagan feasts in the spiritual realm.

We can go a bit further. The reason this issue emerged was likely because the Corinthians were originally taught a sacramental view of baptism and the Lord's Supper. The Corinthians mistakenly took this too far as blanket protection against other sins. They failed to understand that they needed to maintain separation and that the Lord's Supper must be accompanied with the Lord's righteousness. Separation and holiness are thus the true applications of this important passage.

Concerning the objection of associating grace to an outward act, we must tread carefully. Allowing Scripture to speak on its own terms can be damaging to overly systematized theologies. The notion that grace and spiritual power must be divorced from outward acts cannot be found in Scripture. When Jesus was baptized, something truly happened. When we partake in the Lord's Supper, we spiritually bind ourselves to others in the group. This may be a mysterious, unseen reality, but Scripture affirms it (1 Cor. 10:16-22). So this particular objection of ordinance advocates is ultimately founded upon a doctrinal system more so than on Scripture.

As was mentioned earlier, we should not overly restrict sacramental principles to the Lord's Supper and baptism—as important as those two practices are. Sexual relationships, the laying on of hands, and anointing with oil are additional examples of physical acts infused with spiritual power. A generally neglected example of sacramental power is the meeting of the church, to which we turn next.

[2] The Latin expression that a sacrament automatically effects grace, apart from faith, is *ex opere operato*. Literally, "from the work done."

Chapter 28

The local church and membership

And they were all with one accord... Yet none of the rest dared join them. (Acts 5:12-13)

In the previous chapter, we noted that certain outward acts are infused with spiritual power. This "mystery" (*sacramentum*) evades the natural eye and can be only seen with the eyes of faith. One of the most underappreciated mysteries involves the gathering of the saints. Many people find the concept of a church gathering to be boring. The world trains us to chase after novelty; thus seeing the same faces week after week can grow wearisome. But with faith's eyes, assuming the congregation is biblical, the gathering of the saints should be a thrilling experience.

To understand this significance, we need to start at the beginning: the very first place that the word "church" is used in the New Testament. Firsts are important, and this is no exception:

> You are Peter, and on this rock I will build My church, and the gates of Hades shall not prevail against it. And I will give you the keys of the kingdom of heaven, and whatever you bind on earth will be bound in heaven, and whatever you loose on earth will be loosed in heaven...
>
> Moreover if your brother sins against you, go and tell him his fault between you and him alone. If he hears you, you have gained your brother. But if he will not hear, take with you one or two more, that 'by the mouth of two or three witnesses every word may be established.' And if he refuses

> to hear them, tell it to the church. But if he refuses even to hear the church, let him be to you like a heathen and a tax collector. Assuredly, I say to you, whatever you bind on earth will be bound in heaven, and whatever you loose on earth will be loosed in heaven. Again I say to you that if two of you agree on earth concerning anything that they ask, it will be done for them by My Father in heaven. For where two or three are gathered together in My name, I am there in the midst of them. (Matt. 16:18-19, 18:15-20)

Interestingly, the above two passages are the only two recorded instances of Jesus using the word *church.* Yet we tend to shy away from these passages because they are filled with daunting and controversial phrases and concepts: "keys of the kingdom," "this rock," binding and loosing, and church discipline. What is all this about?

We will focus on the meaning of "keys of the kingdom" and "binding and loosing." When making sense of any passage, it helps to start with the easier parts and build upon that clarity to understand the more difficult parts. The context of Matthew 18:15-20 involves church discipline—putting someone out of the church. That is immediately followed by the promise of power to bind and loose. In Matthew 16, the promise is given just to Peter, in chapter 18 to all the disciples. Next follows Jesus' promise of answered prayer and His presence among believers. Because of the juxtaposition, the natural interpretation is that the binding and loosing involves the church's authority to put out of the kingdom or welcome into the kingdom. The parable immediately following Matthew 18:15-20 confirms this understanding of "binding and loosing." In the parable of the unforgiving servant, the servant moves from being loosed to bound because his fellow servants petitioned the Master. Still another passage in Matthew connects this concept to the language of keys, "But woe to you, scribes and Pharisees, hypocrites! For you lock people out of the kingdom of heaven" (Matt. 23:13 NRSV).

The final confirmation of this understanding of binding and loosing comes from a passage written by Paul to the Corinthians, also concerning church discipline: "In the name of our Lord Jesus Christ, when you are gathered together, along with my spirit, with the power of our Lord Jesus Christ, deliver such a one to Satan for the destruction of the flesh, that his spirit may be saved in the day of the Lord Jesus" (1 Cor. 5:4-5). Note the striking language, "when you are gathered…*with the power of our Lord Jesus Christ.*" This agrees perfectly with what was recorded in Matthew: in the context of a passage on church discipline, the highlight is on Jesus' powerful presence. Also, in this passage, the congregation has keys: they can hand this man over to Satan's kingdom.

The inference is that when disciples gather together, Jesus' special power is present for the purpose of affirming (or putting out) those gathered. The gathering of saints in Jesus' name therefore has a sacramental power that few appreciate. As we will see, this concept ties deeply into the notion of membership. Before exploring this further, we will pause to reflect on the state of affairs today.

Wrong beliefs and their consequences

Many today wrestle with the idea of church membership. Should we have it today? Is it even biblical? Much of our trepidation comes from not thinking about the church properly: "Most people in Western societies lump churches into the same category as soccer clubs or charity organizations. Churches are one more kind of voluntary association, we say. Alternatively, we regard churches as a service provider, like a mechanic who services your soul or a gas station that fills up your spiritual tank...It's ironic that we refer to church 'services'...it's as if we are telling people to pull into the church parking lot at 11:00 a.m. and get themselves serviced—'Tune ups for your soul in sixty minutes!' "[1] Thinking about the church as a club or charity organization has multiple unfortunate consequences:[2]

- Participation in the Lord's day gathering is not consistent.
- Professing Christians view the Lord's Supper as their own private, mystical experience and not as a corporate act that spiritually binds them to other believers.
- Believers do not integrate their Monday through Saturday lives with those of fellow saints.
- Believers make major life decisions (moving, selecting an occupation, accepting a promotion, choosing a spouse, etc.) without considering the effects of those decisions on the family of relationships in the church or without consulting the wisdom of the church's leaders and other members.
- Believers buy homes or rent apartments with scant regard for how factors such as distance and cost will affect their ability to serve their church.

[1] Jonathan Leeman, *Church Membership*, Crossway (2012), pp. 20, 22-23. I draw extensively from Leeman's excellent book in this chapter.

[2] List adapted from Leeman, pp. 23-24.

- Christians do not realize that they share responsibility for both the spiritual welfare and the physical livelihood of the other members of their church.

A new vision of the church

If thinking about the church as a club is wrongheaded, how should we correct our error? As we have stated throughout the book, the church should be regarded as a nation or kingdom. Clubs have members, but nations have citizens. Embedding this concept firmly in our minds helps to dispel misconceptions of membership and puts us on track toward a more biblical concept of the church. A provocative, paradigm-shifting vision of the local church has been well stated by analogy: "Just as the Bible establishes the government of your nation as your highest authority on earth when it comes to your citizenship in that nation, so the Bible establishes the local church as your highest authority on earth when it comes to your discipleship to Christ and your citizenship in Christ's present and promised nation."[3] The state is endowed with divine authority to confer or strip citizenship. Similarly when Peter, standing in the place of the church throughout history, is given the "keys of the kingdom of heaven" (Matt. 16:19), the church is given the power to affirm or deny citizenship. The church is certainly fallible, as is the state, or other human authorities such as parents. But Jesus has vested the church with a tremendous authority. And while the church does not make citizens (the Spirit does), it serves an official declaratory function.

An analogy helps us understand the concept. We become citizens of an earthly nation by virtue of where we are born. When traveling in a foreign country, only your embassy can reissue a lost passport or renew an expired one. Your embassy does not make you a citizen, but it officially *affirms* your citizenship. So it is with the church: it does not make citizens, but it officially affirms them. Furthermore, no individual can stand before the nations and self-declare his or her citizenship—it takes an official proclamation by an embassy. Likewise, the church, because it has the keys of the kingdom, has the authority to affirm or deny citizenship. Individuals cannot do this.

Let us press forward the analogy of an embassy. Christians are called "ambassadors for Christ" (2 Cor. 5:20). An ambassador operates out of an embassy. But our embassy does not represent an earthly nation. In-

[3] Leeman, p. 25.

stead the local church represents a place *from the future.*[4] Residing in enemy territory, the church is an embassy of Jesus' present and future reign. Armed with this understanding, the question can be now be answered more richly: "What is church membership? It's a declaration of citizenship in Christ's kingdom. It's a passport. It's an announcement made in the press room of Christ's kingdom. It's the declaration that you are an official, licensed, card-carrying, bona fide Jesus representative."[5]

In its regular gathering (especially through the Lord's Supper, as we will see), the church then officially affirms the citizenship of those present. In addition to this affirmation function, the church strengthens the faith of disciples, offers protection from hostile forces, officially removes impostors, and seeks to protect and magnify the name of King Jesus. In some sense, a two-way dialogue is occurring between the church and an individual. The church body says to the individual, "We recognize your profession of faith, baptism, and discipleship to Christ as valid. Therefore, we publicly *affirm* and acknowledge you as belonging to Christ and the *oversight* of our fellowship."[6] The individual says to the church, "I submit my discipleship to your care and oversight. And I offer my spiritual gifts to build up this local body."

Recognizing citizenship in Acts and the epistles

Jesus' vesting of the keys of the kingdom to the church, with the attendant power to bind and loose, supplies us with a *principle* to understand the church's relationship to affirming citizenship. This principle can be seen throughout the book of Acts and the epistles:

- In Acts 9:26, Paul tried to join the disciples, but they would not admit him. This demonstrates the necessity of having one's citizenship affirmed, namely that a new believer would have to be accepted by the local body. (As we will see, the picture is similar with baptism.) Beyond merely being physically present, there remained a subsequent step of ratification.
- The citizenry was numbered: one hundred and twenty in Acts 1:15; three thousand believers were added in Acts 2:41; five thousand are numbered in Acts 4:4. The phrasing in Acts 1:15 is noteworthy, "the number of names was about a hundred and twenty."

[4] Leeman, p. 28.
[5] Leeman, p. 64.
[6] Leeman, p. 65.

Someone within the early church was recording names and numbers, supporting the concept of a defined affirmation process.

- In the Old Testament, God ordained that the people be numbered and carefully accounted for (see Num. 1:1-4). Given the above examples from Acts, it is reasonable to suppose that God continues to desire a numbering of his people during the New Testament era.
- The word "member" is used explicitly in Scripture, albeit through analogy, "So we, being many, are one body in Christ, and individually members of one another" (Rom. 12:5).
- The concept of church discipline (Matt. 18:15-17; 1 Cor. 5) presupposes the concept of something like membership or citizenship, wherein some people are in and some are out.
- In 2 Corinthians 2:6, "punishment by the majority" is described. A majority represents more than half of a body. Without a body being numbered, such language is illogical.
- Mutual submission cannot be exercised unless one knows to whom one is in submission (Eph. 5:21; Heb. 13:17).
- The metaphor of a family, so commonly employed in the New Testament, is a well-defined, circumscribed entity. When asked to name one's natural brothers and sisters, no one pauses in giving an answer. One's family is not whoever is in the house at the time, but those with whom one has a clear relationship. The case is similar with the metaphor of soldiers; soldiers know precisely who is on their side (Eph. 6:10-18; 2 Tim. 2:4).

Submitting, not joining

Here is another paradigm-shifting statement: Christians do not join churches, they submit to them.[7] As potentially frightening as that might be, this is the language of Scripture. "Submit to one another in the fear of God" (Eph. 5:21). In the fear of God! Because the gathered saints are vested with power *directly from Jesus*, the church is not simply a club which we happen to "join." The church is an embassy of God's kingdom.

Many (perhaps most) churches today are apostate, and Jesus' presence has been removed. Submitting to an apostate church is not submitting to God but to human wickedness. This topic will be addressed later.

Submission to a biblical church especially involves the leaders.

[7] Leeman, p. 30.

"Obey those who rule over you, and be submissive, for they watch out for your souls, as those who must give account" (Heb. 13:17). As off-putting as this verse might be, it is a badly needed correction in our day of freewheeling individualism. Bullying leaders have certainly abused this teaching, but a widespread overcorrection from abusive potential has resulted in anarchy. What does submission look like? We are called to submit publicly, geographically, socially, financially, vocationally, and spiritually:[8]

- Publicly. The relationship between a disciple and a local church should be no shrouded secret, no piece of guesswork. It should be an intentional, well-defined relationship. Providing a model to all shepherds, Jesus knew exactly who His disciples were (see chapter 4 on "Discipleship as intensive companionship").
- Geographically. Insofar as possible, disciples should live as close to one another as possible, "breaking bread from house to house" (Acts 2:46). In an Anabaptist church we attended, my wife and I were melted by the expressions of love where the members cared for one another in very practical ways. Ranging from babysitting during a mother's dentist appointment to sharing meals to garden work, much of this was enabled because the disciples of the congregation intentionally lived near one another.
- Socially. Christians ought to share friendship and affection with fellow believers from their congregations. "Churches should be more than social clubs, but they shouldn't be less."[9] Biblical fellowship transcends barriers of ethnicity, age, and socioeconomic status. Many of us have experienced in high school or college a genuine affection for our friends. Often that withers as time goes on because of busyness or isolation. But through the church, that longing affection should find fulfillment.
- Financially. We share one another's burdens and give sacrificially to help the family of God (see chapter 5, "Equality among brothers").
- Vocationally. At the least, we should select occupations that facilitate time with the brotherhood and the gathering of the saints. This may require making less money or doing work we otherwise might not choose. Even better, working with or employing fellow believers serves as a powerful and biblical means of discipleship and spiritual encouragement.
- Spiritually. Disciples share responsibility in watching over the

[8] List elements from Leeman, pp. 95-102.

[9] Leeman, p. 97.

souls of fellow Christians. They commit to using and developing their spiritual gifts for the service of the body. Christians submit to the authority of the elders and humbly accept counsel from the brotherhood on important matters. They commit to regularly intercede on behalf of their brothers and sisters in the Lord.

Affirming unfamiliar citizens

The apostle Paul presented himself for recognition as a citizen of the kingdom. Initially the saints in Jerusalem declined. They "did not believe he was a disciple" (Acts 9:26). Elsewhere we are urged, "Do not lay hands on anyone hastily, nor share in other people's sins; keep yourself pure" (1 Tim. 5:22). Yet because it is flattering when someone expresses a desire to join our church, we tend toward haste. Months or years later, we regret that haste after understanding the person's character better. Affirming citizenship without sufficient scrutiny can be dangerous. Adding an Achan[10] or a person who stirs up controversy can rob a group of its vitality. Earthly embassies recognize the possibility of fraud; so must we. Representing Jesus' kingdom is a great responsibility not to be taken lightly. While the desire to grow quickly will be a temptation, large numbers will destroy a group more easily than small numbers. We therefore need guidelines for responsible affirmation:

1. Affirmation of citizenship should be a collective decision (Acts 9:26), and not one that rests on a single individual's wisdom. A group discussion among mature believers produces insight far greater than any one individual may possess. Just as discipline should involve a group, affirmation should require a group. This implies that several members of a church would have spent time with the unfamiliar person.
2. For those who are just becoming believers, baptism itself is the public declaration of a new citizenship. Just as individuals cannot attest to their own earthly citizenship but require an embassy to issue their passports, a person cannot baptize himself. The apostolic declaration "repent and be baptized" is thus in itself a proclamation of the authority of the church in affirming biblical faith.
3. Those who have long and complex histories of church attendance require greater wisdom than new believers. Often these people have embedded errors in their thinking or patterns of sin that must be first identified and addressed.

[10] See Joshua 7.

4. The person should demonstrate the fruits of the Spirit. Of particular interest is how the person behaves under trial or stress. Ultimately, a person cannot be truly known without the benefits of time and adversity. Time and adversity expose a person's character far better than static observation or interactions among pleasant company.
5. The unfamiliar person should be questioned on whether he or she agrees with the group's convictions. Documents such as this book are expedient ways to help determine whether or not there is agreement.
6. References should be utilized, particularly from prior churches. Leaving churches under questionable circumstances should be thoroughly investigated. Reference letters are a biblical concept (Rom. 16:1-2; 1 Cor. 4:17; 2 Cor. 8:16-24; Phil. 2:19-30; Acts 9:2; Acts 22:5). Unstable or serial church attendance must be carefully examined.
7. Special attention should be paid as to whether or not the person harbors a pet doctrine or belief that might lead to destabilization or needless controversy in the group.
8. The unfamiliar person should be questioned as to the presence of unrepentant sin or strained relationships in which he or she may have been primarily at fault (Matt. 5:23-24). These issues should be cleared before affirmation at the Lord's Supper. When there are questionable past relationships, effort should be made to hear the counterparties' side of the story. A trail of broken relationships should serve as a bright warning light that there are almost certainly unresolved sin issues in the person's life. Sadly, the business world often does a better job scrutinizing prospective employees than the church does with new members.
9. The unfamiliar person should be observed in his family setting if at all possible. For those who are parents, the spiritual vibrancy and behavior of the children usually reveal more about the parents than any direct conversation with the parents themselves.
10. Because becoming part of a biblical church has financial implications, consideration should be given to outstanding debts, medical liabilities, and other future costs which the body might be called to bear. While being poor is welcomed, many people have used deceit to take advantage of generous disciples. The biblical account of the Gibeonite deception was given for the church's warning.

The goal of this process is for the church with one mind to be able to affirm the candidate's citizenship in Jesus' kingdom. If at the end of this process outstanding issues remain, the church does better to proceed cautiously and not affirm citizenship. Allowing additional time for observation, resolution of potential sin issues, or theological instruction is a far wiser course. A belief in the sacramental power of the Lord's Supper should motivate caution.

One is either an affirmed citizen or not. Care should be taken to practice equality among citizens, without levels or hierarchy. For example, affirmed citizens should be welcomed in the Lord's Supper, brotherhood assistance, and all other aspects of church life.

When churches have their lampstands removed

Many, perhaps most, churches today are so far from God's word that they no longer have Jesus' abiding presence. Jesus said to an erring church, "Remember therefore from where you have fallen; repent and do the first works, or else I will come to you *quickly* and remove your lampstand from its place—unless you repent" (Rev. 2:5). If a church has persisted in a sin for years, despite being called to repentance, this church has likely already had its lampstand removed. This of course cannot be seen with the physical eye and requires spiritual discernment. The standard should be high for testing a church. Jesus says that merely *tolerating* sin is sufficient for disqualification. "But I have this against you, that you tolerate that woman Jezebel" (Rev. 2:20 ESV). Even if the elders are themselves not teaching evil, to tolerate sin is to make Jesus be "against you" (Rev. 2:20).

When genuine disciples maintain relations with diseased churches too long, several symptoms may manifest. First, church meetings may cause a depletion of energy rather than a rejuvenation because of underlying confusion, discomfort, disagreement, or conflict. Second, by binding themselves to the group, disciples "share in other people's sins" (1 Tim. 5:22) and may grow spiritually weak. By partaking in communion, they are spiritually uniting themselves to the group and infecting themselves with leaven. Third, faithful disciples may have their own witness harmed because of their tacit acceptance of sin. After all, to the outside world a person's regular presence in a group serves as an endorsement. Furthermore, when strong believers spread themselves out amongst apostate churches, it only dilutes the strong witness that might occur if faithful saints were united. We are exhorted to come out from evil structures and groups (2 Cor. 6:14-18). "Flee to protect your discipleship, to protect your family, to set a good example for the members left behind, and to serve non-Christians by not lending credibility to the church's ministry."[11]

Apostate churches can be identified by their disobedience to the word. One should especially pay attention to commands of the word that are countercultural. When churches tolerate divorce and remarriage, worldly entertainment, immodesty, jewelry, war, and reject the woman's headcovering, such a church has probably had its lampstand removed, especially if prophets have long since sounded the alarm. Some churches have gone bad through abusive leadership. Manipulation, bullying, hypocrisy, dogmatism, and favoritism are some of the characteristics of these groups. They should be avoided.

If God's true followers everywhere had a holy discontent with the *status quo*, pleading to Him night and day for pure churches, God would open up heaven itself and provide embassies to mark His present and future reign.

[11] Leeman, p. 118.

Chapter 29

Accountability and church discipline

[I] cut off all the evildoers from the city of the LORD. *(Psalms 101:8 NKJV)*

In the previous chapter, we saw that the church has been given the authority to publicly affirm or deny citizenship in Jesus' kingdom. This authority comes with great responsibility because God's honor is vested with His children. Any father's honor rises or falls with the behavior of his children. God's honor therefore depends on how the church exercises its responsibility to declare who are His children, and how those children are disciplined.

Imagine what a child would be like who never experienced discipline. He would be lazy, selfish, and immoral. For this reason, the Bible exhorts us to love discipline. "Whoever loves discipline loves knowledge, but he who hates reproof is stupid" (Prov. 12:1). This truth certainly applies to a group: without discipline, the church is bound to weakness, immorality, and a poor witness.

Yet church discipline is often badly practiced and itself has a tarnished reputation. In most Protestant churches, discipline is typically restricted to blatant doctrinal deviation (such as denying the Trinity) or to sexual sins (such as pornography or adultery). Rarely do accountability and discipline permeate deeper.

Part of the problem is that accountability and church discipline are wrongly viewed in isolation, away from the larger fabric of church life. When there is faithful preaching, biblical standards, and godly example, many problems can be prevented. Discipline that is reactive rather than preventative is sure to be ugly. Consider the sight of parents with unruly children making a scene in public. The children, not having been raised in a loving environment of discipline, act spoiled and rebellious. The exasperated parents are embarrassed or perhaps lose their temper as they try to bring their children into order in public. Such reactive discipline is bound to bring shame upon the parents.

Too often, the expression *church discipline* is used to describe only the very late stages of dealing with an unrepentant person. Church discipline, in such a setting, becomes about the steps in confronting a wayward person. While these steps are certainly an important part of accountability and discipline, in a healthy church these are a small portion of what discipline should entail.

An analogy with medicine is helpful. Most of medicine deals with treating patients *after* they are sick. This focus hurts society's health and pocketbook. Largely because health care costs have rapidly escalated, many people advocate that *preventative* medicine would be a more sensible focus. Creative ways to get people to stop smoking, eat healthy, and exercise regularly would improve the health care system far more than developing the next pill. In the same way, our emphasis should be on "preventative theology"—being part of churches where conflict and sin are not allowed to take root.

When viewed in this way, the previous chapters on biblical standards and strong-group church life are foundational to accountability and church discipline. Intensive discipleship, spiritual teaching, biblical standards, and faithful examples constitute the *majority* of healthy church discipline. If one is not part of a church where these elements are found, heightened conflict and confrontation over sin issues are inevitable.

Even in settings where these elements are present, there will occasionally be the need to handle professing Christians living in sin. As we saw in the previous chapter, "tolerance" of sin is not acceptable (Rev. 2:20). Sin must be confronted. The Bible speaks often about the importance of discipline and purity:

> Like a muddied spring or a polluted fountain is a righteous man who gives way before the wicked. (Prov. 25:26)
>
> Have no fellowship with the unfruitful works of darkness, but rather expose them. (Eph. 5:11)
>
> Moreover if your brother sins against you, go and tell him his fault between you and him alone. If he hears you, you have gained your brother. But if he will not hear, take with you one or two more, that "by the mouth of two or three

> witnesses every word may be established." And if he refuses to hear them, tell it to the church. But if he refuses even to hear the church, let him be to you like a heathen and a tax collector. (Matt. 18:15-17)
>
> I wrote to you in my epistle not to keep company with sexually immoral people. Yet I certainly did not mean with the sexually immoral people of this world, or with the covetous, or extortioners, or idolaters, since then you would need to go out of the world. But now I have written to you not to keep company with anyone named a brother, who is sexually immoral, or covetous, or an idolater, or a reviler, or a drunkard, or an extortioner—not even to eat with such a person. For what have I to do with judging those also who are outside? Do you not judge those who are inside? But those who are outside God judges. Therefore "put away from yourselves the evil person." (1 Cor. 5:9-13)
>
> But we command you, brethren, in the name of our Lord Jesus Christ, that you withdraw from every brother who walks disorderly and not according to the tradition which he received from us. (2 Thess. 3:6)
>
> If anyone does not obey our word in this epistle, note that person and do not keep company with him, that he may be ashamed. (2 Thess. 3:14)
>
> In the last days perilous times will come: For men will be lovers of themselves, lovers of money, boasters, proud, blasphemers, disobedient to parents, unthankful, unholy, unloving, unforgiving, slanderers, without self-control, brutal, despisers of good, traitors, headstrong, haughty, lovers of pleasure rather than lovers of God, having a form of godliness but denying its power. And from such people turn away! (2 Tim. 3:1-5)

Anyone living in unrepentant sin or idleness is to be put out of fellowship. This action is on behalf of four parties[1]:

- For God's glory, to bring honor to Jesus' name.
- For the church's protection, to keep it pure by eliminating the corrupting leaven which easily spreads.

[1] Jonathan Leeman, *Church Discipline*, Crossway (2012), p. 23 and 33.

- For wayward individuals, by showing them the gravity of their state. To not discipline unrepentant sinners is to give them a false hope.
- For the world, to maintain a pure witness so that the church can be a city on a hill.

Discipline for leaders or the divisive

Note that Scripture uses stronger language for false teachers or those who stir up division:

> Now I urge you, brethren, note those who cause divisions and offenses, contrary to the doctrine which you learned, and avoid them. (Rom. 16:17)
>
> As for a person who stirs up division, after warning him once and then twice, have nothing more to do with him, knowing that such a person is warped and sinful; he is self-condemned. (Titus 3:10-11 ESV)
>
> If anyone teaches otherwise and does not consent to wholesome words, even the words of our Lord Jesus Christ, and to the doctrine which accords with godliness, he is proud, knowing nothing, but is obsessed with disputes and arguments over words, from which come envy, strife, reviling, evil suspicions, useless wranglings of men of corrupt minds and destitute of the truth, who suppose that godliness is a means of gain. From such withdraw yourself. (1 Tim. 6:3-5)
>
> Whoever transgresses and does not abide in the doctrine of Christ does not have God. He who abides in the doctrine of Christ has both the Father and the Son. If anyone comes to you and does not bring this doctrine, do not receive him into your house nor greet him; for he who greets him shares in his evil deeds. (2 John 9-11)

God especially hates division. Those who stir up division are therefore far from God's nature; they are especially twisted. Believers are hence counseled to "have nothing more to do" with a divisive person once such a disposition has been exposed. Scripture warns us similarly about false teachers. Such persons are to be avoided and not even to be greeted. The hurdle to become a teacher is high because of the influence that he wields. Naturally, a false teacher has great potential to ruin a person or a group. For this reason, such a person cannot even be granted a toehold.

The mechanics of discipline and restoration

The authority of discipline and restoration lies with the congregation as a whole, not with the leaders. While leaders should play a facilitating role, the New Testament teaches that final authority rests with the congregation. Note the language that Jesus uses: "if he refuses even to hear the church" (Matt. 18:17). Reinforcing this truth, Paul describes how the punishment required "a majority" (2 Cor. 2:6). At the same time, we learn from Matthew 18:15-17 that church discipline should involve as few people as possible in the initial stages of confrontation. By being discrete and sensitive, the sinner is more likely to be restored.

Upon confrontation, many questions will naturally arise regarding what to believe, the existence of a sin pattern, the sincerity of repentance, and reasonable next steps. Scripture could never address all the possible situations that may arise, so those involved should together ask God for wisdom. The interactions of a small group of people generally produce greater wisdom than a lone individual. Thus Jesus' instruction in Matt. 18:15-17 in moving from one person to two or three to the whole church draws out a greater wisdom that pools the strengths of those involved.

Relating to a person under discipline requires wisdom. One has to balance firm disassociation with a loving attitude. An early Anabaptist confession, the Dordrecht Confession, adds helpful insights:

> Concerning the withdrawing from, or shunning the separated, we believe and confess, that if any one, either through his wicked life or perverted doctrine, has so far fallen that he is separated from God, and, consequently, also separated and punished by the church, the same must, according to the doctrine of Christ and His apostles, be shunned, without distinction, by all the fellow members of the church, especially those to whom it is known, in eating, drinking, and other similar intercourse, and no company be had with him that they may not become contaminated by intercourse with him, nor made partakers of his sins; but that the sinner may be made ashamed, pricked in his heart, and convicted in his conscience, unto his reformation. I Cor. 5:9-11; II Thess. 3:14.

> Yet, in shunning as well as in reproving, such moderation and Christian discretion must be used, that it may conduce, not to the destruction, but to the reformation of the sinner. For, if he is needy, hungry, thirsty, naked, sick, or in any other distress, we are in duty bound, necessity requiring it, according to love and the doctrine of Christ and His apostles, to render him aid and assistance; otherwise, shunning would in this case tend more to destruction than to reformation.
>
> Therefore, we must not count them as enemies, but admonish them as brethren, that thereby they may be brought to a knowledge of and to repentance and sorrow for their sins, so that they may become reconciled to God, and consequently be received again into the church, and that love may continue with them, according as is proper. II Thess. 3:15.

Because the goal is spiritual restoration, this matter should be discussed as a group so that parameters and guidelines can be established. In consultation with the brotherhood, Christians can more easily maintain the appropriate balance to win back a wayward soul.

The force and blessing of discipline

Much of the force of church discipline is lost because most groups today are weak-group. But in the first century, to be put out of the church was to lose social, economic, and emotional bonds that we can scarcely understand today.[2] While today, a person put out of one church will just show up at the church down the street and be welcomed with open arms, being put out of a strong-group church is a much more weighty matter. Because strong-group churches cannot be widely found, a person will feel the loss and not easily be able to experience such intense belonging.

There are also spiritual implications to discipline. By being put out of the Lord's Supper, a person loses the opportunity to commune with Jesus in an important way. Being put out of the church has grave implications for an individual's spiritual welfare, to the point that Paul describes this state as being handed over to Satan (1 Cor. 5:5).

---

[2] James Burtchaell, *From Synagogue to Church*, Cambridge University Press (1992), p. 281.

The blessings of biblical church discipline are many. Paradoxically, unity is one of them. Immediately after Ananias and Sapphira were publicly censured and struck down, the Scriptures record that "they were all in one accord" (Acts 5:12). When there are clear teachings and those who violate those teachings are put out, this has the tendency of binding the group together. It also paradoxically increases the respect that the world has for the church. Immediately following the story of Ananias and Sapphira, "None of the rest dared join [the Christians], but the people esteemed them highly" (Acts 5:13). Because of this esteem, the church gains the credibility to function as the city on a hill that attracts the world to its Savior.

Chapter 30

The Regulative Principle

Those who worship Him must worship in spirit and truth. (John 4:24)

The church faces two contrasting visions of the worship of God and the ordering of His house. One view states that we can worship and order the church however we please, so long as it is not forbidden in Scripture—the so-called Normative Principle. A second view states that we can only worship God or order His house in ways that have been positively demonstrated or commanded—the so-called Regulative Principle (RP).[1] Another way of stating the RP is that what Scripture does not command or authorize, it forbids.

The choice between these competing visions will affect decisions concerning holidays such as December 25, musical instruments in worship, and distinctive clerical dress. It will affect the use of crosses, holy water, incense, and images. Church governance will differ under groups that follow the Normative versus Regulative Principle. For example, advocates of the RP reject offices such as cardinal or archbishop and hold only to explicitly scriptural offices like elders and deacons. Our journey in understanding the RP begins with a historic survey.

---

[1] This is sometimes called the Regulative Principle of Worship (RPW). However other matters, such as church governance, fall under the Regulative Principle, so the shorter term is preferred. Though the terms the *Normative Principle* versus the *Regulative Principle* have already been fixed by history, my preferred terminology is different. While I defer to historic nomenclature in this chapter, I prefer the terms the *Innovation Principle* versus the *Pattern Principle*.

Historic advocacy

The early Anabaptists and Protestants were advocates of the RP. The RP served as the centerpiece of a theology that led the Anabaptists and Protestants to argue against the Mass, priestly vestments, images and many other Roman Catholic trappings. Conrad Grebel, a prominent leader of the first Anabaptists, wrote: "Therefore we ask and admonish you as a brother in the name, power, Word, Spirit, and salvation which comes to all Christians through Jesus Christ our Master and Savior, to seek earnestly to preach only God's Word unflinchingly, to establish and defend only divine practices, to esteem as good and right only what can be found in definite clear Scripture, and to reject, hate, and curse all the schemes, words, practices, and opinions of all men, even your own."[2] Elsewhere, Grebel wrote a remarkably clear statement of the RP, "Whatever we are not taught in definite statements and examples [from Scripture], we are to consider forbidden."[3] Grebel's methodology can be summarized as, "Everything must be tested by the New Testament, and what is not found therein as the teaching of Christ and the apostles or as an apostolic practice must be abandoned."[4] Grebel's advocacy of the RP was shared by Michael Sattler, Felix Manz, and other leaders of early Anabaptism.[5] Among the Dutch, Dirk Philips championed the RP.[6] Menno Simons advocated the RP and notes his agreement with the Protestants on this issue:

> Luther writes…that which is not commanded of God in religious matters of faith is forbidden. Again, concerning the 12th chapter of Genesis he says, "That we should not accept any doctrines without certain reasons from the divine word." Daniel writes, "Worship, without the word of God, is idolatry." Philip Melanchthon in a book on the *Jurisdiction and authority of the church*, says, "That all worship which is not instituted of God in his express word, is false and wrong…" For if we read and well consider the Scriptures then we clearly find how pointedly God has

[2] *The Sources of Swiss Anabaptism: The Grebel Letters and Related Documents: Volume 1*, Leland Harder (ed.) Wipf and Stock (1985), p. 286.

[3] Ibid, p. 287.

[4] Harold S. Bender, *Conrad Grebel: The Founder of the Swiss Brethren*, Wipf and Stock (1998), p. 175.

[5] C. Arnold Snyder, *The Life and Thought of Michael Sattler*, Herald Press (1984), pp. 139-143.

[6] *The Writings of Dirk Philips*, Cornelius Dyck, William Keeney, and Alvin Beachy (translators and editors), Herald Press (1992), pp. 83-84.

> commanded us that we shall not institute a religion of our own choice, but that we should do as he has commanded. On account of self-righteousness and self-chosen religion, Israel was severely visited and punished of the Lord.[7]

Protestant leader John Knox advocated the RP by saying, "All worshipping, honoring, or service invented by the brain of man in the religion of God, without His own express commandment, is idolatry."[8] Protestants cherished the RP so dearly that it was expressed in the Westminster Confession: "But the acceptable way of worshiping the true God is instituted by himself, and so limited by his own revealed will, that he may not be worshipped according to the imaginations and devices of men, or the suggestions of Satan, under any visible representation, or any other way not prescribed in the holy Scripture."[9]

The Regulative Principle in other churches

The first example of the RP outside of Scripture is usually credited to Clement of Rome. Perhaps the earliest book composed after the New Testament, 1 Clement was likely written sometime between 80-100 AD.[10] The book addresses a leadership struggle in Corinth. A careful examination of the book's themes reveals a desire for unity rooted in the RP.[11] While the themes of communal solidarity around the apostolic pattern emerge most clearly from a wider reading, chapters 40-44 contain the RP in miniature. Clement describes the exactness of the Old Testament worship form. He writes that we are under more severe judgment if we deviate from God's plan (1 Clement 41:4). When describing the leadership model of the apostles, Clement writes, "Nor was this an innovation" (1 Clement 42:5).[12] He then argues for the per-

---

[7] Menno Simons in "Infant Baptism," *The Complete Works of Menno Simons*, John F. Funk and Brother (1871, reprint by Pathway Publishers in 1983), Second Part, p. 269.

[8] John Knox quoted in Alexander Taylor Innes, *John Knox*, Oliphant Anderson & Ferrier (1896), p. 67.

[9] Westminster Confession of Faith, chapter XXI, heading I.

[10] On dating issues, see *The Apostolic Fathers*, third edition, Michael Holmes (editor and translator), Baker Academic (2007), pp. 35-36.

[11] For an excellent analysis of Clement's arguments, see B. E. Bowe's *A Church in Crisis: Ecclesiology and Paraenesis in Clement of Rome (Harvard Dissertations in Religion)*, Fortress (1988). The book's thematic analysis as opposed to prooftexting make it particularly worthwhile.

[12] Translation by Robert Grant and Holt Graham in *The Apostolic Fathers: Volume II*, Thomas Nelson (1965), p. 71.

manency of the apostolically ordained offices (1 Clement 44:2). One of the great themes of 1 Clement is divinely created order.[13] "Order becomes for Clement a means for preserving the very existence of the church."[14] This order is God's order, over and against human wisdom. Despite Clement's arguments, the ante-Nicene church slowly drifted from the apostolic pattern, leading to corruption and setting the stage for Constantine's more dramatic changes.

The Waldensians were a twelfth century group that stressed radical obedience to the gospel, voluntary poverty, lay preaching, and the translation of the Bible into the vernacular. In their brief Confession of Faith (ca. 1120 AD) of fourteen articles, two articles were dedicated to the RP:

> 10. We have ever regarded all the inventions of men (in the affairs of religion) as an unspeakable abomination before God; such as the festival days and vigils of saints, and what is called holy-water, the abstaining from flesh on certain days, and such like things, but above all, the masses.
>
> 11. We hold in abhorrence all human inventions, as proceeding from Antichrist, which produce distress, and are prejudicial to the liberty of the mind.[15]

Their statement on the RP rings as clear and strong as any found among the Anabaptists or the Protestants. In 1487, Pope Innocent VII issued an edict for the extermination of the Waldensians, leading to tremendous persecution for the next hundred years.

Immersed in Scripture, John Wycliffe (1324-1384 AD) came to the RP while at Oxford University. While best known for his work on the first translation of the Bible into English, Wycliffe wielded his genius in many areas of church life. In particular, Wycliffe saw the peril of innovation in the church. "Throughout his writings, he complains that innovation and infatuation with novelty threaten the integrity of Christianity and the church."[16] He applied the RP to many facets of worship and ecclesiology. For example, he taught against the use of images and musical instruments. He also severely criticized the papacy, long before the Protestant Reformation. Wycliffe used the RP to argue

---

[13] In Greek, *tasso*.

[14] Bowe, p. 108.

[15] William Jones, *The History of the Waldenses: Volume II*, Paternoster (1816), p.45.

[16] Stephen Lahey, *John Wyclif*, Oxford University Press (2009), p. 154.

that the church should not even own property.[17] "What goods come to the church ought automatically to be bestowed upon those in need as a matter of course, without the church's having anything to do with civil *dominum*. This is the ideal for which the church was ordered by Christ, and some of the harshest invective in Wyclif's prose is against the church's inability even to desire to return to the apostolic state. For example, in *Dialogus sive Speculum Ecclesia Militantis*, he attributes all of the clergy's shortcomings to their captivation with property."[18] Like Wycliffe, we should be alarmed at the inability of churches today to "desire to return to the apostolic state." In contrast, churches that hold the RP have a fervent desire to follow that pattern, no matter the cost or how thickly tradition has been overlaid. This hunger for the apostolic pattern fuels an energetic study of the Scriptures. The Lollards, Wycliffe's followers, taught a return to the New Testament model but were persecuted and killed.

Some of the early Baptists came to the RP through exegesis. They succinctly captured the RP in an early confession: "The acceptable way of worshipping the true God, is instituted by himself, and so limited by his own revealed will, that he may not be worshipped according to the imagination and devices of men, nor the suggestions of Satan, under any visible representations, or any other way not prescribed in the Holy Scriptures."[19] Around this time the Baptist John Bunyan, while in prison for preaching without a license, wrote the book *The Pilgrim's Progress*. The book describes the trial of Faithful, accused of describing Vanity Fair as a place of vain worship, and Faithful's testimony of true worship requiring "a divine revelation of the will of God."[20]

In yet another approach, the Puritans came to the RP through meditation on the Son's nature, the story of redemption, and the church. In modern terminology, they arrived at the RP through biblical theology as opposed to systematic theology. John Owen, with characteristic Puritan eloquence, weaves together biblical themes of God's sovereignty, Jesus as builder of the church, and the nature of worship. His *Christologia* and *Worship of God and Discipline of the Churches of the New Testament* are two of several sources that theologically arrive at the RP. Any distillation of Owen's work does injustice to his stirring contemplations on the majesty of God and the beauty of His redemptive work. However, Owen does provides a catechism answering the question, "How is the way of worship made known to us?" He answers, "In and by the

[17] Lahey, chapter 7.
[18] Lahey, p. 215.
[19] The London Baptist Confession of 1689, Article 22, Heading 1.
[20] John Bunyan, *The Pilgrim's Progress*, Penguin (2002 printing), p. 91.

written word only, which contains a full and perfect revelation of the will of God as to his whole worship and all the concernments of it."[21] Owen taught that false worship would mark the apostate church: "The great apostasy of the church in the last days, foretold in the Scripture, and which God threateneth to punish and revenge, consists principally in false worship and a departure from the institutions of Christ; Rev. [xiii] 4, 5. xvii. 1-5."[22]

Jonathan Edwards also affirmed the RP. "God has declared his abhorrence of such worship as is taught by the precept of men without his institution."[23] Elsewhere he writes, "Nothing is to be done in the worship of God more or less but what God has instituted."[24] In this same document, he wisely anticipates the importance of distinguishing between content and circumstance (more on this later).

Alexander Campbell, leader of the nineteenth century Restoration Movement, also held to the RP: "There is a divinely instituted worship for the assemblies of the disciples...But as none but the Lord can prescribe or regulate the worship due to himself and profitable to us; so, if he has done it, human regulations are as vain and useless as attempts to prevent the ebbing of the sea or the waxing and waning of the moon."[25]

Biblical foundations of the Regulative Principle

As demonstrated by diverse groups in history, there are multiple ways to arrive at the RP. Prooftexting is generally the weakest. Biblical theology, the enterprise of allowing the larger narrative of Scripture to speak, serves as a more constructive approach. My capsule summary of an approach rooted in biblical theology would be:

> At creation, God's intent was that creation would function as His temple and that humans would bear His image as priests serving in that temple.[26] Because of the fall, humankind and the earth were marred by sin. God sought to

[21] John Owen, "A Brief Instruction in the Worship of God," available at www.ccel.org/ccel/owen/worship.txt.

[22] John Owen, *The Works of John Owen: Volume XIX*, Thomas Russell (ed.), Richard Baynes (1826), p. 501.

[23] Jonathan Edwards in *The Works of President Edwards: Volume I*, Leavitt and Allen (1852), p. 309.

[24] Jonathan Edwards in *Miscellanies*, 76, available at edwards.yale.edu.

[25] Alexander Campbell, *A Restoration of the Ancient Order of Things*, No. 5 (1824).

[26] See Acts 7:49; Isa. 66:1. This theme is developed in Gregory Beale's *The Temple and the Church's Mission: A Biblical Theology of the Dwelling Place of God*, IVP Academic (2004).

> restore His temple and pure worship through the Mosaic Covenant. Under this covenant, God carefully prescribed the structure of His temple and how Israel could approach Him. Again the covenant was thwarted by sin; the temple was destroyed. Finally God sent His Son to the earth who proclaimed that the Father may be worshipped only in spirit and in truth. Jesus taught that He was God's true temple. Secured to Jesus as cornerstone, the apostles and prophets form the foundation of a structure with a divine blueprint. God can be worshipped rightly when people are found in the temple of His Son and offer themselves as living sacrifices. As throughout the sweep of history, God determines the worship that pleases Him, and the ordering of His temple. Humanity is called to worship through this divinely ordained pattern.

Let us now expand upon this summary. At the first sacrifice recorded in Scripture, Abel's offering is rejected while Cain's is accepted. Here the word *sin* is first mentioned in Scripture (Gen. 4:7). While Scripture is silent on specifics, Cain somehow departs from God's intent and chooses to sacrifice as he pleases.[27] When the Mosaic covenant is established, God dispels the pagan notion that He can be worshipped as humans decide. "The Hebrews were not free to approach God however they pleased, through whatever means they found enlightening, fun, or interesting. Instead God comes out of the gate with explicit commands on the relationship between their making and their worship...No other ancient rule set commanded monotheism and no other system puts such a high importance on the tools and objects used for worship."[28]

After the Ten Commandments are given, a detailed blueprint is given for the Tabernacle. "And let them make me a sanctuary, that I may dwell in their midst. Exactly as I show you concerning the pattern of the tabernacle, and of all its furniture, so you shall make it" (Exod. 25:8-9). Old Testament worship was based on exactly *imitating* the divine pattern that God showed to Moses.

Deuteronomy 12 is an important chapter on the subject of worship. The Israelites are told that they may not worship as they please (v. 8), but must follow what the LORD prescribes. One verse from this chapter is especially relevant to the RP: "Whatever I command you, be care-

---

[27] John Brown's *Hebrews*, Banner of Truth (1961), pp. 493-494 explores Hebrew's commentary on Cain and Abel from the perspective of the RP.

[28] John Dyer, *From the Garden to the City*, Kregel (2012), p. 113.

ful to observe it; you shall not add to it nor take away from it" (Deut. 12:32). The verse is not about adding or removing commands from God's laws in a general sense—that was prohibited elsewhere, namely, in Deuteronomy 4:2. Deuteronomy 12:32 is about the worship of God. Paraphrasing Deuteronomy 12:32, God says, "Regarding my worship, do exactly as I tell you, don't do additional things and don't omit what I've specified." Commentator Matthew Henry explains this verse, "You shall not add thereto any inventions of your own, under pretence of making the ordinance either more significant or more magnificent, nor diminish from it, under pretence of making it more easy and practicable, or of setting aside that which may be spared; but observe to do all that, *and that only*, which God has commanded" (emphasis added). This is of course a restatement of the RP.

Specific examples clarify our understanding of the RP. A famous example is the fate of Aaron's sons, who offered an unauthorized sacrifice before the Lord: "Now Nadab and Abihu, the sons of Aaron, each took his censer and put fire in it and laid incense on it and offered unauthorized fire before the Lord, which he had not commanded them. And fire came out from before the Lord and consumed them, and they died before the Lord. Then Moses said to Aaron, 'This is what the Lord has said: "Among those who are near me I will be sanctified, and before all the people I will be glorified." ' And Aaron held his peace" (Lev. 10:1-3). The passage notes that Aaron's sons were doing that "which he had not commanded them." They were doing something *in addition* to what God had prescribed. Aaron's sons did not sin by breaking a particular command, but by deciding to *innovate* in their worship. They offered unauthorized fire, novel fire, which came from their imaginations and not from God's express will. Despite being sons of the high priest himself, they were struck down. Even Aaron could but hold his peace before such a display of God's holiness.

In Isaiah's day, the people were supposed to offer sacrifices in a particular way. But in addition, they were offering sacrifices in gardens, on altars of bricks. This may have been a well-meaning effort to bolster devotion to God by worshipping in beautiful settings on orderly altars. But God detests these human additions, "I spread out My hands all the day to a rebellious people, who walk in a way that is not good, following their own devices; a people who provoke Me to My face continually, sacrificing in gardens and making offerings on bricks" (Isa. 65:2-3). The people were never told to worship with brick altars in gardens. God was thus provoked because people were "following their own devices" (v. 2). At the core of the RP is the charge to follow God's pattern rather than human devices and imaginations, even if they are well intentioned.

This understanding blends well with another text: "If you make Me an altar of stone, you shall not build it of hewn stones, for if you wield your tool on it you profane it" (Exod. 20:25). When man puts his design into worship, he defiles it.

When God speaks through the prophet Jeremiah about the evils of child sacrifice, He says, "And they have built the high places of Topheth, which is in the Valley of the Son of Hinnom, to burn their sons and their daughters in the fire, which I did not command, nor did it come into my mind" (Jer. 7:31). Note the reason why God describes it as being evil: God did not command it. Rather than mentioning the deaths of the children, certainly an evil consequence, God's stated reason for the wickedness of the deed was that it was not His command. This reason hearkens back to the account of Nadab and Abihu's punishment.

Where do religious innovations originate? Usually they come from the world or other religions. In 2 Kings 16, the tragic story of Ahaz is given. After describing the wickedness of Ahaz in offering child sacrifice and idolatry, Scripture exposes his errant motivations. Ahaz copied a foreign nation by introducing its patterns into the worship of the true God. Why do people suppose that they can improve upon what God has revealed by mixing biblical teaching with the things of this world? Professing Christians have mixed every manner of paganism into God's ordinances. But these are things which "I did not command," says the Lord (Jer. 7:31). Rather than follow human innovation, God calls us to the pattern of Scripture.

In the New Testament, Jesus teaches that human innovation does not please God:

> Then the Pharisees and some of the scribes came together to Him, having come from Jerusalem. Now when they saw some of His disciples eat bread with defiled, that is, with unwashed hands, they found fault. For the Pharisees and all the Jews do not eat unless they wash their hands in a special way, holding the tradition of the elders. When they come from the marketplace, they do not eat unless they wash. And there are many other things which they have received and hold, like the washing of cups, pitchers, copper vessels, and couches. Then the Pharisees and scribes asked Him, "Why do Your disciples not walk according to the tradition of the elders, but eat bread with unwashed hands?" He answered and said to them, "Well did Isaiah prophesy of you hypocrites, as it is written: 'This people honors Me with their lips, But their heart is far from Me.

> And in vain they worship Me, Teaching as doctrines the commandments of men.' For laying aside the commandment of God, you hold the tradition of men." (Mark 7:1-8)

Mark 7:3 must be grasped in order to comprehend the whole passage. Varying translations read "unless they wash their hands in a special way" (NKJV) or "unless they wash their hands properly" (ESV) or "unless they wash their ritually" (LEB). The underlying Greek is simply, "washed with the fist." A method of handwashing was introduced, and religious significance was attached to this practice. This practice did not come from Scripture but was a tradition. But note carefully: *Jesus demonstrates in this passage that His followers are not to partake in religious practices that do not originate from Scripture.* Jesus was an advocate of the RP.

The deed under fire in this passage is quite remarkable. Washing and ritual purity are taught in the Old Testament (Exod. 29:4, 40:30; Num. 8:7). Handwashing was not prohibited. This particular method of handwashing was nowhere prohibited. Washing one's hands in a certain way would not interfere with other commands of Scripture. Moreover, this account takes place outside the temple, in private settings. If there were ever an innocuous religious practice, this was it. Perhaps it began with a good motivation, to remind observers of the importance of purity or keeping the Torah. But Jesus rails against it. Jesus speaks against attaching religious significance to this humanly conceived practice.

We saw earlier that Moses taught the people to follow the pattern which the Lord had given them (Exod. 25:8-9). Looming large in the apostolic understanding of worship, the New Testament twice mentions this teaching (Acts 7:44; Heb. 8:5). The New Testament also affirms the concept of a template being handed down, "For I received from the Lord that which I also delivered to you" (1 Cor. 11:23). The epistles urge the "imitation" of an apostolic pattern (1 Cor. 4:16, 11:1; 1 Thess. 1:6; 2 Thess. 3:6). Paul commends the churches in Thessalonica for becoming, "imitators of the churches of God which are in Judea" (1 Thess. 2:14).

While God formerly dwelt in a temple of limestone and marble, He now dwells in the church. Worship, ordinances, and the governance of the church are thus at God's direction, not our own. "I write so that you may know how to conduct yourself in the household of God, which is the church of the living God, the pillar and ground of the truth" (1 Tim. 3:15). The church is God's house. What person when visiting another's home does not first inquire what the rules of that household are and how he should behave? He does not simply say, "Because there are no prohibitions put before me, I can do as I please." How much more so should we act in accordance with God's revealed will in Scripture in matters of worship and ordering His house?

The loss of the RP in history

In an earlier section, we noted that the RP was the instrument of many of the important reform-minded churches in history. The Waldensians, Anabaptists, Protestants, Lollards, Baptists, Puritans, and Restoration churches advocated the RP. We noted that these groups came to the RP through different approaches.

Yet today few have heard of the Regulative Principle, even among the descendants of those groups. Most modern Anabaptists and Protestants have never read the works of the early Anabaptists or Protestants. They feel little connection to their spiritual heritage. They are thus liable to discard even hard fought truths of their spiritual ancestors. As something like the RP is forgotten and associated practices are eliminated, one is left with a hodgepodge of inconsistent practices. Often I visit Anabaptist churches and see a syncretistic blend of modern evangelicalism with historic Anabaptism. For example, members will hold dearly to nonresistance but sing along to guitar-led worship of contemporary praise songs. Members at such churches do not understand that they have rejected biblical truths that were a prominent part of their spiritual heritage. On the other side, visitors coming to churches that follow the RP may not understand why musical instruments are not used. Without clear understanding of this principle's logic, people grow frustrated in congregations that refrain from using instruments.

By articulating the RP, one has a framework to handle many issues, particularly in seeing where human innovation has elbowed its way into the church. And because so much human tradition has crept into the church over many centuries and now seems normal, one will find great resistance to the RP even among Protestants and Anabaptists. Thus this is a topic that should be broached with carefulness, patience, and love.

We should be clear that the RP is that it is a *principle*, not a mathematical formula. While proponents of the RP agree on core applications, other applications are more controversial. We must pray for wisdom, learn from others, and be willing to ask difficult questions. Let us first consider human innovations that nearly all RP advocates have rejected:

- Icons, statues, or the use of crosses
- "Holy" objects such as holy water or saints' relics
- Distinctive clerical garb of any form (robes, staffs, caps, etc.)
- Musical instruments or incense (more on this later, given the presence of these elements in Old Testament worship)
- Extrabiblical holidays such as Ash Wednesday, Lent, or Christmas
- Rituals or ceremonies such as crossing oneself or using the rosary

However, RP advocates have been less unified about other questions:

- Should the church meeting itself be structured according to the New Testament pattern? For example, should the Lord's Supper involve a weekly, full meal as the apostles did?
- Should we introduce modern age-segregation into our meetings, such as Sunday School?
- Should the church own buildings or lands?

Some groups have followed out the RP to these applications. The early Anabaptists attempted to configure their meetings according to the New Testament pattern. As we have already seen, John Wycliffe wanted the church out of the business of owning land. While there have been areas of disagreement, we will spend more time on consensus applications to better understand the RP and its implications.

Case study 1: Holidays like December 25

In most churches today, observing December 25 is part of what it means to be Christian. For such people, rejecting this holiday is tantamount to embracing a secular or pagan worldview. Their notion of victory is having nativity displays in public areas or hearing "Merry Christmas" instead of "Happy holidays."

But Scripture nowhere mentions such an annual commemoration. Under the RP, because it lacks scriptural warrant, December 25 as a religious holiday should be rejected. It is as simple as that. (Few appreciate that this has been the historic position of groups like the Puritans, the Anabaptists, and the early Protestants.) This would naturally apply to other extrabiblical holidays such as Ash Wednesday, Lent, or Ascension Day. The New Testament gives warrant only for the weekly gathering of the saints on the Lord's day and the observance of the Lord's Supper as a commemoration of His death and resurrection.

Rejecting a religious observance of December 25 is supported by an important biblical passage, "You observe days and months and seasons and years! I am afraid I may have labored over you in vain" (Gal. 4:10-11 ESV). In this passage, set in a larger discussion of circumcision in the church age, Paul bemoans that the Galatian converts are observing various "holy" days. Because of the context and the circumstances of the Galatian believers, nearly all commentators believe that these religious days are references to Jewish holy days in the Old Testament.[29] Paul, while naturally appreciating that those days were given by God in the Old Covenant, rejects observing these days in the New Covenant. This rejection leads to a more precise statement of the RP: In matters of faith, worship, and ordering God's house, the Christian should avoid that which lacks *New Covenant* warrant, that is, *New Testament command or approved apostolic example.*

Let us return to the subject of December 25. If Paul speaks negatively about observing religious holidays described in the Old Testament, once given by God Himself, it is not hard to imagine his reaction to a religious holiday that humans have manufactured.

The word *Christmas* comes from "Christ's Mass." Should we advo cate the celebration of a Mass? Consider the expression "Merry Christmas." Was Christ described as merry, or a man of suffering, living a life of "cries and tears" (Heb. 5:7)? The answer should be obvious to anyone who has read the New Testament. The expression "Merry Christmas" thus sandwiches Jesus' royal title with mischaracterization and Roman Catholic practice.

A corollary of the RP is: *Where man innovates, the law of unintended consequence takes effect. Through the law of unintended consequence, this innovation will hinder advance of the kingdom.* Even a moment's reflections on December 25 confirms this:

- Partakers effectively say to Jesus, "We love you and honor you so much, that we're going to buy presents for ourselves." Does this make sense? Is there another day so marked by materialism? What witness does this provide to the lost?
- By lifting up days like December 25, millions of nominal Christians soothe their consciences by attending services on this "holy day." Millions of non-Christians likewise give homage to Jesus one day per year and receive false comfort from superstitious ceremonies.
- Jesus is presented as a perpetual baby on December 25. Even for ordinary human birthdays, no one does this. Imagine if on your

[29] For example, see Thomas Schreiner, *Galatians*, Zondervan (2010), p. 279.

> birthday, you were presented with a barrage of baby pictures. December 25 relegates Jesus to the comfortable position of the cute baby, not the one who rides on a horse, with His robe dipped in blood, leading the armies of heaven (Rev. 19:11-16).

We can understand something's true nature by its fruits. By departing from the RP with religious holidays, we have reaped the whirlwind.

Case study 2: Instrumental music in worship

In the previous case study, drawing from Galatians, we noted that legitimate religious practice requires New Testament warrant. The church's worship is described in several places (Matt. 26:30; Mark 14:26; 1 Cor. 14:15; Col. 3:16; Eph. 5:19; Heb. 2:12, 13:15). Musical instruments are strikingly absent. Thus musical instruments lack New Testament warrant and should not play a role in the worship of God.

The church has historically held a negative view toward musical instruments in worship. Musical instruments were not used in church worship until 1000-1300 AD.[30] Throughout history, many prominent Christian leaders from diverse denominations rejected the use of musical instruments in worship. The list includes Justin Martyr, Tertullian, Clement of Alexandria, Eusebius, Athanasius, Ambrose, Chrysostom, Jerome, Augustine, Thomas Aquinas, John Wycliffe, Huldrych Zwingli, John Calvin, Theodore Beza, John Knox, John Owen, John Bunyan, John Wesley, Alexander Campbell, and Charles Spurgeon.[31] These men gave diverse reasons for their rejection of instruments, including a desire to avoid Judaizing and paganism. Some explicitly mentioned the RP.

Despite the strong historic support, many objectors howl in protest. Their main objection is founded upon the use of instruments in the Old Testament. Why should the church refrain from using instruments when Israel used them? After all, even David played a harp. Before answering this objection, we should note that those who advocate musical instruments for the church have an intuition and discomfort that using incense or special priestly garb would be too "Old Testament." So they themselves are inconsistent in relying upon Old Testament witness.

The first response to this Old Testament objection comes from the history of God's dealings with humankind. Musical instruments were

[30] Paul Westermeyer, *Te Deum: The Church and Music*, Fortress Press (1998), p. 120.

[31] A good historical survey can be found in John Price's *Old Light on New Worship*, Simpson (2007), chapter 2.

reserved for the temple and not used in the synagogue.[32] Because the church was born from the womb of the synagogue, no specific prohibitions against musical instruments were required, because their absence was assumed. In addition, the thoughtful reader should pause because anytime a practice is associated with the Old Testament temple, it is likely to have been fulfilled through Jesus' work.

The New Testament often witnesses to Old Testament paradigms being fulfilled, leading to their cessation. The obvious example concerns animal sacrifice. But a less obvious example is also instructive. In the Old Testament priests were commanded to wear turbans (Exod. 28:39, 29:6, 39:31; Lev. 8:9, 16:4; Ezek. 24:17; Zech. 3:5). Yet in the New Testament, rooted in a revelation of the Trinity, for a man to pray with his head covered is strictly prohibited (1 Cor. 11:4). Such a radical change should give pause to casual reliance on Old Testament examples for the New Testament believer.

Besides the RP, at least three additional reasons can be given to maintain historic *a capella* worship. First, Israel was in a childish period that required helps and aids. But with the people of God as an adult in the church age, those aids should no longer be required. Relying on childish aids fosters childishness. The state of the churches today reflect this. How many congregations would lose attendance without their praise bands? How many professing Christians would attend worship concerts that were *a capella*? Make no mistake: many come for the emotional titillation generated by the instruments, not for the unadorned worship of God. They are like children searching for thrills. The true prophetic, worshipful spirit can sing to God from the heart. Discarding instruments assists the church to maintain a pure and mature brotherhood.

Second, instruments often serve as a distraction. My wife and I were recently in a church gathering where the instrument playing was so loud that my three-year old son started to cry. Others, surprised by the poor quality of the music, tried to restrain their snickers. Still worse, two unbelievers standing in front of us stumbled at this poorly done cacophony of worldly music applied to sacred language and walked out in disbelief. Consider now the other extreme, when there is very professional music and the heart is stirred. This environment causes people to admire the instrument players (though they may resist the urge) and thus lose focus on the King. Simple *a capella* music is unsurpassed in its ability to focus attention on the words and object of praise.

Third, musical instruments have been fulfilled in Jesus' work. This

[32] Westermeyer, pp. 20-21.

consideration has generally been neglected but emanates from examining the role of instruments in the Old Testament period. "The liturgical use of musical instruments in the OT was a particular function of the priests and Levites—connected with the sacrifice and the ark of the covenant—and therefore part of the ceremonial order that has been fulfilled by the Priestly work of Christ."[33] In the books of Chronicles, we learn that musical instruments were very specific parts of the Levitical and sacrificial system (1 Chron. 15:16, 16:4-6; 2 Chron. 29:25-26). Priests appointed to play instruments were specifically named and numbered (1 Chron. 16:39-42, 23:2-5, 25:1-2). The music was especially associated with the burnt offering (2 Chron. 29:27), but the instruments were to stop once the offering was completed (2 Chron. 29:28). After the offering was completed and the instruments were put away, reverent singing would continue to the Lord (2 Chron. 29:28-30). From a typological perspective, musical instruments should therefore cease after Jesus' sacrifice. More broadly, "the Great High Priest has replaced the earthly priests. All of the outward, external, sense-oriented, tutorial elements are now abrogated—whether instituted under Moses or David."[34]

Other applications of the RP

Space limits the extent to which additional applications of the RP can be explored. The reader is encouraged to labor as we have done above with each of the below applications in greater detail. The reader should explore how the law of unintended consequence has unfolded, how neglecting the RP in each instance has hindered the kingdom, and how Jesus' work relates to the practice. These additional examples of violating the RP include:

- Special clerical dress: The New Testament nowhere offers warrant for this practice. Special vestments in fact violate the larger principle of the priesthood of all believers.
- Using icons, statues, or crosses: they resemble pagan superstition more than biblical faith. Nowhere in the New Testament is there mention of using images or Jesus' cross as a visible symbol of faith. One should pay close attention to how crosses are used today. Crosses are often happily embraced by worldly churches. Some individuals functionally use it as a "rabbit's foot" or talis-

[33] Quoted from Douglas Comin, www.puritanboard.com.

[34] Ibid.

man. Rap singers flaunt ornate gold crosses with other lavish jewelry. Others use the cross as a tattoo. By juxtaposing the cross to immorality, one wonders if demonic forces are trying to tarnish the message of the cross and spoil the witness of Jesus' church. Riding the subway, I often witness sights such as a modestly dressed Muslim family seated next to a woman with a gold or diamond cross glittering light above her exposed chest. Yet this woman probably believes that she is somehow honoring God. It would be far better if true Christianity were associated with simplicity, modesty, and holding the cross as an inward disposition, not an outward show of symbols.

- Youth ministry and age-segregated Sunday school: these are fairly recent innovations (mostly beginning in the 1800s) that are now widespread. The history of the Sunday School movement involved the education of street children, not the children of believers, and was met with great skepticism in the church, with some fearing that it would "destroy family religion."[35] While some good has come from these movements, it has been matched by a great deal of harm.
- Stripping the love feast from the Lord's Supper: most churches have changed the Lord's Supper from its New Testament pattern (more on this subject in a later chapter). They have removed the love feast from the Lord's Supper largely for practical reasons. This model has been exported all over the world by Western churches. Sadly, in some churches in India, churchgoers from Hindu backgrounds will not eat a meal with other church members because of caste prejudice, but they will have communion together! They tolerate passing a plate full of crackers but will not tolerate sharing a meal. The Holy Spirit intended that the Lord's Supper as a meal would destroy those prejudices.[36] Without a meal, these prejudices can remain undisturbed. This represents another example of the law of unintended consequences at work.

[35] S. Brown, *A Weed in the Church*, NCFIC (2011), pp. 101-103. Brown's book represents a rewarding historical and theological exploration of how age segregation and youth ministry have harmed the church and weakened the family.

[36] The meal functioned similarly in the New Testament era. Consider the reason for Paul's rebuke of Peter in Galatians 2:11-13.

Blessings from the Regulative Principle

There is something winsome and refreshing about simplicity. The great prophets of the church age have railed against the thick crust of human tradition that has obscured Jesus and His word. From John Wycliffe to Conrad Grebel, these prophets have called for a return to the simplicity of the New Testament. The Regulative Principle, by speaking against human innovations, sweeps clean the house of God. The Regulative Principle is allied with simplicity. The apostle's words serve as a helpful reminder: "For our boasting is this: the testimony of our conscience that we conducted ourselves in the world in simplicity and godly sincerity, not with fleshly wisdom" (2 Cor. 1:12). Simplicity is contrasted with fleshly wisdom. The Regulative Principle, by opposing innovations of the flesh, keeps the church simple and transparent. Jesus can more clearly be seen without the clutter of the works of men.

The Regulative Principle preemptively strikes at needless conflict and reproach. John Owen wrote, "That principle, that the church hath power to institute any thing or ceremony belonging to the worship of God, either to a matter or manner, beyond the orderly observance of such circumstances as necessarily attend such ordinances as Christ Himself hath instituted, lies at the bottom of all the horrible superstition and idolatry, of all the confusion, blood, persecution, and wars, that have for so long a season spread themselves over the face of the [C]hristian world."[37]

In addition, departing from the RP erodes the church's belief in the sufficiency of Scripture (2 Tim. 3:15-17; Jude 1:3). The RP is closely aligned with the sufficiency of Scripture, *sola scriptura*, and prohibitions against extrabiblical standards. All four serve as the legs of a sturdy table onto which confidence can be laid. They mutually reinforce confidence in God's wisdom and make us hesitant to put confidence in the flesh. To be sure, the RP is no guarantee for unity. The RP can also be handled poorly, without love and grace. Because of its controversial nature and because of areas of uncertainty, we should be cautious, charitable, and humble in our implementation.

While the RP may appear a stifling collar, it should rather be understood as what best strengthens our faith. Consider the content of what we sing: twice in the New Testament we are taught to sing the Psalms in our worship (Eph. 5:19; Col. 3:16). The Psalms offer a far more inspiring body of songs than most of the sentimental, watery, and weak songs used in churches today. Could it be that some of the church's strength

[37] John Owen, quoted in William Orme, *Memoirs of the Life, Writings, and Religious Connexions of John Owen*, T. Hamilton (1870), p. 20.

has been lost because it has given itself over to uninspired and theologically imbalanced praise? How many churches profess to follow the Scriptures and yet their worship lacks the inspired hymns of Scripture itself!

While beyond the scope of this chapter, virtually every example we have discussed above could be understood in this positive dimension. By using the RP, we are strengthening our families and our churches. The reader is encouraged to meditate on the examples above and contemplate how the New Testament paradigm serves to build our faith and increase our trust in the Savior.

Answering objections

People in the New Testament didn't have cars. Does the RP teach we shouldn't drive either?

Opponents of the RP often construct a false opponent and then pummel their deformed caricature. The RP covers the worship of God and the ordering of His house. When Moses provided an exact pattern for the tabernacle of God, he said nothing about what sort of tents the Israelites must live in. When the apostle commended the Thessalonians for imitating the churches in Judea, he was not speaking about the Thessalonians' diet or their choice of sandals. Similarly, the RP is about God's dwelling place; it should not be extended beyond its intended range.

Second, the RP concerns content, not circumstances. Whether an assembly meets at 5 o'clock or 6 o'clock is a circumstance left to their discretion. Whether a group uses emmer or wheat in their love feast is *adiaphora*, a matter of indifference. God leaves these circumstantial matters to our discretion; He provides us with wisdom to best serve His flock.

Objection: Jesus, by participating in synagogue services and Hanukkah, showed He did not embrace the RP.

Some wrongfully imagine that the synagogue was merely a development of the intertestamental period. Because synagogues lack scriptural warrant, as the argument goes, Jesus Himself did not embrace the RP.

However, a more careful reading shows that the synagogue meeting is implied by the Old Testament: "Six days shall work be done, but on the seventh day is a Sabbath of solemn rest, a holy convocation" (Lev.

23:3). This holy convocation represents the origin of the synagogue. The holy convocation was a meeting to pray, hear Scripture, and worship God. While the temple was prescribed as the location of certain feasts and special occasions, *each week* Jews were commanded to meet locally in a holy convocation. Not surprisingly then, the Psalms attest to multiple meeting houses, besides the temple: "They said to themselves, 'We will utterly subdue them'; they burned all the meeting places of God in the land" (Ps. 74:8). The KJV translates this verse as "they have burned up all the synagogues of God in the land." The synagogue was not invented during the intertestamental period; it was present in ancient Israel. It was the means of fulfilling the "holy convocation" commanded by the Lord. The New Testament supports this ancient origin: "For from ancient generations Moses has had in every city those who proclaim him, for he is read every Sabbath in the synagogues" (Acts 15:21 ESV).

Though a nonbiblical writer, Philo independently attests that the synagogue dates back to the days of Moses.[38] Some modern scholars believe that the synagogue was a formalization of the city-gate often described in the Old Testament.[39] Integrating the biblical witness with nonbiblical writers, we can have confidence that the synagogue was authorized by Moses and found in the biblical period. Thus Jesus' participation in the synagogue was obedience to Scripture and not a violation of the RP.

In a similar vein, some claim that Jesus observed an extrabiblical holiday, the Feast of Dedication (also known as Hanukkah), based on the following passage: "Now it was the Feast of Dedication in Jerusalem, and it was winter. And Jesus walked in the temple, in Solomon's porch" (John 10:22-23). Hanukkah was a feast that developed in the intertestamental period as a celebration of the accomplishments of the Maccabean revolt. The passage does not say that Jesus observed the feast. In fact, a more careful reading shows that He did not. First, Jesus is outside the temple proper, in Solomon's Colonnade. Earlier in John's

[38] *The Ancient Synagogue from its Origins to 200 C.E.*, Anders Runesson, Birger Olsson, and Donald Binder (eds.), Brill (2008), p. 209. This book, an anthology of primary sources on the synagogue, serves as a very useful reference on the subject.

[39] Lee Levine, *The Ancient Synagogue: The First Thousand Years*, second edition, Yale University Press (2005), pp. 30-44. Levine's book has become the standard reference on this topic in scholarly circles. Levine, professor at the Hebrew University in Jerusalem, marshals evidence from a variety of sources in his argument, including from early architectural evidence (p. 37) and intertestamental literature (p. 41).

account, in chapter 8, Jesus departs the temple, never to return.[40] Accordingly, John portrays Jesus in chapter 10 outside the temple.

Second, what happens next helps us to understand the significance of Jesus' remaining outside the temple: "So the Jews encircled Him and said to Him, 'How long will You take away our life?' "(John 10:24).[41] The Jewish leaders are angry that Jesus is not partaking in this ceremony. "The Jews are suggesting that Jesus is attempting to destroy Judaism."[42] Far from supporting Jesus' endorsing extrabiblical holidays, this passage teaches the opposite. If Jesus were in the crowd, celebrating with everybody else, presumably He would be in the temple, not outside, and the Jewish leaders would be pleased with Him. Instead, Jesus' actions provoke the religious leaders to anger. Third, John is painting a vivid picture of the true temple, walking outside the old temple. Rather than pay homage to the old temple in an extrabiblical holiday, Jesus points to Himself as the new temple in a bold, symbolic act.

Objection: You advocate singing the Psalms, but the Psalms describe musical instruments. Isn't that a contradiction?

The Psalms also describe animal sacrifices (Ps. 118:27), pilgrimages to Jerusalem (Ps. 84:7), and blowing the trumpet on the new moon (Ps. 81:3). Because these have all been fulfilled through Jesus' work, we can sing them with confidence.

Objection: The New Testament mentions harps in the book of Revelation. This provides warrant for using musical instruments in the church.

This argument suffers from two flaws. First, the book of Revelation uses highly symbolic language. Whether or not literal harps are used in heavenly worship is uncertain. Also, if one accepts the premise, then Christians should wear crowns on earth because that is also described in the heavenly scene.

The second flaw involves eschatological confusion. For the sake of argument, let us suppose that literal harps are used in the next age in heavenly worship. Would that supply warrant for their use in this age?

---

[40] "Jesus' departure from the temple at the end of chapter 8 was final." in "Jesus Forms a Community Around Himself Over Against Official Judaism" (9:1-10:42), IVP New Testament Commentaries, available at www.biblegateway.com/resources/ivp-nt.

[41] A very literal translation.

[42] Leon Morris' view, quoted in Andreas Köstenberger's *John*, Baker Academic (2004), p. 310f.

No. Consider marriage as example. We know that human marriage is done away with in the next age (Matt. 22:30). Does that imply that we should refrain from human marriage today? While certain groups like the Shakers have maintained this position, it is unbiblical. We require New Testament warrant *for the church age* in order to embrace a practice for today.

Chapter 31

The Lord's Supper

They saw God, and they ate and drank. (Exodus 24:11)

The Bible is filled with eating. At the beginning of Genesis, Adam and Eve sin through food. The joy of the marriage supper of the Lamb reverberates through the final chapters of Revelation. When the disciples preached about Jesus, they drew attention to their shared meals, how they "*ate and drank* with Him after He arose from the dead" (Acts 10:40).

Meals are important in virtually every culture, especially the Hebrew one. As families, we recognize the value of eating meals together. Families that do not eat together are considered dysfunctional. When people celebrate an event, they reflexively eat together. Having a wedding without a meal would seem incomplete. People naturally understand that sharing meals is a way to solidify commitments, strengthen relationships, and celebrate good news.

Meals were infused with significance in the ancient world. "To share a meal in the ancient world was to share a life."[1] In the biblical context of a meal, the host offers protection, fellowship, and acceptance.

In the Old Testament, meals would often follow sacrifices. Three basic types of sacrifice were prescribed: sin, burnt, and peace.[2] To understand the Lord's Supper, the peace offering (sometimes translated fellowship offering[3]) is the most important (Lev. 3, 7:11-34). It often

---

[1] Grant Osborne, *Revelation*, Baker Academic (2002), p. 213.

[2] By some counts, there are five basic offerings, including the grain and guilt offerings. But the grain offering is a variant on the burnt offering, and the guilt offering is a variant of the sin offering.

[3] The underlying word is *shelem*, related to *shalom*, and represents wholeness, peace, and restored relationships.

followed the burnt or sin offering (e.g. Exod. 24:11; Num. 7:16-17) and involved sacrificing a portion of an animal and eating the rest in a communal meal. The fellowship offering and the associated meal implied restored relationship and a bond of peace.

When Jesus offered the cup as the New Covenant in His blood, He retrieved language from a climactic passage in Exodus:

> And he sent young men of the people of Israel, who offered burnt offerings and sacrificed peace offerings of oxen to the LORD. And Moses took half of the blood and put it in basins, and half of the blood he threw against the altar. Then he took the Book of the Covenant and read it in the hearing of the people. And they said, "All that the LORD has spoken we will do, and we will be obedient." And Moses took the blood and threw it on the people and said, "Behold the blood of the covenant that the LORD has made with you in accordance with all these words." Then Moses and Aaron, Nadab, and Abihu, and seventy of the elders of Israel went up, and they saw the God of Israel. There was under His feet as it were a pavement of sapphire stone, like the very heaven for clearness. And He did not lay His hand on the chief men of the people of Israel; they beheld God, and ate and drank. (Exodus 24:5-11)

After the Mosaic covenant was given, burnt and peace offerings were made (v. 5). Upon hearing the covenant, the people accepted its weighty terms. The climax of this acceptance was the meal. Moses and the elders ascended the mountain and *ate with God Himself.* God, as the host of this meal, protected those who ate (v. 11). The meal illustrates the bond of peace and fellowship between host and guests.

When Jesus described the cup as the "new covenant in My blood," He was recalling the Exodus event. As the apostles reflected back on that somber evening, the Lord's Supper would have been comprehended as the meal associated with the peace offering. The Lord Jesus would offer His body and blood to bring about reconciliation. Jesus, as host of the meal, expressed fellowship and peace with His disciples. Just as the Israelites ate with God Himself under His protection, so the disciples ate with Jesus.

To understand the Lord's Supper, we should let this imagery of the meal following the peace sacrifice pervade our hearts. Jesus has offered His body and blood on the cross. As host of the Lord's Supper, He now offers protection, fellowship, and acceptance. In the midst of enemy territory, we may therefore say to the Lord, "You prepare a table before me in the presence of my enemies" (Ps. 23:5).

The power of the meal

> The cup of blessing which we bless, is it not the communion of the blood of Christ? The bread which we break, is it not the communion of the body of Christ? For we, though many, are one bread and one body; for we all partake of that one bread...The things which the Gentiles sacrifice they sacrifice to demons and not to God, and I do not want you to have fellowship with demons. You cannot drink the cup of the Lord and the cup of demons; you cannot partake of the Lord's table and of the table of demons. (1 Cor. 10:16-17, 20-21)

Meals have a binding power. Whether the meal honors the Lord or honors a pagan deity, the participants in the meal unite with each other and the one being honored. By partaking of the bread and cup, we commune with Jesus Himself (v. 10).[4] This is the sacramental power of this holy meal. Through it, believers are promised communion and fellowship with Jesus Himself.

The second dimension of unity forged by the Lord's Supper is with other believers. By drinking of the one cup and partaking of the one bread (both important symbols that should be retained), disciples bind themselves to one another. "For we, though many, are one bread and one body; for we all partake of that one bread" (1 Cor. 10:17). For this reason, the Corinthians could no longer eat with the man living in sexual immorality (1 Cor. 5:11). Leaven spreads easily, and the church is to remain pure (1 Cor. 5:7). Those who are unbelievers or professing believers living in sin cannot eat the Lord's Supper, for it would bind the holy to the unrighteous. Jesus confirmed that the Last Supper was for believers alone when He took the bread and "*gave it to the disciples*" (Matt. 26:26).

Determining who is at the Lord's table is part of the official declaratory function that Jesus vested to the church (see chapter 28, "The local church and membership"). Baptism and the Lord's Supper are the two main ways by which the church exercises the "keys of the kingdom." When the church opens the Lord's table to a person, it affirms the heavenly citizenship of that individual. Similarly, when the church turns an

[4] The underlying Greek word is *koinonia*. Some translations read "share in," others "participate in," the blood and body of Christ.

individual away, it is saying that it cannot vouch for that person's citizenship. While this may appear harsh, it should be done for the sake of the Lord's honor, the purity of the church, the individual's soul, and the watching world. Those churches that fail to mark off God's people fail in their primary mandate. The Lord's Supper also looks forward to the marriage supper of the Lamb. The meal should be a "rehearsal dinner" for that great meal; the church is staging this dramatic meal in miniature. Because unbelievers and the impenitent will not be present with the bridegroom at the final banquet, they should be excluded from the church's forward-looking enactment.

Sadly, many churches fail to responsibly exercise their declaratory authority. In some churches, attendees do not even know the names of other congregants, much less their spiritual state; such congregations fall short of being biblical churches. Other churches suffer from poor teaching about leaven and the uniting power described in 1 Corinthians 10:16-21. As the leaven spreads, the church falls deeper into ruin.

By taking the Lord's Supper, a person attests that he or she believes that the other participants are walking with the Lord in holiness (1 Cor. 5). By taking the Lord's Supper with another known to be in sin, a person endorses that sin. Similarly, Paul forbids Christians to eat meals in the pagan temples, because Christians should not "fellowship with demons" (10:20) and thus "cannot eat the cup of the Lord and the cup of demons" (10:21). The principle is the same: a union is effected by these spiritual meals so Christians cannot partake in pagan meals.

Consider this analogy from medicine. To protect the quality of the blood supply, blood donation centers ask prospective donors dozens of questions about their health. The donation center tries to eliminate donors with cancer, hepatitis, and sexually transmitted diseases. Although they rigorously test the blood before giving it to a patient, the tests can fail. Thus standard policy is to screen out potentially diseased blood before it is even collected. Imagine you are a patient needing blood. You walk by a hospital's blood donation center and see prostitutes, drug addicts, and donors with open and weeping sores all donating blood. This would hardly inspire you to accept blood from such a center. Similarly, imagine the sight of a person spiritually uniting themselves to adulterers, the lustful, greedy, violent, and depraved. When a person takes the Lord's Supper, they become spiritually united to other participants. This spiritual reality should provoke thoughtfulness.

At the same time, there should not be a cloud of dread over the Lord's Supper and communion. The meal is supposed to be a celebration of what God has done. Our focus should be on Jesus and serving others—we should not have a morbid fixation on sin. Maintaining a healthy balance between reverence and joy is a challenge that requires the Spirit's guidance.

While the Lord's Supper is normally a local "family meal," visitors should be able to participate. In the meal, the church is attesting not for local membership but for citizenship in Jesus' kingdom. If the visitor is well known to the church and believed to be walking with the Lord, there is no reason to exclude the person. But for a stranger, it is better to be cautious rather than lax and unquestioning.

The Lord's Supper as a family meal

The Lord's Supper consists of the organic union of the love feast (Jude 1:12) and communion (1 Cor. 10:16). We should be careful with our language: the Lord's Supper consists of both portions, not just communion (see 1 Cor. 11:20-34). Indeed, the Lord's Supper is called a *supper*, not a snack. Like the Last Supper, the love feast is a meal. Confirming this, 1 Corinthians 11:21-22 notes that some were eating all the food, leaving little for others, and that some were even becoming drunk. Over time, the church stripped the love feast from the Lord's Supper and lost the significance of sharing a meal. Most modern churches continue in that tradition and have communion as essentially a solitary event, taken in silence or with background singing, without a trace of fellowship with one's brothers and sisters. While historians overwhelmingly agree that the New Testament Lord's Supper involved a full meal, churches have departed from the New Testament model because of expediency or tradition. Especially in larger churches, pragmatic reasons prohibit the partaking of a full meal.

The Lord's Supper should be a time of fellowship. Because it is the Lord's Supper, conversation should be focused on what the Lord has done and what He is teaching. In this sense, it should resemble an intimate family meal.

Confession of sin between believers is an appropriate activity, "Confess your trespasses to one another, and pray for one another, that you may be healed" (James 5:16). This might occur privately between two individuals or among the whole group. There is great joy in uncovering the solitude of sin. The reconciled fellowship of the Lord's Supper should be a highlight of Christian community.

The meal should be a time to seek the welfare of the whole group, especially its weaker members. This was precisely where the Corinthians went wrong. With the rich eating most of the food before the poor arrived, the Corinthian church was violating the purpose of the Lord's

Supper as an expression of peace and fellowship within the body of Christ. The poor members, some of whom were slaves, had work obligations and likely could not arrive at the same time as the wealthier members. In fact, the entire discourse on the Lord's Supper in 1 Corinthians 11:20-34 is bracketed by a concern over the poor brethren. The discourse begins with a charge to not shame the poor among them: "Therefore when you come together in one place, it is not to eat the Lord's Supper. For in eating, each one takes his own supper ahead of others; and one is hungry and another is drunk. What! Do you not have houses to eat and drink in? Or do you despise the church of God and shame those who have nothing? What shall I say to you? Shall I praise you in this? I do not praise you" (1 Cor. 11:20-22). After Paul explains the significance of eating and drinking in an "unworthy manner," the discourse ends with, "Therefore, my brethren, when you come together to eat, wait for one another. But if anyone is hungry, let him eat at home, lest you come together for judgment" (1 Cor. 11:33-34). The word "therefore" points to the action that is expected by understanding the significance of the meal. While the focus of the modern Lord's Supper is largely introspective, the admonition given in verse 33 is outward looking. The Lord's Supper should be a time in which believers examine themselves as to how they are in loving fellowship with one another, particularly the weak and poor among them. Of course, eating with a clean conscience concerning personal sin is important—but the focus of the passage is on concern for the totality of the body.

The purpose of the weekly gathering

The New Testament describes the main purpose of the weekly gathering as partaking of the Lord's Supper. Two passages highlight this truth. "On the first day of the week, when the disciples came together to break bread…" implies that the purpose of the disciples' gathering was to "break bread," a reference to the Lord's Supper (Acts 20:7). Because the purpose of their gathering was to break bread, and they gathered weekly, the Lord's Supper was thus observed weekly. The second passage comes from the epistles: "Now in giving these instructions I do not praise you, since you come together not for the better but for the worse. For first of all, when you come together as a church, I hear that there are divisions among you, and in part I believe it. For there must also be factions among you, that those who are approved may be recognized among you. Therefore when you come together in one place, it is not to eat the Lord's Supper" (1 Cor. 11:17-20). The last sentence has often been misunderstood. Paul is telling them that while the intent of their gatherings should be to eat the Lord's Supper, they are not actually doing so. Another translation is clearer: "When you meet together in the same place, your meeting does not amount to an eating of the Lord's Supper."[5] The intent of their gathering was not reflected in practice. Thus verse 20 implies that when the Christians came together, their purpose was to take the Lord's Supper. And because the assembly was weekly, partaking of the Lord's Supper would be also. The history of the early church confirms this: "The Lord's Supper was a constant feature of the Sunday service."[6]

Some worry that weekly observation of the Lord's Supper would make it so frequent that it would lose its significance and become cheapened. Three responses should be made. First, this was the same argument made by opponents of vernacular translations of the Bible. They said that the Bible's impact would weaken by making it too common. And why is the argument not also made about the entire church gathering? By the same logic, is not a weekly gathering too often? Second, if there is a New Testament pattern established, human wisdom should not topple a divine pattern. We should simply obey. Third, the Scriptures say that as often as we partake of the Lord's Supper, we proclaim the Lord's death until He comes (1 Cor. 11:26). Should that be a biannual event? Rather, a weekly observation harmonizes with the Lord's day being a celebration of the resurrection.

The early Anabaptists revived the practice of the Lord's Supper as a full meal, observed at least weekly. An early document, thought to be written by Michael Sattler, describes how the earliest Anabaptists practiced the Lord's Supper:

> The brothers and sisters should meet at least three to four times a week, to exercise themselves in the teaching of Christ and his apostles and heartily encourage one another to remain faithful in the Lord as they have pledged...All gluttony shall be avoided among the brothers who are gathered in the congregation; serve a soup or a minimum of vegetable and meat, for eating and drinking are not the kingdom of heaven. The Lord's Supper shall be held, as often as the brothers are together, thereby proclaiming the death of the Lord, and thereby warning each one to com-

[5] Translation of 1 Corinthians 14:20 by Anthony Thiselton in *The First Epistle to the Corinthians: A Commentary on the Greek Text*, Eerdmans (2000), p. 848.

[6] Everett Ferguson, *Early Christians Speak: Faith and Life in the First Three Centuries*, third edition, ACU Press (1999), p. 94.

> memorate, how Christ gave His life for us, and shed His blood for us, that we might also be willing to give our body and life for Christ's sake, which means for the sake of all the brothers.[7]

The early Anabaptists took the Lord's Supper at least weekly, just as the book of Acts describes (Acts 2:46, 20:7). Interestingly, they observed the Lord's Supper as an evening meal because of the New Testament pattern.[8] Restoring the Lord's Supper from what lies behind the fog of human traditions to its New Testament pattern requires fortitude inspired by the word of God.

The many dimensions of the Lord's Supper

At the heart of the gospel message is Jesus' death and resurrection, with the anticipation of the consummation of the kingdom. Having the Lord's Supper at the core of weekly gathering offers an anchor to ground participants in the basic gospel message. As churches may veer into other subjects (as important as they may be), they must never lose sight of the gospel message. Jesus in his wisdom gave the Lord's Supper as a means of providing this weekly reminder of hope as an "anchor of the soul" (Heb. 6:19). But this is no vain repetition. The meal offers many facets for reflection: the Lord's Supper as memorial, reconciliation, nourishment, eschatological prelude, and covenant renewal. This meal is so expansive and rich that it extends in multiple directions:[9]

- Downward: We remember God's gift of his Son down to us as the foundation of our salvation. We praise and thank God for His initiative and grace.
- Upward: We look up to the resurrected King who reigns over His people.
- Backward: We remember the Son's death on the cross for us.
- Forward: We look to the future when the kingdom will be fulfilled and we will eat at the marriage supper of the Lamb.
- Inward: We look inward as we renew our covenantal vows and thankfully receive forgiveness and nourishment.

---

[7] *The Legacy of Michael Sattler*, John H. Yoder (translator and editor), Herald Press (1973), pp. 44-45.

[8] Peter Hoover, *The Secret of the Strength*, Elmendorf books (1998), chapter 13. The early Anabaptists contrasted their evening meal with the daytime observance of the Roman Catholics.

[9] F. D. Bruner, *Matthew: Volume 2*, Eerdmans (2007), p. 636.

- Outward: We look outward to fellow believers to whom we bind ourselves, seeking to discern the body rightly.

Maranatha!

Chapter 32

The Lord's day gathering

Whenever you come together, each of you has a psalm, has a teaching, has a tongue, has a revelation, has an interpretation. Let all things be done for edification. (1 Corinthians 14:26)

Historians and biblical exegetes broadly agree on the structure of the original Lord's day meeting.[1] The meeting began with the love feast, usually an evening meal, which was followed by communion—the bread and the cup. (The Lord's Supper represents the organic union of the love feast and communion.) Following communion came the time of singing, exhortation, and teaching when various brothers successively spoke.[2] Communion was therefore the centerpiece of the meeting, flanked by the love feast on one side with public exhortation and singing on the other.

By the end of the second century, the original format of the Lord's day gathering had been substantially modified. The love feast was stripped from the Lord's Supper and moved to a separate meeting. Exhortation became the duty of a few, rather than broadly participatory. These early changes highlight the need to derive one's convictions directly from Scripture.

The purpose of the meeting

As seen in the previous chapter, the church in Acts met on the first day of the week in order to partake of the Lord's Supper (Acts 20:7). To-

[1] For example, see Ben Witherington III, *Conflict and Community in Corinth*, Eerdmans (1995), pp. 241-252.

[2] The book of 1 Corinthians proceeds precisely through this order: the love feast (1 Cor. 11:17-22), communion (11:23-32), and the time of exhortation (1 Cor. 12-14).

day the Lord's day gathering is commonly described as a "worship service." Yet the New Testament never calls the meeting a worship service. Worship is a valid activity for the gathering of the saints, but worship is never stated as the *primary* purpose of the assembly. The purposes that the New Testament gives for assembly are either to partake of the Lord's Supper or to exhort other disciples. "Let us consider one another in order to stir up love and good works, not forsaking the assembling of ourselves together, as is the manner of some, but exhorting one another, and so much the more as you see the Day approaching" (Heb. 10:24-25). The author of Hebrews charges his listeners to consider how they can encourage one another to love and good works, and thus to assemble for exhortation. How many Christian believers during the week are prayerfully contemplating how they can build up the brotherhood on the Lord's day? Sadly, nearly everyone has been conditioned to leave that to the minister, while they remain passive. The New Testament even teaches that our singing should first be directed to others: "Be filled with the Spirit, speaking to one another by means of psalms and hymns and spiritual songs, singing songs and psalms with your hearts to the Lord, giving thanks always for all things in the name of our Lord Jesus Christ to God the Father" (Eph. 5:18-20).[3]

Singing is portrayed as radiating out in two dimensions: first horizontally, to God's people, and next vertically to God. The book of Colossians describes singing in a similar manner: "Let the word of Christ dwell in you richly in all wisdom, teaching and admonishing one another in psalms and hymns and spiritual songs, singing with grace in your hearts to the Lord" (Col. 3:16).

The first audience for psalms, hymns, and spiritual songs is fellow believers! While we rarely use language like "speak to one another with psalms, hymns, and songs" or "teach and admonish others with psalms and songs," these notions are deeply biblical. Both passages place the Psalms at the head of the list, implying that singing the Psalms should be prominent in worship. The Psalms ground us in Scripture, reverent praise, Christocentric meditation, and epic hymns describing the history of God's people. "What we sing becomes the grammar of what we believe."[4] While not widely appreciated, singing has as much or more power than preaching to affect our worldviews. For example, by neglecting the Psalms, most modern churchgoers avoid singing about God's judgment, likely part of the reason the church has progressively

---

[3] Translation taken from Harold Hoehner, *Ephesians*, Baker Academic (2002), pp. 702-713.

[4] Keith Getty, quoted by Joan Huyser-Honig in "Keith Getty on Writing Hymns for the Church Universal," www.worship.calvin.edu.

marginalized this teaching.

The Lord's day meeting should be a time for disciples to exhort and build up the body through the Lord's Supper and through their teachings and songs. This is a calling for every brother (1 Cor. 14:26, Heb. 10:24-25). Rather than emphasizing a "worship service," we therefore should be emphasizing the Lord's Supper and a "meeting of exhortation." Many of us require a significant adjustment in our thinking.

Unbelievers in the meeting

If the Lord's Supper is for believers (see previous chapter), are unbelievers in the Lord's day meeting? If so, how? The New Testament answers: "If the whole church comes together in one place, and all speak with tongues, and *there come in* those who are uninformed or unbelievers, will they not say that you are out of your mind? But if all prophesy, and an unbeliever or an uninformed person *comes in*, he is convinced by all, he is convicted by all. And thus the secrets of his heart are revealed; and so, falling down on his face, he will worship God and report that God is truly among you." (1 Cor. 14:23-25) The context of this passage is the period of public exhortation, which occurred after the Lord's Supper. Paul's careful choice of words shows that it was at this point that unbelievers *came in*.[5] They were not already present for the Lord's Supper; they were coming for the time of public exhortation. Unbelievers then heard the brothers preach, exhort, and sing on the Lord's day.

Two references from the early church validate this understanding. The first comes from the history of the word *Mass*. The word means "dismissal" in Latin. Although the format of the Lord's day gathering had changed by the time the word *Mass* gained currency, the early church would dismiss unbelievers when the bread and the cup were partaken. This practice likely descended from the earliest Lord's day gatherings, when unbelievers were not present at the Lord's Supper. Second, the *Didache* (a document written shortly after the New Testament) verifies that only believers partook of the Lord's Supper: "Let no one eat or drink of your Eucharist except those who have been baptized into the name of the Lord, for the Lord has also spoken concerning this: 'Do not give what is holy to dogs' " (Didache 9:5).[6] Because it is unlikely that others would be watching disciples eat the love feast and share commu-

---

[5] The underlying Greek word is *eiserchomai*, used twice, once in verse 23 and once in 24.

[6] *The Apostolic Fathers*, third edition, Michael Holmes (editor and translator), Baker Academic (2007), p. 359.

nion (imagine having people at your house stand back and watch you eat dinner without themselves eating), it is reasonable to suppose that unbelievers were not present for this portion of the meeting.

Format of the meeting

During the New Testament gathering, after the Lord's Supper, the congregation had a period of exhortation where several brothers would offer a teaching or song (1 Cor. 14:26). Often the elders, prophets, or apostles would give lengthy teachings (e.g. Acts 20:7). These meetings harmoniously displayed the diverse gifts of the congregation. While the modern church meeting is basically filled with spectators, the apostolic church gathering was filled with contributors. 1 Corinthians reveals a great deal about the apostolic church gathering:

1. The brothers led with songs, the public reading of Scripture, and periods of instruction. 1 Corinthians 14:26 uses the term "each one" (some translations say "everyone") implying that all or nearly all of the brothers offer something in the service.
2. Unlike the modern scripted and canned service, New Testament church meetings were participatory and hence more vulnerable to abuse. Yet despite the abuse at Corinth, Paul exhorts them to continue with their participatory meetings, but with order.
3. In this meeting format, the body with its different member functions forms a powerful expression of diversity within unity. Paul's discussion of the body of Christ and the importance of love precede and provide the foundation for the key passage on participatory meetings of encouragement and exhortation. (1 Corinthians 12 and 13 provide the foundation for chapter 14.)
4. Unbelievers would be convicted by their secrets being disclosed by prophetic utterances (1 Cor. 14:24-25). Hence these meetings had powerful evangelistic effects.

Other New Testament passages mention corporate prayer as an activity of their gatherings. "And they continued steadfastly in the apostles' doctrine and fellowship, in the breaking of bread, and in prayers" (Acts 2:42). Jesus says, "My house shall be called a house of prayer" (Matt. 21:13).

The nature of preaching and teaching

Preaching should generally be expository rather than topical. Topical preaching certainly is appropriate and healthy at times. But we are generally instructed to "preach the word" (2 Tim. 4:2). Expository preaching pulls people away from their idiosyncrasies, obsessions, and pet doctrines. Expository preaching can be done poorly, somehow twisting texts to always find the same message. But proper exposition stretches preacher and hearer by forcing both to consider what Scripture presents, not the topics to which they may naturally be inclined.

Preaching through Scripture also makes it more difficult to avoid the hard texts, which we often need the most. What a teacher does not speak on reveals a great deal:

> As we have already seen, any Christian can detect the man who says outrageously wrong things; but is it unfair or uncharitable to say that the vast majority of Christians today do not seem to be able to detect the man who seems to say the right things but leaves out vital things? We have somehow got hold of the idea that error is only that which is outrageously wrong; and we do not seem to understand that the most dangerous person of all is the one who does not emphasize the right things. That is the only way to understand rightly this picture of the false prophets. The false prophet is a man who has no 'strait gate' or 'narrow way' in his gospel.[7]

Scripture is not only true, but its proportions are right. By preaching (and singing) Scripture, we can align our fallen minds to the proportions that the Holy Spirit intended. Again, expository preaching most naturally facilitates the transformation of our minds.

By expositing the Bible, preachers and teachers are more likely to ground their hearers in the storyline of Scripture. Christians should identify the history of Israel and the church as their own story. The Bible's story ought to become our story. This reorientation of identity is a crucial part of transformation:[8]

story → identity → convictions → values → actions

[7] D. Martyn Lloyd-Jones, *Studies in the Sermon on the Mount*, second edition, Eerdmans (1976), p. 500.

[8] This model of transformation was articulated by Steve Green. The following list is quoted from Steve Wilkens and Mark Sanford, *Hidden Worldviews*, IVP Academic (2009), p. 19.

- Story: The central narrative of our life
- Identity: How we see ourselves and present ourselves to others
- Convictions: Those beliefs that make up how reality works for us
- Values / Ethics: What we believe we should do and what we take to be our highest priorities
- Morals / Actions: The realm of doing that includes all of our activities

Story is deceptively powerful to induce transformation. If we practice sound expository preaching while submitting ourselves to God's word, we will naturally drive out error and produce godly change. To get expository preaching right is to get much right indeed.

Order in the meeting

Overseers in the New Testament (also known as elders) maintain oversight in the meeting. Good principles of order include:

1. Similar to the practices seen in Acts, a person should be recognized and given permission to speak. Great harm has been done in meetings where unknown persons spoke foolish, errant, or controversial words. Permission to speak should be granted by the elder-overseers. Strangers should not be allowed to speak.
2. Women are forbidden to speak or teach in the congregation of the saints (1 Cor. 14:34; 1 Tim. 2:11-15). While many today struggle with these commands, we must trust in the Lord's wisdom. Clearly women can prophesy (1 Cor. 11:5) and encourage other believers, but this should occur outside the public time of exhortation on the Lord's day. God in His wisdom has so ordered the functioning of the church.
3. Elders should help to cultivate spiritual gifts by recognizing those with gifts of teaching and encouragement. Those who struggle to speak profitable words should be gently instructed in better ways of edification. "Eyes trying to speak and ears trying to smell quench the Spirit."[9]

The power of such a service—guided by the Spirit, blessed by the diversity of gifts, focused on edification—is a beautiful expression of the body. Though few modern Christians have experienced its power, such a meeting is a large step forward in restoring God's house to its glory.

[9] Matthew Milioni, personal communication.

Chapter 33

Meetings of prayer and fasting

And when they prayed, the place where they were assembled together was shaken. (Acts 4:31)

When the disciples walked with Jesus, they asked Him, "Lord, teach us to pray." Impressed by Jesus' spiritual power, the disciples perceived that this power came through prayer. They did not say, "Lord, teach us to preach" or "Lord, teach us to heal." *Prayer* was the source of the Master's power. The church needs to cry out afresh to Jesus, "Lord, teach us to pray!"

Jesus teaches the disciples a specific prayer (Matt. 6:9-13), which should continue to be prayed today. While it can be abused through vain repetition, Jesus' command is clear. Other prayers should of course be offered (e.g. Acts 4:24-30), but the Lord's prayer should play an important role in the disciple's prayer life.

The Gospel accounts all draw attention to Jesus' prayer life.[1] Jesus would sometimes pray alone, all through the night (Luke 6:12). But Jesus also prayed in groups: "He took Peter, John, and James and went up on the mountain to pray" (Luke 9:28). Jesus would publicly pray for children: "Then little children were brought to Him that He might put His hands on them and pray" (Matt. 19:13). The New Testament draws special attention to Jesus' fervency in prayer: "He had offered up prayers and supplications, with vehement cries and tears" (Heb. 5:7).

The church's life should flow from Jesus' life. To this very day, Jesus' life is marked by prayer and intercession: "Therefore He is also able to save to the uttermost those who come to God through Him, since *He*

[1] Matt. 14:23; Mark 1:35, 6:46; Luke 5:16; John 17.

always lives to make intercession for them" (Heb. 7:25). Jesus lives to make intercession on behalf of His people. So He could tell Peter, "But I have prayed for you, that your faith should not fail" (Luke 22:32). He encouraged His disciples to persist in a life of prayer: "Then He spoke a parable to them, that men always ought to pray and not lose heart" (Luke 18:1). Jesus clearly described His vision for the activity of the church by saying: "My house shall be called a house of prayer" (Matt. 21:13).

Could we say this about our churches? Are they places of prayer? Are they churches of "prayers and supplications, with vehement cries and tears"? Or have "cares of this world, the deceitfulness of riches, and the desires for other things" (Mark 4:19) choked Jesus' word and the spirit of prayer?

Prayer among the apostles

The church was born in a prayer meeting. The apostles learned well from Jesus' example and instructions. Corporate prayer figures prominently in the book of Acts (note how often prayer goes with a plural word like "we" or "they"):

> These all continued *with one accord in prayer and supplication.* (Acts 1:14)

> And they continued steadfastly in the apostles' doctrine and fellowship, in the breaking of bread, *and in prayers.* (Acts 2:42)

> And *when they had prayed,* the place where they were assembled together was shaken; and they were all filled with the Holy Spirit, and they spoke the word of God with boldness. (Acts 4:31)

> We will *give ourselves continually to prayer* and to the ministry of the word. (Acts 6:4)

> Peter was therefore kept in prison, but *constant prayer was offered to God for him by the church.* (Acts 12:5)

> He came to the house of Mary, the mother of John whose surname was Mark, where *many were gathered together praying.* (Acts 12:12)

> Then, *having fasted and prayed*, and laid hands on them, they sent them away. (Acts 13:3)
>
> So when they had appointed elders in every church, and *prayed with fasting*, they commended them to the Lord in whom they had believed. (Acts 14:23)
>
> And on the Sabbath day we went out of the city to the riverside, *where prayer was customarily made*. (Acts 16:13)
>
> At midnight Paul and Silas *were praying* and singing hymns to God. (Acts 16:25)
>
> When we had come to the end of those days, we departed and went on our way; and they all accompanied us, with wives and children, till we were out of the city. *And we knelt down on the shore and prayed.* (Acts 21:5)

Just as Jesus wanted, the apostolic church was a house of prayer. The epistles confirm this disposition by commanding us to "pray without ceasing" (1 Thess. 5:17; see also Rom. 1:9; 1 Tim. 1:3). Paul elsewhere writes, "I desire therefore that the men pray everywhere, lifting up holy hands, without wrath and doubting" (1 Tim. 2:8).

Confession, accountability, and prayer

Scripture commands, "Confess your trespasses to one another, and pray for one another" (James 5:16). Every church should ask if it has fostered an environment where its people are able to confess their sins to each other and receive prayer. Unless the leaders are demonstrating confession, unless there are safe spaces created for confession and prayer, vulnerability and honesty will be difficult. It is harder to confess our sins before other people than before God. Confession develops humility.

Small groups of men or women serve as an excellent place for confession and prayer. Before partaking of the Lord's Supper, there should be space created for confession and prayer. When churches do a poor job of fostering such an environment, sin is allowed to fester and swell in the dark. But when God's people confess and renounce their sins, revival can erupt in the midst of a pure brotherhood. "And many who had believed came confessing and telling their deeds...So the word of the Lord grew mightily and prevailed" (Acts 19:18, 20).

The benefits of God's people praying

Every great move of God has been sparked and sustained with prayer. Through prayer, the church can access power far disproportionate to its numbers. Consider the success of the Moravians. Despite small numbers, they helped usher in a worldwide harvest. This success was likely due to their continual prayer meeting that lasted for a hundred years. The triumphs of men like John Hyde, Charles Finney, and George Müller could be attributed to their life of prayer.

God cannot bless the church until it is humbled through prayer. If God were to simply grant the church success without deep, fervent prayer, the church would quickly become proud and attribute success to its own righteousness. By wrestling with the Lord through prayer, it becomes evident to whom the glory is due.

The church also deepens its affection for the object of its prayer. Suppose that a church is praying for a lost soul. The churches agonizes for this person for weeks or months. If such a person becomes a follower of Jesus and appears in the church's midst, the church will already have a natural affection for this individual. It is the same way with childbirth. After a woman has carried a baby for many months and labored in anguish, she will have a tender love for the newborn.

Prayer joins heaven and earth. When in the presence of great servants of God, when among God's friends in prayer, there is no mistaking the attendant power. Someone who prayed with John Hyde remarked, "I knelt down, and a strange feeling crept over me. Several prayed, and then Hyde began, and I remember little more. I knew that I was in the presence of God Himself, and had no desire to leave the place; in fact, I do not think that I thought of myself or of my surroundings, for I had entered a new world, and I wanted to remain there."[2]

Prayer increases the unity of a church. When Christians hear their brothers and sisters express their hearts, it increases the love which they have for one another. The sympathies and passions of godly Christians spread throughout the church. When other believers hear a person pray repeatedly for a particular object, this concern grows collectively.

The prayerless church is a dead church. With all of the supposed productivity gains from technology and travel, corporate prayer is at

[2] J. Pengwern Jones in *Praying Hyde*, E. G. Carré (ed.), Bridge Publishing (1982), pp. 67-68.

a low point in the West. This reflects the true spiritual state of these churches. Little wonder that modern churches are so anemic and dry.

The ministry of fasting

Fasting has always been a mark of God's people. In the Old Testament, fasting was used to subdue nations (2 Chron. 20:1-30). Prophets like Daniel fasted and were given insight into great mysteries (Daniel 9). Fasting is prominent among the penitent exiles as they return to Jerusalem (Ezra 8:21, 23, 9:5; Neh. 1:4, 9:1). Jesus was welcomed by Anna, a prophetess, who "served God with fastings and prayers night and day" (Luke 2:37).

Jesus Himself fasted for forty days, providing an example for His people. Jesus gave three important teachings on fasting:

- Jesus blessed those who are hungry and proclaimed woes to those who are full (Luke 6:21, 25).
- After He was taken away, Jesus said that His disciples would fast (Mark 2:19-20). Thus Jesus taught that the church age should be marked with fasting.
- Higher levels of spiritual power come only through "prayer and fasting" (Mark 9:29).

Just as we saw with prayer, the disciples followed Jesus' example and teachings. We find fasting among God's people in the book of Acts (Acts 10:32, 13:2-3, 14:23). Paul boasted twice of his frequent fastings (2 Cor. 6:5, 11:27). Fasting seems to grant God's people a special grace as they detach themselves from the things of this world. "Prayer is the one hand with which we grasp the invisible; fasting, the other, with which we let loose and cast away the visible."[3] By detaching ourselves from something so basic as food, God brings us closer to His presence.

One reason to learn self-control of the body is to be able to fast. As food has grown more plentiful and addictive, fasting has diminished. This is part of the Enemy's trap. Christians must be aware of his schemes and strive to master our bodies. "By fasting, the body learns to obey the soul; by praying the soul learns to command the body."[4] Our fasting should reflect our desire for our bridegroom and true home.

[3] Andrew Murray, *With Christ in the School of Prayer*, Fleming Revell Company (1895), p. 98.

[4] Attributed to William Secker.

Chapter 34

Undoing Antioch: on ethnic-specific churches

For God shows no partiality. (Romans 2:11)

Martin Luther King Jr. once said, "It is appalling that the most segregated hour of Christian America is eleven o'clock on Sunday morning, the same hour when many are standing to sing: 'In Christ There Is No East Nor West.' "[1] King's plea was that "the church must remove the yoke of segregation in its own body."[2] Despite this call, over the last thirty years, ethnic churches have grown in number and size, particularly in the United States. Korean-American, Chinese-American, Indian-American, and African-American churches multiply at a rapid rate. Even at universities, rather than assembling as campus-wide fellowships, there has been a growth in "Asian-American Fellowships" or other ethnically-centered campus fellowships.

The growing number of ethnic-specific churches and fellowships is partly due to a change in the demographics of professing Christians. Churches are more diverse than ever, drawing from more ethnicities than ever before. As reported in one magazine, the Campus Crusade fellowship at Yale University is 85% Asian, while the Buddhist gatherings consist mostly of whites![3]

Why have ethnic churches and fellowships proliferated so rapidly in recent times? First, people increasingly are using the church primarily as a social vehicle. For marriages or even close friendships, many

[1] Martin Luther King Jr., *A Testament of Hope: The Essential Writings and Speeches of Martin Luther King, Jr.*, James Washington (ed.), HarperOne (1986), p. 479.

[2] King, p. 479.

[3] "Go Figure," *Christianity Today*, volume 47, no. 7 (June 2003).

people want to remain within their own ethnicity. Many feel that there are unique issues to their particular ethnicity that could not be adequately addressed in multiethnic settings. Often it is parents who pressure their children to remain in an ethnic church to socialize, marry, and have children. Second, many parents feel that by remaining in an ethnic church, they can reap the benefits of their new country while keeping the culture of their homeland.

While these reasons may be convincing to some, they directly oppose core teachings of the New Testament. The very origin of the term *Christian* serves as a useful starting point. The term was first used in the city of Antioch in Syria, after many new believers entered the church from the work of itinerant evangelists from Cyprus and Cyrene. In Antioch, the gospel entered for the first time into a truly multicultural city, unlike the more ethnically homogeneous Jerusalem (see Acts 11:19-26).

The city of Antioch has been the source of a great deal of interest in recent years.[4] One thing is clear about this intriguing city: it was there that non-Jews began pouring into the church. F. F. Bruce calls Antioch "the citadel of Gentile Christianity." Prior to missionaries coming to Antioch, the followers of Jesus were regarded as a sect within Judaism. *After the gospel came to Antioch, for the first time believers in Jesus could no longer be called Jews, for the obvious reason that so many non-Jews were now declaring that Jesus was their Lord.* After Antioch, the followers of Jesus were multiethnic; Jews still comprised a portion of the believers but had been joined by many other ethnicities. A new term had to be used; hence "Christian," meaning "people of the Christ." Antioch thus represents a pivotal moment in church history—when Christianity moved from being a religion closely connected to a specific ethnicity (Judaism) to being a religion for all people.

It is hard to overstate the significance of this watershed event. Paul, not long after this revolution occurred in Antioch, would pen one of the most radical statements written in the first century, "There is neither Jew nor Greek, there is neither slave nor free, there is neither male nor female, for you are all one in Christ Jesus" (Gal. 3:28). Paul often writes that after Jesus' crucifixion and resurrection, faith alone should unite the people of God. Looking at the list Paul makes in Galatians 3:28, it is logically similar to regard one of today's Indian, Chinese, or Korean churches as comparable to how a church of non-slaves or a church of the circumcised would have been viewed in the first century.

This truth can be stated in more theological language: *Ethnic-*

[4] For example, Rodney Stark, *The Rise of Christianity*, Princeton University Press (1996).

specific churches and fellowships represent an eschatological violation. They are a throwback to the period before Jesus' coming. In fact, it is not far from the mirror image (Gentile) error that Paul addresses in Galatians. Paul combats an error that circumcision is required for table fellowship (see Gal. 2:11-12). Even though most people within ethnic churches do not deny that others can be saved outside their group, they functionally partition themselves off from other believers across ethnic and racial lines. As a practical matter, this partitioning includes table fellowship. Especially in a church, partitioning over being "Jew or Greek" (ethnicity), "male or female" (gender), or "slave or free" (socioeconomic status) violates the integrity of the unity in Christ that is articulated in Galatians 3:28.

A natural corollary of this "faith transcending ethnicity" principle is that the church should strive to mirror the demographics of the local population. In the New Testament, churches are referred to by their geographic location. It should be obvious that the church should welcome the heterogeneity of the people present in its particular geographic area. Although a church might have more members of a particular ethnicity by virtue of its location (especially suburban versus urban), there is no reason to embed exclusionary terms such as ethnic labels into its name. This naturally applies to intentionally (sadly, the better word is often exclusionary) ethnic-specific churches or fellowships.

Besides their inherently unbiblical nature, ethnic-specific churches have several attendant dangers. A joke in the Korean Christian community is, "Let's start a Korean church so that we can split." Splitting over secondary issues has been so commonplace in the Korean-American community that this joke is now widespread. This is also common in Indian churches. Full of nepotism, they divide over whether or not to have carpet in the sanctuary, how to distribute the elements during communion, how much English versus Indian language to use during worship, etc. This should not be surprising. *Once lines are drawn in artificial, unbiblical ways such as with ethnicity, other superficial lines will surely follow.*

Another problem with ethnic-specific churches or fellowships is that reasons for attending are often self-centered. It is of course more comfortable to interact with people similar to ourselves. Parents attend because they want their children to marry within their culture. Others go because the environment is similar to what they were accustomed to back in their home country. Yet surely these reasons are basically selfish. Many immigrants forget that the reason that God has brought them to any country is to be a blessing to that land as a whole, not just to their own ethnic group. There is a related danger to religiously segregating ourselves by ethnicity. All cultures have areas where they have greater propensity for sin (for example, the idolatry of academic success in Asian cultures). When people are homogenized, these sins can grow to monstrous proportions as they go unchecked by believers who are culturally blind to them.

It is also difficult to bring newcomers to such an environment if they are not of the ethnicity of the host group without making them feel uncomfortable or changing the dynamics of the group. These churches and fellowships thus straightjacket the members' ability to carry out the Great Commission. A person is forced to say "Go to that other fellowship or church and be blessed there." This is not far from the error that James describes when he writes, "If a brother or sister is poorly clothed and lacking in daily food, and one of you says to them, 'Go in peace, be warmed and filled,' without giving them the things needed for the body, what good is that?" (James 2:15-16). We must bring our neighbors and those with whom we work to our churches, not send them to other places with hopeful wishes.

There are two caveats to this general principle that ethnic-specific churches and fellowships are unbiblical. First, if a person does not understand the local language, it is reasonable to find a church where he or she can understand the language and also contribute. Second, in regions and countries of persecution, foreigners may be legally forced to remain in churches that lack native believers. This final caveat is almost completely irrelevant to churches and fellowships in the West.

Insofar as possible, may our churches reflect the state of heaven, where people of all nations praise God continually. As churches and fellowships continue to divide along ethnic lines, may more believers choose instead to participate in multiethnic churches and fellowships. May we not undo Antioch!

Part V

The Growth of the Nation

Chapter 35

Gospel preaching

Preach the word! Be ready in season and out of season. Convince, rebuke, exhort, with all longsuffering and teaching. (2 Timothy 4:2)

A former teacher of mine once told one of his friends that he was teaching a class on preaching. The friend asked him what dynasty that was. Puzzled, he asked this intelligent woman from Boston what she meant. Eventually it became clear that when she heard the word "preaching," she thought that "Ching" was referring to a Chinese dynasty. One hardly knows whether to laugh or cry at such a story. Perhaps it is fitting that with gospel preaching scarce today, the meaning of the word itself has become obscured.

Preaching is for all Christians. While preaching may connote speaking before a crowd, the underlying Greek word simply means "proclaim." While not everyone may stand behind a pulpit, everyone is called to proclaim Jesus' gospel. One of the recurring themes in Acts is that in virtually every situation Christians (not just the apostles) are placed, they find a way to proclaim the gospel. The verb forms of *preach* and *proclaim* occur about thirty times in the book of Acts alone.[1] Peter spontaneously proclaims the gospel to the crowd at Pentecost. Stephen preaches when he is on trial. Once persecution breaks out, "Those who were scattered went everywhere preaching the word" (Acts 8:4). Philip proclaims the gospel in private conversations. Paul preaches to intellectuals on a hill.

Preaching has two remarkable properties that have special bearing on the church. The first is, "We get what we preach…How we live reveals the gospel we responded to and the gospel we preach."[2] This is

---

[1] This totals the Greek verbs *kerysso*, *katangello*, and *euangelizo*.

[2] Scot McKnight, "Getting the Gospel Right," *Out of Ur*, May 9, 2007.

only sensible. If leaders and members of a church preach a gospel of health and prosperity, it will attract a certain type of person, often the selfish and greedy. If a church preaches about speculative prophecy, it will attract people attracted to titillating mysteries and the paranormal. For this reason, there is great value in expository preaching that is immersed in Scripture and balanced by Scripture.

The second property of preaching is that its method of persuasion not only brings converts in but also leads them out. If a convert was made through an emotional appeal, that same person can be easily moved away through an emotional experience. This is very common in today's churches in the West. Prospective converts are subjected to calculated emotional manipulation. The song sets are carefully chosen to "warm up" the crowd, then excite them with plenty of rhythm, then cool down with contemplative songs in the minor key. The preacher then makes his appeal with a steel-stringed guitar playing in the background. The world persuades by using emotion. The world does this in film, television, sports, or other exciting experiences. Oscillating between emotional highs and lows is the norm. But to proclaim the gospel in this way is a trap. Paul boasts that his proclamation of the gospel was not according to the methods of the world (1 Cor. 1:18-2:5). When worldly methods are used, the world will eventually outdo you. For example, when these converts go to a worldly concert where things are done a little bit better than in church, with more style, flash, and fervor, they will give their hearts over to the world.

Often gospel appeals are primarily about God helping you in this life and then providing a ticket to heaven in the next. This method of persuasion appeals to self-interest. While a convert may be temporarily drawn into a church through selfish devices, it is usually a matter of time until another selfish force draws them away. Eventually church services lose their novelty and become familiar or even boring. Then when a convert is invited to go to the football game with his friends on a Sunday, the same selfish forces which drew him to "accept the Lord" will now draw him away. Many converts fall away today (many estimates are at over 90%) because their basic selfishness was never displaced by the true gospel. Their selfishness merely redirected their interests to religious topics for a season.

Both properties help explain why the fruits of the church are so poor (see chapter 12). A "save me," antinomian gospel has a chokehold on the church.[3] This makes converts easy targets for deception, apathy, and cultural relativism. Poor gospel preaching also puts the church into

[3] John D. Martin has several helpful sermons rebuking what he terms the "save me" gospel.

a weak-group cage.

We get what we preach. Unless we change, the church will remain on a treadmill, expending energy but getting nowhere. Having looked at two properties of preaching—"we get what we preach" and "what persuades people to come in can just as easily lead them out"—we will now examine what preaching should be.

The gospel is distinct from the plan of salvation

In today's churches, the gospel is understood to be synonymous with the plan of salvation. "When we evangelicals see the word gospel, our instinct is to think (personal) 'salvation'...What has happened is that we have created a 'salvation culture' and mistakenly assumed it is a 'gospel culture.' "[4]

But when Jesus proclaims the gospel, He does not go around saying, "Here is how you can go to heaven. Pray this prayer after me..." Instead Jesus *first* talks about the kingdom of God, a new nation, that is coming. As we will shortly see, the apostles proclaim the gospel in a very similar manner. A summons does *follow* the announcement of the kingdom: repent and believe in Jesus. But the gospel at its essence is first the announcement of Jesus' kingdom, not a plan of personal salvation. A plan of salvation certainly flows from this kingdom announcement, but they are not the same. The plan is distinct.

By omitting the announcement of the kingdom and jumping to the plan of salvation, something precious is lost. Perhaps a stronger statement should be made: if one preaches the plan of salvation apart from the gospel announcement of the kingdom, one is not preaching the gospel. Sadly, the summons to repent and believe has in most churches been ripped from its gospel anchor. But the remedy is clear: "The good news is that the more we submerge 'salvation' into the larger idea 'gospel,' the more robust will become our understanding of salvation."[5]

The gospel is framed by Israel's story

Consistent with the principle of the sufficiency of Scripture, the best way to learn gospel preaching is by going to the New Testament. There we find sermons by Jesus and the apostles in the Gospel accounts and

[4] Scot McKnight, *The King Jesus Gospel*, Zondervan (2011), p. 29.

[5] McKnight, p. 39.

the book of Acts. The sermons from Acts are particularly helpful as we see how the apostles preached after Jesus had been crucified and resurrected. We also have the advantage of multiple perspectives: lengthy sermons of Peter, Stephen, and Paul are recorded.

When modern readers read these sermons, they can seem boring. These sermons are intensely historical. So much time is spent telling Israel's story (which we think we already know) that these sermons seem tedious. Peter spends time in two of David's Psalms (Acts 2:25-35). Stephen seems to want to give highlights of two thousand years of Israelite history (Acts 7). Paul also summarizes Israel's history (Acts 13:16-22). The repetition of Israel's story is especially surprising given the Jewish settings of many of these sermons. Weren't the Jews already familiar with the Old Testament?

While a detailed analysis of these sermons is beyond the scope of this chapter, modern boredom from these sermons exposes a disconnect between our understanding of the gospel and the apostles' understanding. The gospel is not "a solution to an individual, existential, private sin-problem" but instead "the resolution of a story-problem, namely Israel's Story in search of a Messiah-solution."[6] We have failed to understand that the gospel is framed by a larger story, namely the story of Israel and the ancient covenants. Telling this story, not simply relating abstract propositions, is how one proclaims the gospel of Jesus.

Jesus anticipated that His gospel would be set in the larger story of His ministry, teachings, and deeds. After a woman anoints Jesus' head with a costly jar of perfume, He says, "Assuredly, I say to you, wherever this gospel is preached in the whole world, what this woman has done will also be told as a memorial to her" (Mark 14:9). Jesus envisioned the gospel traveling with the stories of His life! "We dare not permit the gospel to collapse into the abstract, de-storified points in the Plan of Salvation."[7] To strip the story of Israel and the story of Jesus' life (not just His death) from our gospel proclamation is to part ways with the apostolic pattern. Interestingly, the sermons in Acts lay greater stress upon the resurrection than the crucifixion. Because Jesus was coronated king at the resurrection (Acts 13:33; Rom. 1:4), this emphasis on the resurrection fits beautifully with the stress on kingdom. In chapter 1, we defined the gospel in the context of the larger story:

> **The Good News of the Nation**: God's intention at creation was for humanity to benevolently rule the earth. But because Adam and Eve rejected God's command, the Lord

[6] McKnight, p. 37.
[7] McKnight, p. 51.

> chose Abraham, Isaac, Jacob, Moses, and David to be instruments by which He would establish His own nation through covenant to bless the world and draw humanity to Himself. Because Israel failed in its mandate, Jesus founded a new nation—the church—with Himself as the reigning king to accomplish what Israel did not. Jesus' nation is marked by righteousness and peace. Joining this new nation involves following a radical new "constitution," the covenant of King Jesus, and requires a radical break from one's previous lifestyle. Disciples are baptized into a new social order, the church. Through Jesus' death and resurrection, members of the new nation receive liberation from Satan, forgiveness of sins, the power of the Spirit, and eternal life. The good news of Jesus' reign culminates with His nation emerging victorious, and His citizens being co-regents with Him forever. All other nations and their kings will eventually be conquered, and all will declare that Jesus is the King of kings and Lord of lords.

Seen from another perspective, the gospel is good news because of three interlocking truths:

- The world finally has a righteous king. A new nation under King Jesus' leadership has been birthed. Citizens of this new nation live the abundant life and demonstrate to the world the radiant presence of God among them.
- Israel's story has been brought to fulfillment. Jesus' death is the ultimate sacrifice foreshadowed by the Torah and the prophets. What was promised to the ancient prophets finds its realization in Jesus as the seed of Abraham, the true Israel, the new Moses, the greater David, and the last Adam.
- The decay of this world has been undone through the resurrection of King Jesus. At the resurrection, He was coronated King over all and imparts sin-crushing, death-overcoming power to His citizens. (Personal salvation is certainly a very important part of this gospel, but it is not the centerpiece, as we have often been told. The centerpiece is King Jesus.)

The plan of salvation is centered around Jesus

Modern preaching has a deep problem: it does not proclaim the gospel but an invitation to personal betterment. Modern preaching is therapeutic, not demanding. This was not always so in history. I once read about a man in the 1800s who approached a preacher with a concern that he had blasphemed the Holy Spirit and was eternally lost. While the preacher did not believe that he had committed such sin, his answer stunned me. The preacher told the man, "Serve God anyway." This idea of serving God irrespective of personal benefit was disruptive to my thinking because I held a man-centered gospel, not a Christ-centered gospel. I thought that we choose to believe and live as we do primarily for the reward. But this anthropocentric gospel is not the Christocentric gospel of the New Testament.

Most preachers today proclaim the gospel basically as a "save me" message. Highly self-centered, this notion of the gospel fails under closer scrutiny. Jesus Himself directly addressed this distortion: "For whoever desires to save his life will lose it, but whoever loses his life for My sake will find it" (Matt. 16:25).

Yet most false gospels are all about saving me. While it is certainly correct that the true gospel saves, this benefit follows a deeper decision to serve God first. By losing ourselves, we save ourselves. Scripture affirms that we are not called to primarily seek our own benefit:

> Seek first the kingdom of God and His righteousness. (Matt. 6:33)
>
> Incline my heart to your testimonies, and not to selfish gain. (Ps. 119:36)
>
> Let no one seek his own, but each one the other's well-being. (1 Cor. 10:24)
>
> He died for all, that those who live should live no longer for themselves, but for Him who died for them and rose again. (2 Cor. 5:15)
>
> You ask and do not receive, because you ask amiss, that you may spend it on your pleasures. (James 4:3)

Moses and Paul went as far as praying that their own salvation could be sacrificed if it could bring salvation to others (Exod. 32:31-32; Rom. 9:3)! To be sure, few truths are more glorious than receiving personal salvation. And God loves to repair broken marriages, provide us with jobs, and heal our bodily illnesses. But true salvation comes from seeking God's glory and kingdom, not one's own interests. The "save me" gospel has failed because it is unbiblical. One gets neither abundant life now nor salvation in the next life. The "save me" gospel, as opposed to the "Jesus' kingship" gospel, produces selfishness, laxity, and a hedonism that the modern church now reaps. The gospel of Jesus' kingship produces abundant life because followers willingly lose their lives.

The gospel is corporate and strong-group

The principle that "we get what we preach" has powerful ramifications in the area of community and strong-group thinking. When the modern individualistic plan of salvation is accepted (not founded upon the gospel announcement of kingdom or nation), the new convert looks around and thinks, "Who are all these people around me?" But when the gospel of the kingdom is proclaimed, the new convert *needs* to find fellow citizens for the message to be authenticated. New disciples rejoice in their hearts when they see Jesus' nation—they see that the kingdom has come! Much of the New Testament has this corporate focus; this focus originates from the gospel itself. The gospel of God's nation attacks weak-group thinking at the start of the journey of the faith. The gospel of the kingdom is the foundation of a biblical, strong-group church.

Having framed the gospel in the context of Israel's story and the ancient covenants, new disciples will see themselves standing in the stream of God's covenant activity coursing through history. When the gospel is properly proclaimed, disciples gain a sense of solidarity with God's chosen people throughout history. This was the basic polemic in the sermons of the book of Acts. In their presentations of Israel's history, the early Christians were saying, "We are the true people of God. We now take up the mantle of the prophets of old."

Reading the Bible takes on a new dimension when one views oneself in solidarity with the men and women in Scripture. As with the Corinthian church, we can meditate on Israel's history and refer to the prophets and patriarchs of old as "our fathers" though we may not be ethnically Jewish (1 Cor. 10:1; see also Rom. 4:16). Those who understand the gospel of the kingdom are far more motivated to study church history and understand contemporary missions. Church history and missions become our family story. Seeking to join this great cloud of witnesses, believers will be passionate to understand the history of their new nation that spans millenia and national boundaries.

Paul describes his ministry in Ephesus simply as "preaching the kingdom" (Acts 20:25, see also Acts 28:23, 31). How many hearers of a modern gospel message would describe what they heard in those terms? The term "kingdom" implies a king, subjects, dominion, covenant, and obedience.[8] Unless a person hears a message that could be described as the "gospel of the kingdom," it may well not be the gospel at all.

The gospel polarizes and elicits strong reactions

Whenever the gospel was preached in the book of Acts, listeners reacted strongly. Polarization was the norm. Even in our age of lukewarmness, the true gospel will elicit strong devotion or bitter antagonism.

Proclaiming the true gospel requires boldness. Of course, belief in God, the atoning death of His Son, and His resurrection are alien beliefs for the world. But Christians were not persecuted by the Roman imperial forces for holding a private, closet religion—but rather because Christians taught that Jesus was the true King. Teaching about another nation requires boldness because it threatens the powers and *status quo*. A riot began in Thessalonica because they preached that there was another king besides Caesar: "These who have turned the world upside down have come here too. Jason has harbored them, and these are all acting contrary to the decrees of Caesar, saying there is another king—Jesus" (Acts 17:6-7).

The gospel requires boldness and leads to polarization because of the attendant call to repentance. The call to repentance figures prominently in the sermons of Acts.

> And with many other words he testified and exhorted them, saying, "Be saved from this perverse generation." (Acts 2:40)

> God, having raised up His Servant Jesus, sent Him to bless you, in turning away every one of you from your iniquities. (Acts 3:26)

> Truly, these times of ignorance God overlooked, but now commands all men everywhere to repent, because He has appointed a day on which He will judge the world in righteousness by the Man whom He has ordained. (Acts 17:30-31)

> When Felix came with his wife Drusilla, who was Jewish, he sent for Paul and heard him concerning the

[8] The expression "obey the gospel" is found in Rom. 10:16; 2 Thess. 1:8; and 1 Pet. 4:17.

> faith in Christ. Now as he reasoned about righteousness, self-control, and the judgment to come, Felix was afraid. (Acts 24:24-25)
>
> I was not disobedient to the heavenly vision, but declared first to those in Damascus and in Jerusalem, and throughout all the region of Judea, and then to the Gentiles, that they should repent, turn to God, and do works befitting repentance. (Acts 26:19-20)

This preaching bore fruit. It caused people to burn their books (Acts 19:19) and disrupted economies (Acts 19:24-27). Most preaching today is not bold because it fails to speak against widely practiced sins. People can tolerate denouncing sin in general or certain sins that even the world recognizes as wrong, such as lying or adultery. But a line is crossed when specific sins are raised of which they are guilty. Observe what happens today to those who speak against worldly entertainment, jewelry, or divorce and remarriage. These sins are widely practiced, so those who speak against them will encounter fury, just as God's prophets always have. Gospel preaching in the New Testament elicited antagonism and persecution. The comfortable gospel preached in nearly all modern churches of the West can thus be easily recognized as false.

Conclusion

Preaching serves as a barometer of a church's health. We have looked at five aspects of gospel preaching:

1. The gospel is distinct from the plan of salvation. At the same time, the plan of salvation flows from the gospel. When the gospel is accurately proclaimed, the plan of salvation is strengthened.
2. The true gospel is framed by Israel's story. The gospel is the story of Jesus' words, deeds, crucifixion, and resurrection. Special focus is put upon Jesus' exaltation as king at the resurrection.
3. Even the plan of salvation should be centered on Jesus, not around me.
4. The kingdom gospel is corporate and strong-group, marked by the language of another nation.
5. Preaching the gospel requires boldness. The gospel describes a rival nation and calls for repentance from widely accepted sins. The true gospel thus elicits a strong reaction from its hearers.

At the close of gospel preaching, the apostles issued a decisive call to action. That call was for baptism, to which we turn in the next chapter.

Chapter 36

Baptism into one body

As many of you as were baptized into Christ have put on Christ.
(Galatians 3:27)

Because the church is the consequence of God's action in Christ, our ecclesiology should flow from our Christology.[1] As described in one of the foundational chapters of this book (chapter 8, "Principles of faithful biblical interpretation"), a Christocentric interpretation of Scripture involves both order and focus. To unpack Scripture's view of baptism, we should therefore begin with Jesus Himself.

In the Gospel according to Matthew, Jesus' first recorded words come at His baptism (Matt. 3:15). His last recorded words in the book, at the Great Commission, include a command to baptize (Matt. 28:18-20). Firsts and lasts are important in Scripture, suggesting a great deal about the significance of baptism.

What happened when Jesus was baptized? This much we can confidently say: *something actually happened.* That is, Jesus' baptism was no mere memorial of a past event. At this baptism, *the Father* opens the heavens, *the Spirit* lights upon Him as a dove, and *the beloved Son* is announced before the world. This Trinitarian imprint extends to the Great Commission where Jesus commands His disciples to baptize in the name of the Father, Son, and Spirit. The Trinity "has an affinity for baptism."[2]

If Jesus' example is normative for His followers, then it is reasonable to infer that baptism for His followers should be more than a symbol. This observation lays the foundation for a sacramental understanding

---

[1] Everett Ferguson, *The Church of Christ*, Eerdmans (1996), p. xx.

[2] F. D. Bruner, *Matthew: A Commentary, Volume 1*, Eerdmans (2007), p. 108.

of baptism. The outward act sheaths a powerful spiritual reality. Scripture in fact draws special attention to reception of the Spirit at baptism: "Repent, and let every one of you be baptized in the name of Jesus Christ for the remission of sins; and you shall receive the gift of the Holy Spirit" (Acts 2:38). Other texts conjoin the Spirit to water and baptism (John 3:5; 1 Cor. 12:13; Titus 3:5). Of course, the Spirit first appears in Scripture as hovering over the waters (Gen. 1:2). So too now He hovers over the new creation waters of baptism. Neither should the symbolism of a dove over the water be missed. Noah's dove hearkens us back to a renewed creation; now the dove of the Spirit takes believers forward into a new creation.[3]

Corroborating the emphasis of new life, baptism is portrayed as identification with Jesus' death and resurrection (Rom. 6:3-4). But like other great scriptural symbols, baptism has multiple facets. While the controlling motif is Jesus' death, burial, and resurrection, other resonances with Old Testament imagery can be found. They include cleansing, conflict, journey, and refreshment.[4] "Immersion into water—with both its shocking and pleasurable sensations—can evoke…a washing away of what is unclean, an encounter with a hostile force, a passing through a boundary marker, and reinvigoration."[5] Ananias draws upon the imagery of cleansing when he tells Paul to "wash away" his sins at baptism (Acts 22:16). This sacramental view of baptism was held by the ante-Nicene church, some of the early Anabaptists, and the Restoration churches.[6]

The church's declaration in baptism

You cannot baptize yourself. Someone else, a citizen of Jesus' kingdom, must validate your profession of faith by baptizing you. This seemingly obvious statement is laden with significance. We saw in a previous chapter (chapter 28, "The local church and membership") that Jesus vested the church with the keys of the kingdom, which is a power to

[3] Bruner, p. 110.

[4] Paul Fiddes in "Baptism and Creation" in *Reflections on the Water*, Paul Fiddes (ed.), Smyth & Helwys (1996), pp. 51-57.

[5] Fiddes, p. 57.

[6] For the early church, see Everett Ferguson, *Early Christians Speak: Faith and Life in the First Three Centuries*, third edition, ACU Press (1999), chapter 3. For the early Anabaptists, see Hans-Jürgen Goertz, *The Anabaptists*, Routledge (2008), chapter 3. For the Restoration churches, see *The Encyclopedia of the Stone-Campbell Movement*, Douglas Foster (ed.), Paul Blowers (ed.), Anthony Dunnavant (ed.), D. Newell Williams (ed.), Eerdmans (2005).

validate citizenship much as an earthly embassy validates citizenship. Baptism is the first declaration of citizenship by the church. Thus "repent and be baptized" should be thought of as a call for individual decision followed by the church's ratification. Both individual and collective components are present. The church's declaration that begins at baptism is then renewed weekly at the Lord's Supper.

The analogy of marriage is also helpful. Followers of Jesus are under the New Covenant. Covenants have a component of public declaration. After a man and a woman agree privately to commit their lives to another, they publicly declare this vow at the wedding. Baptism is much like this public wedding: "Christian baptism is like Christian marriage. Both include a *promise* to be faithfully joined (the ethical component) and both *bring about* the joining (the sacramental component). In both Christian baptism and Christian marriage a disciple promises to be a real Christian in fidelity to another, and *just as importantly* the disciple is also *joined* to a person who will *help* the disciple to be faithful."[7] Seen in this light, an unbaptized professing Christian is a bit like a person claiming to be married without having had a wedding!

The concept of synecdoche

Synecdoche (pronounced syn-NECK-deh-kee) refers to a part standing for the whole.[8] For example, the expression "all hands on deck" refers to people by a specific body part. Another example is the expression "nice set of wheels," which uses wheels refer to a car.

When we look at the conversions in the book of Acts, we find several elements portrayed: faith, baptism, forgiveness, receiving the Spirit, and sometimes the laying on of hands and speaking in tongues. But sometimes the order varies. "Which is the normative order of conversion: repentance, water-baptism, forgiveness and reception of the Spirit (Acts 2:28,41); believing, water-baptism, laying on of hands and reception of the Spirit (Acts 8:12-17); reception of the Spirit, speaking in tongues and water-baptism (Acts 10:44-48); believing and water-baptism (Acts 16:31-33); or believing, water-baptism, laying on of hands, reception of the Spirit and speaking in tongues (Acts 19:1-6; see also 9:17-18; 22:16)?"[9] These events are all part of an integrated composite, a multifacted complex. This clustering explains why Scripture uses synecdoche to describe conversion. Romans 10:9 describes verbal

[7] Bruner, p. 104.
[8] In contrast, a merism uses the poles or multiple parts to describe a whole.
[9] A. Cross quoted in Brandon Jones, *Waters of Promise*, Pickwick (2012), p. 63.

confession as securing salvation. Galatians 3:27 describes baptism as putting on Christ; 1 Peter 3:31 says that baptism "saves." Mark 6:12 and Acts 17:30 link repentance to salvation. None of these contradict one another when one understands that each passage uses synecdoche. In each, one part stands for the whole complex of events that together comprise conversion. One can speak of any part as causally related to salvation because it is supposed to travel together with the other parts. The idea that a person would confess Jesus as Lord and not be baptized is alien to the New Testament. Similarly foreign is the idea that a person would be baptized without faith. Indeed, baptism without faith is invalid (an argument against infant baptism, to be discussed later). Faith should be regarded as the centerpiece of this composite but is not a lone traveler. When one understands synecdoche, many foolish arguments can be averted about apparent contradictions between these passages.

If we were to look for a standard, Jesus' example and explicit apostolic instruction (for example Acts 2:38) should be our source. These passages contend for a high view of baptism, wherein something is actually occurring, particularly the reception of the Spirit. But the flexibility seen in Acts (also in the Gospel accounts) should give us pause about hasty judgment over others' experiences of conversion coming from overly rigid expectations around sequence. The book of Acts also reminds us that these events generally occur as a cluster in time (not separated over months or years), which should inform our practice and expectations.

When baptism should occur

In many Protestant and evangelical groups the altar call has taken the place of baptism. Other groups separate baptism from repentance and profession of faith by months or years, departing from the New Testament model.

As we have just seen, baptism was expected immediately, alongside repentance and calling upon the name of Jesus. These should form an integrated composite. Typically we see only the elapse of a few hours between preaching and baptism. Peter attests to the close link between repentance and baptism on Pentecost: "Repent, and let every one of you be baptized in the name of Jesus Christ for the remission of sins; and you shall receive the gift of the Holy Spirit" (Acts 2:38). So too Ananias instructed Saul: "And now why are you waiting? Arise and be baptized, and wash away your sins, calling on the name of the Lord" (Acts 22:16).

Philip did likewise with the Ethiopian eunuch: "Then Philip opened his mouth, and beginning at this Scripture, preached Jesus to him. Now as they went down the road, they came to some water. And the eunuch said, 'See, here is water. What hinders me from being baptized?' Then Philip said, 'If you believe with all your heart, you may.' And he answered and said, 'I believe that Jesus Christ is the Son of God.' So he commanded the chariot to stand still. And both Philip and the eunuch went down into the water, and he baptized him (Acts 8:35-38)." Paul and Silas modeled this pattern with the Philippian jailer who was baptized the night of his conversion. This example is particularly notable because he likely had never encountered Christians before, so the teaching he could have received preceding baptism was limited to several hours: "So they said, 'Believe on the Lord Jesus Christ, and you will be saved, you and your household.' Then they spoke the word of the Lord to him and to all who were in his house. And he took them the same hour of the night and washed their stripes. And immediately he and all his family were baptized" (Acts 16:31-33).

The administrator of the baptism must of course ascertain the legitimacy of the baptismal candidate. The church's carrying of the keys of the kingdom is no small matter. Preaching lasted several hours in biblical times (Matt. 15:32; Acts 20:7), affording some time to adequately explain repentance and faith. However, there is no New Testament precedent for months, years, or membership classes before baptism.

Against infant baptism

Roman Catholic and many Protestant groups practice infant baptism, drawing heavily on the Old Testament analogy of circumcision. Scripture however teaches believer's baptism (sometimes called confessor's baptism). The arguments against infant baptism include the following:

- With infant baptism, the integrated composite of repentance, forgiveness of sins, water baptism, and reception of the Spirit is violated. The synecdoche of Galatians 3:27 becomes nonsensical. The New Testament witness concerning the significance of baptism is thus obliterated.
- To have an infant undergo a rite associated with participating in the death, burial, and resurrection of Jesus makes little sense. Moreover, the sprinkling of a small amount of water so often done at infant baptism fails to symbolically capture the drama of the death and resurrection of Jesus.

- The infant cannot make an "appeal to God" or a "pledge to God" (1 Pet. 3:21). Several senses of Peter's important passage on baptism are nullified, including the dramatic statement "baptism now saves you."
- Biblical theology, the study of the larger narrative of Scripture, speaks against infant baptism. While beyond the scope of this chapter to develop, a beautiful presentation has been articulated elsewhere with implications for infant baptism.[10]
- Jesus blessed children (Matt. 19:13) but neither baptized them nor commanded their baptism.
- Infant baptism is nowhere mentioned in the New Testament. Hence the Regulative Principle would forbid the practice. Since Christian disciples were certainly having children during this period, the absence of instruction around the baptism of children is glaring.
- Recognizing the biblical deficiencies of infant baptism, proponents of infant baptism often create events like "confirmation" to reconnect personal faith to public testimony. This manufacturing of new rites further violates the Regulative Principle.
- To the objection that the Philippian jailer's household included infants, the passage says that "he rejoiced, having believed in God *with all his household*" (Acts 16:34). Unless we are prepared to imagine infants who believe in God, the objection fails.
- The Bible never states that baptism functions in the church age as circumcision did in the Old Testament.
- In Galatians, if Paul believed that baptism replaced circumcision, he would have made such a statement. Instead, he makes an entirely different argument.
- If baptism replaced circumcision, the Jerusalem council (Acts 15) would have surely connected baptism to circumcision given the context of the debate—yet they did not.
- The true antitype of circumcision is spiritual regeneration of the heart (Phil. 3:3; Col. 2:11-12).
- The covenantal arguments for infant baptism are weak and have been refuted elsewhere in detail.[11]
- Salvation by faith is undermined by infant baptism.
- The convoluted chain of who had faith at the baptism of an infant spun a web of controversy in the medieval church. Augustine in-

[10] See Leonard Verduin, *The Anatomy of a Hybrid*, Eerdmans (1976).

[11] See Stephen Wellum in "Baptism and the Relationship between the Covenants" in *Believer's Baptism: Sign of the New Covenant in Christ*, Thomas Schreiner and Shawn Wright (ed.), B&H Academic (2007).

troduced the idea that it was the faith of others, *fides aliena*, that was a prerequisite for baptism. "If *fides aliena* solves the problem of the infant's lack of faith, it opens up a new question, who actually does the believing? The early scholastics reckoned with the possibility that parents or sponsors may not really believe. In this case, the act of believing devolves upon the church as a whole, as Augustine had said. But what if the entire church was in error? Then, said the early scholastics, it is the faith of the *ecclesia triumphans*, the church already in heaven, that suffices. But the church triumphant does not need faith; how can it 'believe'?"[12] This Pandora's box testifies to the illegitimacy of the position.

- Some advocates of infant baptism (especially Calvinists) teach that infants become members of the covenant community but are not yet regenerate. Splitting regeneration from covenant entry cannot be found in the New Testament. Moreover, a host of secondary exegetical problems develops wherein the church by necessity becomes a mixed group of the regenerate and the unregenerate. This was perhaps the most important distinction between the Anabaptists who sought a pure, disciplined church of believers from the Protestant vision of a state-church of mixed character.
- The early Lutheran position teaches that the baby is actually regenerated and has faith (*fides infantium*).[13] While solving the Protestant problem of removing personal faith from the act of baptism, this creates the incredulous position that infants can understand and believe the gospel. Other advocates of infant baptism (especially Wesleyan) teach that infant baptism removes original sin.[14] This notion also lacks biblical support.
- The implications for child rearing are significant. As one advocate for believer's baptism wrote, "We do not say to our children, 'Be a good Christian child,' but rather, 'Repent and believe the gospel.' "[15] Which seems more biblical?
- Using the argument of recognition by fruits, the churches that

[12] Jonathan Rainbow in "Confessor Baptism" in *Believer's Baptism: Sign of the New Covenant in Christ*, Thomas Schreiner and Shawn Wright (ed.), B&H Academic (2007), p. 191.

[13] See Rainbow, pp. 192-196. Modern advocates slightly modify the position but teach infant baptism as regenerative. As a Lutheran, Robert Kolb presents this view in *Understanding Four Views of Baptism*, Zondervan (2007), chapter 3.

[14] See Thomas Oden, *John Wesley's Teachings: Volume 3 (Pastoral Theology)*, Zondervan (2013), chapter 7.

[15] Timothy George in *Believer's Baptism: Sign of the New Covenant in Christ*, Thomas Schreiner and Shawn Wright (ed.), B&H Academic (2007), p. xix.

have practiced infant baptism are usually antinomian in tendency. Very few of Jesus' hard teachings are practiced in such settings. Members generally live worldly lives.

- Further developing the test of fruits, countless millions have been baptized as infants (especially in historically Roman Catholic countries) and receive a false hope. Seen in this light, infant baptism has the demonic consequence of providing false assurance to those who live wicked lives.
- Those who practice believer's baptism have historically been the persecuted, suffering church (the Waldensians, the Lollards, the early Anabaptists, and the early Baptists). As highlighted before (see chapter 8), the suffering church serves as a guidepost to biblical truth.
- 1 Corinthians 7:14 notes that children born to believing parents are in some sense sanctified, without mentioning baptism.
- The church, for its first hundred and fifty years, upheld believer's baptism.[16]
- When infant baptism was developed, particularly by Augustine, it was associated with a "theology of coercion" and the state-church.[17]

Infant baptism, with its attendant hermeneutic, represents a continued threat to the pure faith of Scripture. If a church gets infant baptism wrong, the door has been opened to a flood of error. Even some Calvinists like Spurgeon have called it an "abomination."[18] We should answer as Philip did when questioned on what prevents baptism: "If you believe with all your heart, you may" (Acts 8:37).

How should baptism be performed

The Greek word for baptism means to dip, soak, or wash.[19] This definition naturally suggests baptism by immersion. This is corroborated

[16] Even proponents of infant baptism assent that the early church practiced believer's baptism. Kurt Aland's *Did the Church Baptize Infants?*, Westminster Press (1963) is one such example. The best survey of the history of baptism in the early church can be found in Everett Ferguson's *Baptism in the Early Church*, Eerdmans (2009).

[17] Verduin, pp. 101-121.

[18] Charles Spurgeon, *The Soul Winner*, Cosimo (2007), p. 184.

[19] See *A Greek-English Lexicon of the New Testament and other Early Christian Literature*, third edition (BDAG), Frederick Danker (ed.), Univ of Chicago Press (2000). This lexicon notes that the word means to "put or go under water in a variety of senses." See also Friberg's lexicon.

by New Testament example. After His baptism, Jesus comes up from the water: "It came to pass in those days that Jesus came from Nazareth of Galilee, and was baptized by John in the Jordan. And immediately, coming up from the water, He saw the heavens parting and the Spirit descending upon Him like a dove" (Mark 1:9-10). Philip and the eunuch both go down into the water, and come up out of the water—language that implies they were in a body of water and most consistent with immersion: "So he commanded the chariot to stand still. And both Philip and the eunuch went down into the water, and he baptized him. Now when they came up out of the water, the Spirit of the Lord caught Philip away, so that the eunuch saw him no more; and he went on his way rejoicing" (Acts 8:38-39).

John also selected locations because there was much water, again most consistent with immersion. "Now John also was baptizing in Aenon near Salim, because there was much water there. And they came and were baptized" (John 3:23). In the epistles, the language of being "buried with Him" in baptism is also most consistent with immersion (Rom. 6:3-4; Col. 2:12). The picture of going under the water visually demonstrates our participation in Jesus' death. Coming out of the water reflects the resurrection in newness of life.

In circumstances where immersion is not possible, pouring serves as a reasonable second choice. Pouring can be linked to the language of pouring out of the Holy Spirit. One of the earliest Christian writings after the New Testament advocates immersion as the best option; if this is not possible, then it advocates pouring (see Didache 7:1-5). This is a sensible and irenic stance. In the case of pouring, a large amount of water should be used, such that the person could justifiably say that they have been "washed." The tiny amounts used in some pourings would better be called sprinkling, a word not associated with water baptism.

Conclusion

In light of the significance of the public declaration of entering the church, how tragic it is that baptism has been obscured in so many ways. And how eager we should be to practice it rightly: to identify with Jesus should be at the heart of the Christian life. Similarly, baptism is a powerful testament to Jesus' identification with us:

> The first thing Jesus does for the human race is *go down with it* into the deep waters of repentance and baptism. Jesus' whole life will be like this. It is well known that Jesus *ends* his ministry on a cross between thieves; it deserves

to be as well known that he *begins* his ministry in a river among sinners. From his baptism to his execution Jesus stays low, at our level, identifying with us at every point, becoming as completely one with us in our humanity as, in the church's teaching, he is believed to be completely one with God in eternity. Jesus' 'at-one-ment' with the human race, visible here at baptism is as impressive and important for human salvation as Jesus' at-one-ment with the heavenly Father.[20]

[20] Bruner, p. 101.

Chapter 37

Family life

For I have chosen him, that he may command his children and his household after him to keep the way of the LORD by doing righteousness and justice. (Genesis 18:19)

Strong churches depend upon strong families. Church growth depends upon biblical families. Being the first institution ordained by God, the family holds a special place in the Scriptures. Because of its divine origin, the family has a unique ability to reflect God's attributes. Few sights are as winsome as a godly family. Being in the presence of a loving, warm family melts the hearts of believers and unbelievers alike. Observing a loving family silently convicts an unrighteous heart and encourages a pious heart. Strong families are the backbone of the church.

Singleness

While it may seem odd to begin a chapter on family life by discussing singleness, it is necessary because many churches have fallen into unbalanced positions. When a religious group takes a position of excess or abuse, another group often reacts by swinging to an opposite extreme. Protestant groups have erred by overreacting to Roman Catholic teachings on virginity. The Roman Catholic church contradicts Scripture by making Mary a perpetual virgin and demanding that its priests be celibate.[1] Protestant groups have over-reacted to the Roman Catholic exaltation of celibacy by looking upon those who are single and celibate as second-class citizens. The New Testament speaks against both of these extremes.

Jesus of course lived a celibate life, so those who imitate this lifestyle have noble ground on which to stand. Paul was glad for his celibacy and extols its advantages (1 Cor. 7:7, 32-38). He plainly teaches that it is advantageous to be single so that one may serve the Lord with less distraction. There should be no reason therefore to look down on those who are single or pity them for not marrying. We should instead think as Paul did: a person who chooses singleness for the Lord's service is to be applauded. Undue pressure has likely caused some young people to be married whom the Lord would rather have in His undistracted service. Of course, those who desire marriage also desire a good thing—the church should hold both callings as noble. The church as a whole needs correction and balance on this issue.

Children and their training

God instructed the first couple to multiply and fill the earth. Godly offspring are elsewhere described as a purpose of marriage (Mal. 2:15). Yet we live in an era in which children are shunned or despised. Governments like China forcibly limit childbearing. Somewhat surprisingly, college-educated white women in America have the same number of children as women in China.[2] Despite greater wealth, the advantages

[1] Responding to these errant Roman Catholic positions should be done with Scripture. Matthew 1:25 records that Joseph did not know Mary (a euphemism for marital intercourse) *until* after Jesus was born, implying that he did eventually "know" her. The Gospel accounts also record that Jesus had brothers (Matt. 12:46). While Catholics maintain they were cousins, New Testament Greek has a word for cousin that is used elsewhere (Col. 4:10) and this word is not used about Jesus' brothers. On the celibacy of priests, the qualification to be an elder is being the husband of one wife and having well-behaved children (1 Tim. 3:2-5). Ironically the Roman Catholic church's current requirement for celibacy among its priests itself represents an overreaction to nepotistic abuse.

[2] "For more than three decades, Chinese women have been subjected to their country's brutal one-child policy. Those who try to have more children have been subjected to fines and forced abortions. Their houses have been razed and their husbands fired from their jobs. As a result, Chinese women have a fertility rate of 1.54. Here in America, white, college-educated women—a good proxy for the middle class—have a fertility rate of 1.6. America has its very own one-child policy. And we have chosen it for ourselves." Taken from "America's Baby Bust," by Jonathan Last, *Wall Street Journal*, February 2, 2013.

of modern medicine, and the conveniences of modern technology, the birthrate in America has fallen from seven children per woman in 1800 to about two today. This is not restricted to America: fertility rates around the globe are plummeting, with many countries experiencing population contraction. About 20% of all pregnancies worldwide end in abortion.[3] Over forty million babies per year are killed in abortion,[4] amounting to over one baby per second. Throughout the world, children are seen as threats to the rainforest, drains on natural resources, hindrances to career advance, inhibitors of freedom, financial burdens, and emotionally depleting hardships.

Despite the culture's protests, children are a blessing to be welcomed. When God made Adam and Eve, He blessed them. Note the connection of blessing to bearing children: "So God created man in His own image; in the image of God He created him; male and female He created them. Then God blessed them, and God said to them, 'Be fruitful and multiply' " (Gen. 1:27-28).

This pattern repeats throughout the Scriptures. After the flood, God blessed Noah and his sons. Again blessing was linked to childbearing. "So God blessed Noah and his sons, and said to them: 'Be fruitful and multiply, and fill the earth' " (Gen. 9:1, also see 9:7). Hundreds of years later, God's blessing to the people of Israel began with multiplication: "And He will love you and bless you and multiply you; He will also bless the fruit of your womb and the fruit of your land, your grain and your new wine and your oil, the increase of your cattle and the offspring of your flock, in the land of which He swore to your fathers to give you" (Deut. 7:13). In this passage, material blessings *follow* the blessing of children. Today's society would have it the other way around: establish material prosperity first and then have children. In a very long list of blessings promised for obedience, bearing children was again the *first* blessing promised to Israel: "Blessed shall be the fruit of your body" (Deut. 28:4). The Psalms celebrate this truth:

> Behold, children are a heritage from the LORD,
> the fruit of the womb a reward.
> Like arrows in the hand of a warrior
> are the children of one's youth.
> Blessed is the man
> who fills his quiver with them! (Ps. 127:3-5)

[3] G. Sedgh et al. "Induced Abortion: Incidence and Trends Worldwide from 1995 to 2008." *Lancet*, 379:625-632 (2012).

[4] Data from the Guttmacher Institute, www.guttmacher.org/pubs/fb_IAB.pdf.

Children are the honor and pride of the godly family. Hannah's husband Elkanah comforted her by saying, "Am I not better to you than ten sons?" (1 Sam. 1:8). That expression, almost unthinkable today, captures how God's people regarded children. In the New Testament, Jesus had at least four brothers (Matt. 13:55) and multiple sisters, implying that Mary had at least seven children.

In addition to the implications for an individual family, the strength and honor of a nation were connected to its population size and growth: "In a multitude of people is a king's honor, But in the lack of people is the downfall of a prince" (Prov. 14:28). Christians should be known for large families (through birth or adoption), as we believe God's word that they are blessings. We should seek to be a growing and vibrant nation for King Jesus. To bring another image of God into this world is a great honor. Unfortunately the church has imbibed the world's values and attitudes toward children. Christian couples show little to no difference with respect to family size when compared to their non-Christian peers. Much of the church uses the same contraceptive instruments as the world. Few realize that until the twentieth century, every church denomination was opposed to contraception. The sin of Onan was to take pleasure in sexual relations without being willing to bear children (Gen. 38:8-10). Onan's judgment therefore speaks against the modern permissiveness of contraception. Some have even argued that contraception opened the door to abortion through an implicit devaluation of children.

To the shopworn line that the environment cannot handle more children, there is a good answer: "The world has enough for everyone's need, but not for everyone's greed."[5] The world likely cannot support everyone's living as most do in the West. But the earth can likely support a vastly higher population of those who live a simple lifestyle.[6]

Raising children requires sacrifice and humility. Children are powerful magnifying glasses. They expose our hypocrisies and weaknesses. Honestly acknowledging our own flaws in our children is humbling. Yet children also acquire our strengths. While beyond the scope of this book, proper child training should incorporate intense prayer, mentorship, and study.[7] Because of their exposing powers, children's behavior represents one of the best litmus tests for the health of a church.

---

[5] Quotation attributed to Mohandas Gandhi.

[6] For example, Harvard biologist E. O. Wilson has noted that the earth's population capacity could increase fourfold with a move to a plant-based diet.

[7] For more, see Lloy Kniss, *Practical Pointers for Training Your Child*, second edition, Christian Light Publications (2004) and Steven and Teri Maxwell, *Keeping Our Children's Hearts*, Communication Concepts (2004).

The spiritual vitality, obedience, love, and submissiveness of a congregation's children speak volumes more than a statement of faith.

Most parents today send their children off to government schools where they are effectively raised by the state. Parents have pushed off the bulk of parenting onto others. In one of the passages that many ignore or explain away, the Bible says, "Train the young women to love their husbands and children, to be self-controlled, pure, working at home, kind, and submissive to their own husbands, that the word of God may not be reviled" (Titus 2:4-5 ESV). The argument of cultural relativism (see chapter 9) has been leveled against this passage for decades. No matter what the evasive tactic, the Christian pattern is clear: mothers are charged to work at home. Society often puts this role down in favor of more "glamorous" positions. But managing a home and raising children is a far more influential role than the occupations that the world exalts. The refrain from the famous poem rings out, "The hand the rocks the cradle is the hand that rules the world."[8] Homemaking has inestimable power to change the world. This power aligns well with Jesus' example of focusing on the few to most effectively change the world (see chapter 4).

In the New Covenant, fathers' hearts are inclined to their children. "He will turn the hearts of the fathers to the children, and the hearts of the children to their fathers" (Mal. 4:6). Children do not receive the leftovers of a father's time—they get the best. Children are at the center of a father's thoughts and affections. The world jokes about "deadbeat" fathers or workaholic fathers. This humor comes from men's sinful inclination to neglect their children for other activities. But biblically, fathers have the responsibility for the direction and training of their children (Eph. 6:4). A powerful mark of the Holy Spirit's presence in a father is his passion for his children. This mark explains why the Scripture says that overseers must have submissive, reverent children (1 Tim. 3:4). Children expose the character of their fathers.

The marriage bond

God designed marriage for the purpose of companionship. He also designed it as the vehicle for children. Outside of discussions on divorce, the lengthiest passage on marriage in the New Testament teaches that human marriage should reflect the relationship between Jesus and the church (Eph. 5:22-33). This is the deep truth about marriage: it is intended to reflect an eternal, perfect union. The one-flesh union should

[8] The refrain from William Ross Wallace's poem.

reflect the unity of Jesus and His church: "For we are members of His body, of His flesh and of His bones. 'For this reason a man shall leave his father and mother and be joined to his wife, and the two shall become one flesh' " (Eph. 5:30-31). Marriage should be a living metaphor of Jesus' relationship to His church. Husbands and wives should therefore embrace the roles of Jesus and the church, respectively. While many deem this to be archaic and outmoded, the case is exactly the opposite. Jesus' relationship to His church is eternal, not something from the first century. Cultural relativists who want to grant husbands and wives the same functions sever the metaphor and obliterate the deep purpose of marriage.

The husband is called to be the head of the marriage—to take on Jesus' role. Whenever a husband reads of Jesus' words or deeds in Scripture, he should ask himself, "What would it mean for me to act in this way toward my wife?" The husband should seek to outserve and outlove his wife. Husbands are to protect, provide, and lead. Today's culture does its best to challenge that paradigm. We live in an age of emasculation, where many men are passive, weak, and preoccupied with the trivial. Many men shed their convictions for the sake of a girlfriend or wife. But the biblical pattern is for husbands to wash their wives in the word by teaching them from the Scriptures (Eph. 5:26). How many husbands have taken up this duty? The world needs more men who can boldly serve as heads of their homes. While many wince at the idea of headship, Jesus' leadership balances authority with loving service. Such a great responsibility should make husbands cry out daily for wisdom and strength.

The wife should submit to her husband. When a wife does this in the right spirit, it disarms the husband and humbles him, helping him to love his wife more. Similarly the husband who loves his wife, and truly lays down his life for her, helps his wife to submit.

One day every Christian husband and wife will dine at the marriage supper of the Lamb and behold the majestic Bridegroom and His loving bride in all their splendor. We will see then with our eyes the authentic relationship of which all Christian marriage is a copy. While all human marriages will be dissolved in that grander union, may the erstwhile marriage partners be able to whisper across the table, "We painted a good picture."

Chapter 38

Education and occupations

Everyone when he is fully trained will be like his teacher.
(Luke 6:40 ESV)

We will spend most of the wakeful hours of our lives either in school or at work.[1] The sheer number of hours spent at these tasks is bound to impact our spiritual lives. As noted in chapter 4, discipleship is closely related to our companionship. Because so much socialization and companionship come from our educational and occupational environments, they play significant roles in discipleship. Without proper discipleship, the church's growth will be stunted. Despite these powerful connections, the church has done a poor job in developing a practical theology of education and work.

Jesus gives a foundational spiritual law: "Everyone when he is fully trained will be like his teacher" (Luke 6:40 ESV). Teachers produce students like themselves. Students and apprentices become like their teachers. This principle is the great natural law of training through education or work. We become like those who train us; this principle can be used for great blessing or harm.

Education

The Enemy wants children. He wants children that are not his own. His skill at kidnapping is unrivaled. As the most expert kidnapper in history, Satan has accomplished what any criminal would envy: he coaxes parents to voluntarily give their children to him. Many parents, unbeknownst to them, are sending their children to destruction.

[1] By the term "work," I mean either homemaking or work outside the home.

At low points in their history, some Israelites sacrificed their children to a Canaanite god called Moloch (2 Chron. 28:3, 33:6; Jer. 7:31). One can hardly believe that any parent would do such a thing. Modern minds look down on such primitive behavior with disgust. Yet most parents are oblivious to today's "child sacrifice" in which they might be participating. While some children survive the flames, most do not.

To send a child into the state's system is to send that child to a rival power with its own agenda. Parents entrust the mind, emotions, and sensibilities of their children to ungodly influences while these little ones are most vulnerable. That child will effectively be raised by their teachers and peers for most of their waking hours. When the parent asks how the child's day went, they receive the bare answer, "Fine." The child will soon look to peers for approval instead of parents.

In biblical times, parents educated their children (Deut. 6:7; Eph. 6:4). Sons were apprenticed by their fathers, and daughters by their mothers. While the Greek model took children out of the home to be educated by the state (in the so-called gymnasium), this was recognized as sin by the Jews. In the intertestamental period, the author of 2 Maccabees condemns the high priest, Jason, for bringing Greek education into Judaism (2 Macc. 4:7-22). One way that Greek education corrupted Jewish youth was the stress on athletics. The Greek gymnasium was a place of sporting events—quite similar to today's colleges and universities. Even the Jewish priests were seduced by these games:

> [Jason] took delight in establishing a gymnasium right under the citadel, and he induced the noblest of the young men to wear the Greek hat...The priests were no longer intent upon their service at the altar. Despising the sanctuary and neglecting the sacrifices, they hurried to take part in the unlawful proceedings in the wrestling arena after the signal for the discus-throwing, disdaining the honors prized by their ancestors and putting the highest value upon Greek forms of prestige. For this reason heavy disaster overtook them, and those whose ways of living they admired and wished to imitate completely became their enemies and punished them. (2 Macc. 4:12, 14-16 NRSV).

Many people complain about the spirituality of young people today. Moans of weariness go up because instead of being at home with the family, young people would rather play video games, go to the mall, or spend time with their friends. None of this should be a surprise, for it is Jesus' natural law of training exerting its force. The children are becoming like their worldly teachers and peers. Those few spiritually strong youth who emerge with godly vibrancy do so *in spite* of their education, not because of it.

When parents stand before the Lord on the last day, they will have to give an answer for the influences that their children felt at school. Delegation of responsibility to the state does not imply absolution of responsibility. Parents are responsible for whatever instruction, images, and examples their children received at school. Many parents falsely imagine that they know what their child is being exposed to. The reality is usually otherwise. Unfortunately, even most "Christian" schools have many of the same problems as the public schools—sometimes worse, because the same evils are done under a Christian name. When contemplating the temptations, snares, and false teaching that children are subject to outside the home, Jesus' words should sober us: "Whoever causes one of these little ones who believe in Me to sin, it would be better for him if a millstone were hung around his neck, and he were drowned in the depth of the sea. Woe to the world because of offenses! For offenses must come, but woe to that man by whom the offense comes!" (Matt. 18:6-7)

A biblical education is grounded in the fear of Lord (Prov. 9:10). The parents, especially the father, are charged with the duty of educating their child (Eph. 6:4). This naturally implies some form of home-schooling. Unusual circumstances might dictate the child being at some form of Christian school, but this should be the exception. Homeschooling implies that both spouses cannot work outside the home. While some may say they need the additional income from two parents working, the Lord will prove faithful to those willing to trust Him. Many homeschooling parents have testified that while sacrifice was required, the Lord always met their needs. Families will likely have to make material sacrifices, but what is gained far surpasses earthly riches or comforts.

The first purpose of education is discipleship. Because of the intensive companionship involved in homeschooling, parents naturally become their children's disciplers and friends. With the fear and knowledge of the Lord at the foundation of Christian education, a child's mind remains clear—unlike their peers whose minds are progressively twisted from repeated exposure to sin. Especially through high school, children who are homeschooled and shielded from worldly influences better retain their innocence and natural youthful qualities. Less jaded and cynical than their peers, they have the ability to learn with the acuity of a young, supple mind. This served Daniel and his three associates well, as they were called "gifted in all wisdom, possessing knowledge and quick to understand" (Daniel 1:4).

College is widely recognized as the place that children leave the faith. While the seeds of rebellion had been planted long before, the spiritual influences of the college environment are profound. The late teens and early twenties are crucial years of identity formation. What message is conveyed by putting our youth at the feet of brilliant but worldly teachers? We encourage our youth to please their professors by getting good grades and recommendations from them. Imagine getting this message and hearing eloquent professors expound their views of art, sexuality, agnosticism, evolution, and the meaning of life. Even if the student has an intuitive sense that these professors' views might be wrong, can most eighteen year olds stand up to accomplished scholars with doctorates and skillfully debate them in the classroom? Instead, young people effectively become these professors' disciples, having been encouraged to do so by their parents. Jesus' law of training then works its power in all realms, including spiritual. Academic learning has served as a Trojan horse for spiritual destruction.

While I was in the Protestant church, I spent two years teaching organic chemistry to Harvard University students. For seven years, I lived in a Harvard dormitory as a mentor. I watched with my own eyes the faith trajectories of students sent there by well-meaning parents. Tragically, most lost their faith. While there were a precious few who managed to escape with some measure of faith, they too suffered damage. While their parents proudly hailed their accomplishments at graduation, I wonder what speech the Lord would give at such an event.

Not only was the spiritual fruit disastrous, the quality of the education was poor. This statement surprises many who would expect Harvard to have one of the best education systems in the world. Because most students were interested in getting the highest possible grades, they would search out the easiest classes and professors. Often their final transcripts were a confused jumble of unrelated courses (a course on Japanese cooking was especially popular during my years at Harvard). More importantly, few students learned proper discipline. Yes, they worked hard, but it was almost always due to forced deadlines around which they would frantically crunch. Very few students learned how to discipline and motivate themselves to learn a field of study thoroughly and systematically. A churning blend of hard work, laziness, procrastination, and partying marked their lives. The college life is a life of emotional extremes, not of steady and patient discipline. Education has failed to impart to our children even basic elements for being a successful lifetime learner.

Jesus calls us to love God with all our mind, a command that should make followers of Jesus the most committed people in the world to studying and learning. And Christians can educate their children in a more effective manner than the world. After having attended some of the top schools in the country, I am convinced that motivated parents can provide their children with a better education than graduates receive from the most prestigious colleges. Besides having discipleship as the primary goal, parents can do a better job than the world at producing knowledgeable and disciplined youth who can earn an honest living. A Christian education should surpass the education of the world in terms of quality and depth. Committed parents can teach their children the necessary self-discipline to learn effectively. Christian parents can ground education in a scriptural worldview. This is easier than ever before because of unparalleled access to high quality books (e.g. grammar, writing, history, math, and science). For higher education, emergent trends at the advanced level (such as remote courses and certification programs) have promise in providing a superior education to today's typical university system. I have personally seen examples of homeschooled children receiving a better education than students at elite colleges.

How to best disciple and educate our youth is a gauntlet that has been thrown at our feet. We need much more prayer, discussion, and study of this important subject. We need spiritual writers and speakers to articulate a vision for Christian education. Armed with a biblical understanding, the families of this generation have the opportunity to reproducibly impart excellent discipleship and scholarship. Our prayer should be that kingdom Christians rise to the challenge.

The social pressures to conform in education are high. Education is a god in many cultures, particularly Asian ones. Unlike shameful traps like pornography, the idol of education has corrupted these cultures in a pernicious way: vain pursuits can draw acclaim. Much of the family's identity will come from the children's grades, academic accomplishments, school prestige, and eventual occupation. This excitement over worldly education robs families of the zeal and identity that should come from standing in God's family. Paul counted his previous accomplishments as rubbish in comparison to knowing Jesus. Families that value righteousness, discipleship, and sacrifice for the Lord tend to produce children who seek first the kingdom. In contrast, families that draw identity from education are more likely to send their children onto a track of worldly pursuits that will rob their children of the time, interest, and energy to wholeheartedly pursue the Lord.

For the world, education is the first step on a journey. The world seeks to put children on its path, to make them crave its rewards and pleasures. By so doing, children will spend their lives chasing after vanities, the deceitfulness of wealth, hollow amusements, and lives of comfort. The following track is often followed by the families of professing Christians:

1. Parents expose their children to television, movies, the internet, video games, and worldly magazines at a young age. The children's early sense of beauty, humor, and values then comes from the world.
2. Children are then placed in a public school, where nearly all their peers have these worldly sensibilities and begin to judge one another according to these values.
3. Fairly quickly the children crave the approval of their peers, above even their parents, and so fall deeper into folly.
4. By the teenage years, the world's educational system will introduce another set of values involving security, prestige, and accomplishment. This may involve expectations of attending a certain college, having an enviable home, and achieving honors in one's field.
5. Many will go to college, living away from home for the first time, and taste both hard work and recklessness. The pressure to get a respectable job will intensify. Lavish dinners and award ceremonies await those who succeed. Meanwhile, the world continues to shape the sensibilities of young people regarding music, beauty, recreation, humor, friendship, lifestyle, and security. Many men will become enslaved to pornography during these late teenage years and descend into spiritual laxity.
6. After college (or perhaps graduate or professional school), having incurred financial debt, graduates will get a job that can help relieve their debts and also provide funds for their desired lifestyle. By this time, they are becoming accustomed to eating out in restaurants, lavish vacations, and a comfortable lifestyle. Wanting to maintain this, they work hard in their jobs while sometimes despising them.
7. Such a person marries someone else on the same path, perhaps even in a "Christian" setting. In reality, both are gliding away from the King.
8. Having further progressed along their job paths, they are ascending a professional ladder. They simply could not leave after having so much "invested" into their careers. And so they continue, digging themselves deeper into a spiritual hole.
9. Now having children, they have further justification to continue in their spiritual direction for fear of disrupting the family. The

pursuit of security, savings, and comforts are quietly intensified.

10. A sense of separation from the world is lost, and while financially comfortable, they are spiritually dead. Their children are spoiled. They might find a church filled with people in a similar lifestyle who exhort one another to be "lights" in their workplace, an impossible task because their lifestyle betrays the commands of Jesus.
11. Caught in this web, they are given over to a strong delusion, and either justify what they do on religious grounds, or quietly abandon King Jesus altogether, leaving the next generation with little hope to ever know what kingdom living could be.

Occupations

One purpose of education is preparation for a job—for being a productive member of society. A person's choice of occupation plays an immense role in one's spiritual development. Four basic principles will now be sketched toward a practical theology of work.

Principle 1: Labor should provide for one's needs without turning into the pursuit of riches. One obvious goal of an occupation is the provision of income to supply a person's needs. If someone chooses not to work, neither should he eat (2 Thess. 3:10). But on the other side, there is a trap associated with the power to earn money: "And having food and clothing, with these we shall be content. But those who desire to be rich fall into temptation and a snare, and into many foolish and harmful lusts which drown men in destruction and perdition" (1 Tim. 6:8-9). Far too many people choose a pursuit of riches. They are not content with food and clothing, but seek to store up treasure on earth. With the extra money come snares. Family time diminishes. With the greater prosperity come large houses, expensive cars, fine dining, and extravagant vacations—things which keep our hearts bound to this world. Children become spoiled and spiritual vitality dries up.

Principle 2: We should match a person's gifts and strengths to appropriate work without having that person draw identity from his or her occupation. On one side, God has fitted individuals with diverse strengths that are suited for differing occupations. Some are skilled with numbers and attention to detail that make them good accountants. Others are skilled craftsman who enjoy laboring with their hands. These different personalities will naturally be more fulfilled in differing roles. But far too often, career fulfillment is romanticized and takes on an unhealthy role. Especially through the education process, selecting a career becomes a matter of great angst. A person begins to draw identity from his or her career. Career becomes a top priority and receives a person's best time. Men size each other up by asking about their line of work. Education and culture often induce women to pursue a career and abandon their biblical calling of motherhood. Career leads to a deferral of marriage and childbearing. These attitudes are never found in Scripture. Believers are called to seek first the kingdom, not their own fulfillment through career. "Christianity should be our career."[2]

Principle 3: We should seek honest work that betters society without being delusional about its impact. Work is a noble activity. God Himself is a worker who loves to create and provide. Being made in the image of God, we work and should take satisfaction in our work. Work and business should exhibit God's attributes of provision and righteousness. Honest work is thus part of holiness. Christians have no role in worldly businesses with sinful goals or practices. Changing occupations will often be a part of repentance and following Jesus. (Note the biblical examples of fortune tellers, tax collectors, idol makers, and prostitutes.) Besides obviously evil industries like tobacco or gambling, most modern occupations in retail fashion, book selling, or high finance would require the repentance of changing jobs. Work should be infused with honesty, integrity, and God's attributes. Christians should have jobs that render spiritual satisfaction at the end of a day's labor.

At the same time, we should not be delusional about the impact of our occupation. Some occupations like mothering and homemaking have very profound spiritual significance. But usually the jobs that are the most admired have little spiritual impact. I remember well having my "bubble burst" about what can be meaningfully achieved in medicine. While there were definite rewards to healing the body, it quickly became apparent that spiritual issues were often the root of the problem (gluttony, addiction, violence, etc.). Because of severe time constraints, it was nearly impossible to address the real issues. I often felt that medicine was a glorified bandage covering deeper spiritual problems. I often mused over Thoreau's adage, "For every thousand people hacking at the leaves of evil, there is one striking at the root." Medicine was only hacking at the leaves—and I knew it. Another physician, D. Martyn Lloyd-Jones, put it this way when questioned about why he left medicine:

> "Ah well!" I felt like saying to them, "if you knew more about the work of a doctor, you would understand. We but spend most of our time rendering people fit to go back

[2] David Bercot, personal communication.

> to their sin!" I saw men on their sick beds, I spoke to them of their immortal souls, they promised grand things. Then they got better and back they went to their old sin! I saw I was helping these men to sin and I decided that I would do no more of it. I want to heal souls. If a man has a diseased body and his soul is all right, he is all right to the end; but a man with a healthy body and a diseased soul is all right for sixty years or so and then he has to face an eternity of hell. Ah, yes! we have sometimes to give up those things which are good for that which is the best of all—the joy of salvation and newness of life.[3]

Very few people have this level of honesty. Too often young people dream of improving access to health care, clean water, or education for the poor—which are all good things. But they delude themselves as to the relative importance of these matters in and of themselves. Often educated young women travel the globe in these pursuits, having been seduced away from their higher calling of motherhood. A useful rule of thumb is this: if others are impressed by your job title or career, there is a high likelihood that your actual occupational kingdom impact is low. There is an inverse correlation between positive kingdom impact and pay (or prestige). Professional athletes, music stars, and world travelers have tremendous acclaim but make little positive impact. Mothers, teachers, or fathers who work with their sons in a home business have the potential to make great impact from God's perspective. Paradoxically, significant kingdom advances occur in quiet, obscure, and unglamorous ways.

Principle 4: We should seek to work with fellow believers while retaining opportunities to preach the gospel. If possible, working with fellow Christians is desirable for accountability and discipleship. Because we are all naturally discipled by those with whom we spend time, the secular work environment is a pull away from spiritual mindedness. Most people cannot withstand this constant tug, and they succumb to the snares of the world. But on the other hand, we are designed to be soldiers, and the opportunity to interact with those outside the household of faith sharpens our skills and makes us aware that we are strangers living in a foreign land. Work environments also provide excellent opportunities for being "a city on a hill." An ideal scenario would therefore be working with fellow believers in a business where they can be challenged by and witness to unbelievers. Scenarios where believers are

---

[3] D. Martyn Lloyd-Jones, quoted in Iain Murray, *D. Martyn Lloyd-Jones: the First Forty Years, 1899-1939*, Banner of Truth (1982), p. 80.

isolated make it hard to maintain a vibrant faith.

These four principles form the rudiments of a practical theology of labor. As a concluding thought, our educations and occupations provide opportunities to prepare us for spiritual battle. Whether we are mothers or welders, our occupations teach us a great deal about ourselves, interpersonal skills, and general principles of wisdom. This has great value in advancing the kingdom. Jesus often used parables from ordinary work to teach spiritual principles. When understood rightly, our homes and workplaces provide excellent training grounds for the everlasting work of advancing God's kingdom. Indeed, they are decisive battlegrounds of kingdom work.

Chapter 39

Church organization and denominations

[I pray] they all may be one, as You, Father, are in Me, and I in You; that they also may be one in Us, that the world may believe that You sent Me. (John 17:20 21)

Denominations are declining with respect to influence and loyalty. Professing Christians typically evaluate a prospective church for the engaging preaching, the worship style, the age and status of its members, the degree of fellowship, and the location. Little weight normally is given to the theology of that church. In today's mobile society, it is not uncommon for a person to attend Methodist, Presbyterian, and Lutheran churches within a few years and scarcely be able to describe the doctrinal differences.

A further contributor to the decline of denominations is the rise of ecumenicalism. Many believe that the *primary* problem of the church is needless splintering into hundreds of denominations. People are more likely than ever not only to forgo a denomination but also to blame denominations for much of Christianity's woes.

The causes of divisions

Historically divisions have arisen for one or more of the following reasons:

1. Interpersonal conflicts. While not often the stated reason for a split or new denomination, honest examination will reveal jealousy, pride, and lack of forgiveness as a common root problem.

2. Poor leadership. Overbearing leaders or leader-centered groups have high potential for factions and splits (see chapter on "Servant-leadership and the offices").
3. Lack of clarity around the group's vision and principles. Often groups start without a clear foundation. Perhaps those groups were founded as a reaction to error and not with their own positive vision. When troubles come, such houses on weak foundations will fall in the storm.
4. Not embracing the Regulative Principle. The Regulative Principle gives immense stability to God's churches. Because so few understand and implement the principle, it subjects the governance of the church to human wisdom. Humans are thus placed at the foundation of a church. Having such a weak and unstable foundation, such churches eventually split.
5. Extrabiblical standards. The Jewish concept of "fence around the Torah" has ironically been adopted by supposedly New Testament churches (see chapter on "The commandments of men"). Yet these fences are by their very nature arbitrary and sow the seeds for subsequent division.
6. Drift from a group's original confession or charter. Sometimes a group drifts from its founding principles that were rooted in Scripture. A righteous minority will want to return to these principles while the majority may not. A breakaway of the minority leads to a new denomination.
7. Doctrinal disagreement. While less common than supposed, sometimes genuine differences in belief arise, spawning a new church or denomination.

The Regulative Principle and denominations

As the matter of denominations entails the ordering of God's household, the Regulative Principle firmly applies (see chapter on "The Regulative Principle"). Because the church is God's household, humans may not determine how to order it. The church's mandate is to implement the pattern of the New Testament, not to innovate: "We also thank God without ceasing, because when you received the word of God which you heard from us, you welcomed it not as the word of men, but as it is in truth, the word of God, which also effectively works in you who believe. For you, brethren, became imitators of the churches of God which are in Judea in Christ Jesus" (1 Thess. 2:13-14). The churches in Thessalonica, hundreds of miles from Jerusalem and remote in culture and language, were praised because they *imitated* the Judean churches. So we today should also imitate those practices. It is therefore disturbing that discussions around denominations are often centered on *pragmatic* concerns. Instead effort should be expended to rediscover New Testament patterns for the purpose of imitation.

The New Testament describes the church as a building (Eph. 2:19-22) built upon a foundation of Jesus and the apostles. A builder who deviated midway on a Victorian building into a Greco-Roman or Gothic plan would construct a ridiculous structure that passersby would mock. Perhaps much of the aspersion cast upon denominations is for this reason: inconsistency and deviance from an original blueprint.

New Testament divisions

Many people feel that denominations are a modern problem and that in New Testament times were more idyllic because there was only one church. Contrary to that belief, divisions and parallel groups to the apostolic churches can be found in the New Testament, even during the time of Jesus: "Now John answered and said, 'Master, we saw someone casting out demons in Your name, and we forbade him because he does not follow with us.' " (Luke 9:49). Paul encounters division in Corinth as believers rallied around various leaders (1 Cor. 1:12, 1 Cor. 3:1-4). While personalities apparently played a large role in Corinth, Paul elsewhere prophesies that division will come through rank falsehood: "Also from among yourselves men will rise up, speaking perverse things, to draw away the disciples after themselves" (Acts 20:30).

Since the problem began very early, one cannot dismiss division and denominations as a modern problem and wistfully look back to the day when the church was united. Instead, recognizing that schisms and denominations have always been present, one should turn to Scripture for wisdom. Paul's response to the Corinthian situation should be our model. After remarking that their sectarian spirit is from the flesh (1 Cor. 3:1-4), Paul seizes upon the metaphor of temple. Because the church is God's temple, with Jesus as its foundation, "let each one take heed how he builds on it" (1 Cor. 3:10). And, "If anyone defiles the temple of God, God will destroy him" (1 Cor. 3:16). Next Paul proceeds to denounce worldly wisdom, because "the wisdom of this world is foolishness with God" (1 Cor. 3:19). He plans to send Timothy, "who will remind you of my ways in Christ, as I teach everywhere in every church" (1 Cor. 4:17). The argument is a model of the Regulative Principle: the church being God's house should be based on His design; human wisdom should be regarded as foolishness in these matters; and the church everywhere should follow the apostolic pattern. This naturally begs the question, "What is the apostolic pattern?"

The apostles in inter-church organization

New Testament church governance was remarkably simple. Within a given church, there were elders and deacons (see chapter 26 on "Servant-leadership and the offices"). Between the churches, the apostles and their delegates circulated to ensure doctrinal integrity, faithful obedience, and economic solidarity.

The goals of doctrinal integrity and faithful obedience *across all of the churches* pervade the epistles. For example, regarding the headcovering, Paul writes, "If one is inclined to be contentious, we have no other practice, nor do the churches of God" (1 Cor. 11:16).[1] One of his lines of argument is that the headcovering was the uniform practice of God's churches. The epistles contain other examples where the apostles strive for faithful obedience among all the churches. 1 Corinthians opens with such an awareness: "To the church of God which is at Corinth, to those who are sanctified in Christ Jesus, called to be saints, *with all who in every place* call on the name of Jesus Christ our Lord" (1 Cor. 1:2; see also 1 Cor. 4:17, 11:16). The letter was not merely to Corinth, but to those who in every place call on Jesus' name. Similar statements are made by other church leaders (1 Pet. 1:1; James 1:1). A desire for inter-church unity fueled the apostles.

The apostles also collected funds for poor churches, by urging prosperous churches to share their burden (Gal. 2:10; 2 Cor. 8:13-15). Economic solidarity between Jewish and Gentile churches played a particularly important role in expressing that the dividing wall had been broken down (Eph. 2:14).

Are there apostles today?

The word *apostle* comes from a Greek word that simply means messenger. The word is used in two distinct senses in the New Testament. The first sense applies to the twelve men appointed by Jesus Himself. Qualifications of being such an apostle are having seen Jesus personally (Acts 1:21-22; 1 Cor. 9:1) and being chosen directly by Him (Gal. 1:1). The authenticity of these apostles was validated by their miracle-working power (2 Cor. 12:11-12; Acts 2:43). They also are described

[1] Author's translation.

as the foundation of the church (Eph. 2:20). In this sense, because of the necessity of having been with Jesus (Acts 1:21-22) and because a foundation cannot be laid again, there are no such apostles today.

But the word *apostle* is used more broadly than just the twelve. Jesus Himself is called an apostle (Heb. 3:1). In Acts 14:14, Barnabas is called an apostle, though he was not one of the twelve. 1 Thessalonians 2:6 names the authors of the letter—Paul, Silas, and Timothy—as apostles (cf. 1 Thess. 1:1). 2 Corinthians 8:23 names Titus and two other brothers "apostles of the churches."[2] Men like Barnabas, Silas, Timothy, and Titus serve as particularly important examples, because the word *apostle* (or messenger) was used about them as we might use the word *missionary* today. "Paul occasionally uses 'apostle' in a general way to simply mean 'messenger' (Phil. 2:25; 2 Cor. 8:23), and more often to refer to accredited missionaries (e.g. Rom. 16:7)."[3] The New Testament sometimes uses "apostles of the churches" as a distinguishing expression from the twelve apostles of Jesus (2 Cor. 8:23).

The word *missionary* is not used in the Bible, yet that is the term that many instinctively use to describe the apostolic functions of evangelism and church planting. So in this sense, there are apostles today who are messengers of the gospel into new areas.

But using the English word *apostle* as a title for today is probably unwise. The word is liable to cause confusion, mistrust, and pride. Instead, a helpful nomenclature is to use the term apostle only for the twelve, and *messenger* for those who plant churches and circulate among them.

In the New Testament model, messengers (that is, apostles or missionaries) are not those who assume leadership of the local church. That role is given to elders and deacons. Messengers stay for a period, evangelize, help found the church, and ensure that local leadership is appointed. Paul stayed in Corinth for two years fulfilling this function, and in Ephesus for three years. Then he moved on. *Elders stay; messengers go. Elders provide stability; messengers provide mobility.* Messengers are called to plant churches and circulate among them, but not to assume final local authority. As one contemplates the messengers described in the New Testament—Paul, Barnabas, Silas, John Mark, Timothy, and Titus—one cannot help but notice that members of this group are often young (1 Tim. 4:12) and single (1 Cor. 7:7), consistent with their being itinerant and suffering hardship. Furthermore, the roles of evangelist and messenger have tremendous overlap (2 Tim.

---

[2] Many translations read "messengers of the churches," although the Greek word is identical to that for apostles.

[3] Douglas Moo, *The Epistle to the Romans*, Eerdmans (1996), p. 41. See also pp. 923-924 for apostle as "commissioned missionary" or "traveling missionary."

4:5). The work of a messenger can thus be summarized:

1. They are heavily involved in evangelism.
2. They help plant churches and establish local leadership.
3. They circulate between churches to ensure doctrinal unity and faithful obedience to the King's commandments.
4. They help deliver funds to needy churches.

The New Testament nowhere suggests that these roles would no longer be needed. In fact, because of greater confusion, the church today perhaps needs these functions as much as the first century church!

How are messengers appointed? Similar to the appointment of elders (see discussion in chapter 26, "Servant-leadership and the offices"), messengers are recognized, not manufactured. Because messengers are visionaries who found churches, their gifting by God should be evident. They should be those who zealously desire doctrinal unity and faithful obedience, as did the messengers of the first century.

Neither elders nor messengers have a superior position in a hierarchy. When elders are first appointed, messengers play an important role (Acts 14:23; Titus 1:5). However, the messengers are themselves commissioned by the elders (1 Tim. 4:14). So the interdependence of these groups of men testifies to the ultimate headship of King Jesus alone.

An international brotherhood

A group of congregations with their associated elders, deacons, and circulating messengers constitutes an *international brotherhood* as described in the New Testament. A local congregation and their leaders have the ability to leave such a brotherhood (3 John 1:9-10 describes such a situation), because ultimately the affairs of a congregation are determined by its local membership. However, the free association of congregations—with the blessing and cooperation of circulating messengers—has biblical precedent as described above. The goals of this free association are doctrinal unity, faithful obedience, and economic solidarity.

Balancing structure with liberty is always challenging. Many have veered off into either extreme. While the Roman Catholic, Episcopal, and Greek Orthodox churches have created vast structures that have no biblical warrant, their failings have produced a counter-reaction of celebrating looseness of form and structure. Out of a reaction to denominational failings, the modern house-church movement, the Emergent churches, and the "independent" churches have swung to an opposite error with its own set of tragic consequences. They tend to be isolated, ingrown, and arrogant. They oppose anything that smacks of denominations, including circulating messengers who facilitate unity in doctrine and practice. Such revolts are far from the New Testament vision.

Aiming for a biblical balance point, an international brotherhood contrasts with both the modern denomination and the independent church in the following ways:

1. An international brotherhood is nothing more than the collection of congregations with their elders, deacons, and messengers. A denomination, on the other hand, is an organization that sits above the congregations. It often has its own governance, its own staff, its own committees, its own buildings, and an independent life of its own. The New Testament provides no basis for the additional structure.
2. When making important decisions and applications of Scripture, the elders and messengers, met together with the "whole church" (Acts 15:6, 22). So an international brotherhood operates between churches in a coordinated fashion. No precedent, however, is given for a supra-organizational structure that hands down decisions.
3. A useful clue whether or not a group has crossed over into denominationalism as opposed to a New Testament brotherhood is the presence of fees that a denomination collects or buildings that a denomination owns. While the Vatican is the most extreme example of this phenomenon, even Protestant and evangelical groups have unfortunately veered into this error.
4. A church that is part of an international brotherhood stands in greater economic solidarity with its fellow churches than in the denominational model. In most denominations today, the degree of economic solidarity between churches is tragically weak. Modern denominations do a poor job at binding churches together because they are institutional, impersonal structures that lack the kindred spirit of a family or strong-group. An international brotherhood, in contrast, with its circulating messengers and greater unity in doctrine and praxis, naturally leads to greater affection and sympathy between churches.
5. When Peter tells Jesus that that have left everything to follow him, Jesus responds by saying, "There is no one who has left house or brothers or sisters or father or mother or wife or children or lands, for My sake and the gospel's, who shall not receive a hun-

dredfold now in this time—houses and brothers and sisters and mothers and children and lands, with persecutions—and in the age to come, eternal life" (Mark 10:29-30). In a healthy brotherhood, a disciple should be able to come to a new city and be received with the hospitality of lodging and family. Ironically, errant groups like Mormons and Jehovah's Witnesses have done a better job at this than most orthodox Christian groups and their denominations. Naturally, independent groups have failed the most in this area.

6. The parable of the sheep and the goats (Matt. 25:31-46) describes blessing Jesus' poor and persecuted brethren. The international brotherhood has this cause placed into its very heart, and so seeks to unify churches economically. Paul's ministry fulfilled this: "They [the apostles] desired only that we should remember the poor, the very thing which I also was eager to do (Gal. 2:10)." By collecting funds from the churches in Macedonia and Greece to serve the famine-striken Judean churches, the brotherhood lived out its calling.
7. As discussed at the beginning of the chapter, denominations are waning in influence, partly because of ecumenical thinking. In contrast, an international brotherhood preserves a sense of strong-group boundary. The New Testament repeatedly affirms doctrinal unity, faithful obedience, and economic solidarity as essential qualities of God's churches. These goals presume knowing who is within the group of congregations and who is without. So an international brotherhood is demarcated, consistent with New Testament practice (1 Cor. 11:16; 2 John 1:10). A brotherhood is birthed from the desire to follow God's commands and to take care of the household of God. Separation is an inevitable result. "It is better to divide around truth than unite around error."[4]

Relating to other groups

The New Testament gives instructive examples of relating to other groups: "Now John answered and said, 'Master, we saw someone casting out demons in Your name, and we forbade him because he does not follow with us.' But Jesus said to him, 'Do not forbid him, for he who is not against us is on our side' " (Luke 9:49-50). Jesus Himself does not forbid this other person from ministering under his name, because

[4] Attributed to Edward John Carnell.

there are only two states—being against Jesus or for Him. Similarly, Paul does not fret when people preach King Jesus out of wrong motivations: "Some indeed preach Christ even from envy and strife, and some also from good will: The former preach Christ from selfish ambition, not sincerely, supposing to add affliction to my chains; but the latter out of love, knowing that I am appointed for the defense of the gospel. What then? Only that in every way, whether in pretense or in truth, Christ is preached; and in this I rejoice, yes, and will rejoice" (Phil. 1:15-18). Yet in the same letter he also says, "Beware of dogs, beware of evil workers, beware of the mutilation!" (Phil. 3:2) Paul gives similarly strong warnings and rebukes elsewhere (Acts 20:30; Gal. 1:8; Col. 2:8, 2 Cor. 11:14-15; Titus 1:10-11, 3:9-11; 2 Tim. 4:3-4), as do John (2 John 1:7, 10) and Peter (2 Pet. 2:1, 3:16). Jesus Himself spoke similarly (Matt. 7:15, 23:13-35; Rev. 2:2). Synthesizing these passages, other groups who are preaching the true King outside of one's own group, even with wrong motivations, are not to be hindered or spoken against. However, when their gospels cross into falsehood, strong rebukes should be given. Furthermore, no greeting or relationship should be offered by any Christian to false teachers. Ravenous wolves have no place near Jesus' flock.

Guarding against stagnation

A New Testament church should naturally be expanding and stretching. Stagnation breeds complacency and deadness. The curse of Babel afflicts church groups that isolate themselves from other believers and build monuments to themselves. When one reads the book of Acts and the epistles, one is impressed by how much travel believers undertook between cities and churches. Conversely, history teaches us that when many generations of believers are fixed to a given location, it is likely that they will spiritually stagnate.

Besides the curse of Babel, where there is too high a density of Christian groups, a spirit of jealousy and competition take root. Once that happens, much evil flows: "For where jealousy and selfish ambition exist, there will be disorder and every vile practice" (James 3:16 ESV). Once Paul saw healthy churches flourishing in an area, he would leave and pursue unreached areas. Families like Aquila and Priscilla apparently did likewise. If young people are not living in a challenging spiritual environment, they will likely express their God-given desire for battle in ways such as sports, worldly entertainment, or foolish hobbies. Guarding against complacency, followers of Jesus should be strangers and pilgrims on this earth.

Chapter 40

The strategy to conquer the world

Your people will offer themselves freely on the day of Your power. (Psalms 110:3)

Just as Jesus gave his disciples radical commandments for living in the Sermon on the Mount, He also gave them a radical model of ministry. The church today must be attentive to Jesus' vision for how His church should advance, lest it fail in flesh-driven efforts.

Immediately after Jesus selected the twelve apostles, He gave an extended discourse on how the disciples were to spread the kingdom in a sermon of commissioning, found in Matthew 10:5-42. This very important sermon contains Jesus' instructions for how to spread the gospel. Combining the words of Jesus with how the apostles followed those words offers today's disciples a vision for the biblical expanse of Jesus' nation.

Preaching the kingdom

"And as you go, preach, saying, 'The kingdom of heaven is at hand' " (Matt. 10:7). The expansion of the kingdom centers on preaching the gospel. Social work, starting hospitals, or serving in soup kitchens are activities that have a place, but should be subordinate to preaching. When Jesus fed the five thousand, He did so *after* He had preached and taught. There are no examples of Jesus healing or feeding apart from His preaching and teaching. Often today's missions try to draw people with social services, food, or buildings. Much later, if ever, is the kingdom of heaven proclaimed. Because of this divorce of preaching and serving, such ministries do not follow Jesus' example.

Not only do Jesus' disciples not use money or resources to draw people into the kingdom, Jesus made this impossible for the apostles by instructing them: "Provide neither gold nor silver nor copper in your money belts, nor bag for your journey, nor two tunics, nor sandals, nor staffs; for a worker is worthy of his food" (Matt. 10:9-10). The apostles had to rely upon God's provision—not upon bringing money into a city and lavishing riches upon the population. Indeed Paul is described as working to provide for himself (1 Thess. 2:9). Their model was not to give money to those they ministered to. As Peter said, "Silver and gold I do not have" (Acts 3:6). Instead of money, the apostles offered a far more valuable gift: preaching the kingdom of heaven.

An urban vision

Jesus sent the apostles into the cities of Israel: "When they persecute you in this city, flee to another. For assuredly, I say to you, you will not have gone through the cities of Israel before the Son of Man comes" (Matt. 10:23). This verse is particularly important because going through cities is envisioned as occurring right up until the Son of Man comes. This vision was not merely for the twelve, but for his disciples until the end of the age.

As was His practice, Jesus led by example. Immediately after the commissioning sermon, Matthew writes, "Now it came to pass, when Jesus finished commanding His twelve disciples, that He departed from there to teach and to preach *in their cities*" (Matt. 11:1). Jesus' commissioning of His apostles to the cities was thus followed by Jesus' doing ministry in the cities. This proximity of teaching and example emphasizes the theme of urban ministry. Jesus even describes the purpose of his earthly ministry as preaching to the cities: "I must preach the kingdom of God to the other cities also, because for this purpose I have been sent" (Luke 4:43).

Some wrongly imagine that Israel was a rustic, depopulated area and that the cities of Greece and Rome were dense and urban. Josephus, the first century Jewish historian, writes about Galilee: "Moreover, the cities lie here very thick, and the very many villages there are here are every where so full of people, by the richness of their soil, that the very least of them contain above fifteen thousand inhabitants."[1] Small cities

[1] Flavius Josephus, *The War of the Jews*, Book III, chapter 3.

in Galilee had 15,000 people! Thus Jesus' ministry was more urban than most imagine.

Did the apostles follow Jesus' commission to the cities after the resurrection? The answer is a resounding yes. In the book of Acts, the apostles strategically brought the gospel to the leading and most populous cities of the Empire. The most populous cities of the first century were:[2]

1. Rome: 650,000-1,000,000 people
2. Alexandria: 400,000 people
3. Ephesus: 200,000 people
4. Antioch: 150,000 people
5. Apamea: 125,000 people
6. Pergamum: 120,000 people
7. Sardis: 100,000 people
8. Corinth: 100,000 people

Of the eight leading cities, at least six had churches established within fifty years of the resurrection. What most do not appreciate is the incredible density of these cities. Rome and Antioch are estimated to have had approximately 200 persons per acre. This compares to about 25 persons per acre in Chicago and San Francisco, and 100 persons per acre in Manhattan.[3] And of course modern cities have skyscrapers and are free of livestock!

The apostles were following Jesus' example and commands by going to these cities and establishing churches. The book of Acts serves as a chronicle of the urban expansion of the church, beginning in Jerusalem, followed by Samaria, Antioch, Lystra, Thessalonica, Athens, Corinth, Ephesus, and Rome. By "invading" these cities, the disciples of Christ gained notoriety. In Thessalonica, the Jews complained that, "These who have turned the world upside down have come here too" (Acts 17:6). The disciples established such a dominant presence in the cities, that, paradoxically to modern sentiment, the Christians were the city-dwellers while the pagans lived in the country. Thus *pagan* comes from the Latin word *paganus*, meaning "country dweller," and the word *heathen* refers to "people of the heath."

As Jesus commanded, the early disciples functioned as a city on a hill, commanding attention across the world. To be sure, one should

---

[2] Statistics from taken Rodney Stark, *The Rise of Christianity*, HarperSanFrancisco (1997), p. 131. While Stark gives 650,000 as the population for Rome, other historians put the number closer to one million.

[3] Stark, pp. 149-150.

not say that every Christian is called to the city. There is a place for rural ministry. However, based on Jesus' commands and example, as well as the apostolic pattern, we can say that the church *as an institution* is called to the city.

The strategic value of cities

There are several pragmatic arguments why the church should preserve the New Testament's emphasis on urban ministry:[4]

- Today's world is becoming increasingly urbanized. Today more than half of the world is already urban. By 2050, 85.9% and 64.1% of the developed and developing world, respectively, are projected to be urban.[5] Even apart from the biblical paradigm, if the church is going to reach the world, it must focus on the cities.
- High density creates opportunity. In the suburbs or remote areas, people tend to live comparatively isolated lives. The high density of the urban environment (so-called urban compression) provides much greater opportunity for ministry. "Urban compression then creates the opportunity to realign affiliations and relationships while increasing the exchange of ideas. These two factors and many others make high-density environments a strategic point of leverage for doing missions where the good news can be proclaimed with greater efficiency and effectiveness in a rapidly shifting world."[6]
- Cities are filled with receptive people. Students and immigrants are among the most open people to the gospel; they tend to be found in cities. Moreover, cities tend to erode *status quo* village values. Many evangelists to Latin American countries testify that dominant family structures undermine the ability of the gospel to take hold. In the city, people have an openness to consider new ideas and patterns. In cities, people can more easily reconfigure their relationships. Being a more fluid environment, cities are thus more conducive to the strong-group message of total resocialization into the people of God.

[4] Partially adapted from Alan McMahan's "The Strategic Nature of Urban Ministry" in *Reaching the City*, Gary Fujino, Timothy Sisk, and Tereso Casiño (eds.), William Carey Library (2012).

[5] Data from the United Nations (business.un.org) and the World Health Organization.

[6] McMahan, p. 3.

- Cities demands a well-reasoned gospel. Cities are filled with educated, sophisticated individuals. Yet the New Testament describes "casting down arguments and every high thing that exalts itself against the knowledge of God" (2 Cor. 10:5). The apostolic church successfully met this challenge. Too often modern churches are filled with individuals who are not competent in warfare against the world. Thus our spiritual harvest in the city is an indicator of our training and preparedness.
- The city demands spiritual warfare. Cities are known for their confluence of evil forces.[7] Paul spent more time in Ephesus than any other city during his missionary journeys. Ephesus was the center of worship of the goddess Diana (also called Artemis) and filled with attendant evils. His church planting effort served to bind the powers of evil and liberate its inhabitants to faithfully follow Jesus. Indeed, cities are the primary battlegrounds between God's church and the powers of the Enemy.[8] To neglect these battlegrounds is to lose the war.
- The city is a place for meeting needs. Cities tend to be places of extremes. Great wealth and great poverty are often found side by side. Antioch, the launchpad of Paul's missionary journeys and the place where Christianity first became multicultural, was a very dense city filled with poverty, crime, and sickness. "Any accurate portrait of Antioch in New Testament times must depict a city filed with misery, danger, fear, despair, and hatred. A city where the average family lived a squalid life in filthy and cramped quarters, where at least half of the children died at birth or during infancy, and where most of the children who lived lost at least one parent before reaching maturity. A city filled with hatred and fear rooted in intense ethnic antagonisms and exacerbated by a constant stream of strangers. A city so lacking in stable networks of attachments that petty incidents could prompt mob violence. A city where crime flourished and the streets were dangerous at night. And, perhaps above all, a city repeatedly smashed by cataclysmic catastrophes: where a resident could expect literally to be homeless from time to time, providing that he or she was among the survivors."[9] Places like Calcutta, Mexico City, and Nairobi are precisely the cities where the gospel can shine the brightest.

[7] This idea is developed more fully by Robert Linthicum's chapter "Our City as the Abode of Satanic Principalities and Powers" in *City of God, City of Satan: A Biblical Theology of the Urban Church*, Zondervan (1991), pp. 64-79.

[8] Linthicum, p. 23.

[9] Stark, pp. 160-161.

"To cities filled with the homeless and impoverished, Christianity offered charity as well as hope. To cities filled with newcomers and strangers, Christianity offered an immediate basis for attachments. To cities filled with orphans and widows, Christianity provided a new and expanded sense of family. To cities torn by violent ethnic strife, Christianity offered a new basis of social solidarity. And to cities faced with epidemics, fires, and earthquakes, Christianity offered effective nursing services."[10]

- To reach the city is to reach the world. When Paul evangelized Ephesus, others carried the gospel to surrounding cities apart from his efforts. The seven letters in Revelation were to precisely these cities (Smyrna, Philadelphia, Laodicea, etc.). If the church can take a prominent place in the cities, the gospel can naturally spread to the whole world.

Sheep among wolves

The majority of Jesus' sermon of commissioning (Matt. 10:5-42) prepared the disciples for the persecution that they would endure in these cities. While a lengthy passage, it merits careful reading from the perspective of urban ministry:

> Behold, I send you out as sheep in the midst of wolves. Therefore be wise as serpents and harmless as doves. But beware of men, for they will deliver you up to councils and scourge you in their synagogues...Now brother will deliver up brother to death, and a father his child; and children will rise up against parents and cause them to be put to death. And you will be hated by all for My name's sake. But he who endures to the end will be saved. When they persecute you in this city, flee to another...A disciple is not above his teacher, nor a servant above his master. It is enough for a disciple that he be like his teacher, and a servant like his master. If they have called the master of the house Beelzebub, how much more will they call those of his household! Therefore do not fear them...Therefore whoever confesses Me before men, him I will also confess before My Father who is in heaven. But whoever denies Me before men, him I will also deny before My Father who is in heaven. Do not think that I came to bring peace on

[10] Stark, p. 161.

> earth. I did not come to bring peace but a sword. For I have come to "set a man against his father, a daughter against her mother, and a daughter-in-law against her mother-in-law"; and "a man's enemies will be those of his own household." He who loves father or mother more than Me is not worthy of Me. And he who loves son or daughter more than Me is not worthy of Me. And he who does not take his cross and follow after Me is not worthy of Me. He who finds his life will lose it, and he who loses his life for My sake will find it. (Matt. 10:16-17, 21-23, 24-26, 32-39)

The implication was that the disciples would be betrayed by their relatives who resided in these cities. Many verses from the above passages have been used lightly by Christians, to the extent that we almost do not hear their meaning. Placing these verses in the original context of the disciples' commissioning into cities gives them fresh meaning.

Churches have often fallen into one of two extremes. Some live in the city but are worldly, so the world loves them as their own. Others flee the city for a comfortable life. Still others flee the city for the sake of separation, sometimes with good motivations. But separation must be possible in the city, as attested by the New Testament example. Some choose compromise; others choose survival. Neither option is the New Testament pattern.

The choice for urban ministry, especially for families, can be a difficult one. George MacDonald's poem expresses the tensions well:

> I said "Let me walk in the fields;"
> He said "Nay, walk in the town;"
> I said "There are no flowers there;"
> He said "No flowers, but a crown."
> I said "But the skies are black,
> There is nothing but noise and din;"
> But He wept as He sent me back.
> "There is more," He said, "There is sin."
>
> I said "But the air is thick
> And fogs are veiling the sun;"
> He answered, "Yet souls are sick
> And souls in the dark undone."
> I said "I shall miss the light
> And friends shall miss me, they say."
> He answered, "Choose to-night,
> If I am to miss you, or they."

I pleaded for time to be given,
He said "Is it hard to decide?
It will not seem hard in heaven
To have followed the steps of your Guide."
I cast one look at the fields,
Then set my face to the town;
He said "My child, do you yield?
Will you leave the flowers for the crown?"

Then into His hand went mine,
And into my heart came He,
And I walk in a light divine
The path I had feared to see.

The New Testament offers a third way—invading, faithful soldiers marked with suffering. The church's mandate is to adopt this New Testament vision for an expansive, worldwide brotherhood birthed in persecution and suffering.

Appendix: Forward for the King

In the Preface we began with Psalms 48 and described how the church can be likened to a city. Our tour of the city-state of the King is now complete; hopefully it has been educational and inspiring. Most tour guides now give their pleasant farewells and depart—but I cannot. If the vision of this book resonates with you, I ask you to go from being a tourist to being a fellow laborer with me in helping the King build His great city. Do not allow complacency and inertia to stifle the stirrings of the Spirit. Do not remain unequally yoked with evil. Some of you may be called to church planting. Others may be in godly churches that are discussing their vision. Others may be thinking about moving to a new location. But neither churches nor believers should be independent. Followers of Jesus need each other for accountability, prayer support, and wisdom. If you would like to discuss becoming part of an international brotherhood as described in this book, please write to info@followers-of-the-way.org (the dashes are necessary) or write to Followers of the Way, 52 Oakland St, Medford MA 02115 USA.

We are living in one of the most exciting periods in church history. While sin abounds, grace abounds much more. God is calling and empowering His people to be witnesses of His true kingdom to every nation and tribe. Maranatha!